D1083809

Joseph Alois Schumpeter is one of the great intellectual figures of the twentieth century. His contribution to the study of entrepreneurship and innovation, to the theory of economic development and business cycles, his writings on the evolution of capitalism into socialism, and his *magnum opus* on the history of economics all had a major impact not only on economics, but on the social sciences in general.

In this major scholarly study the distinguished Japanese economist Yuichi Shionoya presents a new analytical interpretation of Schumpeter's accomplishments. Taking account of all aspects of Schumpeter's work, Shionoya provides an entirely original reconstruction of the Schumpeterian framework, encompassing both theory and metatheory. By concentrating on Schumpeter's views on methodology and on his idea of a universal social science, Shionoya reveals Schumpeter's synthetic approach, which he argues was achieved by applying an instrumentalist methodology and the tools of sociology to the evolution of society as a whole. Throughout the book the originality of Schumpeter's work is examined in the light of the intellectual environments in which he lived, Austria, Germany, and the United States in the first half of the twentieth century.

This book is a major contribution to the history of economics and of the social sciences. It casts new light on Schumpeter's thinking, and should be a standard reference on Schumpeter scholarship for years to come.

SCHUMPETER AND
THE IDEA OF SOCIAL SCIENCE

Historical Perspectives on Modern Economics

General Editor: Craufurd D. Goodwin, Duke University

This series contains original works that challenge and enlighten historians of economics. For the profession as a whole, it promotes better understanding of the origin and content of modern economics.

Schumpeter and the idea of social science

A METATHEORETICAL STUDY

YUICHI SHIONOYA

Hitotsubashi University, Professor Emeritus

CAMBRIDGE
UNIVERSITY PRESS

Published by the Press Syndicate of the University of Cambridge
The Pitt Building, Trumpington Street, Cambridge CB2 1RP
40 West 20th Street, New York, NY 10011–4211, USA
10 Stamford Road, Oakleigh, Melbourne 3166, USA

Originally published in Japanese as *Shumpētā-teki shikō*
by Toyo Keizai Inc., Tokyo 1995
and © Toyo Keizai Inc.
First published in English by Cambridge University Press 1997 as *Schumpeter and the idea
of social science*
English translation © Cambridge University Press 1997

Printed in Great Britain at the University Press, Cambridge

A catalogue record for this book is available from the British Library

Library of Congress cataloguing in publication data

Shionoya, Yuichi, 1932–
Shumpeter and the idea of social science: a metatheoretical study / Yuichi Shionoya.
    p.   cm.
Includes bibliographical references and index.
ISBN 0 521 43034 8 (hardback)
1. Schumpeter, Joseph Alois, 1883–1950.
2. Economics – History – 20th century.
3. Social sciences – History – 20th century.
I. Title.
HB119.S35S54   1997
330'.092 – dc20   96–26542   CIP

ISBN 0 521 43034 8 hardback

CE

Contents

Contents

Figures

Preface

Joseph Alois Schumpeter is generally acknowledged as one of the first-rank economists of the twentieth century. Textbooks of micro- and macroeconomics, however, do not incorporate Schumpeter's thought into the corpus of standard theories. Books on the history of economics, too, rarely assign a chapter to him alone. In most cases, his name can be found only in the index, and that sometimes leads us only to footnotes. If this treatment is valid, it means that Schumpeter did not shape an original paradigm or a school in economics.

On the other hand, monographic studies on Schumpeter display a strong admiration for his work, but he is treated in a way that curiously parallels the one described above. Such accounts emphasize his uniqueness, yet it's a uniqueness that cannot be recorded in the principles and history of economics. Just as biographical analyses that portray the subject as having produced a single brilliant achievement, these studies regard Schumpeter's work as a unique historical event or a work of art that is not reproducible, instead of as a scientific finding that is more or less universal and transposable.

Both the benign neglect and enthusiastic praise of Schumpeter seem to reflect a more basic fact. Whereas Schumpeter developed a comprehensive understanding of the social world that went beyond the prevailing structure of economics, people can see his work in no other way than through the framework of contemporary mainstream economics and thus cannot appreciate his entire body of work. Twentieth-century economics has been developed by combining the macroeconomics of John Maynard Keynes with neoclassical microeconomics. This is how most economists of this century have interpreted and practiced their profession. It is just another example of the autointoxication of mainstream economists that they cannot incorporate Schumpeter's ideas into their systems.

If Schumpeter's own frame of thought is to be taken seriously, we must consider all of his work, cast new light on his texts, and offer revised interpretations, rather than reading him in snatches – taking up, for instance, only his theory of economic development or his thesis on the demise of capitalism. With the passage of time and a change in expositors, Schumpeter's thinking can be reconstructed as a paradigm. This book intends to present such a reconstruction.

I believe that I have formed a considerably different picture of Schumpeter's world. Of course, this is my construction, not his own, because without subjective construction there is no interpretation. But, in developing my argument, I wholly depended on his psyche and on materials that have been little noticed even by Schumpeterians. Therefore, the view represented in this volume reproduces his world as it would have been visualized if whole sections of his work had been duly organized according to his principle ideas and if the internal demands of his work had been faithfully met. Among his neglected materials, I drew on Schumpeter's *metatheories*, a set of concepts comprising the methodology of science, the sociology of science, and the history of science. Based on the metatheoretical framework, I tried to reconstruct his *theories*, a set of thoughts incorporating economic statics, economic dynamics, and economic sociology. It is shown that for Schumpeter, the pair of tripartite research areas constituted a "two-structure approach to mind and society" that is comparable, in social research, to Marx's economic interpretation of history.

The conventional picture of Schumpeter is, metaphorically speaking, like viewing a distant mountaintop, that is recognized as being one of the highest in the world. The topography at the foot of the mountain has not been explored until now. I used the various features of Schumpeter's metatheoretical framework as the tools with which to climb the mountain from the foot to the top.

My interpretation might be criticized for being too well ordered and artificial. Yet in science theoretical models imposed on reality are always systematic and artificial creations of the human mind, and both the depiction and the reconstruction of theories and thought are in themselves theoretical activities. Moreover, my characterization is free from arbitrary exaggeration or distortion of Schumpeter's work. Because a constructed theory, if it is to be accepted, must fit the facts, I have empirically tested my own theories using his materials.

I prefer anti-mainstreams to mainstreams in science. Although the mainstream has enough scientific reasons to represent the movements of the times, it possesses simultaneously a nonscientific power by which it neglects and conceals its own defects. The establishment of mainstreams is a contemporary social phenomenon. The contention of anti-mainstreams serves to mirror the defects of mainstreams and sometimes includes a powerful motive for challenging new ideas for a new era. Originally, the ideas of Marx, Keynes, and Schumpeter were anti-mainstream. Among the concepts of these giants, Schumpeter's paradigm of social science – what I call a "universal social science" – is little known. It was the soul underlying and leading the body of his work. This book aims to bring to light the entire picture of his idea of social science.

I have undertaken this study because Schumpeter's view of social science has important implications for the future of economics. Throughout the twentieth century economists have been engaged in the analytic process of isolating narrowly defined economic phenomena from complex social phenomena. Though not diminishing the achievements of economics, it is now necessary to look at society as a whole and pay attention to the social embeddedness of an economy and the unity of social phenomena. After Marx, no other economist but Schumpeter has met the demands of the times. If one criticizes Marx, one must have an alternative position. To this end, the Schumpeterian style of thought or mind-set provides a clue to a universal social science, and it should be identified as reproducible and transposable. Instead of writing a treatise on social science by myself, I tried to do so through an interpretation of Schumpeter. Therefore the purpose of this book goes beyond a contribution to Schumpeteriana.

Half a century after Schumpeter's death, his work seems to be proving its worth in numerous ways. When the world becomes less preoccupied with short-term problems, social scientists shift their attention to lofty problems regarding changes in the economic and political systems of civilization. Schumpeter's thought on the transformation of the capitalist system, in its most basic sense, throws light on the challenges that the world has been facing since his death, that is, the breakdown of the communist regime, the growth of the capitalist economy in the United States, Europe, Japan, and East Asia, and the hardships inherent in the welfare state in developed countries. Schumpeter's idea of a universal social science and his underlying style of thought provide not a ready-made doctrine but an approach to solving these grand problems.

I have been interested in Schumpeter for a long time. As a university student, I first read his *Epochen der Dogmen- und Methodengeschichte* – painstakingly – to learn the German language together with the history of economics; since then, it has always been fun for me to read Schumpeter. Ichiro Nakayama of Hitotsubashi University and Seiichi Tobata of Tokyo University, who were Schumpeter's pupils at Bonn, contributed to the spread of his ideas in Japan by translating his many works. When I was on the economics faculty at Hitotsubashi, they asked me to revise their translation (first published in 1937) of *Theorie der wirtschaftlichen Entwicklung*, which took me several years. We published the new translation in 1977. Then in 1983 the economic academic community worldwide commemorated the Marx, Keynes, and Schumpeter centenary, and before long we saw the resurgence of Schumpeter. In spite of the growing literature on him, I felt that I had something different to say about Schumpeter.

Every year since 1987 I have submitted a paper on Schumpeter at the History of Economics Society meetings held in North America. The International Schumpeter Society, founded in 1986, has also become a useful forum for exchanging ideas. When almost half of this book was written, I took office as president of Hitotsubashi and thus lost three years of research time from 1989 to 1992. But in 1993–94 I spent a delightful year of research in the United States at the National Humanities Center, Research Triangle Park, North Carolina, where I not only resumed the thread of thought in a wonderful environment, but also learned a lot from thirty Fellows of the humanities and the social sciences from around the world. Duke University, neighboring the Humanities Center, is the mecca of the history of economics studies, and I benefited from various comments at its workshop. I am particularly grateful to Craufurd Goodwin, who kindly brought me to the National Humanities Center and made possible the publication of this book by Cambridge University Press with his constant encouragement.

Through all these interchanges I am indebted to many who have aided in the production and improvement of this book by raising particular points, including Karl Acham, Jürgen Backhaus, Roger Backhouse, Nicholas Balabkins, Humberto Barreto, John Bethune, Stephan Böhm, Martin Bronfenbrenner, Bruce Caldwell, Bob Coats, Kurt Dopfer, Wade Hands, Arnold Heertje, Abraham Hirsch, Claude Jessua, Peter Koslowski, Heinz Kurz, Richard Langlois, Uskali Mäki, Neil de Marchi, Marguerite Mendell, Laurence Moss, the late Horst Claus Recktenwald, Fritz Ringer, Bertram Schefold, Christian Schmidt, Vincent Tarascio, and E. Roy Weintraub. I owe a very special debt to Mark Perlman, Richard Swedberg, and Wolfgang Stolper for their careful reading of the entire manuscript and their helpful comments and suggestions, not all of which I could incorporate because of the need to hold down the overall length of the book. The Japanese version of this volume was published in 1995 and favorably reviewed, as far as I am aware, by Takenori Inoki, Hirotaka Kato, Masahiro Nei, Tosimaru Ogura, and Kiichiro Yagi and hailed as a very ambitious work. Their positive appraisal has sustained my confidence in developing the English version.

Although several of the chapters in this book grew out of my previously published articles, chapter 4 draws heavily on an article "The Sociology of Science and Schumpeter's Ideology," in Laurence S. Moss (ed.), *Joseph A. Schumpeter, Historian of Economics*, Routledge, 1996. I am grateful to the publishers for permission to use the material here in slightly revised form.

Finally, I would like to thank Mrs. Stevie G. Champion for her wonderful copy-editing. With my style of thinking nurtured by the Japanese language, her literary talent and patience have been invaluable in helping convey to the English reader what I mean to say without serious obstacles I hope.

CHAPTER 1

Introduction

Schumpeter once wrote: "Not the first, but the last chapter of a scientific system should deal with its methodology" (1908, xv). This means that in science one cannot effectively discuss methodology independently of concrete problems and actual practice. Now that all of Schumpeter's work is available, it is possible, in light of this precept, to examine his methodology for the purpose of understanding and evaluating his whole body of work. The aim of this book is to reconstruct Schumpeter's contributions to the social sciences from a methodological point of view.

The purpose of the book

Schumpeter was interested in pairs of grand problems such as statics and dynamics, development and cycles, economic development and sociocultural development, theory and history, science and ideology, economic systems and political systems, the economy and civilization, and mind and society. Thus, he was invariably conscious of broad perspectives on problems and developed an overall approach to their resolution in order to give a global picture of reality. Although he stressed the need to restrict the scope of a study, Schumpeter always considered questions in a wider context. He mastered the achievements of other scholars in many fields and, at the same time, went beyond existing scientific knowledge to put forward a new understanding of concepts. His grasp of issues was global as well as multifaceted, and his use of methods was synthetic as well as analytic.

A universal social science

Schumpeter's studies, extending over numerous disciplines and schools, contain ideas that appear so inconsistent that they might create the impression of cynicism, eclecticism, and occasionally even paradoxy. Because Schumpeter opposed the viewpoint of policymaking in economics and was fond of advocating novelty, he has sometimes been considered insincere. This is so, to a great extent, because his rich and unified body of thought, if apprehended only in bits and pieces without perceiving the underlying unity of his overarching theory, can lead to a serious misunderstanding of that thought. The essence of Schumpeter's work lies not so much in his separate scientific treatment of the component parts of a whole, as in his capacity to generate comprehensive designs, ideas, or insights that assign each component its proper place in the total picture. One cannot adequately evaluate the significance of his individual scientific achievements without recognizing his global vision of the economy, society, and science. It is my view that such recognition will be obtained through methodological investigation.

There is no need to argue methodology in the case of scholars who are content to work within an existing paradigm to solve an ordinary set of problems with standard techniques. To understand the rationale for Schumpeter's thinking, however, one must reconstruct a scientific system by examining his implicit habits and styles of thought through methodological study. These steps are all the more necessary because Schumpeter deliberately avoided reflecting upon his own scientific system. Although he accomplished a large-scale work on the history of economics, he did not place his system of thought in history by sticking to what he called "my principle of effacing myself in this book" (1954a, 1019).[1] But he did not conceal his blueprint at all times. It can be discovered and explicated. Schumpeter's system of thought, if interpreted accurately and reconstructed methodologically, can be regarded as based on the research program of a "universal social science" (1926b, 365).[2]

The Schumpeterian style of thought

Over time Schumpeter's achievements in particular areas may become obsolete, as does any scientific work. Although he did not leave a system or a doctrine that would be embodied in economics textbooks and a school that shared it, his characteristic point of view, on the most primitive level of cognition, which might be labeled a "Schumpeterian style of thought," will survive insofar as the efforts of social science will continue. A mind-set, a style of thinking, or an inclination of thought in a scholar precedes his design, idea, and vision about external objects and lies as tacit knowledge on the side of a subjective agency. While Schumpeter emphasized the importance of having a vision before constructing a theory, he also drew attention to implicit habits of thinking that precede both vision and theory (1949a). He admitted that vision originated from personal tastes and peculiarities.[3] This is the reason why an outstanding biography of a scholar will succeed in linking his character and achievement. Schumpeter himself demonstrated remarkable skill in writing biographical essays on eminent economists.[4]

This book is not a biographical study of the man Schumpeter; rather, it is intended to portray his style of thought, which can be generalized and thus shared with social scientists, through the interpretation of his work. In other words, I am more interested in the Schumpeterian style of thought than Schumpeter's thought *per se*.

How, then, can one formulate conceptually what may be called the Schumpeterian style of thought? I got a hint from the concept of *habitus* as it is represented by the French sociologist Pierre Bourdieu (Bourdieu 1977, 1990a). The Latin *habitus* means condition, habits, disposition, deportment, or character, but it is better identified with a mental habit or a habit-forming force. Bourdieu defines *habitus* as "systems of durable, transposable dispositions, structured structures predisposed to function as structuring structures" (Bourdieu 1990a, 53). The aim of this concept is to intermediate between two extreme approaches in the social sciences, namely, individualistic subjectivism and supra-individualistic objectivism. *Habitus* is not only a personal propensity but also can be held socially in common; it not only generates and organizes an image of the world as the object of study but also can be reproduced socially through institutional devices such as education and the formation of schools. The concept of *habitus*, together with the concept of the "intellectual field," provides the framework of Bourdieu's sociology of science, which will be a useful reference in this study of Schumpeter.

In the light of these concepts, Schumpeter's characteristic work and activities are interpreted as his habitual practice, and the organizing principles responsible for his practice should be found in his entity. These principles, however, were formed and applied in a social space called the intellectual field and are transposable between individuals. It is my contention that the practice of the Schumpeterian mode of thought, thus viewed, was not a singular, one-time phenomenon confined to one individual; rather, it is a method of social science that can be repeated, experienced, and transposed through an appropriate formulation.

A methodological perspective

Contrary to the general opinion among economists, Schumpeter was extremely conscious of method and methodology. As the methodologist Fritz Machlup pointed out (Machlup 1951, 95), one of his earliest articles was "Über die mathematische Methode der theoretischen Ökonomie" (1906) and one of his last articles was "The Historical Approach to the Analysis of Business Cycles" (1949c). His first book, *Das Wesen und der Hauptinhalt der theoretischen Nationalökonomie* (1908), was a serious work of methodology, and his posthumous publication *History of Economic Analysis* (1954a), which was originally intended as a revision and translation of his earlier study *Epochen der*

Dogmen- und Methodengeschichte (1914a), was an overall evaluation of economics with regard to not only the content of economic doctrines but also the methods of economic analysis. Still other important studies demonstrate his methodological perspective. Nevertheless, Schumpeter's methodological work has been almost completely neglected. Even his archetypical *Das Wesen* has not received a proper place in the history of economic methodology.[5]

If Schumpeter is viewed from the standpoint of his famous work, *Theorie der wirtschaftlichen Entwicklung* (1912), or its English version, *The Theory of Economic Development* (1934), or his most widely read book, *Capitalism, Socialism and Democracy* (1942), he might be considered as unfamiliar with methodology and philosophy. Moreover, if he is evaluated on the basis of his occasional remarks on the sterility of methodological debates, he might be regarded as even hostile to methodology and philosophy. The following observation gives the impression that he was opposed to philosophy: "Economics is not a philosophy of economy, nor is it a view of essence. We must be less philosophical so that economics may become more productive. Even if economics used metaphysical elements, these are indifferent to the knowledge of specialized science" ([1932] 1952, 603).

In fact, however, Schumpeter was reared in the intellectual atmosphere of Austria and Germany at the turn of the century. His student life was dominated by a classical education at the Austrian Gymnasium, and both the *Methodenstreit* between Carl Menger and Gustav von Schmoller on theoretical versus historical methods and the debate between the Austrian school of economics and the Austro-Marxists on the working of a capitalist economy made a profound impression on him. Although he was imbued with the historicism and idealism prevalent in German thought, he started work on positive economics following Anglo-Saxon and Austrian positivism. Accordingly, he often pretended indifference or sometimes hostility to the Germans' favorite philosophical speculation, but his penchant for method and methodology was apparent throughout his academic life. It was his fundamental habit of thought.

This book will discuss his contributions to methodology, which he himself used generally to clarify the nature of science and specifically to integrate theory and history in economics, and attempt a reconstruction of the background of his thought and the framework of his analysis. In this book methodology is utilized as a tool for organizing Schumpeter's many-sided achievements and is not considered independently from his substantive work.

It follows that my attempt to identify the Schumpeterian style of thought and to construct a bird's-eye view of the Schumpeterian cosmos will raise some basic questions beyond a study of Schumpeter's economic thought. First, the investigation of Schumpeter's methodology will mean a clarification of his idea of social science, which goes well beyond the narrow concept of economics. No contemporary economist has tried to establish a system of thought broader than Schumpeter's, with the exception of Friedrich von Hayek, Kenneth Boulding, and a few others. Indeed, his methodology gives us a rare frame of reference for our own perspective on economics. Schumpeter's viewpoint is timeless.

Second, in order to understand and evaluate Schumpeter's methodology it will be necessary to place it in the context of the philosophy of science of his time as well as our own. Although he did not speak as an expert philosopher of science, his work is worthy of serious examination. Through this inquiry we can expect not only to gain a clarification of his methodology but also to see how his thinking was rooted in the stream of thought preceding the heyday of logical positivism and how his methodology deserves our attention because of its contemporary relevance.

The metatheoretical framework

For convenience's sake, I have used the term "methodology" only in a symbolic and representative sense. To be precise, I will refer to "metatheory," or "metatheoretical framework," a part of which is methodology. It is, of course, necessary to clarify the meaning of metatheory in order to approach Schumpeter's theoretical work from this point of view and establish the conceptual framework of this inquiry. In presenting the metatheoretical framework, which covers the view of science as comprising normative, social, and historical activities, I have kept in mind recent developments in the philosophy of science since the decline of logical positivism.

Three metatheories

The first element of the metatheoretical framework is the *methodology of science*. Here one must distinguish between method and methodology; although related, they are two distinct things. For Machlup it was very problematic that people often confused the two, calling something methodology when they were only speaking of methods (Machlup 1963, 204). The explication of methods is not necessarily methodology. Methods in science consist of a series of rules and technical procedures relating to concept formation, setting of assumptions, building of models, formulation of hypotheses, observation of facts, testing of theories, and the like. Methodology, on the other hand, involves a philosophical inquiry into the reasons why certain methods are utilized and gives criteria for appraising theories derived by certain methods. In this sense scientific methodology is a synonym for the philosophy of science; it provides a normative prescription for science as well as a philosophical analysis of science. Different methodologies can justify one and the same method, whereas different methods can be justified by one and the same methodology.

Methodology must be linked with the *sociology of knowledge* – the second element of the metatheoretical framework – because science does not work with methods alone. As the terms "problems and methods" or "scope and methods" indicate, science needs to define the scope of the subject matter to which methods are to be applied. The choice and setting of problems, which are prescientific acts, depend on the visions of scientists working in a society. Based on neo-Kantian philosophy, Heinrich Rickert (1902) and Max Weber (1904) called this relationship "value-relevance" (*Wertbeziehung*). Because the formation of a scientist's vision of what is important takes place in a social process that is historically conditioned, values, ideologies, and institutions affect the choice and setting of problems in the prescientific stage. The effects of social factors are not limited merely to the choice of problems; they may also extend to methods of science. This is the theme of the sociology of knowledge or the sociology of science. Broadly speaking, the sociology of science is concerned with the relationship between thought and society.

The third element, the *history of science*, deals not only with the historical development of scientific achievements addressed to the "problems" and assisted by the "methods" of science, but also with the historical evolution of the relationship between science and society. In other words, the history of science describes not only scientific activities that are under the control of the abstract rules of procedures, but also those activities that are not scientific in themselves but are conducted in relation to science within a specific context of social circumstances. By so doing the history of science is concerned with all those factors, which both the methodology of science and the sociology of science deal with, from the historical point of view, and supplies the place for testing empirically what these two disciplines advocate.

Thus my conceptual framework for dealing with science consists of three components: the methodology of science, the sociology of science, and the history of science. Their relationships are depicted in Figure 1.

This framework includes not only the *methodology of science* concerning the precepts of science, but also the *sociology of science* concerning the practice of science in society and the *history of science* concerning the evolution of science in history. I call this system the "metatheoretical framework." Since the fall of logical positivism, the philosophy of science has moved toward the sociology of science and the history of science, so that the three disciplines are integrated in a comprehensive study of science. Schumpeter's idea of social science was defined by the overlapping interests of philosophers, sociologists, and historians, and his substantive work in social science was constructed in a correspondingly cosmic fashion. All three disciplines can be called metatheories in that they deal with a theory or science from different angles, that is,

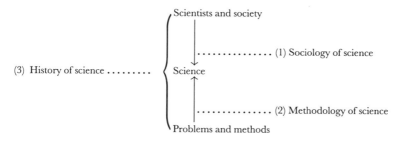

Figure 1   *The metatheoretical framework*

from the perspective of philosophy, sociology, or history. Metatheory is contrasted with substantive theory, to which it is addressed.[6]

Apart from Schumpeter's substantive examination of the economy and society, my framework covers all of his work on metatheory. His major contributions in these three fields are represented by *Vergangenheit und Zukunft der Sozialwissenschaften* (1915) and "Science and Ideology" (1949a), *Das Wesen und der Hauptinhalt der theoretischen Nationalökonomie* (1908), and *History of Economic Analysis* (1954a). Among his metatheories, the best known and the most esteemed come from his studies in the history of economics. But his work involving the sociology of science and the methodology of science was also significant. In Part I of *History*, he planned to discuss the sociology of science and the methodology of science as an introduction to the history of science, but he did not complete it. Nevertheless, he worked in all three fields. Thus, the metatheoretical framework for organizing Schumpeter's wide-ranging studies in this book is his own, and on the basis of this framework I have attempted to reconstruct his total work.

Theory and metatheory

Now, let us consider Schumpeter's substantive theory in contrast to the metatheory. As will be explained in chapter 3, his theory about economic society encompasses economic statics, economic dynamics, and economic sociology. Having constructed the statics and dynamics of an economy, Schumpeter developed his idea of a universal social science by assuming that an economy was embedded in a society as a whole and by approaching this task by means of economic sociology. Today's studies on Schumpeter, though they often neglect his contribution to static theory, do evaluate his work on economic development, technological innovation, entrepreneurship, and economic sociology.[7]

How then can one explain such an economist's invariable interest in metatheory? Specifically, how did the author of *The Theory of Economic Development* come to be the author of the *History of Economic Analysis*? It might be said that economists are naturally drawn to the history of economics. In the case of Schumpeter, however, there was a deeper reason. In his idea of a universal social science, both the development of an economy and the development of thought were social phenomena to which he applied parallel treatments. He intended this concept to replace Marx's social theory based on the economic interpretation of history. Just as Marx's theory, another version of a universal social science, addressed the relationship between production (substructure) and a system of ideology (superstructure), so Schumpeter focused on the interrelationship between the economy and ideas. Schumpeter's interest in both economic development and scientific development was not accidental; his work on the history of economic thought was not merely the hobby of an erudite scholar.

Thus viewed, it is suggested that in Schumpeter's idea of a universal social science, a set of substantive theories (economic statics, economic dynamics, and economic sociology) is matched with another set of metatheories (methodology of science, history of science, and sociology of science) with a parallel structure. First, the methodology of science is concerned with the static structure and rules of science; second, the history of science deals with the dynamic development of science; and third, the sociology of science involves scientific activities as social phenomena. If the two sets of thought are likened to buildings, we can envision two intellectual buildings – one for economy and one for science, respectively; they have three stories, and their third floors are linked by a passage representing sociology. I call Schumpeter's total system of thought the "two-structure approach to mind and society."

In this way, the concepts of metatheories, which I have introduced to organize and interpret Schumpeter's substantive theories on the working of an economy, play the part of a universal social science and analyze the working of thought as a social entity. Viewed from this perspective, the past and present studies that consider Schumpeter's system of economics in terms of economic statics, dynamics, and economic sociology at most and that never integrate his work on the history of economics – let alone his achievements in the methodology of science and the sociology of science – are obviously flawed.

The plan of the book

Figure 2 shows the structure of this book based on the metatheoretical framework.

Chapter 2 provides an overview of Schumpeter's life, career, and activities; it demonstrates how his character and the circumstances of the time in which

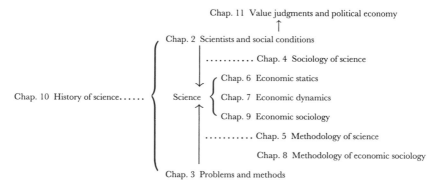

Figure 2   *The structure of this book*

he lived shaped his prescientific outlook and influenced the directions of his scientific work. The substantive and methodological ideas of science do not emerge in a vacuum. Because science is a kind of social activity, social and historical conditions always play a role in the performance of science in addition to the efforts and contributions of scientists. What kind of vision did Schumpeter embrace when he launched his economic studies at the beginning of the twentieth century? By illuminating his personality and social circumstances and using the sociology of knowledge, we can better understand his work.

What kind of problems and methods did Schumpeter draw upon to implement his vision? In chapter 3 I will argue that he created a unique, comprehensive research program that distinguished between three problem areas: statics, dynamics, and sociocultural development. With regard to methods, he identified four: theory, history, statistics, and economic sociology. From a combination of the problems and methods thus distinguished came his varied achievements in substantive theory, consisting of economic statics, economic dynamics, and economic sociology (considered in chapters 6, 7, and 9 respectively). Underlying his research program was the idea of integrating theory and history, an approach that was distinctly influenced by ideology inherent in the German intellectual field.

Chapters 4 and 5, corresponding with chapters 2 and 3, explore Schumpeter's sociology of science and methodology of science, both of which have been least discussed in the Schumpeter literature. Chapter 4 focuses on the relationship between science, ideology, and schools of thought and examines the structure of Schumpeter's ideology concerning the three research fields of statics, dynamics, and sociocultural development. Chapter 5 takes up his maiden work, *Das Wesen und der Hauptinhalt der theoretischen Nationalökonomie*, and interprets his methodology as instrumentalism, which was first developed to lay a foundation for neoclassical economics but later functioned as an anchor in his attempt to construct a universal social science designed for the integration of theory and history.

The most characteristic feature of Schumpeter's methodology is that its argument is not confined to an abstract or general level but is united with concrete problems and methods. Thus chapters 6, 7, and 9 deal with his economic statics, economic dynamics, and economic sociology, which are concerned with circular flow, economic development, and sociocultural development, respectively. These bodies of theory are widely recognized as his specific contributions, but locating them within our metatheoretical framework will clarify the logical connection between them and dispel existing misinterpretations about them. For example, Schumpeter's theory of technological innovation in economic development is particularly well known, but it is only one aspect of the total picture that he wanted to describe; thus it is linked with discussions of economic sociology and yet does not deny the logic of economic statics.

Having started from a foundation of neoclassical economics and engaged in basic methodological work in order to establish this young science on a secure basis, Schumpeter then tried to supplement it with dynamic economics. However, as Schumpeter was also brought up in the traditions of German historical economics, German cultural sociology, and Marxian socialist thought, he did pay attention to the historical, social, and institutional aspects of an economy; the outcome was his economic sociology. Chapter 8 examines whether his instrumentalist methodology is valid for economic sociology, and in this connection considers the relationship between Schumpeter, Schmoller, and Weber with regard to the methodology of economic sociology or historical science.

Chapter 10 is concerned with the history of economics. Schumpeter's monumental *History of Economic Analysis* has been regarded as the most authoritative work in this field, but, contrary to what is generally believed, I contend that it is not a description of the developments in economics in the narrow sense, which converged in the establishment of the general equilibrium theory. As Figure 1 (see page 7) shows, his history of science, while focusing on science, describes the interplay between the evolution of the relationships between society and scientists addressed by the sociology of science, on the one hand, and the development of problems and methods addressed by the methodology of science, on the other. Thus Schumpeter's concept of the "filiation of scientific ideas" (1954a, 6), a key term in his history of economic analysis, is conceived as the development of economic theories embedded in the sociological and methodological inquiries of science. What is noteworthy is his view that scientific activities are not only passively conditioned by social factors that pose the theoretical problems to be solved at a specific time, but also affect the course of events of a society because the ideas of scientists and philosophers are ultimately powerful as a directive for understanding and organizing the society; thus the history of science constitutes a part of the history of society as a whole. This explains why he was so interested in the history of economics. Schumpeter's two-structure approach to mind and society is really the scheme to grasp the interactions between thought and society.

It is erroneous to regard Schumpeter simply as a scholar. For a short time he was finance minister of Austria and then chairman of a bank. Although unsuccessful in these posts, he had wished to be a politician or a "consultant administrator" (1954a, 159) who influenced the policy of a nation. In view of the practice of university professors in Austria at that time – his teachers Eugen von Böhm-Bawerk and Friedrich von Wieser became finance minister and commerce minister, respectively – his ambition was not unreasonable. After his disappointing experiences outside academe, he often pretended indifference to politics. But Schumpeter, the universal social scientist, could not abandon his interest in politics and economic policy. This aspect of Schumpeter was recently most intensively and excellently explored by Wolfgang Stolper (1994). In order to incorporate this picture of Schumpeter into my conceptual framework, chapter 11, without going into the details of his political activities, focuses on his *Weltanschauung*, his world outlook, which is a reflection of his ideology at the practical level (as distinguished from the scientific level) as well as his habits, inclinations, and values. Discussions of his value judgments lead specifically to his political concept of economy and provide a counterpart to chapter 4, where ideology is regarded as a prerequisite of scientific activities. The chapter also examines the relationship between science and policy and his attitude toward policymaking.

In conclusion, chapter 12 comments on the significance of the Schumpeterian style of thought. Schumpeter is ranked among the greatest economists of the twentieth century. If so, in what sense did he succeed? Whereas the conventional view seems to be either one of benign neglect or uncritical praise, we must admit that in fact he failed to immediately influence the course of events in history. To use his unique style of rhetoric, if he is ever to succeed, he will succeed because of his short-term failures. Against the stream and fashion of the times, he continued to raise fundamental questions that the social sciences should address:

But there comes a moment when the atmosphere changes. The significance of the unreflectively utilized viewpoints becomes uncertain and the road is lost in the twilight. The light of the great cultural problems moves on. Then science too prepares to change its standpoint and its analytical apparatus and to view the streams of events from the heights of thought. It follows those stars which alone are able to give meaning and direction to its labors. (Weber [1904] 1949, 112)

Will Schumpeter be regarded as such a guiding star to the social sciences?

Schumpeter said that great ideas are revived. This was his insight into the history of ideas. He also observed that great ideas need not be perfect or faultless in their fundamental design and theoretical formulation. It is due to "a power of darkness" that great ideas keep their vitality and enjoy revivals (1950a, 3). This book intends to shed light on the structure of the power of darkness in Schumpeter.[8]

Schumpeter and his surroundings: an overview

In the latter half of the nineteenth century the Habsburg monarchy with its glorious history of six hundred years enjoyed the last epoch of brilliance as the Austro-Hungarian Empire. Vienna, the capital, was the cultural center of Europe; there from the 1880s to the 1910s, many great thinkers, artists, and scientists prevailed in the fields of literature, painting, music, philosophy, natural science, psychology, and social science.[1] After triggering World War I, however, the Empire was defeated and collapsed.

The crucial moment

Joseph Alois Schumpeter took his place in the intellectual history of Vienna at the turn of the century. He was born on 8 February 1883 in Třešt' (pronounced 'trdʒeʃtə), a small Moravian town in the Austro-Hungarian Empire.[2] (The Germans called the town Triesch, but that name is no longer used.) Třešt' lies at the basin of the Bohemian–Moravian Highlands, 120 kilometers southeast of Prague and halfway between Prague and Vienna. When the multiracial Austro-Hungarian Empire disintegrated from within after World War I, the independent state of Czechoslovakia was formed from Bohemia, Moravia, and Slovakia. Třešt' celebrated its six hundredth anniversary in 1949, and the Schumpeter family occupies an indispensable place in the town's history. After World War II Czechoslovakia belonged to the socialist bloc, but it was split into Czech Republic and Slovak Republic with the fall of Eastern European socialism at the end of the 1980s. Today Třešt' belongs to the Czech Republic and has a population of 6,700. It is an industrial town with small factories, but a castle and two churches retain the image of earlier days.

The economist Schumpeter is presumed to have represented the thirteenth generation of Schumpeters, who settled in Třešt' in the early sixteenth century.[3] On the whole, his paternal ancestors had been rich and prestigious middle-class provincial businessmen; many of them were textile merchants or manufacturers, and sometimes they served as mayors or councilmen of the town, where several religious monuments donated by the family remain. The tenth generation (that of Schumpeter's great-grandfather) started manufacturing woolen cloth in the 1830s, and the eleventh generation (Schumpeter's grandfather) greatly improved and enlarged the factory. The grandfather had seven daughters and four sons (the twelfth generation); two sons died in infancy and the elder son inherited the factory. The latter's brother Josef Alois Karel (1855–87), who was fifteen years younger, was the economist Schumpeter's father.

Schumpeter's mother Johanna (1861–1926) was the daughter of Julius Grüner, a surgeon in Jihlava. Jihlava (the German name was Iglau) is 10 kilometers north of Třešť and a much bigger city; in the early 1990s its population was 50,000. The Grüner family, which had produced doctors in Jihlava for two generations, was also well respected. Johanna's grandfather, Franz Julius Grüner, was director of the town's hospital as well as a botanist who specialized in research on moss plants. Johanna's father succeeded him as hospital director.

The children of the tenth generation of Schumpeters found their spouses in larger neighboring towns such as Jihlava, Třebič, and Telč. Indeed, the wealth and fame of the Schumpeter family made marriage possible with members of the intellectual strata of those more advanced towns.

Schumpeter's parents were married in 1881, and their first son, the economist, was born in 1883. Although his paternal ancestry included many businessmen, it apparently had not produced any intellectually prominent figures. Thus, it would seem that Schumpeter had inherited his high intelligence from his maternal side.

A year after his birth, the Roman Catholic Josef and Johanna had another son who was born dead. According to the Třešť registry, the family lived at the house numbered 52 (now reportedly 462 Rooseveltova Street).[4]

To high society

In 1887, when Schumpeter was four years old, his father died, and the next year he and his mother moved to Graz, where he attended school for four years. In 1893 they went to Vienna; there his mother married Sigmund von Kéler, a retired *Feldmarshalleutenant* (Lieutenant General) in the Austro-Hungarian army who was thirty-three years older than she. Austria had the most rigidly aristocratic society in Europe. Generals from *Feldmarshalleutenant* upwards belonged to the upper upper class or the "first society" and were ranked just below peers, cabinet ministers, and high civil servants (Streissler 1982, 61).

Little is known about the life Schumpeter's family led during this period, but the change in their circumstances enabled him to attend the Theresianum

(1893–1901), the elitist school in Vienna. This great transformation in his life had a remarkable influence on his career. If his father had not died so young, and if his mother had not then married a prominent former official, Schumpeter probably would have lived in obscurity in the little-known town of Třešť. His mother's remarriage was crucial to producing the scholar Schumpeter, for it connected him with the elite of high society, enabling him to cultivate his intelligence and to become intimately acquainted with the aristocratic lifestyle. Unlike those born into society, an upstart is apt to make himself conspicuous. Although there is no doubt about Schumpeter's intellectual gifts, his rise to a higher social plain may have influenced his tendency to show off and his extreme self-consciousness.[5] Johanna's second marriage ended in separation in 1906, when Schumpeter was twenty-three, as if it had been intended only to provide her son with an opportunity to pursue a better way of life.

The early years, 1901–1924

In 1904 Schumpeter, blessed with opportunities and propitious circumstances, graduated from the Theresianum and entered the University of Vienna, which at that time ranked with Cambridge and Stockholm as a center of economic research.[6] There Carl Menger, one of the founders of Marginalism, initiated through his *Grundsätze der Volkswirtschaftslehre* (Menger 1871) the Austrian School of Economics. According to Friedrich von Hayek, Vienna was nothing until the university reform of 1867; after that, it began to flourish, reaching its highest level of growth from the 1890s up to 1914 (Hayek 1994, 49). Menger retired in 1903 and went into seclusion for the remaining twenty years of his life. Meanwhile, his pupils Böhm-Bawerk and Friedrich von Wieser started to work at the University of Vienna as members of the Austrian School's second generation.

When Schumpeter enrolled at Vienna, economics was taught by the Faculty of Law (Rechts- und Staatswissenschaften). According to the registration records of lectures (1901–5) and his curriculum vitae at the Habilitation (1909), Schumpeter first studied the law generally and the history of land tax in Lower Austria in the seminar of Siegmund Adler, professor of history. Then he attended Robert Meyer's seminar on public finance, Eugen von Philippovich's seminar on public finance, and finally Böhm-Bawerk's seminar on economics, Friedrich von Wieser's seminar on economics, and Theodor von Inamma-Sternegg's seminar on statistics.[7] Before World War I Böhm-Bawerk's seminar was known as the intellectual center of the Austrian School; not only students but also prominent intellectuals and government officials sat in on his session – among others, Ludwig von Mises, Felix Somary, Otto Bauer, Rudolf Hilferding, and Emil Lederer. Bauer, Hilferding, Lederer,

Viktor Adler, Friedrich Adler, Max Adler, and Karl Renner, who studied at Vienna during this period, later became the leaders of Austrian socialism and were called Austro-Marxists.[8] In seminars Schumpeter witnessed the clash between neoclassical economics and Marxian economics, especially Böhm-Bawerk's attack of Bauer. Thus, at the center of the Austrian School Schumpeter studied the new economic theory as well as Marxian theory, statistics, history, and law. His starting point was economic and legal history.

In light of Schumpeter's lifelong academic activities, his early learning experiences are significant. In his curriculum vitae submitted to the University of Bonn in 1925, he wrote:

Already at the time of the Theresianum, I had developed sociological interest together with philosophical ones, but at the university my first field of research was legal and social history especially from an economic point of view. Then I made a sharp turn to economic theory of the Austrian (Menger) School; I was looked upon above all as its representative (and problem child) and my work in economics is based on its theoretical ground, although subsequent development followed the direction of Walras, Pareto, and Edgeworth ("mathematical school") and my own results were compatible with other approaches. After 1912, these interests receded behind sociological ones, which led to different opinion of Schmoller's research field.[9]

Schumpeter was not drawn to the narrow field of theoretical economics; rather, it must be stressed, he had a great interest in history, sociology, and philosophy from the beginning.

The decade of sacred fertility

Schumpeter's study of economics, from the time he began work at Vienna until his death in 1950, can be divided into two twenty-five-year periods. After graduating from the university in 1906, he made his debut in the academic world as a young theoretical economist. His early trilogy, *Das Wesen und der Hauptinhalt der theoretischen Nationalökonomie* (1908), *Theorie der wirtschaftlichen Entwicklung* (1912), and *Epochen der Dogmen- und Methodengeschichte* (1914a), dealt with static economics, dynamic economics, and the history of economics, respectively, and put forward a system of basic theoretical economics. In particular, *Entwicklung* made him world famous. The central purpose of the book was to identify the fundamental phenomenon of economic development with the innovations of entrepreneurs. Schumpeter completed all three volumes by the age of thirty. Arthur Spiethoff, his colleague at Bonn, referring to the early trilogy in an obituary essay, remarked: "What is more amazing than that a man of 25 or 27 should shake the very foundations of his science, or that a man of 30 should write the history of that discipline!" (Spiethoff 1949, 291).

In his sparkling obituary of Böhm-Bawerk, Schumpeter wrote: "The fact that has been often surmised, discussed, and more and more clearly established by biographical research – namely, that the roots of important original achievements, especially those of a theoretical nature, are established when authors are in their twenties – is confirmed in the case of Böhm-Bawerk" (1914b, 463–64).[10] Schumpeter often spoke of "that period of sacred fertility" (1921, 203) and found in the ideas and visions scholars entertained in their twenties the inexhaustible source of vitality in their later years. In the case of Böhm-Bawerk, Schumpeter noted that when his former teacher returned to the University of Vienna (after serving in the ministry of finance for fifteen years) to harvest the fruits of his early creative years, "the essential elements and the basis of his life work were not fundamentally changed since he had once developed them" (1914b, 463). All of this also applied to Schumpeter himself in that his work in the second half of his career can be seen as an effort to bring his work in the first half to fruition.

In appearance, Schumpeter was completely self-assured; he possessed aristocratic tastes and surprised others by doing the extraordinary.[11] To mystify people, he would talk about his three ambitions as a youth: "I wanted to be the greatest lover in Vienna, the greatest horseman in Austria, and the greatest economist in the world, but I failed to achieve one of the three."[12] Although he earned his reputation as an excellent theorist while still young, self-consciousness and ambition always impelled him to care about success and fame. What sustained him was his remarkable precocity, erudition, and superhuman endeavors.

During the period of his early trilogy Schumpeter was not accepted by the first-rank universities. In 1907–8 he practiced law at the International Mixed Tribunal in Cairo and worked as a financial adviser to the Egyptian princess. In 1909–10, through the intervention of Böhm-Bawerk, he was appointed professor at the University of Czernowitz, located in the eastern borderland of the Austro-Hungarian Empire (now in the Ukraine); in 1911–18 he became a professor at the University of Graz near Vienna. In Austria and Germany, at that time under the influence of the German Historical School, theoretical economists like Schumpeter were isolated from academic circles. He never obtained a permanent position at the University of Vienna.

Meanwhile in 1907, while traveling in England, Schumpeter married Gladys Ricarde Seaver, whose father was said to be a dignitary of the Church of England. His biographers disagree about her age, but apparently she was twelve years older than Schumpeter.[13] The marriage was a failure, and they soon lived apart and finally divorced in 1920. About Gladys nothing more is known.

During this period Schumpeter lived in Graz, where he lectured on economic theory, public finance, and economic policy; after 1915 he also gave special talks on "The Problems of Social Classes" and "Economic Democracy." Previously, he had spoken on "State and Society" at the University of Czernowitz (1910–11) and on "The Theory of Social Classes" at Columbia University, in New York (1913–14), where he was an exchange professor. His interest in the problems of social classes produced an important article, "Die sozialen Klassen in ethnisch homogenen Milieu," in 1927. Schumpeter had been exploring the frontier of theoretical economics and was a defender of mathematical economics, but at the same time he was drawn to economic sociology; he published sociological works such as *Die Krise des Steuerstaates* in 1918 and "Zur Soziologie der Imperialismen" in 1918–19.

Consultant administrator and pamphleteer

After World War I the German socialist government established the Socialization Commission in Berlin for planning the nationalization of industries; its chairman was Karl Kautsky. Schumpeter, together with Hilferding, Lederer, and others, was appointed to the commission.[14] In Austria a coalition government of the Social Democratic Party and the Christian Social Party was established under Prime Minister Karl Renner, and Foreign Minister Otto Bauer recommended that his old friend Joseph Alois Schumpeter be named finance minister. This position seemed to be fully compatible with Schumpeter's ambition. As minister he worked on the finance plan for the reconstruction of the postwar economy but resigned after seven months as a result of the political strife.[15] Although he was not a socialist, he developed an ardent interest in socialism from the experience of this period and soon shaped a vision on the transformation of the economic system from capitalism to socialism.

In 1920, after spending two semesters at the University of Graz, Schumpeter became president of the Biedermann Bank in Vienna. Schumpeter sought to make a lot of money by borrowing from the Bank for private investment in business. Due to a series of business failures in the postwar depression, he lost money and fell into debt; the Bank was also in trouble, and he resigned in 1924. Worried about repaying his creditors, Schumpeter contributed articles on current economic policy to the *Deutsche Volkswirt* in order to earn money over the next several years.[16]

During the decade of World War I three professorships became vacant at the University of Vienna owing to the retirement of Böhm-Bawerk, Phillipovich, and Wieser. The first of these appointments was taken by the economic historian Carl Grünberg, who was soon succeeded by another historian, Degenfeld-Schönburg. Of the remaining two posts, Schumpeter and Ludwig von Mises were regarded by outsiders as most deserving, but instead the chairs were offered to Othmar Spann and Hans Mayer (Craver 1986, 2–3). After the war Schumpeter remained outside academe for seven years (1919–25).

Although he aspired to work in the public sphere, his activity in this field proved a failure. In 1943, on his sixtieth birthday, when asked about his three famous ambitions by his young colleagues at Harvard, he replied that he actually had had five ambitions: the other two were "to be an accomplished connoisseur of art, and to be successful in politics" (Morgan 1983, 4). In fact, Schumpeter was interested in painting and church architecture. His enthusiasm for painting is indicated by his remark on the history of painting that he made in chapter 11 of his *Capitalism, Socialism and Democracy* (1942) in describing the cultural complements of the capitalist economy. But this might not have extended beyond his personal taste. Schumpeter was more serious about politics. In the *History of Economic Analysis*, when examining economic thought in the seventeenth and eighteenth centuries before the emergence of the Classical School, he discussed "Consultant Administrators" and "Pamphleteers" (1954a, 159). Moreover, in the midst of his creative period he had worked in the worlds of politics and banking. This, then, was not necessarily a "great waste" (Allen 1991, 2, 87), that he bitterly repented of, because his postwar activities were related to his practice of economics as a consultant administrator and a pamphleteer, although he may have preferred to be finance minister over consultant administrator and pamphleteer for the sake of earning a living.

The later years, 1925–1950

The first half of Schumpeter's professional life produced remarkable achievements as well as vicissitudes. He had already published his early trilogy and established a vision of an economic society and an image of what economics should be. After a detour of seven years, he devoted the second half of his career to academic work, developing and expanding his ideas of the earlier period and thus demonstrating the unity and consistency of his research program. In scientific terms, he sought a sociological and historical view of society. This was in marked contrast to his image as such an avant-garde theoretical economist that even the German academic community gave him a cold shoulder. His ultimate goal, then, was to integrate theory and history.

The second half of his life did not begin smoothly, however, for in 1924–26 he was in the depths of despair both socially and personally. It is necessary for a man who has earned a good reputation in his youth to maintain his status by becoming more productive as time goes on; the more ambitious he is, the keener is his sense of duty to perform. Moreover, his achievements must now reflect a more rigid scientific formulation of the ideas developed earlier. Because Schumpeter was sensitive to external success and public opinion, he not only worked very hard in private but also experienced irritation and anguish. In later life he sometimes felt a deep sense of failure.

The Bonn period

In 1925, after leaving politics and the Bank, Schumpeter married Anna Josefin Reisinger; he was forty-two years old and she, twenty-two. On his return to Vienna from Graz to enter the public service, he had lived initially with his mother in an apartment at Doblhofgasse 3; Anna's father, while managing a small store that sold chandeliers and ornaments, was also the caretaker of their apartment, where Schumpeter and Anna met. In the postwar turmoil Anna had lost a bank job and for two years worked as a housemaid in the French provinces.[17] In 1923 she returned to Vienna, where she saw Schumpeter again and they fell in love. The latter half of Schumpeter's life began with his marriage to Anna, whose existence was all-important to him; indeed, his devotion to her would be lifelong, continuing after her death.

Also in 1925 Schumpeter obtained a professorship at the University of Bonn. Just before this he had been offered a similar post at Tokyo University as the successor to Emil Lederer, a proposal that he received with enthusiasm. When the chance of Bonn came up, however, he declined the invitation from Japan.

Schumpeter moved to Bonn in the winter semester of 1925 and began a new life. But only a year later he suffered heavy blows. In July 1926 his mother died in Vienna. Then in August his wife died after giving birth to their son. The child also succumbed after several hours. After Anna's death, Schumpeter, in his frenzy and grief, adopted an unusual, lifelong habit. Anna had kept a diary from 1919 to 1926. Every day from then on Schumpeter would copy her daily entry into a single notebook, which he maintained for the twenty-four years preceding his death. Not only at the top of every page of this diary, but also on his lecture notes and his famous yellow slips of paper, he always wrote "O Mutter und Herrin – o seid über mir!" (O Mother and Mistress – please protect me!) in the Gabelsberger shorthand, followed by words of prayer that he would succeed in his work; sometimes there were words of irritation and despair, sometimes words of relief and thanks. His mother and his wife became, so to speak, his guardian angels, the anchors of his later life. Although this practice illustrates Schumpeter's prodigal use of time, it was a secret device that sustained his inner life in the face of solitude and distress.[18]

Welcoming Schumpeter to the economics staff at Bonn were Arthur Spiethoff, Karl Dietzel, and Herbert von Beckerath. Spiethoff, who was ten years older than Schumpeter, became a close friend. He had started his career as the assistant of Gustav von Schmoller, the leader of the German Historical

School, and was counted among the school's third generation; he had gained a reputation for his empirical studies of business cycles and taught the principles of economics at Bonn. Schumpeter gave lectures on the history of economics, public finance, monetary theory, and sociology (especially the theory of social classes). In the area of theoretical economics, he taught an introduction to mathematics for economics during the 1929 summer semester and statistical methods for economics during the 1931 winter semester.

Schumpeter's main focus during the Bonn period was to develop the ideas of *Entwicklung* both theoretically and empirically, and for this purpose he thoroughly revised the book and published the second edition in 1926. Further development of the volume's propositions required him to perform two tasks: first, to construct a monetary theory, and second, to analyze business cycles. According to Schumpeter, the fundamental phenomenon of economic development was the innovation of entrepreneurs, and the means that enabled innovation was the credit created by banks; therefore, a dynamic theory of money was needed. On the other hand, he believed, because innovation produced economic development by causing business cycles, it was also necessary to provide a historical and statistical analysis of the cyclical development process.

In Bonn, Schumpeter devoted his efforts to the first task, the study of money. Just at this time, however, John Maynard Keynes brought out *A Treatise on Money* (1930), a book that Schumpeter felt preempted his own analysis. He continued the study but could not work out a satisfactory result and finally discarded the project in 1935. After his death the manuscript was published as *Das Wesen des Geldes* (1970).

The Harvard period

In 1932 Schumpeter resigned his post at Bonn and moved to Harvard University as professor. He felt uncomfortable and empty leaving the cultural world of Europe to live in the United States, but the intellectual climate of Harvard attracted him, particularly in view of his empirical research on business cycles. At that time Vienna and Berlin were the centers of business cycle study, but there were no opportunities for his appointment at either university. Thus he spent the last two decades of his life – during his fifties and sixties – at Harvard, which was then enjoying its golden age of economics. Although Schumpeter is not counted among the practitioners of the Austrian School, he was the first Austrian economist to emigrate to America in the 1930s, while the first Austrian economist to emigrate was actually Friedrich von Hayek to London in 1931. After the move, he published only in English. He had planned to translate his major work, *Entwicklung*, into English, but the translation was actually done by Redvers Opie, an Oxford don and Frank

Taussig's son-in-law, who had graduated from Harvard and stayed at Bonn; it was published by Harvard University Press in 1934 just after Schumpeter's arrival. Had he remained in Germany and continued his research in the same manner as before, writing largely in German, it is doubtful whether he would have had such a profound influence in his field, although before World War II German was undoubtedly an international language in the circle of economists.

After much effort, Schumpeter at last published his two-volume *Business Cycles* in 1939. Although an ambitious work with a lofty subtitle, "A Theoretical, Historical and Statistical Analysis of the Capitalist Process," it was almost totally ignored by economists, who were preoccupied with Keynes's revolutionary theory of depressions and unemployment in his *General Theory of Employment, Interest and Money* (1936). *Business Cycles*, while addressing the same questions, leaned toward historical description and did not appeal to practitioners. After abandoning his money study when preempted by Keynes's *Treatise on Money*, Schumpeter had devoted all of his energies to *Business Cycles*. But again, Keynes stood in his way. For him, this must have been humiliating.

After arriving in the United States, Schumpeter resided at the home of Professor Frank Taussig, at 2 Scott Street, Cambridge, until he married Elizabeth Boody Firuski in 1937. The couple lived at 7 Acacia Street, Cambridge, and sometimes stayed at her home in the village of Taconic, Connecticut. Fifteen years younger than Schumpeter, Elizabeth was an economist and a graduate of Radcliffe College; this was her second marriage. She had studied eighteenth-century English trade for her doctoral dissertation and then political and economic problems of the Far East, including Japan. From 1935 to 1940 she held an appointment at Harvard's Bureau of International Research. She edited *The Industrialization of Japan, Korea, and Manchuria, 1936–1940* (1940), and her dissertation was published posthumously as *English Overseas Trade Statistics, 1698–1808* (1960).

Schumpeter's next book, *Capitalism, Socialism and Democracy* (1942), was written in a short time, but it was a great success and won a popular audience. This volume analyzes the consequences of economic development in the context of the evolutionary capitalist system, not capitalism as an economic system but capitalism as a social and cultural system. Rejecting the notion that capitalism would fall because of its economic failure, he argued that the very success of capitalism in economic terms would erode its foundation and give rise to socialism. The book, whose basic ideas go back to *Die Krise des Steuerstaates* (1918), is a final synthesis of his work in sociology during the first half of his career.

In the last ten years of his life, Schumpeter was absorbed in writing a history of economics. After publishing *Epochen* in 1914, he had constantly received offers to translate it into English but always refused them because he planned to write a new version after bringing *Epochen* up-to-date.[19] The history of economics was his favorite subject, and at Harvard he taught a course on the history of economic thought from 1938 to 1948. His writing project, starting from 1941, continued to expand in scope and was still in progress nine or ten years later. On his death huge bundles of unfinished manuscript were found in several places; Elizabeth Boody Schumpeter compiled and edited them in a *magnum opus* entitled the *History of Economic Analysis* (1954a) containing over 1,200 pages of fine print.

It can be argued that *History* reflects what Schumpeter had learned, what he thought, and what he wanted to accomplish in the social sciences. In later years he would tell his friends that, although he wanted to write five more books, the preparation of *History* prevented him from doing so. Apparently the themes of those five books would have been cultural history, logic, the relationship of economic concepts to the wider social world, and three semisociological works with a strong flavor of the history of ideas (Goodwin 1983, 613). Yet the history of economics enabled him to consider all of the history of theory, thought, philosophy, methodology, and biography; social background; and so forth. Thus *History* posited as its objective what he understood by a "universal social science" and described its evolution. It was nothing less than a synthesis of all that he had learned throughout life. Indeed, no work on the history of economics has surpassed his *History*.

Business Cycles, *Capitalism*, and *History* can be called Schumpeter's later trilogy; they are an extension of the work he initiated in the first half of his career. The latter two volumes were especially successful. In his last decade, in contrast with the preceding one, he was able to work comfortably – without suffering from an inferiority complex – on the evolution of capitalism and the history of ideas, areas where he had a comparative advantage. But he was not happy. It was the era of Roosevelt's New Deal and Hitler's Nazism. Schumpeter was critical of Roosevelt and remained silent about Hitler, but he hated Stalinism. He found himself isolated in the political and intellectual atmosphere that then prevailed in the United States.[20]

On 8 January 1950, at the age of sixty-seven, Schumpeter died of a stroke in his sleep at Taconic. In the Schumpeter Papers at the Pusey Library of Harvard University are several bundles of telegrams and letters of condolence that were delivered after his death. In view of the enormous amount of time and effort he expended so that his students might develop their own ideas based on his firm belief in the "third decade of sacred fertility," and despite all the obituaries extolling his accomplishments, nothing is more moving or better demonstrates what Schumpeter regarded as his purpose than the following telegram from the graduate students at Harvard:[21] "In our hearts, our minds and our work we will always be part Schumpeterian. That is the measure of our debt to Professor Schumpeter. We will miss him as a teacher, as an inspiration for scholars and most, as a friend. Please accept our deepest sympathy."[22]

The intellectual field and Schumpeter's *habitus*

In 1883 Marx died and Keynes and Schumpeter were born. In 1983, the year of their centenary, memorials for the three great economists were held at various places in the world. They are comparable in that they developed, although in quite different ways, large-scale economic theories that were somehow concerned with the fate of capitalism. With what kind of thought was Schumpeter brought up? To what kind of thought did he commit himself in order to develop his theory? Although Keynes and Schumpeter faced the same problems raised by the capitalist economy in the first half of the twentieth century, namely, the instability of capitalism, they were reared in different intellectual circumstances, which caused different prescientific conditions. It was the claim of Schumpeter's sociology of science that, when one begins to consider what is important and relevant in constructing the image of society, one must rely first on the framework of thought established by precursors. And it was Schumpeter's view that new additions to the thought of precursors and new combinations of their ideas lead to innovation in science.

The intellectual field and habitus

What intellectual circumstances applied to Schumpeter? Instead of vague expressions such as intellectual circumstances, social milieu, or social background, I shall use a concept that has specific meaning and structure in the context of the sociology of science: that of the "intellectual field" as defined by Bourdieu (Bourdieu 1984). This concept and *habitus* (a set of dispositions created by objective conditions and personal history) make a pair. Bourdieu calls the various areas in social life "fields," one of which is the intellectual field. A field is a social space within which competitive struggles take place over specific stakes (capital); the activity or practice of the agents in a field is explained by the *habituses* of the agents. Capital in the intellectual field is called cultural capital (legitimate knowledge). The intellectual field at a given time is made up of agents, individuals, or schools assuming various intellectual positions.[23]

The characteristics of the intellectual field can be summarized as follows: (1) The intellectual field is a historical given, and its constellation of theories confronts individual scientists as objectively given. (2) The intellectual field is characterized by the configuration of various positions that represent the distribution of power held by schools and theories. (3) The intellectual field is influenced by various social factors, but it is relatively autonomous in the sense that it has its own logic and rules. (4) The significance of a specific theory is defined by its place or position in the intellectual field; this is the positional or relational attribute of knowledge. (5) The intellectual field is the total result of intellectual activities produced by the complex of specific *habituses*. As demonstrated in chapter 4, characteristics (1)–(3) are not different from Schumpeter's view, but Bourdieu emphasizes (4)–(5).

The sociology of science traditionally deals with the circumstances under which the individual talents, psychology, economic interests, and social positions of scientists influence their ideas outside the area in which the philosophy of science governs the rules of scientific procedure. In contrast, the theory of the intellectual field denies that the biographical features of individuals and their social positions are directly linked to intellectual performance; it also rejects the view that the interpretation of a text is possible by its internal analysis alone. Rather, it asserts that there are some other factors between society and knowledge as well as between individuals and knowledge. The intellectual field and the *habitus* together constitute the mediating link between the subjective world of individuals and the social world; from this link knowledge is generated. The relationship between the intellectual field and the *habitus* in Bourdieu resembles the relationship between schools and ideology in Schumpeter's sociology of science. The state of competition between schools represents the intellectual field, and the *habitus* or ideology is the spiritual presupposition of agents working in the field.

Figure 3 illustrates the basic structure of the problem. The *habitus*, consisting of a set of durable and transposable dispositions, links the objective conditions of a society with the subjective conditions of an agent. It represents the structure of the human capacity to generate habitually scientific work as practice; it is shaped socially as it is placed in the intellectual field, although it belongs to the personality of an agent. The *habitus* does not produce the practice technically; thus, Bourdieu emphasizes strategy as a game having some latitude, whereas Schumpeter emphasized vision as the subjective precondition of scientific work. Strategy and vision are auxiliary concepts for explaining the process of scientific production by the *habitus* and help to reject the mechanistic and objectivistic view of the social world. The practice thus produced takes place in a society in the form of competition for the position of cultural capital. In this context Schumpeter recognized the existence of scientific schools, whereas Bourdieu is more concerned with the scheme of education. All of these activities constitute the intellectual field, which, in turn, redraws the objective conditions that will be given to future generations.

If we adopt the notions of the intellectual field and the *habitus*, Schumpeter's work cannot be considered without an investigation of the intellectual field he was facing. At the same time, what he intended and aspired to should be

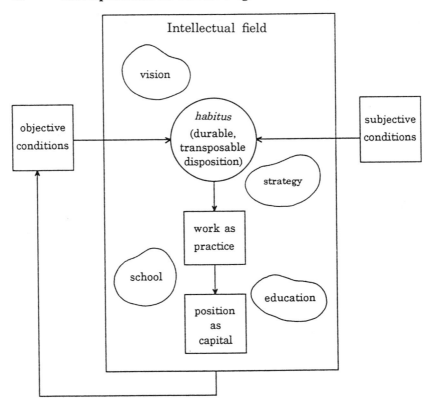

Figure 3   *The intellectual field and* habitus

discussed on the level of *habitus*, which transcends his individual tastes or peculiarities and can be generalized to something like methods of scientists.

Neoclassicism, Marxism, and historicism

Objectively given thought in the intellectual field has no meaning to scientists unless they make a response – that is, unless they accept or reject it. This is the function of the *habitus* vis-à-vis the intellectual field, and through this function a specific image of the problem to be studied by a scholar will be constructed. Schumpeter showed strong interest in the intellectual products of the past in a wide area of the social sciences. His erudition is well known, yet it is not a matter of taste but of material for scientific work. Three important elements in the intellectual field are crucial to an understanding of his work: neoclassical economics, Marxism, and German historical economics. On a more basic level of philosophy and methodology beyond the distinction of schools in economics, Schumpeter was committed to positivism and historicism.

Neoclassical economics, Marxism, and the German Historical School existed in the German and Austrian intellectual field of economics with different relative importance. They represented the positions of elaboration, development, and criticism of British classical economics, respectively. Rather than choose any one, Schumpeter took all of them seriously; his attitude toward them was as follows.

First, neoclassical economics, generated by the Marginal Revolution in the 1870s, elaborated classical economics technically and reconstructed it from the dynamic study of improving national wealth to the static study of resource allocation. Although Schumpeter started from the perspective of Austrian economics under the influence of Eugen von Böhm-Bawerk and Friedrich von Wieser, he firmly supported Léon Walras's concept of general equilibrium as the Magna Carta of economic theory. His position was derived not from the thought within economics but from the methodological reflection of advanced natural science, especially that developed by Ernst Mach (see chapter 5).

Second, based on the Walrasian version of static neoclassical theory Schumpeter wanted to build a dynamic theory, borrowing the idea of evolution from Karl Marx. Marx, inheriting classical economics, especially that of David Ricardo, established a grand theory of social development. Although different, neoclassical economics and Marxian economics had in common their attempt to advance the internal development of classical economics. Schumpeter accepted the concepts of Walras and Marx as the basic ideologies (see chapter 4).

Third, in contrast to neoclassicism and Marxism, the German Historical School challenged classical economics from a transcendental viewpoint. In keeping with its political and ethical orientation, it advocated the historical approach, which had not been established as a paradigm in economics in spite of the emphasis of historical observations by Adam Smith, as opposed to the theoretical approach of classical economics and its successors. The *Methoden-streit* between Carl Menger and Gustav von Schmoller, which took place in Germany and Austria in the 1880s, was a fierce controversy between theory and history. Although Schumpeter was a theoretical economist, he maintained a deep interest in the historical approach because he was first trained in legal and economic history. He developed a methodology that served to resolve the conflict between theory and history, and he used economic sociology to integrate theory and history. The Historical School represented a development of historicism, a characteristic of nineteenth-century German thought, and contained idealism at its core (see chapter 8).

Between positivism and historicism

The intellectual field during the *Methodenstreit* was defined by a confrontation between two basic philosophies: positivism and historicism. It is to be noted that among German academic scholars of the humanities and the social sciences between about 1890 and 1930, avowed positivists were rare, although certain types of empirical and historical research were influenced unconsciously by positivism (Ringer 1969). Positivism and the specialization of knowledge were constantly criticized as heterodoxy to the German tradition of idealism and holism. Surprisingly, with its appointment of Schumpeter, Bonn was the only German university that hired a modern economist during this period. Ludwig von Mises recalls that among the hundreds of scholars who taught economics at German universities between 1870 and 1934, only Schumpeter was acquainted with the works of the Austrian and Lausanne Schools and with modern Anglo-Saxon economics (Mises 1978). Mises probably overstated the facts, but one cannot exaggerate Schumpeter's boldness in openly advocating and defending positivism and mathematical formalism in economics under such circumstances, although he never failed to support historicism at the same time.

The scale and structure of Schumpeter's *habitus* embraced various streams of thought as well as positivist and historicist positions. Special tools were needed to implement these apparently conflicting thoughts; this would explain why Schumpeter developed a unique system of social science.

It is useful to compare Schumpeter and Keynes in light of the intellectual fields into which they were born. Keynes was brought up in Cambridge; for him the weight of Marxism and the German Historical School in the intellectual field was insignificant; for neoclassical economists, only Alfred Marshall, not Walras and Menger, was central. In contrast, Schumpeter faced and reacted to various positions in economics; the intellectual field in Germany and Austria was variegated, and the context of his *habitus* was far more complicated. For Schumpeter, who was once a cabinet member of a coalition government under a socialist chancellor, Marxism and socialism were not the literature, but the actual experience. Keynes constructed his theory in conjunction with neoclassical economics; it was macroeconomic theory in contrast to neoclassical microeconomic theory. Schumpeter, on the other hand, developed, first, a theory of economic development in contrast to neoclassical static theory, and, second, economic sociology in contrast to economic theory proper. The competition between Keynes and Schumpeter was about the superiority of Keynes's macrotheory versus Schumpeter's development theory in understanding and diagnosing the instability of the contemporary capitalist economic system. Keynes took hold of the economics world in those days, but evaluation of these compelling theories had to depend on conditions only explainable by the sociology of science.

Schumpeter's achievements, which went beyond the scope of economics, must be interpreted relationally in the configuration of ideas with Marxism and the German Historical School, both of which had significant weight and authority in the intellectual field relevant to him. Schumpeter's economic sociology, furthermore, should be related to the stream of German sociology. From the beginning of the twentieth century to the establishment of the Nazi regime, sociology developed impressively in Germany, for it was hoped that sociology could reintegrate the social sciences, which had become specialized and separate. Thus, elements of the German intellectual tradition such as historicism, holism, and idealism naturally flowed into German sociology, but at the same time the opposing positivist elements were made a part of it by Max Weber and Karl Mannheim.

The German and Austrian intellectual fields did not always reject positivism. From the end of the nineteenth century to the early twentieth century, the two countries were rather a hotbed of positivist philosophy with regard to natural science. Schumpeter was amazingly sensitive to this direction and therefore rejected the metaphysical elements specific to the Austrian School of economics. Furthermore, German historicism did not, after all, oppose facts and experiences but stood against theoretical and analytic methods because it emphasized the idiographic notion of reality stressing historical development. Indeed, a methodological bridge was needed between historicism and positivism, and Weber and Schumpeter contributed to this effort.

Schumpeter had one foot in German historicism and the other foot in the world of Anglo-Saxon positivism. His intellect did not allow him to choose between theory and history, and so he was challenged to make a theoretical formulation of history and to build a bridge between the pure theorists like Walras and the Historical School. For this reason the scope of his ideas was sometimes too broad to be amenable to analysis. Thus, when he arrived at the central ideas of innovation, leaders, money, and business cycles in his theory of economic development, he undertook a sociological study of these ideas rather than subjecting them to detailed analysis and formulation within the confines of economics. His scientific orientation was to a "universal social science" that was compatible with the German intellectual field, although he was not a member of the German Historical School.

Another factor supported this orientation. As a supporter and a proponent of mathematical economics, Schumpeter studied mathematics industriously but did not enjoy success in this area, for he lacked the mathematical mindset. It can be argued that he was so absorbed in comprehending objects as a whole that he was incapable of making the simplifying assumptions that are necessary to develop a mathematical formulation (Minsky 1992). At the same time, however, the lack of an analytic orientation was responsible for his holistic, all-encompassing vision. Ernst Mach, an admirer of Schumpeter, said about the economy of thought: "The greatest perfection of mental economy is attained in that science which has reached the highest formal development, and which is widely employed in physical inquiry, namely in mathematics. Strange as it may sound, the power of mathematics rests upon its evasion of all unnecessary thought and on its wonderful saving of mental operations" (Mach [1882] 1898, 195). Schumpeter's mental activities were full of waste and extravagance. He called the mathematical mind as well as the lack of it "ideology"; according to him, vision is determined by ideology. In Bourdieu's terminology, these factors belong to the *habitus*.

Schumpeter's idea of social science was to grapple with historical phenomena, the research object of historicism, using positivist methods. Through this approach he intended both to remove the restrictions of a positivist social science and to prevent a historical social science from contenting itself with relative knowledge. His idea of social science was the combined product of the German and Austrian intellectual fields of the early twentieth century and his personal *habitus*. His pursuit of the idea of social science meant the establishment of a social *habitus* that would yield a "universal social science."

CHAPTER 3

The scope and methods of Schumpeter's research program

Schumpeter's first book, *Das Wesen und der Hauptinhalt der theoretischen Nation-alökonomie* (1908), was a recapitulation of neoclassical static theory from the methodological point of view. He then developed a skeleton of dynamic theory in *Theorie der wirtschaftlichen Entwicklung* (1912) and, after a long struggle, worked out a theoretical, historical, and statistical analysis of capitalist economic development in *Business Cycles* (1939). Finally, in *Capitalism, Socialism and Democracy* (1942) he provided an account of the evolution of the capitalist system by including not only economic but also political, social, and cultural factors. If we distinguish between Schumpeter's writings on the economy and society and his metatheoretical pieces, *Wesen*, *Entwicklung* and *Business Cycles*, and *Capitalism* are his major substantive works on economic statics, economic dynamics, and economic sociology, each of which deals with one of three areas of research, that is, the static state, the dynamic state of the economy, and sociocultural development as a whole, respectively.

A fragment of the sociology of culture?

What is the relationship between these three areas of research? Following the accepted view that Schumpeter's distinct contribution was the theory of economic development, it might be thought that the neoclassical static theory he discussed in *Wesen* was merely a body of thought to be superseded by his dynamic theory, namely *Entwicklung* and *Business Cycles*, and that *Capitalism* was a mere impromptu in sociology written for a popular audience. But Schumpeter's statics, dynamics, and economic sociology should be interpreted as constituting a system that addresses his constructed image of the world. This chapter argues that such an interpretation can be derived from Schumpeter's own research program, which was set forth in the first German edition of *Entwicklung* but has been long forgotten.

A research program of a theoretical system must posit problems as the object of study, on the one hand, and select methods as the means of study, on the other. Thus "problems and methods" or "scope and methods" in science characterize the concrete practice of a theory. Schumpeter selected four methods in economics (i.e., theory, statistics, history, and economic sociology) to study three different aspects of the research object (i.e., the static state, the dynamic state, and sociocultural development). By combining scope and method it is possible to reconstruct Schumpeter's research program, although he did not consciously define it in this way.

Chapter 7 of the first edition of Entwicklung

The scope of research in Schumpeter's system is identified in the final chapter (chapter 7) of the first German edition of *Entwicklung*.[1] In that chapter, entitled "The Overall Configuration of the Economy," Schumpeter first summarizes the preceding chapters, then locates them in the wider context of social life and attempts to provide a comprehensive explanation of the development of a society as a whole. He considers such areas as the economy, politics, social relations, the arts, science, and morality. In this respect Schumpeter's argument offers an important viewpoint for the comprehensive recognition of social phenomena, namely applying the static–dynamic dichotomy to all these areas and gaining a picture of the overall development of a society through the interactions between them. Chapter 7 consists of 86 out of the 548 pages in the book.[2]

Unfortunately, Schumpeter omitted chapter 7 from the second and subsequent German editions; the English translation (1934), which is based on the second German edition, does not contain this chapter. In his preface to the second German edition Schumpeter explained the reason for the omission: the chapter included "a fragment of the sociology of culture" (1926a, xi) and had unexpectedly attracted a great deal of attention, most of it adverse. He thus feared that the readers' attention would be diverted from his major contribution to economic theory. In chapter 7 Schumpeter went so far as to present a broad view of the development of society as a whole, including economic development as one element in that process. Because he believed that what his discipline needed above all at that time was an "analysis of the purely economic features of capitalistic society" (1934, ix) as an addition to static economic theory, it was more important for him to receive recognition for his theory of economic development than for his broad vision of social development. He omitted chapter 7 not because he found it incorrect, but because his readers preferred "a fragment of the sociology of culture" to "the problems of dull economic theory" against his expectations.

The most direct evidence of Schumpeter's continuing adherence to the views expressed in chapter 7 is his explicit declaration in the preface to the English edition:

I keep to the distinction [between statics and dynamics], having repeatedly found it helpful in my current work. This has proved to be so even beyond the boundaries of economics, in what may be called the theory of cultural evolution, which in important points presents striking analogies with the economic theory of this book. (1934, xi)

Also, in *Business Cycles*, after the exposition of dynamics and statics, the process of innovation and that of its absorption, he remarked:

The writer believes, although he cannot stay to show, that the theory here expounded is but a special case, adapted to the economic sphere, of a much larger theory which applies to changes in all spheres of social life, science and art included. (1939, 1, 97)

Whether chapter 7 is "a fragment of the sociology of culture" or not, it includes an important clue to Schumpeter's research program of a "universal social science," and for this reason it is most unfortunate that it has not become the object of scholarly investigation. My purpose here is to throw light on this forgotten chapter and to reconstruct his research program in four steps: how are the individual areas of the social sciences established? what is the static phenomenon in each area? what is the dynamic phenomenon in each area? and, what does the development of all social areas look like? This examination will show that the concept presented in the omitted chapter was not a mere passing thought but provided the framework for Schumpeter's subsequent work.

The types of man and research areas

Suppose that social scientists without any knowledge of the conventional practice of the social sciences were confronted with social phenomena that appeared to be part of a chaotic yet indivisible whole. In that case their first task would be to identify and establish distinct research areas for separate disciplines. For example, how can economists identify economic activity as the object of their inquiry?

The classifying hand

On the opening page of chapter 1 of *Entwicklung*, Schumpeter writes:

The social process is really one indivisible whole. Out of its great stream the classifying hand of the investigator artificially extracts economic facts. The designation of a fact as economic already involves an abstraction, the first of the many forced upon us by the technical conditions of mentally copying reality. A fact is never exclusively or purely economic; other – and often more important – aspects always exist. Nevertheless, we speak of economic facts in science just as in ordinary life and with the same right; with the same right, too, with which we may write a history of literature even though the literature of a people is inseparably connected with all other elements of its existence. (1934, 3)

There is by nature no independent economic area; it is artificially constructed by the force of abstraction. In the passage above, Schumpeter states that the manner in which an area is constructed for economics depends on "the classifying hand of the investigator" ("die ordnende Hand des Forschers"). The English word "classify" is not entirely correct in this context, and the meaning of the German verb "ordnen" (put in order) should be emphasized; the investigator extracts an area of economic facts so that the constructed area itself may exhibit some order. This is an important and fundamental idea from the methodological point of view. Any research area can stand only if it can exhibit order within itself, and order is constructed by scientific thought. To put it differently, scientists should identify the object of research in anticipation of the fact that order can be established by means of the rules of scientific procedure.[3]

The contents of order naturally vary according to individual sciences and even individual models within a science. Particular order described by a science is expressed by the contents of a theoretical model.

Areas of social science

Let us examine Schumpeter's approach to the identification of research areas. He contended that different types of man should characterize different areas of social inquiry. If an area of social activity is to be established as the object of science, the type of man peculiar to the area should first be specified and then the area's state of affairs should be explained autonomously in terms of the group behavior of the specified type of man. This is the assumption of so-called methodological individualism, which holds that the pattern and structure of a society should be explained by the deliberate acts of individuals.[4]

Although Schumpeter admitted that man always has diverse motives, interests, and needs simultaneously, he justified the isolation of human types on two grounds. First, in each area of social life, one can find characteristic people whose main activities actually belong to that area. Thus in the economic area, a distinctive type of man called *homo oeconomicus* (economic man) is identified, and his acts (maximizing behavior) specify and delimit the area of economic facts (exchange relations). The fact that such a type of man is not necessarily a product of one's imagination but is found in varying degrees in actual groups of people, such as workers, entrepreneurs, farmers, and merchants, provides the justification for delimiting the economic area. Similarly, the existence of distinctive groups of people, such as artists, politicians, and scientists, provides us with a prima facie reason for distinguishing separate areas of social inquiry. Second and more important, the behavior of a specified type of man is so different from that of other types that it has acquired a sufficient degree of independence and autonomy to enable a distinction to be drawn.

When Schumpeter described the total picture of a society, he talked about an analogy between economic and noneconomic areas. According to him, economics had been most successful in establishing an economic order by the assumption of *homo oeconomicus* and his maximizing behavior; in other areas of the social sciences the specification of area, the definition of actor, and the formulation of behavior was still very much lacking. Schumpeter's approach to areas outside economics was based on an analogy from the economy, and assumed comparisons or similarities between economic and noneconomic areas. As we shall see, metaphors are used step by step to create similarities between the two. The most important point of analogy is the dichotomy of static and dynamic, which, as far as the social sciences were concerned, he believed had been satisfactorily established only in economics. But the dichotomy was introduced into economics in the nineteenth century from zoology. He thus conceived of the concept of the static–dynamic dichotomy for the economy as a special case of the general hypothesis of homology, with static and dynamic phenomena visibly distinguished in every sphere of social life.

In relation to this problem, in *Capitalism* Schumpeter attacked and turned upside down the classical political theory of democracy. The classical theory regarded democracy as an institutional arrangement for realizing the people's will to promote the common good. On the contrary, he maintained, that doctrine was merely a statement of normative judgment, not a description of the actual state of affairs in the political field under democracy. Based on his observation of human nature in politics, he viewed democracy as representing the competitive struggles of politicians for political leadership. He identified a type of man in politics and defined politicians' behavior as apart from political philosophy, according to the analogy of the competitive struggles of economic agents for profits in markets.

The analogy of the statics–dynamics dichotomy

According to Schumpeter, it is necessary, as the second step of any research program, to describe the state of affairs in a specified area as an orderly state. He recognized that the establishment of a unique state of affairs in an area of social life is brought about by both a set of exogenous factors and a specified type of human behavior endogenously governing the area.

The logic of statics

It is well known that order in the static state of an economy is represented by the concept of equilibrium. According to neoclassical static theory, given the quantity of available resources, consumer tastes, the techniques of production, and the social structure, the behavior of *homo oeconomicus* will uniquely bring resource allocation into equilibrium – that is, equilibrium prices and quantities of various goods and factors of production – through the play of individual self-interest and the workings of a competitive market mechanism. This is the essence of economic statics, and Schumpeter analogously applied the same procedure to other areas to explain the static state of the social life in question.

Schumpeter observed that if in a certain area of social life a state of equilibrium can be uniquely determined to correspond to exogenous data, the area in question is logically so self-sufficient that an autonomous and independent science can legitimately be assumed for that area. If and only if a unique equilibrium can be proved for an area can the state of affairs in that area be taken to be a cosmos, not a chaos. The significance of the analogy, Schumpeter argued, was as follows:

> At any point in time every area of social life is determined by given data, and these data are analogous to those data which determine an economy at any point in time according to the method of statics. This recognition signifies the dawn of the scientific understanding of human phenomenon. It has now become common knowledge – and a commonplace. (1912, 537–38)

To put it differently, the method of statics reduces unknown factors in a specific area to known factors outside the area. In the case of an economy, Schumpeter wrote:

> When we succeed in finding a definite causal relation between two phenomena, our problem is solved if the one which plays the "causal" role is non-economic. We have then accomplished what we, as economists, are capable of in the case in question, and we must give place to other disciplines. If on the other hand, the causal factor is itself economic in nature, we must continue our explanatory efforts until we ground upon a non-economic bottom ... Always we are concerned with describing the general forms of the causal links that connect economic with non-economic data. (1934, pp. 4–5)[5]

In this description, "the general forms of the causal links" represent the fundamental task of economic theory in a narrow sense. But the tools of economic analysis include not only economic theory but also historical method. Since both economic and noneconomic phenomena are really historical experiences, the task of history is to recognize the individual forms of the causal links by explanatory hypotheses (see page 45 below).

At first glance, the static method in the social sciences might appear to lack autonomy, because it explains the state of affairs in a specific area by making reference to exogenous data. But this is not true. It is the essential task of statics to explain what the endogenous variables in a specific area will be when the data are given; the autonomy of a science is found in the peculiarities of an explanation in deriving a unique state of affairs from the given data. The substance of a static state varies naturally according to the area of research in question. In the economic area, individual households and firms are assumed to act in a predetermined manner (the maximization of utility or profits) under the given data. When the data change, the agents will adapt to the changes. In a static state, "every one will cling as tightly as possible to habitual economic methods and only submit to the pressure of circumstances as it becomes necessary" (1934, 8–9). The static equilibrium in an economy is expressed as a "circular flow" if a time element is taken into account; the quantity and pattern of a national product remain constant as the process of production follows the same route year after year. Even if changes occur in the circular flow of an economy resulting from changes in the data, they will occur continuously and in small steps within a fixed framework; therefore they can be treated by the method of economic statics. The thrust of Schumpeter's approach to a universal social science in this stage is that the conception of the static state as the adaptive and routine activity within a fixed framework can be applied to noneconomic areas as well.

The logic of dynamics

The third step in his research program is concerned with the identification of the phenomenon of dynamic development as distinct from the static state or the circular flow. According to Schumpeter, in every branch of social activity, forces are working to change the data from within the areas; they destroy the framework of those activities that are merely adaptive to the existing data. This is the phenomenon of dynamic development. In order that an area of social life may be established as the object of scientific inquiry, it is not enough that there should be a distinct type of man peculiar to the area and that an equilibrium can be found in the area when the exogenous conditions are given. It is also necessary that the area should have its own mechanism of development that creates innovation from within itself and of itself destroys the existing order.

Schumpeter's *Entwicklung* describes the mechanism of economic development as the process of innovation, which takes various forms, such as the introduction of new products, new methods of production, new markets, new sources of supply, or new forms of industrial organization. Its central concepts are the entrepreneur as the carrier of innovation and bank credit as the means of innovation. Thus Schumpeter's development concept consists of three elements: innovation, its carrier (entrepreneur), and its means (credit). Again the analogy of development is applied to other areas. Indeed, each area of social life has its own mechanism, its own type of carrier, and its own means of innovation, but the essential feature is the same: the type of man defined as a "leader" overthrows the existing order and creates a new direction. The entrepreneur is a special kind of leader in the economic sphere. The leader is in marked contrast to the majority of people in a particular area who only take adaptive and routine actions. Schumpeter believed that such a contrast exists not only in economics but also in the arts, science, politics, and so on.

Different human types are thus distinguished to identify different areas of social life, and then leaders and average people are distinguished in each area. Schumpeter wrote:

> In every area there are persons of a static disposition and leaders. The former are characterized by the fact that they essentially do what they have learned, that they move within the traditional framework and their views, disposition, and behavior are determined by given data in their area. The latter are characterized by the fact that they see something new, that they alter the traditional framework of their activity and the given data of their area ... Everywhere the two types are divided by a sharp line, which contrasts those persons who develop new trends in culture, new schools, and new political parties with those who are developed by trends in culture, schools, and political parties. (1912, 542–43)

It is interesting to note that Schumpeter regarded scientific activity as a type of social activity, thus asserting that the same procedures of a universal social science could be applied to the scientific arena. An interpretation of the sociology of science and the history of science from this point of view will produce illuminating results, as I demonstrate in chapters 4 and 10.

Human elements

It is not surprising that Schumpeter should emphasize the human element in the dynamic phenomenon. All three steps of his research program are consistent on this point: first, the identification of a research area requires defining the types of man peculiar to an area; second, the static theory for an area depends on the behavior, under exogenous conditions, of the average man thus defined; and third, dynamic theory relates to the behavior of men of unusual ability who dismantle the given conditions. But we must note that the argument of human element was first introduced in *Entwicklung*. In *Wesen*, which was concerned with static theory, Schumpeter eliminated all human elements and confined himself to the investigation of the interrelationship among goods, without an emphasis on the type of average people peculiar to the static state. The treatment of the human element is contrasting in the two books.

Schumpeter pointed out that the static–dynamic dichotomy was first introduced to economics from zoology, not an analogy from mechanics (1934, xi). Even if the notion of statics depended on a mechanical analogy, the emphasis of the human element in the dynamic state was not consistent with mechanics.

Schumpeter presents an important view of the relationship between statics and dynamics, found only in chapter 7 of the first German edition of *Entwicklung*, that whereas static phenomena have an equilibrium, dynamic ones do not. He writes:

> It follows from our entire thought that a dynamic equilibrium does not exist. Development in its ultimate nature disturbs an existing static equilibrium and does not have a tendency to return to a previous or any other equilibrium. Development alters the data of a static economy ... Development and equilibrium are opposite phenomena excluding each other. Not that a static economy is characterized by a static equilibrium and a dynamic economy by a dynamic equilibrium; on the contrary, equilibrium exists only in a static economy. Economic equilibrium is essentially a static equilibrium. (1912, 489)

This interpretation reflects Schumpeter's epistemological view that, because a scientific explanation is incomplete without the reduction of phenomena to a state of equilibrium, dynamic theory cannot stand without the support of static theory. This problem may have something to do with the possibilities for the mathematical formalization of dynamic phenomena. It is often asserted, as Elizabeth B. Schumpeter noted, that "he envisaged a theory which might some day synthesize dynamic economics in the same way that the Walrasian system summed up static economics" (1954a, vi). Indeed, Schumpeter worked hard to master mathematics and mechanics, but there are conflicting views about his intentions. Arthur Smithies said that "throughout his life Schumpeter gave an inordinate amount of his time to the study of mathematics and to the encouragement of its study by others ... He always retained the forlorn hope that mathematics might produce the dynamic counterpart of the Walrasian system" (Smithies 1951, 15). Gottfried Haberler, in contrast, stated: "He [Schumpeter] ... was willing to make limited use of them [mathematical models] for the explanation of minor oscillations around the great waves of economic development, but he felt that they are just as incapable of explaining the great economic rhythm as the ripples caused by high winds on the surface of the sea are incapable of influencing the great rhythm of the tide" (Haberler 1951a, 40–41).

The last quotation above from chapter 7 suggests that Schumpeter's failure to formalize the process of economic development in mathematical terms was at least not inconsistent with his conception of development. In his view, economic development is a deviation from static equilibrium, and a theory of economic development is justified only by recourse to a static theory dealing with the ultimate effects of innovation on the economy in terms of the equilibrating mechanism. His conception of economic development as a deviation from, and a disturbance of, a static equilibrium, as well as his presumption that economic development does not contain equilibrating forces within itself, was based on the epistemological nature of the static–dynamic dichotomy, as seen in chapter 4.

Sociocultural development as a whole

Schumpeter tried to apply a unified procedure of inquiry to all areas of social life. If he was successful in the attempt, applied to these areas, then we are left with a set of separate social sciences. The fourth and last step, the most ambitious, in Schumpeter's research program, was to integrate all areas of social life. The question he raised at this stage was:

In spite of the relative independence of all areas, why is there such an important truth – indeed, the truth which we cannot so much prove exactly as perceive – that every element in every area, at any time, is connected with every element in every other area, that all situations in all areas determine each other and depend on each other? If we call the aggregate of these areas the *social culture* of a nation and the totality of its development *sociocultural development*, we can ask: how does our approach explain that the social culture of a nation at any given time is in a unity and the sociocultural development of a nation always has a unifying tendency? (1912, 545–46)

As shown below, the unfamiliar terms *social culture* or *sociocultural development*, as Schumpeter used them, are best understood in the context of the German sociology of culture in the early twentieth century. To put it simply, the sociology of culture was based on the idea of dividing various areas of social life into ideal, cultural fields and real, social fields; social culture represented a totality of the interaction between the dichotomized fields.

Interaction between society and culture

Between the different areas of social life there must be complicated interrelations whose analysis requires what might be called an interdisciplinary approach. According to Schumpeter, those interrelations can be examined from either a static or a dynamic viewpoint. First, when an area is examined in isolation, static theory provides us with a causal explanation in the sense that the state of affairs in that area is explained by reference to the conditions given for other areas, and that the state of affairs in the isolated area, in turn, is seen as data conditioning other areas. But when all the areas of social life are considered as a whole, the value of such a causal explanation (i.e., endogenous variables are influenced by exogenous variables) is reduced, because the walls separating the areas must now be removed, and every factor in every area must be simultaneously regarded as endogenous. Thus, Schumpeter proposed to substitute functional relations for causal relations when all variables are to be seen as endogenous or as generally interdependent:

In fact, the next step of understanding is to substitute the "general interdependence" for the "observation of causal relations." For a theory of static facts this is a purely advantageous and decisive progression. Instead of viewing every area as the result of other areas, there now emerges the conception that the total state of social life is a result of the total state in a preceding period. And this entails a widening of our theoretical horizon. But in this case, the theory of development loses its ground. For the transition from one state to another can take place only according to the static rule. (1912, 541)

This situation might be designated general interdependence or general equilibrium on a large scale, where the equilibrium in all areas should be compatible. Schumpeter calls this situation the "static unity of cultural level" (1912, 546). Insofar as we maintain a static viewpoint, even the extension of our perspective beyond a single area will not promote the understanding of social evolution.

When a dynamic viewpoint is adopted, on the other hand, the interrelations among areas involve reciprocal effects of innovation: innovation in one area has an impact on innovation in another area. Thus economic development influences the noneconomic areas and brings about social change. Analogously, it is supposed that dynamic performance in one area more or less influences other areas. In the dynamic process, the interrelations among the areas are different from those considered from the static point of view. Schumpeter described how such interrelations work: innovation in one area raises the social rank of successful leaders and influences social organizations; it affects the social values concerning what is important, valuable, and desirable; and it ultimately changes the presumptions and conditions of human action in all areas. Whereas various developments in all areas of social life at first sight appear to be independent of each other because they are carried out by different leaders in different areas, it is Schumpeter's recognition of social classes that makes developments in all areas an interrelated unity. Schumpeter's theory of social classes plays a pivotal role in integrating all social areas. If the integration could be adequately formulated, we would have a universal or all-encompassing social science addressed to sociocultural development. Schumpeter concluded:

Thus, through the combination of relatively independent developments, what appears, if seen from enough distance, as unified cultural development comes into being. Thereby we release things from rigid causal chains and restore life to them. And in this overall view of cultural development the economy also is given a specified place. (1912, 547)

The plan of a universal social science

Schumpeter pointed to the possibility of a unified social science that fuses not only split branches of social science but also conflicting theoretical and historical approaches into a coherent, epistemologically grounded mode of social inquiry. I contend that Schumpeter's *Capitalism* was an attempt to carry out the universal social science program that he had described thirty years before. Specifically, it deals with the interrelations among economic and noneconomic areas. In that book Schumpeter concludes that capitalism will collapse as a result of its economic success, because the successful economic development of capitalism will attenuate the innovating forces in the economy by creating political, social, and cultural environments that are hostile to capitalism. When the economic area is regarded in isolation, the innovating forces that will change its conditions appear to emerge from within that area; but when we take into account other areas as well, we find that the innovating forces will become stronger or weaker in response to the situations in neighboring areas. This reasoning, central to *Capitalism*, depends on the concept of the reciprocal interactions of dynamic forces on a large scale, which is distinct from that of the "static unity of cultural level" or static interdependence on a large scale. Yet it was not in *Capitalism* that he introduced this theme. The seminal idea for that book was clearly stated in his *Die Krise des Steuerstaates* (1918) and "Sozialistische Möglichkeiten von heute" (1920–21). Thus *Capitalism* should not be viewed as the product of casual effort, but as a work that was carefully formulated over a long period. It should not be judged by its success or failure in predicting the future of capitalism, but by its contribution to the understanding of the social and economic process as a whole and to the practice of a universal social science.

Schumpeter did not fully develop the logic of sociocultural development in *Entwicklung*, which only presented the formal structure of statics and dynamics as economic analysis. The work in a wider perspective remained a vision for the twenty-nine-year-old. In his later academic life he attempted to give substance to that early vision of sociocultural development and to develop the methods to achieve his research program.

A chronological examination of Schumpeter's major work might convey the impression that his interest shifted from pure economic theory to empirical, historical, and sociological studies in an attempt to broaden his scientific horizons. It is often observed that scholars sometimes follow such a process as their scholarship matures. But this was not the case with Schumpeter. At the beginning of his academic life he already entertained the idea of a research program with a broad perspective and continued to work in that vein.

Theory–mathematics and history–statistics

When a science has a certain scope, area, or object of study, its substantive contents are revealed by the methods or techniques that are applied in that study. For the methods together with the object of study show concretely how the object is analyzed and what propositions are derived.

Four methods

In part I of *History of Economic Analysis* (1954a), Schumpeter enumerates four basic methods of economics: theory, statistics, history, and economic sociology. The first three concepts are not new. For example, Carl Menger in his methodological study distinguished between two points of view in economic research, that is, individual phenomena and their relationships, on the one hand, and types and their typical relationships, on the other, and defined that to the former (historical science) belong history and statistics, to the latter (theoretical science) theory (Menger [1883] 1985, 37–38). Schumpeter's uniqueness lies in the enumeration of economic sociology. Economic sociology, in contrast to the other three methods, goes beyond mere economic analysis in the sense that it explicitly deals with institutions which are exogenously given in economic analysis. I call the fourth method "institutions" or "institutional analysis" in order to interpret economic sociology as one of the theoretical systems (comparable with economic statics and dynamics) derived from the combination of a method and an area of study.

I shall discuss all four methods in conjunction with Schumpeter's three areas of study – the static state, the dynamic state, and sociocultural development – in order to clarify the total task of his research program and the specific positions taken therein and, above all, to demonstrate that the relationship between theory and history fundamentally characterizes the nature of different approaches contained in the program.

Mathematical thinking

For the sake of convenience in explaining the structure of theory as a method, I shall regard "mathematics" as a separate technique in economic analysis.

There is no doubt that Schumpeter considered mathematics to be a part of logic, which constitutes theory. In economics, "mathematics" is a supplementary means of theory and "statistics" is a supplementary means of history, but mathematics and statistics play a very important role in integrating theory and history. Let us observe more closely the relationship between the methods of "theory–mathematics" and "history–statistics."

Scientists start from hypotheses, assumptions, axioms, and presumptions, which are sometimes expressed by mathematical symbols. Then, by mathematical deduction from a set of assumptions conclusions are derived; these conclusions are called principles, theorems, and laws. A theory consists of a totality of assumptions and conclusions. If observational data are available to support the conclusions, an empirical test of the conclusions will be provided. Through the process of an empirical test, theory–mathematics comes into contact with history–statistics.

Schumpeter did not insist that all the logic of economic theory must be represented by mathematics. When he contributed an article, "The Common Sense of Econometrics," to the first issue of *Econometrica*, the journal for the Econometric Society, he indicated what might be unbecoming as a slogan of the newborn science:

> Much of what we want to know about economic phenomena can be discovered and stated without any technical, let alone mathematical, refinements upon ordinary modes of thought, and without elaborate treatment of statistical figures. Nothing is farther from our minds than any acrimonious belief in the exclusive excellence of mathematical methods, or any wish to belittle the work of historians, ethnologists, sociologists, and so on. (1933a, 5)

He believed that mathematical methods do not reveal the substantive contents of the object but pursue the formality of thought, which is required for the rigorousness and wide possibilities of deduction. When they are not able to grasp the substantive relationship, one must rely on usual language.

In one of his earliest articles, "Über die mathematische Methode der theoretischen Ökonomie" (1906), Schumpeter found in the use of mathematics the possibility of economics becoming an exact science and argued that mathematical methods are available in economics because economic concepts such as labor, commodities, time, price, interest, and so on are quantitative (1906, 33). Later he described the same idea in the *Econometrica* article:

> There is ... one sense in which economics is the most quantitative, not only of "social" or "moral" sciences, but of *all* sciences, physics not excluded. For mass, velocity, current, and the like *can* undoubtedly be measured, but in order to do so we must always invent a distinct process of measurement. This must be done before we can deal with these phenomena *numerically*. Some of the most fundamental economic facts, on

the contrary, already present themselves to our observation as quantities made numerical by life itself. (1933a, 5)

That is not all. Schumpeter believed that mathematical thinking represented not only technical tools but a fundamental attitude of scientists. When he touched upon Spinoza, a seventeenth-century philosopher, in *History of Economic Analysis*, he quoted a sentence from the latter that economists ought to repeat on their deathbed: "I have sedulously tried to deal with the subject of this science with the same serene detachment to which we are accustomed in mathematics" (1954a, 126–27).

A theoretical hypothesis and an explanatory hypothesis

In order to discuss the relationship between theory and history, it is important to define them first so as not to use the terms indiscriminately. Schumpeter distinguished between "simplifying schemata or models" and "explanatory hypotheses" for individual phenomena, regarding the former as theories and the latter as once-and-for-all hypotheses for historical description (1954a, 14–15). Theories are general tools of thought for all economic problems, not *ad hoc* hypotheses to explain only individual cases. He wrote:

They [theories] do not *embody* final results of research that are supposed to be interesting for their own sake, but are mere instruments or tools framed for the purpose of *establishing* interesting results. (1954a, 15)

As we shall see in chapter 5, he clearly recognized this point in *Wesen*. In his view, theories do not describe facts individually but schematically. In other words, there is a difference between historical description and theoretical description. Historical description merely provides catalogues of facts by sorting them out, whereas theoretical description gives schemata or models by transforming them (1908, 42).

The ways in which theories transform facts are unlimited; theories are distinguished from one another depending on whether they grasp facts statically or dynamically or in the form of sociocultural development. There is a system of theory that has nothing to do with historical facts; that system is economic statics. Its scope is established by drastically abstracting historical facts to make clear its universal economic logic. Therefore, in the scope of economic statics only the method of theory–mathematics is applicable. Schumpeter called statics "pure economics" (1908, xix), "economics as economic logic" (1908, 613), and the "logic of economic phenomena" (1908, 134). Theories applied to this area are abstract, formal, and universally valid, but the method of history–statistics is not applicable here because actual facts are excluded. In the static area the separation of theory and history is a methodological imperative.

Historical thinking

The method of history–statistics, on the other hand, is required in economics because actual facts, when they are the object of economics, have two characteristics: historicity and quantitativeness. The object of economic dynamics is such a world. In *History* Schumpeter contends:

> The subject matter of economics is essentially a unique process in historic time. Nobody can hope to understand the economic phenomena of any, including the present, epoch who has not an adequate command of historical *facts* and an adequate amount of historical *sense* or of what may be described as *historical experience*. (1954a, 12–13)

Needless to say, historical facts can be represented by statistical time series, but historical description is not exclusively dependent on statistical quantity in the same way as mathematics is not omnipotent in theory. Insofar as history is represented by statistics, however, theory–mathematics and history–statistics cooperate in the following way. In the sense that mathematics contributes to a logical construction of theory, just as statistics contributes to a quantitative construction of history, the position of mathematics in theory, I argue, parallels the position of statistics in history. Mathematical terms in a theoretical construct represent abstract, general magnitudes of economic variables, while statistical records represent their historical, specific magnitudes. Therefore, to the extent that theoretical models contain quantitative variables, it is possible to bring theory into contact with history through the medium of mathematics and statistics. For example, when an economic theory deals with economics variables, such as prices, wages, profits, consumption, and investment, it can be given empirical, historical expression if statistics are available for the variables. Theory and history overlap in the area where mathematical terms are statistically quantified. This is the basis of econometrics and econometric history (or cliometrics). We may say that in natural science, theories are applied to experiments through the statistical quantification of theoretical terms. History in social science can be compared to, and also distinguished from, experiments in natural science; history is a once-and-for-all experiment of theories in social science.

Integration of theory and history by statistics

The contact of theory with history in this form involves a feedback process, which consists of testing theoretical hypotheses in light of historical observation, on the one hand, and of formulating new hypotheses in light of fact-findings, on the other. In reality, however, works in econometrics and cliometrics have tended to be one-directional, moving from theory to history with little or no feedback. It can be asserted that in contemporary economics, neoclassical theory leads historical inquiry and expels, as it were, the traditional interests and methods of history.[6] We should recognize the limitation of this approach in terms of the mediation between theory and history through mathematics and statistics: the application of theory to history will yield no more than is expected by theory.

If, on the contrary, we place a relative stress on history rather than theory, starting from a vague vision of reality, we can imagine a process in which fact-findings in history offer new subjects for theoretical inquiry, even through the mediums of mathematics and statistics. Moreover, we find that it is possible to interpret theory more loosely as historical hypotheses than neoclassical economics does and to utilize, for the construction of new theories, diverse historical materials of a nonstatistical nature. History-led theory is what the German Historical School actually proposed, and Schumpeter's work is most illuminating in this respect.

In his later years Schumpeter wrote that if he started economics afresh and he was told that he could study only one of the three methods, he would choose history (1954a, 12). Although he was greatly inclined toward the historical method, it was in his nature that he could not remain in an extreme position. In contrast to his earlier warning to the effect that the predilection for mathematical economics should not exclude the historical approach, Schumpeter cautioned in a later article, "The Historical Approach to the Analysis of Business Cycles":

In order to protect the following comments from a not unnatural misunderstanding, I want to make it quite clear right away that I have no wish to advocate the historical approach to the phenomenon of business cycles at the expense, still less to the exclusion, of theoretical or statistical work upon it. As my own attempts in the field amply prove, I am as much as anyone can be convinced of the necessity of bringing to bear upon the study of business cycles the whole of our theoretical apparatus and not only aggregative dynamic schemata but also our equilibrium analysis. (1949c, 25)

In *Business Cycles* (1939), subtitled "A Theoretical, Historical, and Statistical Analysis of the Capitalist Process," Schumpeter based his research on the central contention that economic development features in historical reality as business cycles, and he mainly dealt with a statistical time series of this phenomenon. The time series is evidently located in the overlapping area between theory and history. But Schumpeter's historical analysis is not limited to the scope of inquiry supported by statistics. In a section of *Business Cycles*, entitled "The Fundamental Importance of the Historical Approach to the

Problems of the Cyclical Process of Evolution," he described the relationship between history, statistics, and theory as follows:

Since what we are trying to understand is economic change in historic time, there is little exaggeration in saying that the ultimate goal is simply a *reasoned* (= conceptually clarified) *history*, not of crises only, nor of cycles or waves, but of the economic process in all its aspects and bearings to which *theory* merely supplies some tools and schemata, and *statistics* merely part of the material. It is obvious that only detailed *historic knowledge* can definitively answer most of the questions of individual causation and mechanism and that without it the study of time series must remain inconclusive, and theoretical analysis empty. (1939, 1, 220; emphasis mine)

As we shall see, this remark manifests the essential spirit of the German Historical School. His comment concerning the goal of his research – "filling the bloodless *theoretical* schemata and *statistical* contour lines with live *fact*" (1939, 1, 222; emphasis mine) – is also an aspiration of that school. Summarizing the impact of historical research on economics in his important methodological article, Gustav von Schmoller, the leader of the younger Historical School, had observed:

Historical research has created the conceptions of the historical development of nation, of man, and of economic institutions. It has properly brought economic research into contact with morals, law, the state, and the causes of cultural development in general. It has shown how to inquire into collective phenomena in addition to the conclusions starting from individuals and their self-interest. It has shown how to do a proper synthesis in addition to an analysis. It has given, for the first time, a proper complement to an isolating abstraction by showing how to regard the results of the abstraction as part of a coherent whole. Thus, what used to be faded abstraction and dead schema has recovered blood and life. (Schmoller 1911, 464–65)

From the above we can conclude that, in his approach to capitalist development, Schumpeter was dissatisfied not only with descriptive history but also with abstract theory and that he wanted to engage in a form of theoretical research whose framework was fully expanded by historical experience. Contrary to the writing of historical monographs about a limited time and place, which was most often the preoccupation of the Historical School economists, the analysis of capitalist economic development essentially requires theory and statistics. But they are not enough.

One of Schumpeter's key concepts, "reasoned history," "conceptually clarified history," or "*histoire raisonnée*," which is by itself rather ambiguous, seems to require a more sophisticated method than the use of statistics in order to integrate theory and history. The method that is directed to meet this demand is institutional analysis (or economic sociology), the fourth method in Schumpeter's toolbox of economic analysis, and in his opinion it is borrowed from the German Historical School.

scope	method				theoretical system
	1. theory	2. statistics	3. history	4. institution	
1. statics	O				economic statics
2. dynamics	O	●	O		economic dynamics
3. sociocultural development	O		O	●	economic sociology

Key:
O   Primary method
●   Supplementary method

Figure 4   *The scope and methods of Schumpeter's research program*

To summarize (see Figure 4), Schumpeter identified the static state, the dynamic state, and sociocultural development as unique phenomena or problems to be addressed by scientific methods. The circle in the first row of Figure 4 indicates that he applied theory to the static phenomena; the second row shows that he utilized both theory and history in addressing the problems of dynamics through the intermediary of statistics. Thus Schumpeter's *Wesen* deals with the application of neoclassical theory to static phenomena, his *Entwicklung* is a theoretical contribution to dynamic problems, and his *Business Cycles* is an attempt to integrate theory and history through statistical methods. His fourth and last method (institutional analysis) and his third theoretical system (economic sociology) are considered in the next section.

Economic sociology or the theory of institutions

Definition of economic sociology

When Schumpeter added economic sociology to his analytical toolbox in the manuscript of *History* (1954a), he had not fully clarified its location in his system of thought. But he was actively concerned with this discipline throughout his life, and its aim is clear. *Capitalism* (1942), as well as three essays on the tax state, imperialism, and social classes (1918, 1918–19, 1927a, respectively), are his major works in economic sociology. In *History* he paid particular attention to various attempts in the past to develop an economic sociology, although the book has often been thought to describe the progress of economic analysis in the narrow sense.

Economic theory regards the institutional framework of economic life as exogenously given. According to Schumpeter, however, institutions such as private property, free contract, and government regulation are dealt with not only by descriptive economic history but also by "a sort of generalized or typified or stylized economic history"(1954a, 20). The latter method is called economic sociology and means the generalization, typification, and stylization of history by means of institutional analysis. This is what Schumpeter meant by "reasoned history." He explained the relationship between economic theory and economic sociology as follows:

> To use a felicitous phrase: economic analysis deals with the questions [of] how people behave at any time and what [are] the economic effects ... they produce by so behaving; economic sociology deals with the question [of] how they came to behave as they do. If we define human behavior widely enough so that it includes not only actions and motives and propensities but also the social institutions that are relevant to economic behavior such as government, property inheritance, contract, and so on, that phrase really tells us all we need [to know]. (1954a, 21)

Assuming that social institutions condition the behavior, motives, and propensities of individuals, and that institutions change through the interactions among individuals in a historical process, as Schumpeter believed, then economic sociology deals with the institutional givens of economic theory and their changes in history.

Economic sociology, a theoretical analysis of the development of institutions, addresses a wider object of sociocultural development. But it does not deal with the totality of interactions between all the areas; rather, it summarizes the interactions between economic and noneconomic areas by focusing on the institutional factors that are closely associated with economic activities. In this sense, economic sociology is an approximation of the study of sociocultural development.

Integration of theory and history by institutions

According to this wide perspective, it is not mathematics–statistics but the analysis of institutions that mediates between theory and history, as is shown in figure 4. Analogically speaking, the concept of institutions resembles that of statistics with regard to the position of supplementary means to theory and history. Just as statistics assigns historically specific figures to theoretical variables, so the concept of institutions applies historically specific rules to theoretical models. The difference lies in the scope of the theories. Further methodological inquiries of the concept of institutions will be undertaken in chapter 8.

In Schumpeter's view the source of economic sociology was the German Historical School, and economic sociology corresponded to old institutional economics, an American variant of German historicism. He included both in economic sociology. The so-called new institutional economics, however, aims to integrate theory and history through the analysis of institutions that is based on neoclassical economics. In this sense, it is not economic sociology in Schumpeter's research program.

From the sociology of culture to the sociology of knowledge and economic sociology

In calling his idea of a universal social science "a fragment of the sociology of culture," Schumpeter suggests its origin and nature. Since the sociology of culture reflected the outlook of German thought in the early twentieth century, it is possible to understand Schumpeter's concept in relation to the German intellectual field. The position of the sociology of culture at that time reveals much about the relationship between the intellectual field Schumpeter encountered and his *habitus* as far as various aspects of sociology were concerned. Specifically, it is important to note at this point of the argument the reason why Schumpeter included the sociology of science as well as economic sociology within his system of a universal social science.

The sociology of culture (or cultural sociology) is a branch of social science that was established early in this century in opposition to the formal (or pure) sociology of Georg Simmel and Leopold von Wiese. Simmel abstracted from the concrete and substantive aspects of society with which the specific social sciences had been concerned and regarded the formal elements of spiritual interactions within society as the object of sociological investigation. Thus, formal sociology focused on the forms of dominance, subordination, struggle, imitation, division of labor, representation, exchange, and so forth independently of the substantive purposes and interests involved in these behaviors. This concept was further developed by Wiese and Alfred Vierkandt. Wiese expressed the formal nature of sociology by the term *Beziehungslehre* (relation theory).

The sociology of culture was developed from the very German responses to formal sociology: historicist repulse and the desire for totality. The concept of culture was worked out as a *Weltanschauung* of the philosophy of history and as a reaction to a critical split in the *Weltanschauung*. Although there are diverse approaches to cultural sociology, it is generally concerned with social conditions that determine cultural phenomena. According to Karl Mannheim's definition, cultural sociology is a "theory of the general interconnectedness of happenings in the social and cultural domains."[7]

Schumpeter called his idea "a fragment of the sociology of culture" because he was concerned with the interdependence of the social and cultural areas. Within the conceptual framework of cultural sociology, he considered the totality of the various areas in society "social culture" and the interrelated developments of these areas as a whole "sociocultural development."

Among the proponents of cultural sociology at the time were Alfred Weber, Max Weber, Wilhelm Dilthey, Ernst Tröltsch, Max Scheler, and Mannheim, but Scheler and Mannheim in particular established the sociology of knowledge from that discipline. Scheler ([1926] 1992, 166–200) divided sociology into two parts: cultural (the sociology of culture) and real (the sociology of real factors); he described the former as the sociology of human activities directed toward spiritual and ideal goals and the latter as the sociology of human activities directed toward real and instinctive goals. Cultural sociology encompassed knowledge, religion, art, law, and so forth as its objects; real sociology included blood (kin), power, economy, and their changing organization. The underlying notion of the division was that it is the main task of sociology to characterize social phenomena with reference to these two poles and to examine the kinds and orderly sequence of reciprocal effects of ideal and real factors. This division corresponds to Marx's distinction between the superstructure and the substructure, but Scheler rejected Marx's unilateral determination of the superstructure by the substructure. Among the ideal components he included were Auguste Comte's three factors (i.e., religious, metaphysical, and positive knowledge), which for Scheler, did not shape the phases of knowledge development but coexisted simultaneously as the kinds of knowledge. The social theories of Marx and Comte resembled the sociology of culture in aiming for a total understanding of the various areas in society but were criticized by Scheler and other proponents of the sociology of culture.

The sociology of knowledge as part of the sociology of culture pays special attention to knowledge among cultural phenomena and analyzes the ways in which knowledge is socially and historically conditioned, placing the epistemology of science within a social process. This approach means that at the root of knowledge lies the perspective (*Weltanschauung*) and values held by people in a society; it thus opposes the positivist epistemology subscribing to the universal validity of scientific knowledge.

Just as the sociology of knowledge, with its emphasis on the social conditioning of knowledge, developed from the sociology of culture espoused by German sociologists, so economic sociology unfolded from the sociology of culture to deal with the total interrelationship between cultural and social factors, focusing on the influence of institutions on the economy as a real factor. In Schumpeter's mind, the development of economic sociology was based directly on the tradition of the German Historical School. He was concerned with the sociology of knowledge as well as economic sociology, both of which evolved from the German sociology of culture. It is worth noting that Schumpeter worked in both fields, which had a common origin in the German sociology of culture and were the outgrowth of the sociological approach to the interaction between ideal and real factors in society.

Although Schumpeter's general idea of a universal social science was to create a three-layer structure consisting of statics, dynamics, and sociocultural development for each field of social life, in his actual work he focused on the economy and science. For him the economy was the focal point of real factors and science was thus in the locus of ideal factors. Thus Schumpeter fashioned two three-layer structures of thought, one for the economy (economic statics, economic dynamics, and economic sociology) and one for science (methodology of science, history of science, and sociology of science); I call his total system of thought the "two-structure approach to mind and society." The two structures, whose third floors (economic sociology and sociology of science) were the offshoots of cultural sociology, can be seen as the minimal essential version of a universal social science.

CHAPTER 4

The sociology of science and Schumpeter's ideology

What is science?

In part I of the *History of Economic Analysis* (1954a), Schumpeter gives several versions of the definition of science before launching into an investigation of the history of economic analysis over a period of more than two thousand years. The first definition reads as follows:

(1) A science is any kind of knowledge that has been the object of conscious efforts to improve it. (1954a, 7)

By this definition science and other kinds of knowledge are distinguished. In order to talk about "conscious efforts to improve," it is necessary to make explicit which rules the scientific efforts should follow and by what criterion the scientific improvement can be judged. Schumpeter mentions two distinctive characteristics of the rules of procedure in empirical science:

[The rules of procedure] reduce the facts we are invited to accept *on scientific grounds* to the narrower category of "facts verifiable by observation or experiment"; and they reduce the range of admissible methods to "logical inference from verifiable facts." (1954a, 8)

This description represents a broad viewpoint of positivism in that the rules of procedure in science are essentially based on empirical observation and logical analysis. If the rules of procedure are only relevant to the investigation of scientific activity, the nature and progress of science will be judged exclusively by those rules.

Schumpeter argues that science is distinguished from an ordinary way of thinking in that it follows such special styles of thinking as the use of methods and techniques regulated by certain epistemological criteria. If one accepts this point, the second definition will follow:

(2) A science is any field of knowledge that has developed specialized techniques of fact-finding and of interpretation or inference (analysis). (1954a, 7)

According to Schumpeter's classification, theory, mathematics, history, statistics, and economic sociology are "specialized techniques" in economics. While history and statistics are the techniques that are used for the acquisition of "facts verifiable by observation or experiment," theory and mathematics are the techniques that make possible "logical inference from verifiable facts." Economic sociology is regarded as a more complex technique that involves a generalization of institutional data.

While the second definition clearly shows that science is equipped with certain kinds of methods and techniques to which "the conscious efforts to improve" are devoted, it implicitly means at the same time that scientific work is the job of special groups of trained experts. If one wishes to give a sociological definition of science, referring to the group of experts who are specialized in the cooperative work of controlling and improving the socially shared scientific stock of knowledge, the third definition will follow:

(3) A science is any field of knowledge in which there are people, so-called research workers or scientists or scholars, who engage in the task of improving upon the existing stock of facts and methods and who, in the process of doing so, acquire a command of both that differentiates them from the "layman" and eventually also from the mere "practitioner." (1954a, 7)

This definition leads to the field that is called the sociological investigation of science or the sociology of science. What Schumpeter had in mind as the task of inquiry into the sociological aspect of science was the following:

[The sociology of science] analyzes the social factors and processes that produce the specifically scientific type of activity, condition its rate of development, determine its direction toward certain subjects rather than other equally possible ones, foster some methods of procedure in preference to others, set up the social mechanisms that account for success or failure of lines of research or individual performances, raise or depress the status and influence of scientists (in our sense) and their work, and so on. (1954a, 33)

These aspects of science cannot be explained by the logical criteria of science and demand a different kind of research, the sociology of science (or knowledge).

Schumpeter sets forth other definitions: (4) "science is refined common sense," and (5) "science is tooled knowledge" (1954a, 7). In definition (4), the emphasis is on refinement rather than common sense, and the purpose of refinement is to transform common sense into "techniques that are not in use among the general public" (1954a, 7). In a 1931 lecture in Tokyo, Schumpeter used a similar expression:

Science or theory is nothing but systematised and refined common sense, a technique, learned by experience, of getting hold of the world, not as practical life does, in every given practical instance, but in a way which will hold good for many or all instances of a given class of phenomena. ([1931b] 1982, 1052)

This definition is of interest in that it indicates how science emerged historically, as will be seen in chapter 10. Science, he believed, began with a discussion of practical problems in which people were interested; while the knowledge they held at the outset with respect to the problems in question was the result of the application of common sense or unsystematic thought, it grew over time into techniques that were inaccessible to ordinary people. As I shall discuss in chapter 5, definition (5) represents his concept of instrumentalism in the philosophy of science: that science is a general instrument for understanding reality and is in itself neither true nor false.

The philosophy of science and the sociology of science

In summary, Schumpeter argued, on the one hand, that, as in definition (2), science is the object of the philosophy of science or methodology of science because it has certain rules of procedure and, on the other, that, as in definition (3), science is the object of the sociology of science because it is carried out by groups of experts and is thus socially conditioned. Ernst Nagel ingeniously characterized science as an "institutionalized mechanism for sifting warranted beliefs" (Nagel 1961, 490); he believed that any account of this function of science requires both the epistemological criteria to distinguish between valid and invalid theories and the modes of behavior of scientific groups that are more or less compatible with these criteria. It is within these perspectives of the two disciplines, the philosophy of science and the sociology of science, that Schumpeter defined the notion of science.

The philosophy of science has traditionally discussed the status, structure, and function of science, and it is likely to be concerned with the form rather than the substance of science and with the logical nature of an ideal theory *per se*. On the contrary, the sociology of science draws attention to the actual activity of science that is carried out in social surroundings and tries to clarify empirical and dynamic phenomena such as growth and decline, acceptance and rejection of specific sciences. Schumpeter was interested in the sociological aspect of science not only because he thought that social factors influence science, positively or negatively, but also because the sociology of science, as well as economic sociology, constitutes a part of a "universal social science."

In light of Schumpeter's concept of a "universal social science," sociology is the first approximation of the interactions between various aspects of social life: the sociology of science deals with the relationship between thought and society, and economic sociology (the sociology of economy) with the relationship between the economy and society. These two sociologies were Schumpeter's major attempts to define sociology. Instead of investigating the intricate network of interrelations between each branch of society, sociology is a parasite, so to speak, of any developed branch of science and depicts the relationship between that branch and other branches lumped together; thus, the sociology of science rests on the philosophy of science, and economic sociology rests on economic theory. Specific sociologies usually criticize their parasitized sciences for the limitation of scope, but their parasitism is impossible without the latter.

According to the Marxian economic interpretation of history, the economy and thought represent the substructure and superstructure of the society respectively, and the latter is merely a reflection of the former. This is no doubt a biased view. Schumpeter's two sociologies are alternative approaches to the central problem of Marx's social theory, namely the evolution of the society as a whole. In order to overcome the Marxian bias and still admit the social conditioning of knowledge, it is necessary to consider economic sociology in addition to the sociology of science and to take into account the bilateral interactions between the superstructure and the substructure.

This chapter deals with Schumpeter's sociology of science based on his notion of science as well as on its relationship with economic sociology, as described above. In his view, two major social factors influence science: ideology and school. The latter half of this chapter identifies the structure of his basic ideology with reference to his substantive work.

Science, vision, and ideology

In his presidential address to the American Economic Association in 1948, entitled "Science and Ideology," Schumpeter observed that scientific inquiry in the broad sense consists of two stages, namely the formation of vision and the building of a model, and argued in what sense and to what extent the former influences the latter. The first stage is to perceive as the object of an inquiry the set of related phenomena to be analyzed. This requires a judgment of what is important and relevant in understanding natural or social phenomena. Such perception and judgment is called vision. The second stage is to analyze the material conceived by the vision according to the scientific rules of procedure. The recognition and collection of facts leads to the building of concepts and an analytic apparatus, and vice versa. As a result of the feedback between factual and theoretical research, scientific hypotheses and models are formulated. The same argument is also developed but unfinished in chapter 4 of part I of *History*.

Logical positivism

From the standpoint of a logical positivist philosophy of science, the context of discovery and the context of justification are distinguished, the former representing the setting of problems and the discovery and growth of theories and the latter representing the formulation, justification, and appraisal of theories. This distinction was introduced by Hans Reichenbach (Reichenbach 1938, 6–7) to define the proper domain of the philosophy of science as the context of justification. Schumpeter's distinction between vision formation and model building can be interpreted as corresponding to the context of discovery and that of justification, although a vision is one of the factors working in the context of discovery.

Standard accounts explain the contrast between discovery and justification in the following way.[1] Discovery concerns the origin and invention of scientific theories and hypotheses, whereas justification concerns their construction, testing, confirmation, and evaluation. Problems in the context of discovery are the concern of psychology, sociology, and the history of science, whereas logical problems in the context of justification are the subject matter of the philosophy of science. Discovery is subjective, but it is only descriptive. Justification is objective, but it is also normative because it gives the criteria for the evaluation and acceptance of a theory. Discovery deals with the initial selection of facts for study; justification evaluates whether the facts give the objective evidence for hypotheses.

In this view, factors concerning the genesis of theories are irrelevant to the philosophical analysis of science; the philosophy of science is concerned only with the logical nature of a completed theory, because it is believed that no logical method could be applied to the discovery of a theory. As Reichenbach put it, "the act of discovery escapes logical analysis; there are no logical rules in terms of which a 'discovery machine' could be constructed that would take over the creative function of the genius" (Reichenbach 1951, 231).

Admittedly, the philosophy of science should identify the normative rules of science, as does the grammar of language, but at the same time the rules should explain the actual practice of scientists. Critics of logical positivism claimed that epistemological elements that govern the dynamic process of discovery, evolution, and acceptance or rejection of a theory should also be a legitimate concern of the philosophy of science.[2] This claim is based on at least two major points. First, logical positivism contends that a nonanalytic (factual) statement has meaning only if it is verifiable by observational evidence. But with regard to this most fundamental proposition, the critics claimed that it is impossible to distinguish strictly between theory and observation because we can observe facts only on the assumption of a theoretical framework. This is the thesis of the theory-ladenness of observation. If this is the case, scientific work must be conducted by means of a perspective that governs what is an important problem and what is a desirable answer; this perspective is a *Weltanschauung* (viewpoint, style of thought) and is not necessarily neutral to the context of justification. Second, contrary to the contention of logical positivism, observation is not enough to determine the validity of a theory on account of the problem of induction. This is the thesis of underdetermination of theory by evidence. As a result, it is possible to build many theories from a given observation, and a theory is accepted in fact based on various criteria other than the principle of verification. Even a test of confirmation and falsification does not mean a simple once-and-for-all evaluation, and a theory continues to exist with tenacity through the endless modification and proliferation of auxiliary assumptions even if it is falsified.

The most important consequence of this criticism of the positivist philosophy of science is that serious attention has been given to the dynamics of scientific growth and persistence, and to the social and cultural circumstances in which scientific activity is actually carried out. In this way, the scientific interests of philosophers, sociologists, and historians have overlapped. Contemporary philosophers such as Karl Popper (1935), Norwood Hanson (1958), Thomas Kuhn (1962), Imre Lakatos (1970), Paul Feyerabend (1975), and others have contributed to this stream although there are striking differences among them. Against this background the sociology of science has shown a new upsurge since the 1970s in the work of Barry Barnes (1974), David Bloor (1976), and Michael Mulkay (1979), to name a few.[3] In addition, Pierre Bourdieu has a unique perspective comparable to Schumpeter's.

The relationship between vision and ideology

In distinguishing between vision and model, Schumpeter did not mean that each stage is independent of each other. He emphasized instead, as most contemporary philosophers do, that the former influences the latter, and took out some solid factors from the black box of the discovery process in which mere intuition and irrationality seemed to prevail.

Schumpeter focused on ideology as a specific factor in the vision formation stage; he introduced the concept of ideology in the following remark:

There exist in our minds preconceptions about the economic process that are much more dangerous [than value judgments] to the cumulative growth of our knowledge and the scientific character of our analytic endeavors because they seem beyond our control in a sense in which value judgments and special pleadings are not. Though mostly allied with these, they deserve to be separated from them and to be discussed independently. We call them ideologies. (1949a, 347)

He stressed that he was not going to discuss the problem of value judgments, which might be suggested by the topic "science and ideology." He also did not agree with the Marxian notion of ideology that a system of ideas depends on the class interests of the proponents.

Although Marx's theory of ideology contributed to the sociology of knowledge that developed in the interwar period, the sociology of knowledge already had freed itself of the Marxian bias. Karl Mannheim, the leader of the German sociology of knowledge, defined the key term of the discipline *Seinsverbundenheit des Wissens* (knowledge is existentially related) not as *Interessiertheit* (interest-orientedness) but as *Engagiertsein* (committedness) (Mannheim [1925] 1952, 183–84).[4] Committedness means that knowledge is indirectly correlated with social existence so as to shape a total configuration of the world and the human mind. Mannheim maintained that social existence is linked with thought through the structure of "perspective," which signifies the meaning of the concepts used, the structure of categorical apparatus, models of thought, the level of abstraction, the presupposed ontology, and so forth. "Perspective" is a *Weltanschauung*, style of thought, and intellectual viewpoint, which in turn depends on various social factors (Mannheim [1931] 1936, 244). Schumpeter similarly dealt with ideology in terms of an open-ended relationship with society.

Although some points in his argument might suggest that Schumpeter regarded vision and ideology as interchangeable,[5] his basic intention was to distinguish between them. According to him, vision is a preliminary image of problems in a prescientific stage. In order to draw such an image, one does not start from scratch but from some existing ideas:

We start from the work of our predecessors or contemporaries or else from the ideas that float around us in the public mind. In this case our vision will also contain at least some of the results of previous scientific analysis. However, this compound is still given to us and exists before we start scientific work ourselves. (1949a, 350)

Such a preconception is ideology; ideology is likely to be incorporated into vision because scientific work takes place in a socially continuous process. Vision is indispensable to science, but ideology can be dispensed with in principle. In fact, however, they are combined, and vision is shaped by ideology.

For Schumpeter, "*ideologies are not simply lies*; they are truthful statements about what a man thinks he sees" (1949a, 349). "It [ideology] does not exclude delusions of a wide variety of types," but at the same time "ideologies *may* contain provable truth up to 100 per cent" (1949a, 351). The important point is that although ideology is a prescientific or extrascientific view of the economic process, it is also a prerequisite of scientific research. Ideology is expected to be tested or falsified by the rules of science in a subsequent stage of the scientific act, but Schumpeter emphasized that such anti-ideological safeguards are not always effective. Thus, the sociological questions he raised were the following:

How far, then, does it [ideology] fail to disappear as it should? How far does it hold its own in the face of accumulating adverse evidence? And how far does it vitiate our analytic procedure itself so that, in the result, we are still left with knowledge that is impaired by it? (1949a, 351)

These questions cannot be answered in a general and macroscopic way, but should be explained individually with regard to some major systems of thought in the history of science.

By using the term *ideological bias*, Schumpeter points out that ideology is uncontrollable and dangerous to science. Why is it so? As mentioned, science is knowledge for which it is possible to talk about progress based on certain criteria, and it is different from value judgments or policy recommendations. And what is more, Schumpeter deliberately separated values and policy from ideology. He emphasized the fundamental role of ideology in the formation of vision:

[Vision] embodies the picture of things as we see them, and wherever there is any possible motive for wishing to see them in a given rather than another light, the way in which we see things can hardly be distinguished from the way in which we wish to see them. (1954a, 42)

Of course, there are many facts that no one can deny, and many rules of procedure in science are free from the effects of ideology; but Schumpeter observed that the scope of science that can be protected from ideological bias is fairly limited because the more fundamental "the way in which we see things" is, the more difficult it is for scientific rules to compare and appraise these perspectives. This is the problem of incommensurability; the typical example is the relationship between the subjective theory of value and the labor theory of value. Each value theory can criticize the other on the basis of its own rules of procedure and its power for solving its chosen problems, but the other theory is effective in relation to its underlying vision. Two value theories are the results of two incommensurable visions and ideologies.

The problem of ideological bias occurs not only in the case where vision and theory are consistently linked, but also where they are not. Since vision is an image of things that is to be formulated according to certain rules, the part of vision that is not successfully formulated in the model-building stage is irrelevant and redundant to science and, so to speak, leftover material that is not processed. Such a vision is merely an illusion or a *Weltanschauung* and sometimes vanishes. But it sometimes has a life of its own outside science and exerts an influence as political value judgments or social beliefs. Occasionally, it continues to exist in disguise in science as if it were science; Schumpeter called these cases the "victory of ideology over analysis" or "sterilization of science by ideology" (1949a, 355). Furthermore, there is a possibility of the rebirth of a defunct ideology because the ideology may be revived repeatedly when scientists try to form a vision. Thus, ideology works as an important factor constituting what Schumpeter called "the process of the Filiation of Scientific Ideas" in the history of science (1954a, 6).

What is the significance of Schumpeter's argument concerning ideology? Although he distinguished two stages of a scientific act, vision formation and model building, he admitted that all scientists do not necessarily begin from the formation of their own visions (1954a, 45–46). They begin to work within the existing system of science and take underlying vision and ideology for granted; sometimes they are never aware of this fact. On the contrary, those who bring about a revolution in existing science never fail to begin from the formation of their own vision. Thus continuity and discontinuity of science are explained. In his study of the history of economics, Schumpeter tried to pinpoint the visions underlying the great systems of thought that correspond to Kuhn's paradigms or Lakatos's research programs. We are thus led from the problem of vision and ideology to another problem of the sociology of science, namely the behavior of groups of scientists and schools.

Schools and the development of science

In the last year or two of his life Schumpeter wrote about the problem of ideology in the sociology of science in "Science and Ideology" and part I of *History*. But in his neglected book *Vergangenheit und Zukunft der Sozialwissenschaften* (1915), which presented his farewell address at the University of Czernowitz in 1911 before he left for Graz, he discussed the history of the social sciences in the formative period and included a chapter entitled "The Outcomes of Conflicts between Schools – Towards the Sociology of Science." This was an attempt to explain the sociology of science before Max Scheler and Karl Mannheim introduced it in the 1920s and the 1930s, and it is notable for its discussion of the schools represented by groups of scientists especially from the viewpoint of the historical development of science. Schumpeter's 1931 lecture at Kobe University on a *Weltanschauung*, schools, and methods was also an interesting attempt to define the sociology of science (1931a).[6] He might have intended to discuss these problems relating to schools as well as the problem of ideology in chapter 4 ("The Sociology of Economics") of part I of *History*, but his description was unfinished.[7] However, it is not difficult to reconstruct his view on the problem of schools from the material available.

Are there schools?

There is a perception that Schumpeter claimed that there are or should be no schools in economics, probably owing to his characteristic view about methodological tolerance in his first book *Wesen*. In an article in the widely read *Economic Journal*, he made the following remark that would be circulated as an epigram peculiar to him: "within serious economic theory there are no such things as 'schools' or differences of principles, and the only fundamental cleavage in modern economics is between good work and bad. The basic lines are the same in all lands and in all hands" (1928, 363). But this is not a correct way to represent his view on the sociology of science. Nothing is clearer than his own explanation on this point:

I am sometimes credited with the saying that there are *no schools in economics*. By this I mean that there are now no differences as to fundamental standpoints among serious economists. I do not deny the existence of schools in the sense which we have first defined. And I do not deny the existence of schools in the sense for which Universalism is an example. Only in the first case I hold that the differences are much less important than fervent disciples like to make out. And in the second case I deny that the phenomenon comes within the realm of science. (1931a, 9–10)

What, then, is his definition of schools? In the same article, he stated:

There is *one* meaning to the word "school," which is incident to the very life of science: groups of disciples gather round some teacher or some institution. By being interested in similar problems, by being taught similar ways of handling them, by exchanging and assimilating their views and results, they acquire a sort of mental familylikeness ... The history of Science is a fascinating study which unveils to us the ways of the human mind. And it has a neighboring field of research, which is developing slowly and is perhaps more fascinating still. It may be called the *Sociology of Science*, and consists of the study of Science as a social phenomenon, for example, of how the scientific profession developed, from what social groups its members come, how their social origin and position influences upon [*sic*] their work and so on. In this study, the phenomenon of grouping, which we call scientific schools, is of primary importance. (1931a, 7–8)

According to Schumpeter, various schools in neoclassical economics and even the German Historical School stand on common ground with respect to the fundamental viewpoint of science in spite of their different theoretical structures. On the other hand, he maintained that conflicts in a political view and *Weltanschauung* that camouflage science do not belong to science and referred to Othmar Spann's holistic approach as Universalism. Schumpeter ardently believed that economics should be advanced to an objective technique that all practitioners must accept whatever purpose they might have. By saying that there were no schools among serious economists of his day, he meant that there was *one* science of economics just as we have *one* science of electricity.[8]

In short, Schumpeter argued, as the ultimate ideal of the philosophy of science, that there can be no schools. Nevertheless he admitted that scientific schools were established as a matter of fact and regarded them as a most interesting phenomenon in the sociology of science. These two contrasting theses brought about an important problem for him.

The logic of things: between the philosophy of science and the sociology of science

Schumpeter accepted scientific schools because they were part of the machinery of dynamics of scientific activity:

How such schools arise and decay, how and why they fight each other and how their success or defeat determines the directions in which scientific endeavour moves, all this explains to a considerable degree why we have just the sort of science which we do actually have and why it is that not other lines of thought, just as promising in themselves, have been followed. Schools in this sense will probably always exist, for they are intimately linked up with the fundamental sociological phenomenon of Leadership. (1931a, 8)

No doubt when Schumpeter talked about leadership in science he had in mind an analogy from entrepreneurs in economic development. He distinguished between statics and dynamics in each area of social life; while the static state is governed by an established order, the dynamic state involves the destruction and substitution of an old order by a new one. In a scientific field, he who has achieved a revolution in science and acquired a wide group of supporters becomes a leader of a school. Schumpeter regarded the Ricardians as a genuine school: "There was one master, one doctrine, personal coherence; there was a core; there were zones of influence; there were fringe ends" (1954a, 470). He also accepted the Keynesian school as a sociological entity, that is:

A group that professes allegiance to One Master and One Doctrine, and has its inner circle, its propagandists, its watchwords, its esoteric and its popular doctrine. Nor is this all. Beyond the pale of orthodox Keynesianism there is a broad fringe of sympathizers and beyond this again are the many who have absorbed, in one form or another, readily or grudgingly, some of the spirit or some individual items of Keynesian analysis. (1951a, 288)

He said that analogous cases in the history of economics were the Physiocrats and the Marxists.

Between schools a controversy often develops concerning differences in basic approaches, problems addressed, causal relations, and so on. According to Schumpeter, controversy is the life of science; without it, science does not progress. The state of affairs in economics he actually faced at the turn of the century was characterized by bitter disputes between schools. Apparently in the scientific world conflict, dispute, and disharmony were dominant instead of compromise, cooperation, and harmony. He believed, however, that at a deeper level of scientific activity consistent development was achieved because of the common recognition of the basic nature of science. Thus he claimed the following philosophical thesis:

This is one of the cases, so often found in all fields of human history, where the "arbitrariness," "accidentalness," "uncertainty," etc., of actual individual phenomena are paired with the irresistible impression of "regularity," "uniformity," "necessity," etc., of the totality grasped by observers. (1915, 94)

For Schumpeter this was the central question of the history of science. He attempted to explain this thesis by paying attention to the modes of behavior of schools, on the one hand, and the methodological ideals of economics, on the other.

With regard to the modes of behavior of schools, Schumpeter observed that in the perspective of eternity (*sub specie aeternitatis*), schools are so much driven by vanity and narrow-mindedness that they are apt to emphasize trivial points and criticize others. When a leader creates intelligible and provocative slogans and identifies his foes, he can easily appeal to a wide circle of people; moreover, schools often maintain philosophical and political beliefs that can be supported by still wider circles of people. Although Schumpeter admitted that schools are the products of innovative scientific leaders, he sometimes spoke of schools in a pejorative fashion: the word *school* also means a group of fish; he used to say that schools were only fish shoals.[9] In fact, in view of his analogy of statics and dynamics to science, a school is a group of imitators, like fish in shoals, running after leading entrepreneurs.

On the other hand, with regard to the regulative idea of science, he did not take a simplistic view of cumulative scientific development that is prescribed by any rationalist philosophy of science. His first explicit statement about the development of science was:

"Nature does not make a jump" (*Natura non facit saltum*) – Marshall opened his book with this thesis as a motto, and in fact it adequately represents the characteristics of the book. But I disagree that the development of *culture*, especially of knowledge, takes place just in leaps and bounds. Vigorous jumps and stagnation, overflowing hope and bitter disillusion alternate, and even if the new is rooted in the old, development is not steady. Our science indicates this. (1908, 8)

In his unfinished *magnum opus*, written in the final years of his life, Schumpeter addressed almost the same subject in the same vein:

Scientific analysis is not simply a logically consistent process that starts with some primitive notions and then adds to the stock in a straight-line fashion. It is not simply progressive discovery of an objective reality – as is, for example, discovery in the basin of the Congo. Rather it is an incessant struggle with creations of our own and our predecessors' minds and it "progresses," if at all, in a criss-cross fashion, not as logic, but as the impact of new ideas or new observations or needs, and also as the bents and temperaments of new men, dictate. (1954a, 4)

This process of specialization [of science] has never gone on according to any rational plan – whether explicitly preconceived or only objectively present – so that science as a whole has never attained a logically consistent architecture; it is a tropical forest, not a building erected according to blueprint. (1954a, 10)

To sum up, the sociological activity of member of schools, on the one hand, is too shortsighted to shape a well-ordered history of science by itself, and the logic prescribed by the philosophy of science, on the other, is too unrealistic to depict an actual history of science by itself. Nevertheless, Schumpeter considered the possibility that through the sociological activities of scientific groups the logical direction of science is approximately realized. In other words, he took sides neither with an irrational model nor a rational model of scientific development on an abstract level but attempted to integrate both from a historical point of view. It can be argued that he seemed to believe in an invisible hand in history, something like his idea about the integration of statics and dynamics through business cycles.

How is such a belief possible? Schumpeter emphasized "the existence of given facts we cannot change" (1915, 99), which consist of the historically given objects and apparatus of science, namely the "problems and methods" of science. For scientists, these data are a given; problems, once addressed, cannot be forgotten, and doctrines, once established, cannot be easily dismissed. A vein of ore, once discovered, continues to be patiently explored over time. Streams of great ideas in particular never dry up. He called the tenacity of these moments "a great truth" (1915, 90). For Schumpeter, the development of science takes place zigzag through dialogues of present scientists with history, that is to say, through the rediscovery and reinterpretation of past ideas. In essence, these dialogues are required by the roles of vision and ideology in science. Past thoughts, as unchangeable given data, are repeatedly revived as ideologies and serve to reproduce a continuous scientific framework.

Indeed, in an actual field of science one wants to change existing theories drastically if possible, and in proposing a new theory, one creates a sandstorm and a battle cry under a new slogan. Sooner or later, however, the new is absorbed into the old to accomplish the latter, and a trend of uniform development of science follows. Schumpeter called the inevitable forces by which individual conflicts and diversities in science are coordinated into a totality so as to form a uniform development in a certain direction "the logic of things" (1915, 102). The direction destined for economics is to integrate the logical analysis and empirical observation, as is implied in his notion of science.

The above was Schumpeter's hypothesis which would be put to the test. Despite apparent conflicts between schools, they rest on common ground concerning the fundamental notions of science (this is the reason Schumpeter believed that there were no schools in economics), so that, in spite of discontinuities at first sight, a continuous development of science can be seen from a distance. In *History* he called this process, which leads, after all, to a uniform, although not linear, development of science, "the process of the Filiation of Scientific Ideas." This is "the process by which men's efforts to understand economic phenomena produce, improve, and pull down analytic structures in an unending sequence" (1954a, 6), and a description of this process is taken to be the main purpose of writing a history of science. Thus, starting from his concern with the sociology of science and building upon his component ideas, we have arrived at what Schumpeter regarded as the task of the history of science.[10]

Issues in the sociology of science

In order to develop the problems of the sociology of science based on Schumpeter's views on ideology and schools, I shall address three issues. I have stated that his scientific work covers three fields, namely economic statics, dynamics, and economic sociology, and his metatheory includes three areas, that is, the sociology of science, the methodology of science, and the history of science. Against this backdrop, I shall argue first, how his sociology of science is related to the methodology of science; second, how it influences the history of science; and third, how it is concerned with substantive theories, economic statics, dynamics, and economic sociology.

Overcoming relativism

One of the basic characteristics of the modern philosophy of science after the fall of logical positivism has been the effort to fill a gap between the logical explanation of science in the philosophy of science and the actual scientific activities described by the history of science. Imitating Immanuel Kant's famous dictum, Imre Lakatos stated: "Philosophy of science without history of science is empty; history of science without philosophy of science is blind"

(Lakatos 1971, 91). Schumpeter's viewpoint might be seen as anticipating the current stream of thought, but in order to understand his thought in the historical context one must recognize how much he was influenced by the German sociology of knowledge. Compare Lakatos's dictum above with the following manifesto of Max Scheler, one of the pioneers of the sociology of knowledge:

> Epistemological study is judged to be empty and unfruitful without the simultaneous study of social and historical developments of the supreme types of human knowledge and cognition; however, the history and the sociology of human knowledge would remain without direction, support, and ultimate foundation if these attempts were not directed by clearly conscious and epistemologically valid beliefs – as Condorcet and A. Comte first attempted on a large scale. (Scheler 1926, v)

The aspect of the current philosophy of science represented by Lakatos and Thomas Kuhn might be seen as an acknowledgment of the tenet of the German sociology of science in the 1920s. Schumpeter began with such a sociology of science.

When he discusses the sociology of science in part I of *History* (1954a, 33) and in his article "Science and Ideology" (1949a, 348), Schumpeter referred to Scheler and Mannheim. He seemed to regard Mannheim as more relevant than Scheler. Whereas Scheler is classified as representing the phenomenological sociology of science, Mannheim is classified as exemplifying the historicist sociology of science, each reflecting a different approach to the sociology of science.[11] The perspective of Scheler was metaphysical and static in that he sought for the essential and the eternal beyond facts. While the sociology of science is principally concerned with the social conditioning of knowledge, the aim of the discipline in his case was to find essential knowledge that was not subject to historical contingency. Schumpeter would not have shared this view.

Mannheim observed the relationship between thought and society as objective or existential and accepted the influences of social process not only as the external moments of thought but also as the cores of thought. He interpreted the social conditioning of thought not as "relativism" in the sense that objective, universal truth does not exist, but as "relationism" in the sense that truth cannot be formulated except within the framework of an existential correlation between knowledge and society (Mannheim [1931] 1936, 254). How to overcome epistemological relativism is an important task that the sociology of science must address as a result of the recognition of the social conditioning of thought.

Mannheim considered the objectivity of existentially conditioned thought in the following ways. First, uniform criteria could be applied to different theories that have the same perspective. Second, for those theories that have different perspectives, a certain formula is required to understand the structural differences between their cognitive styles and to transform or translate the one to the other (Mannheim [1931] 1936, 270). This means that objectivity could be obtained by a roundabout method, but there is no assurance of overcoming incommensurability. Schumpeter wrote on relativism:

> Roughly up to the middle of the 19th century the evolution of "science" had been looked upon as a purely intellectual process – as a sequence of explorations of the empirically given universe or, as we may also put it, as a process of filiation of discoveries or analytic ideas that went on, though no doubt influencing social history and being influenced by it in many ways, according to a law of its own. Marx was the first to turn this relation of interdependence between "science" and other departments of social history into a relation of dependence of the former on the objective data of the social structure and in particular on the social location of scientific workers that determines their outlook upon reality and hence what they see of it and how they see it. This kind of relativism – which must of course not be confused with any other kind of relativism – if rigorously carried to its logical consequences spells a new philosophy of science and a new definition of scientific truth. (1949a, 348)

Unfortunately, in this context Schumpeter did not provide a definition of "a new philosophy of science" and "a new definition of scientific truth." In other words, he did not pursue the consequence of his position on the sociology of science for the philosophy of science. But if we interpret his stand on the philosophy of science as instrumentalism, as in chapter 5, we can deduce the relationship between his viewpoint and relativism. Those theories that have different perspectives reflecting different social processes appear, at first sight, unable to claim objectivity. But according to Schumpeter's instrumentalism, a theory is an instrument and should be evaluated in light of its effectiveness in dealing with the problems it addresses, within whatever perspective it is constructed. The forward-looking view of a theory (for what it was made) is much more important than the backward-looking view (how it was made). The notion of effectiveness provides an alternative criterion to what is ordinarily conceived of as truth. This is the interpretation of Schumpeter's above remark on relativism.

Internal and external history

Starting from Schumpeter's definition of science, we have seen that science, in his view, is both the object of the philosophy of science, because it has certain rules of procedure, and the object of the sociology of science, because it is carried out by groups of scientists and is thus socially conditioned. As a result, it must be emphasized, in writing the history of science in *History* Schumpeter claimed that science has two aspects: therefore, the history of science is properly written as internal and external history. If there is no contradiction between the two aspects of science, then there is no contradiction between the internal and external history in his projected work. The meaning of this positing of the problem is, first, that the history of science is not a mere chronological or encyclopedic description of doctrines but requires a conceptual framework based on the philosophy of science and the sociology of science. Thus, *History* should not be consulted piecemeal like a guide to individual theories and authors; to use Schumpeter's favorite term, it is a "reasoned history" of economics. Second, since the contents and methods of science are combined with historical and social factors, the philosophy of science and the sociology of science should not be fixed and ahistorical. Various theories appearing in the history of science are treated as the test of different methodologies and sociologies of science.

It is now clear that the three metatheories, that is, the philosophy of science, the sociology of science, and the history of science, established here as the framework for studying Schumpeter, are interrelated in light of his view of science. He investigated the history of science to pursue their interrelationship in the context of actual economic theories.

The vision of a long-term process

Schumpeter's discussion of ideology at the vision formation stage in economics was actually confined to a discussion of the founders of the great theoretical systems or the leaders of schools, such as Adam Smith, Karl Marx, and John Maynard Keynes. What kind of research problems, then, should be chosen as objects of vision? According to Schumpeter, it is in long-term change that the vision or the image of an economic process plays an important role. This idea is noteworthy in order to pinpoint concretely the locus of vision in his system of thought. He explained:

When we are concerned with nothing more ambitious than to formulate the way in which – on the plane of pure logic – economic quantities "hang together," that is, when we are concerned with the logic of static equilibrium or even with the essential features of a stationary process, the role of Vision is but a modest one – for we are really working up a few pretty obvious facts, perception of which comes easily to us. Things are very different when we turn to the task of analyzing economic life in its secular process of change. It is then much more difficult to visualize the really important factors and features of this process than it is to formulate their modi operandi once we have (or think we have) got hold of them. Vision (and all the errors that go with it) therefore plays a greater role in this type of venture than it does in the other. (1954a, 570)

In the long-term economic process a large number of factors change, and there are many alternative hypotheses with regard to assuming a causal relationship and drawing a historical scenario. Moreover, the verification or falsification of a theory of economic development requires an accumulation of long-term experiences, without which any theory of the long-term process would be no more than a vision. Any work on the total development of capitalist society must be concerned with a long-term process, and Schumpeter admitted that in this case vision and ideology might survive without a crucial check. Here the relevance of the sociology of science to economic statics, dynamics, and economic sociology is different. The rhetoric that characterizes Schumpeter's writings is interpreted as a device to approach and challenge those problems of a long-term process that are only amenable to such a means of cognition as vision and intuition. Rhetoric is the art of constructing and communicating visions in the prescientific stage; for Schumpeter, it was to be located in the toolbox of economics in addition to theory, history, statistics, and economic sociology.

The balance of this chapter delves into the problem of Schumpeter's own vision. The problems of the philosophy of science and the history of science will be addressed in chapters 5 and 10, respectively.

Walras as ideology

Schumpeter proposed a double dichotomy: the static state versus the dynamic state as different economic phenomena, and statics versus dynamics as different economic theories; there is no direct correspondence between the two dichotomies. Schumpeter's model of statics is a version of neoclassical equilibrium theory; basically, it is a timeless model of economic equilibrium established under certain conditions, but if time is taken into account, it also relates to a stationary state or a circular flow that repeats itself year after year on the same scale and with the same pattern. A model of an equilibrium or stationary state assumes the constancy of natural, social, and institutional conditions, as well as the constancy of preference, technology, and the quantity and quality of productive resources. This model is characterized by the nonexistence of saving and investment and by a zero rate of production interest. In addition, Schumpeter's notion of the static state includes the growth process with steadily increasing populations and capital. Under steady economic growth, changes are limited to the quantitative expansion of an existing economy and do not include doing something new or differently. In other words, under a constant production function an increase in productive resources causes a change in the economy but is absorbed without much disturbance; this state of affairs is dealt with by static theory. Schumpeter would have included the economic growth theory, which was developed after World War II by Roy Harrod and Robert Solow but not by Simon Kuznets and Walt W. Rostow, in his notion of economic statics.

Statics versus dynamics

For Schumpeter, dynamic phenomena are characterized essentially by innovation. He included everything else within the scope of the static world characterized by adaptation. In this sense his method was an extreme isolation and purification of dynamic phenomena, which he called "economic development." Economic development, in his view, is caused by "innovation," broadly defined as the introduction of new commodities, new methods of production, new markets, new sources of supply, and new forms of industrial organization. The impact of innovation on the static model is that it changes the data of an economy from within, alters the existing channels of the economy, and causes peculiar disturbances known as "business cycles." Schumpeter called all the changes and repercussions in the economy brought about by innovation "economic development."[12]

In this fashion Schumpeter's models of circular flow, the stationary state, and the growth process, not to mention static equilibrium, which are all covered by the static model, seem to play only a part in making a dynamic process conspicuous, but he neither regarded the static model as unrealistic in comparison with the dynamic model nor denied its significance in economics at all. He raised three questions concerning statics–dynamics relations (1912, 511): first, should static theory be replaced by dynamic theory? Second, should static theory be supplemented by dynamic theory because it is merely a first approximation to reality? And third, do static theory and dynamic theory describe separate facts? To the first question, Schumpeter gave the following negative answer:

It can be understood that dynamics should destroy or modify a lot of things. However, it is a mere subfortress or an extension, as it were. The core of static theory should not be replaced by an idea of development. (1912, 511)

The reason for this remark is given in his affirmative answers to the second and third questions. He considered that statics is an abstract model not only because it deals with the price mechanism of markets regardless of the differences in organizational form but also because it excludes the phenomenon of development. In this sense dynamics, as a theory of development, is closer to reality. But statics is never replaced by dynamics, for the two theories are different apparatuses that address different problems (static phenomena and dynamic phenomena, respectively). It follows that to ask which is correct or realistic is pointless.

Schumpeter further extended the static and dynamic dichotomy; thus he now had four pairs: first, two theoretical apparatuses: static theory and dynamic theory (theory of development); second, two real processes: circular flow, steady growth, the tendency toward equilibrium, and the adaptation to innovation, on the one hand, and a change in the circular flow and in the growth process, the deviation from equilibrium, and endogenous and discontinuous innovation, on the other; third, two types of individuals: mere manager and entrepreneur; and fourth, two periods in economic life: the depression period, when the liquidation and reorganization of an economic system takes place, and the boom period, when there is a deviation from an existing economic pattern. The third point is further generalized to ordinary man versus leader, or, in terms of human motivation, the satisfaction of hedonistic wants versus the pursuit of excellence, creation, and victory. All these elements were regarded as real.[13]

Methodological significance of the dichotomy

The static–dynamic dichotomy or the stationary–evolutionary dichotomy is the most basic vision about the economic as well as the social world in Schumpeter's work. He stated that the proof of economic equilibrium is "the magna charta of economic theory as an autonomous science" (1939, 1, 41). In neoclassical economic theory, given some exogenous data, the prices and quantities of various goods and factors of production – that is, the pattern of resource allocation – are uniquely and interdependently determined. Schumpeter argued that if in a certain area of social life a state of equilibrium can be determined to correspond to exogenous data, the area in question is logically so self-sufficient that one can legitimately assume an autonomous and independent science for that area. A social area can be taken to be a cosmos and not a chaos only if a unique equilibrium can be proved under exogenous conditions from outside that area. In this sense, economic theory is justified to have an orderly world as its subject matter on the basis of the general equilibrium framework.

Also, Schumpeter's view that although static phenomena have an equilibrium, dynamic ones do not, offers an important key to an understanding of the static–dynamic dichotomy. Innovation is merely the destruction of equilibrium. Therefore, the world of dynamic phenomena cannot be an object of scientific inquiry unless it is located epistemologically on some axis of coordinates as a framework of reference and unless it is actually linked with some mechanism of restoring the order. The concept of equilibrium growth is used in economic growth theory, but, as mentioned above, Schumpeter certainly would have included this concept in a static model. After all, even innovation is a case of a change in data, and its effects on the economy are analyzed in terms of an equilibrating mechanism, which works to adapt economic structures to innovation or to absorb the effects of innovation into the economy.

Paradoxically speaking, Schumpeter could grasp the dynamic phenomena of equilibrium destruction cognitively because he believed in the immanent stability of the capitalist economy. Whatever destructive forces may emerge in the economy, markets can be relied on to adapt to them and absorb their effects to establish a new equilibrium. This was his notion of economic order. When seen as the objects of inquiry, static and dynamic states are two separate phenomena, but when seen as the methods of inquiry, static and dynamic theories are not independent; it is statics that makes economics, including dynamic theory, possible as an autonomous science. Dynamics can add new propositions about development phenomena with the aid of statics. In this sense, too, equilibrium analysis is the Magna Carta of economic theory as an autonomous science.

It was Léon Walras who first established equilibrium analysis in economics. Schumpeter, who all along regarded Walras as "the greatest of economic theorists" (1935b, 348), wrote:

To Walras we owe a concept of the economic system and a theoretical apparatus which for the first time in the history of our science effectively embraced the pure logic of the interdependence between economic quantities. (1937, 2)

It is to be noted that in light of Schumpeter's concepts of economic analysis, consisting of theory, history, statistics, and economic sociology, he praised Walras most highly as the pure economic theorist, saying that "so far as pure economic theory is concerned, Walras is in my opinion the greatest of all economists" (1954a, 827). However, whether Schumpeter's evaluation did justice to Walras, who had worked to develop a political economy for social reform, is a different matter.

Schumpeter discussed in greater detail the reasons why equilibrium analysis is essential to an understanding of the economy and summarized the following points (1939, 1, 68–70): (1) However abstract equilibrium theory may be, it gives "the bare bones of the economic logic." (2) Equilibrium theory provides a description of the response apparatus of an economic system to changes in the data, whether exogenous or endogenous. (3) The concept of equilibrium is indispensable as the standard of reference, whether for analytic or diagnostic purposes. (4) The primary relevance of the equilibrium concept depends on the existence of a tendency toward equilibrium in the real world. While points (1)–(3) relate to Schumpeter's view about the significance of equilibrium theory as an analytic tool, point (4) is concerned with his outlook on the equilibrating capacity of the real world and must be distinguished from (1)–(3).

With regard to points (1)–(3), Schumpeter thought that equilibrium theory sustains epistemologically the whole structure of economics. Concerning point

(4), then, he stressed that the capitalist economy, while embodying factors of disturbance, is self-adjusting through alternating booms and depressions. In his empirical analysis of business cycles, he noted:

What matters to us is precisely the presence or absence of an actual tendency in the system to move toward a state of equilibrium: if this concept is to be useful as a tool of business-cycle analysis, the economic system must strive to reestablish equilibrium whenever it has been disturbed or, to put the same thing in the language of a principle associated in physics with the name of Le Chatelier, it must tend to move, in reaction to every disturbance, *in such a way as to absorb the change* ... Common sense tells us that this mechanism for establishing or reestablishing equilibrium is not a figment devised as an exercise in the pure logic of economics but actually operative in the reality around us. (1939, 1, 47)

The idea of equilibrium and order

In short, Schumpeter praised Walras's general equilibrium theory in two respects. First, it established the conceptual framework that represented the interdependence of economic variables, and it clarified the mechanism of economic order by which all economic variables are interdependently determined under given exogenous conditions without recourse to any logic involving outside factors. For Schumpeter, the discovery of general equilibrium made economics a genuine science. Second, economic equilibrium is not a fiction; the forces moving toward equilibrium are working in markets in spite of apparent disturbances, and the economic system is regarded as stable after all. Of course, the recognition of the self-adjusting mechanism of markets did not begin with Walras; it is linked with the name of Adam Smith, who found in market activity an order as if created by an invisible hand. But the importance of Walras is that he used his conceptual apparatus to describe the order.

Thus, on the form and content of economic analysis, namely on the idea of equilibrium and order, Schumpeter accepted Walras's view. This might be called the Walrasian preconception or ideology W in Schumpeter.

Criticism of the received view

In view of Schumpeter's ideas on static–dynamic relations, we must be careful how we treat his critique of Walrasian statics and his concern with dynamic phenomena. The common interpretation of Schumpeter in this respect is that he deals with statics only as the object of critique, and that he starts with an analysis of circular flow or static state in the exposition of his theory of economic development only for the purpose of making the process of dynamic change conspicuous in contrast to stationary conditions. I believe that such an interpretation is superficial.

Thus, struck by its poetic form, Paul Samuelson calls the exposition of the circular flow in the first chapter of *Entwicklung* a "parable" (Samuelson 1943, 61). Among the most recent arguments is the one by John Elliot in his introduction to the English version of Schumpeter's *Theory of Economic Development*:

Schumpeter's analysis of the circular flow in a deeper sense is not intended to be either descriptive or prescriptive; that is, it neither accurately describes actual capitalist economies nor provides normative benchmarks for evaluation of capitalist economic performance. Instead, it constitutes a useful mental experiment by asking what a capitalist market economy *would* be like *if* the dynamic, revolutionary changes of economic development were absent. The austerity of the circular flow model is justified by Schumpeter on the suggestive ground of its corollary implication that the pulsating processes of real-world economic life are better explained from an explicitly dynamic and evolutionary perspective. (Elliot 1983, xviii–xix)

Elliot refers to a similar interpretation by R. C. McCrea (1913), the early reviewer of Schumpeter's first German edition. McCrea even says that Schumpeter's equilibrium analysis is a *reductio ad absurdum*. In this fashion, the misunderstanding began at the time the book was published. These interpretations of statics, such as parable, mental experiment, and *reductio ad absurdum*, no doubt contradict Schumpeter's points on equilibrium analysis, and in themselves do not take into account the deeper methodological problem that dynamics cannot be constructed without the foundation of statics.

On the other hand, Wolfgang Stolper's view is different from conventional ones: he is quite right in emphasizing the role of equilibrium as well as that of innovation as central to Schumpeter's theory of development:

To me, understanding the nature of the equilibrium is as central a part of understanding Schumpeter's approach to evolution as is the role of the entrepreneur. The equilibrium may be quite dynamic in the technical sense of the word. It is a concept which describes all the adaptive forces in an economy, forces which are very strong and which serve not only to keep an economy from going off in all directions or from exploding, but which, by the same token, require special efforts to break out of ... So the "equilibrium" in the Schumpeterian case and its characteristics are neither just a methodological principle ... nor something the economic system is passing through as the cycle is moving up and down. It is a firm and important part of reality, explaining behaviour and adjustments. And to escape from it, i.e. to destroy it, requires more than routine [*sic*]. (Stolper 1982, 31, 33)

Stolper is right in recognizing that equilibrium is neither a mere fiction nor a rhetorical device but an important part of reality, but his interpretation is insufficient in that he neglects the methodological role of equilibrium analysis in the sense described here.

A Lakatosian interpretation

It is illuminating to summarize the relationship between statics and dynamics in Schumpeter's work with the aid of current methodological concepts. Lakatos's methodological view (Lakatos 1970) seems most appropriate to interpret Schumpeter. He calls a series of theories, as a unit of describing a science, a "scientific research program" that has both the negative and positive heuristics as methodological principles; the negative heuristic is concerned with the maintenance of a "hard core" and the positive heuristic with the development of a "protective belt." The hard core is a set of propositions, accepted by the believers of the scientific research program, that are immune from empirical tests, and the negative heuristic has the role of preventing this hard core from being exposed to critiques and anomalies. It is the role of the positive heuristic to deal with the critiques and anomalies arising from the gaps between observation and theory and to extend the scope of the application of a theoretical hypothesis with regard to the explanation and prediction of reality. The positive heuristic actually works through the construction of a protective belt, which consists of auxiliary hypotheses, observation hypotheses, initial conditions, and so forth to protect the hard core from being refuted.

A scientific research program does not mean a single theory but a series of theories constituting a vast protective belt around the hard core. The hard core is irrefutable; only the protective belt, which is directed to the explanation and prediction of reality, is refutable. If a series of theories in the protective belt can predict and discover novel facts that have not been expected, the research program in question is called progressive. Whether a program is progressive or not is the criterion for determining the superiority of the program. However, since a judgment of progressiveness takes a long time, Lakatos stressed the hindsight elements in appraisals of theories and regarded the existence of competing research programs as normal in science. This consideration led him to emphasize the importance of methodological tolerance, which is also an important consequence of Schumpeter's methodology.

If one can interpret, as Roy Weintraub did, the development of the general equilibrium theory since Walras as a scientific research program in Lakatos's sense, the hard core in the program will consist of the fundamental propositions of price theory and the underlying belief in the price mechanism.[14] Weintraub defines as the positive heuristics: (1) go forth and construct theories in which economic agents optimize, and (2) construct theories that make predictions about changes in equilibrium; and as the negative heuristics: (3) do not construct theories in which irrational behavior plays any role, (4) do not construct theories in which equilibrium has no meaning, and (5) do not test the hard-core propositions (Weintraub 1985, 109). Is it possible to locate Schumpeter's contribution of the theory of economic development within the framework of what Weintraub calls a neo-Walrasian research program?

My interpretation that Schumpeter's dynamics depends on statics in the methodological sense can be expressed by the Lakatosian terminology. Thus, Schumpeter accepted the hard core of the general equilibrium theory as the Walrasian ideology W and developed his propositions about economic development, $W+$, as a protective belt in order to approach the reality of the capitalist economy.[15] Specifically, in Schumpeter's thought, the basic assumptions of price theory and the belief in the price mechanism are accepted as the hard core (the negative heuristic (5)). His dynamic theory, guided by the positive heuristics, aims to develop economic theory through a progressive problem shift. Although dynamic phenomena destroy equilibrium, the market forces are conceived to restore equilibrium positions (the positive heuristic (2) and the negative heuristic (4)). The question whether the entrepreneurial activity in Schumpeter's dynamic process is an optimizing, rational behavior (the positive heuristic (1) and the negative heuristic (3)) seems problematical. Although the entrepreneurial activity is not an optimizing behavior in a narrow sense, it is not an irrational behavior. Schumpeter's dynamic theory can be seen as expanding the neo-Walrasian research program by developing a protective belt, not within the framework of, but on the basis of static theory. Far from rejecting it, his dynamic theory depended on static theory. Weintraub's specification of the heuristics seems to be narrow if it excludes the possibility of a protective belt that may be beyond static theory. For Schumpeter, statics and dynamics are not only separate tools addressed to different objects, but also are the complements, as the hard core and the protective belt respectively, in the construction of the Walrasian scientific system. They play different methodological roles, that is, the negative and positive heuristic respectively.

Marx as ideology

Schumpeter started from *Wesen*, which was a recapitulation of economic statics, and explored the area of economic dynamics in *Entwicklung* and *Business Cycles*. In view of his program of universal social scientific research, however, his theory of economic development marked only a halfway position toward his goal. Had he remained within the area of economics, he might have regarded it as a satisfactory contribution. However, his concern with the totality of social phenomena always prompted him to go beyond economics. Thus, finally, in *Capitalism, Socialism and Democracy* (1942), he went as far as establishing as the object of his inquiry a wider area that included politics, society, and culture as well as the economy, and discussed the historical evolution of the capitalist system in terms of the interrelationships between economic and noneconomic areas. This wider perspective gave Schumpeter an opportunity to complete a more satisfactory theory of evolution. In this sense, the theory of economic development in *Entwicklung* and *Business Cycles* might be called a halfway house between *Wesen* and *Capitalism*.

The idea of endogenous development and destruction

That his theory of economic development was half finished in a wider perspective can be ascertained from his treatment of the concept of innovation, the central idea of the theory. Schumpeter repeatedly argued that the innovation of the entrepreneur alters the customary channels of the economy from within the economic system, but it is merely a sort of rhetoric. Innovation appears to be an endogenous variable in the sense that it is carried out by the entrepreneur, but it is still an exogenous variable in the sense that it cannot be analyzed further from the standpoint of economics. It is, as it were, a change in an exogenous variable emerging within the economic system. The following remark by Schumpeter admitted this:

[This book] is not at all concerned with the concrete factors of change, but with the method by which these work, with the *mechanism of change*. The "entrepreneur" is merely the bearer of the mechanism of change. (1934, 61)

In other words, he did not intend to analyze innovation but to describe various economic phenomena accompanying innovation. Despite his rhetoric, the fact that innovation was treated as exogenous in the system of economic analysis limited the applicability of his theory of economic development as the analysis of sociocultural development as a whole.

Only in the overall perspective could an endogenous explanation of capitalist development be possible. When Schumpeter limited himself to the economic area, he defined capitalism as a set of three economic institutions, that is, market mechanism, private ownership, and bank credit. When he took a broader view, however, he conceived of capitalism as a civilization, including a political system, class structure, ways of thinking, value systems, science and art, lifestyles, and so on. According to this conception, interrelationships among various areas of social life form a grand general equilibrium, so to speak. The evolution of capitalism must be explained through changing interrelationships among these areas. Economic development theory conceived in the economic area is not sufficient to indicate the historical behavior of capitalist society as a whole and is therefore no match for Marx's analysis of capitalism. Although Schumpeter claimed the similarity of his theory of economic development with Marx's with respect to the idea of endogenous changes, he admitted that "my structure covers only a small part of his [Marx's] ground" (1934, 60).

Schumpeter thus adhered to the idea of analyzing the process of change in capitalist society as a whole rather than from just an economic perspective. This idea was inspired by Marx. Schumpeter praised Marx so highly because he sympathized with the form and content of Marx's social analysis.

First, concerning the formal aspect of analysis, Schumpeter thought well of the Marxian view that economic systems evolve endogenously in the context of historical time. He even said that his concept and aim were exactly the same as those of Marx; their common idea was "a vision of economic evolution as a distinct process generated by the economic system itself" (1937, 3). In other words, it was "the idea of a theory ... of the actual sequence of those patterns or of the economic process as it goes on, under its own steam, in historic time, producing at every instant that state which will of itself determine the next one" (1950a, 43). In Schumpeter's mind, Marx's idea of immanent evolution was comparable, in terms of scientific values, to Walras's discovery of general equilibrium.

Second, with regard to the substantive content of analysis, Schumpeter accepted Marx's general vision of decaying capitalism. In Marx's scenario, capitalism would fall, through the revolution of the proletariat, after increased aggravation of its inherent contradictions. Schumpeter thought, in contrast, that capitalism must decline because of its economic success. The means of inference was entirely different between them, but they agreed that capitalism has a historical existence and does not continue to work like a perpetual motion machine. Schumpeter regarded this vision as a truly great achievement:

The grand vision of an immanent evolution of the economic process – that, working somehow through accumulation, somehow destroys the economy as well as the society of competitive capitalism and somehow produces an untenable social situation that will somehow give birth to another type of social organization – remains after the most vigorous criticism has done its worst. It is this fact, and this fact alone, that constitutes Marx's claim to greatness as an economic analyst. (1954a, 441)

The rather poetic repetition of the word *somehow* in this passage indicates that Schumpeter did not accept Marx's causation for several crucial aspects of society and replaced it with his own.

Schumpeter accepted Marx's ideology of endogenous evolution and the self-destruction of capitalism. I call this Marxian preconception or ideology M in Schumpeter. He wanted to describe the total process of capitalist development on the basis of Marxian ideology M. Schumpeter's theory of social development, which was finally developed in *Capitalism* and constructed in a manner consistent with this ideology, might be called $M+$.

Criticism of the economic interpretation of history

According to Marx's materialistic or economic interpretation of history, the forces of social evolution can be found in the conflict between the physical productive forces and the overall social relations of production. Schumpeter considered this view to be of "first-rank importance" and summarized its essential points in the following propositions (1954a, 439): (1) All the cultural manifestations of a society are ultimately functions of its class structure. (2) A society's class structure is ultimately and chiefly governed by the structure of production. (3) The social process of production displays an immanent evolution.

In Marx, the class structure of capital and labor is the axis of production relations; it governs the process of capital accumulation and exploitation of labor in relation to the productive forces, on the one hand, and determines the superstructure including the social, political, and cultural processes, on the other. In this sense, the class structure is an important link between the superstructure and substructure, thus forming a monolithic system of economics and sociology in Marx. Schumpeter observed that Marx's theory of social classes was incorporated as a submodel in the framework of the economic interpretation of history but rated it as least valuable because its exclusive emphasis on class struggle was patently wrong; therefore he claimed the separation of economics and sociology within Marx's universal social science.

Schumpeter formulated propositions (1)–(3) so as to minimize the Marxian tone. His appraisal was as follows. Regarding (1), Schumpeter denied the Marxian causation that the superstructure is unilaterally determined by its economic foundation and class structure and merely admitted a functional relationship between them. Rather, in Schumpeter's analysis of capitalist evolution the reverse relationship – the superstructure governs the economic process – is crucial. As for proposition (2), Schumpeter claimed that class structure is also determined by diverse factors other than economic ones; for example, he regarded the symbiosis of the bourgeois with the feudal nobility in the early modern ages as a characteristic of the superstructure in the capitalist system. He also paid particular attention to dynamic phenomena; the contents of classes, he maintained, change like "a hotel or an omnibus, always full, but always of different people" (1951b, 165). Finally, with respect to proposition (3), Marx's thesis was that capital accumulation and class struggle proceed around the notion of classes so that the framework of capitalism will finally collapse. Schumpeter rejected all of these analytic apparatuses and scenarios of Marx and accepted only his general vision of immanent social evolution and self-disintegration of the capitalist economy.

Despite his claim that the two were similar, Schumpeter accepted neither

Marx's labor theory of value nor his theory of social classes, but only a general view that "the social process of production displays an immanent evolution (tendency to change its own economic, hence also social, data)" (1954a, 439), as is shown in proposition (3). This inheritance was no longer worthy of the label "economic interpretation of history"; Schumpeter jettisoned the Marxian substance of proposition (3) because he rejected propositions (1) and (2).

Interactions between economic and noneconomic areas

The bases of Schumpeter's social scientific research, therefore, were partly Walrasian ideology W (markets function interdependently so as to achieve general equilibrium, and thus capitalist economy is essentially stable) and partly Marxian ideology M (markets develop by their momentum and thus capitalist economy will break down). In fact, Schumpeter thought it necessary to refer to two great names, Walras and Marx, in order to explain his goal in the study of economic change (1937, 2). More than a few authors writing about Schumpeter have criticized the paradox and inconsistency in his admiration for, and indebtedness to, both Walras and Marx. This criticism is rooted in the popular misinterpretation of his statics–dynamics dichotomy that fails to understand the coordination of statics and dynamics in Schumpeter's thought; it is no wonder that this misinterpretation is now extended to relations between economic and noneconomic areas in a wider perspective of universal social science.

Social events are related to each other, not only simultaneously but also intertemporarily. Simultaneous relationships are the subject of the Walrasian general equilibrium theory; intertemporal relationships are the theme of the Marxian theory of evolution. Both relationships are necessary like the abscissa and provide the ordinate to explain any event at any point in time. But, it must be remembered, a theory of evolution must cover not only the economic area but also other social areas, because in a historical process the assumption of *ceteris paribus* is not valid. The contradiction of the two ideologies W and M is apparent only on an abstract level. The apparent contradiction is refuted by the idea, based on historical experience, that the very success of the capitalist economy will produce noneconomic factors that are inconsistent with it; these factors will in turn worsen the economic performance of capitalism. Although the economy can work successfully by itself, the impact of external factors will ultimately spoil it. Accounting for the fact that the changes in noneconomic factors are the result of economic development, we can assume a grand general equilibrium between the economic and noneconomic spheres and its evolution over time. This was Schumpeter's integrated vision of W and M.

In Schumpeter's *Capitalism*, it is innovation, not class structure, that mediates bilateral interactions between economic and noneconomic spheres.

Furthermore, the concept of innovation is linked, in unique ways, to Walrasian ideology and Marxian ideology respectively, so as to construct $W+$ and $M+$. First, despite the destructive and destabilizing effects of innovation, the capitalist economic system has a remarkable adaptive capacity to absorb them and to revitalize itself. Second, despite the growth- and welfare-promoting effects of innovation, the capitalist economic system cannot survive indefinitely. In each case, it is claimed that, despite the effects of innovation, other forces (toward the equilibrium of markets and toward the fall of the system) will eventually govern the process because the auxiliary assumptions leading to $W+$ and $M+$ must be consistent with the basic ideologies located at the hard core.

Keynes and Schumpeter

Since Walras and Marx are unmistakable ideological presuppositions of Schumpeter's thought, one must examine the structure of his vision in light of their theories. But it is also important to shed light on Schumpeter's vision from outside by referring to John Maynard Keynes. Both Schumpeter and Keynes, born in the same year, were concerned with the problems of inflation, deflation, unemployment, and business cycles caused by the instability of the capitalist economy in the first half of the twentieth century. Interestingly enough, they approached these problems from different directions and developed different theories to analyze the instability of capitalism. Keynes succeeded in constructing a new theoretical apparatus and redrawing the intellectual field of economics. It may be that the competition between the two economists was mostly in Schumpeter's mind; at least to Schumpeter, Keynes was a tough rival. In order to understand the nature of Schumpeter's ideology, it is useful to compare him with Keynes in the context of the intellectual field at that time.

Different visions

Schumpeter and Keynes developed different views; Keynes's were accepted, whereas Schumpeter's were not. But Schumpeter, with confidence, continued to be critical of Keynes as he examined the limits of Keynes's theory.

At its hard core, neoclassical microeconomic analysis is concerned with the problem of resource allocation under the assumption of the full utilization of resources. The largest contribution of Keynes's theory was to reject the fundamental notion of neoclassical economics, namely the belief in the long-term stability and harmony of the capitalist economy, which was formulated in Say's law, and to establish, as a tool with which to analyze the unstable reality, the framework of macroeconomic analysis, which addresses the fluctuations of effective demand. The essence of Keynesian economics, it can be argued, is captured in the following phrases:

This *long run* is a misleading guide to current affairs. *In the long run* we are all dead. Economists set themselves too easy, too useless a task if in tempestuous seasons they can only tell us that when the storm is long past the ocean is flat again. (Keynes 1923, 80)

Keynes maintained that capitalism, if left alone, could not escape from difficulties and would decay because the capitalist economic system has inherent defects with regard to the saving and investment mechanism. The framework of equilibrium analysis and the corresponding picture of a stable economic order constituted Walrasian ideology in Schumpeter. Thus Keynes and Schumpeter disagreed on this most basic level of vision.

Moreover, Keynes's method of building preconception differed from that of Schumpeter's. Keynes built a vision from the observation of an actual economy and attempted to deviate from traditional thought through the theoretical formulation of a vision. It might be better to say that he constructed a vision using a gap between traditional thought and reality. On the contrary, Schumpeter believed in the continuity of great ideas and inherited the thoughts of Walras and Marx in the form of vision. Most neoclassical economists at that time similarly looked at reality with a preconception of the inherent stability of capitalism, but they did not pay much attention to the gap between their preconception and unstable reality. While both Schumpeter and Keynes were concerned about the anomaly in neoclassical theory, Schumpeter claimed the viewpoint of dynamism in order to explain the gap, whereas Keynes tried to resolve it.

Schumpeter's idea of decaying capitalism was not necessarily based on the observation of facts, such as the Great Depression, but largely on Marxian thought. He pursued the logical consequence of capitalist development to theorize this thought. The nonempirical nature of Schumpeter's ideology should be stressed, but it is not correct to say that his ideas were always idealistic. In *Business Cycles* he made strenuous efforts to base his ideas on an empirical analysis of the historical process; in the broader perspective of sociocultural development, however, vision inevitably played a greater role than observation and analysis.

Against Keynes

Schumpeter's criticism of Keynes can be summarized in three major points. First, Schumpeter distinguished between economic theory as science and economic policy as practice and asserted that: "No science thrives ... in the atmosphere of direct practical aim, and even practical results are but the by-products of disinterested work at the problem for the problem's sake"

(1933a, 6). To him, economists' conflicting answers to current policy issues and loss of credibility was a result of the confusion between theory and practice. In the discussion of practice, value judgments were introduced and a viewpoint obstructive to scientific inquiry was often adopted. Although the discipline of economics emerged historically from the discussion of practical problems, the progress of economics was made possible by its separation from politics and ethics. Schumpeter regarded this recognition as the regulative idea of science and maintained that it was a pillar of the studies in the history of science.

When Keynes's *General Theory* (1936) was published, Schumpeter immediately responded to its political orientation. In his review of *General Theory*, Schumpeter contended that Keynes was offering, in the garb of general scientific truth, policy recommendations that held meaning only with reference to the practical exigencies of a unique historical situation. He wrote:

This sublimates practical issues into scientific ones, divides economists ... according to lines of political preference, produces popular successes at the moment, and reactions after – witness the fate of Ricardian economics – neither of which have anything to do with science. (1936a, 791–92)

This appraisal anticipated the immediate triumph of Keynesian economics and the later controversy between the Keynesians and the Non-Keynesians (such as the Monetarists, the libertarians, and the rational expectation school).

Indeed, one characteristic of Schumpeter's thought is its independence from a policy viewpoint, but this requires a careful interpretation. In fact, he warned economists against indulging in hasty policy discussions without a fundamental understanding of situations from a long-term perspective; it is a mistake to say that he was not interested in policy. The following remark in his preface to *Business Cycles* clearly indicates this position:

I recommend no policy and propose no plan. Readers who care for nothing else should lay this book aside. But I do not admit that this convicts me of indifference to the social duty of science or makes this book – including its historical parts – irrelevant to the burning questions of the day. What our time needs most and lacks most is the understanding of the process which people are passionately resolved to control. To supply this understanding is to implement that resolve and to rationalize it. This is the only service the scientific worker is, as such, qualified to render. (1939, 1, vi)

Nor does Schumpeter deny the application of science to diagnoses and recommendations; he even says:

I am speaking of science which is technique that turns out the results which, together with value judgments or preferences, produce recommendations, either individual ones or systems of them – such as the systems of mercantilism, liberalism and so on. (1949a, 349)

The sum total of practical recommendations together with the underlying schema of social values is called "political economy" and is distinguished from economics (1954a, 1141).

Schumpeter thought, on the one hand, that science should be a neutral technique that could or should be used regardless of one's objectives, as was seen in natural science; he wished that economics could progress to such a stage. But, on the other hand, he admitted that where the procedural rules of science do not work, science must be influenced by ideology, and that theories must be built so as to be consistent with a scientist's goals and perspectives. Furthermore, insofar as Schumpeter held an instrumentalist philosophy of science, he had to accept this in principle. In this sense, the second and third points of Schumpeter's criticism of Keynes clearly reflect the basic differences in their ideologies.

The second criticism focused on Keynes's aggregate analysis. According to Schumpeter's preconception, an economic system can be analyzed only in terms of the general interdependence of microeconomic variables. From this viewpoint, Keynes's macroeconomic analysis considered some variables that related directly to practical problems and ignored all others for the sake of simplicity; thus, as in a tautology, it established simple macro relations among selected variables to arrive at the conclusions that Keynes desired. Schumpeter called this "the Ricardian Vice" (1954a, 473); David Ricardo was the first theoretical economist who constructed models artificially on the basis of simplifying assumptions.

In Schumpeter's interpretation, Keynes's vision was that, although investment opportunity had declined, saving habits persisted, causing capitalism to fall into chronic functional disorder. In order to develop this vision within a theoretical apparatus, Keynes constructed a model by means of three macroeconomic functions: the consumption function, the efficiency-of-capital function, and the liquidity-preference function. Schumpeter, at last, said:

If we place ourselves on the standpoint of Keynesian orthodoxy and choose to accept his vision of the economic process of our age ... then there can be little objection to his aggregative analysis that produced his results. (1951a, 282)

He admitted the consistency of Keynes's theory with his original vision but exclaimed: "What a *cordon bleu* to make such a sauce out of such scanty material!" (1951a, 281).

Schumpeter, however, disagreed with Keynes's vision about the fall of capitalism. And macroanalysis, too, he considered to be an expedient for policy linked with this vision. His skepticism of macroanalysis was consistent, and as late as 1939 he stated that "the saving-investment mechanism, as such, does not produce anything that could qualify for the role of an explanation of crises or depressions" (1939, 1, 78).

The third criticism concerned Keynes's short-term analysis. For Schumpeter, the waves of boom and bust were as natural in a capitalist economy as the beats of the heart or the ebb and flow of the tide, and it was silly to let oneself be affected by temporary economic fluctuations without realizing the mechanism of capitalist development at work. Unemployment was essentially a temporary phenomenon that characterized the period of adaptation subsequent to the prosperity phase. In contrast, Keynes took this phenomenon seriously and made the vanishing of investment opportunity a vital point of his argument. But his explanation of the investment process seemed to Schumpeter entirely unrealistic; Keynes's reasoning that the lack of inducement to invest would produce unemployment had no greater practical importance than a statement that "motor cars cannot run in the absence of fuel" (1936a, 794).

While Keynes dealt only with some aggregate variables, ignoring all other factors, what was most intolerable to Schumpeter was Keynes's assumption that methods of production and the quantity and quality of capital equipment were not allowed to change. Under Keynes's theory, Schumpeter wrote:

All the phenomena incident to the creation and change in this [industrial] apparatus, that is to say, the phenomena that dominate the capitalist process, are thus excluded from consideration. (1951a, 283)

It may be argued that this was not a criticism but the view of a well-fed Harvard professor who knew little about unemployment and cared even less about those who were starving. Schumpeter's emphasis on the long-term characterized the "protective belt" that defended his Walrasian ideology that the capitalist economy was stable in the long run. However, verification or falsification of a theory of sociocultural development is not easy because, from his point of view, "a century is a 'short run' " (1950a, 163). Therefore, one cannot always expect that the underlying ideology of a long-term theory will become extinct. It follows that when in the name of science Schumpeter criticized Keynes generally for his practical orientation and specifically for his aggregate, short-term analysis, he himself was not free from the ideological bias underlying his own general equilibrium approach with its long-term perspective. His assessment of Keynes cannot be understood independently from his own ideology.

For good or for evil, Keynes's theory dominated the intellectual field. His demand management policy has been widely applied in the revival of capitalism, which was once thought to have lost its self-adjustment mechanism. After World War II a full employment policy took hold in developed countries as a part of their economic system. The third quarter of the twentieth century is sometimes called the "Age of Keynes" (Hicks 1974, 1). As Schumpeter died in 1950, he did not experience the heyday of the Keynesian economic system but witnessed Keynesian economics in vogue. Anyway, he anticipated the problems that such an era would face, and in fact, this was Schumpeter's last blow against Keynes. According to Schumpeter, Keynes, in order to overcome the alleged malfunction of capitalism, broke down the conventional belief that saving, as a part of the bourgeois scheme of life, and unequal distribution of income and wealth, as a necessary evil for progress, were social virtues; this was, Schumpeter declared, the essence of the Keynesian Revolution (1951a, 290). However, the renouncement of allegiance to the bourgeois scheme of values was the most basic noneconomic factor leading to the fall of capitalism. Thus, for Schumpeter, the very success of Keynes's theory, which aimed at the revival of capitalism in the short run, proved to be helping the fall of capitalism over the long term. This was the severest critique that Keynes ever received.

At the Highgate Cemetery in London there is a huge tomb of Karl Marx; on it is inscribed an epitaph of his words, the eleventh thesis on Ludwig Feuerbach: "Philosophers have only interpreted the world in various ways. But what is important is to change it."[16] This represents well the madness and ardor of Marx, who sought to overthrow capitalism by revolution. A suitable epitaph for Keynes, who worked for the reform of capitalism through rational policy, might be his declaration, "In the long run we are all dead." Unlike Marx's cry for revolution and unlike Keynes's claim of control, Schumpeter's uniqueness lay in his insight into the logic of events in the long run. Those who advocate changing reality, whether revolutionists or reformists, sharply grasp an aspect of some things but are unlikely to account for others. Schumpeter could not tolerate this mode of thought. I would choose as his epitaph the words of Julius III (1443–1513), which Schumpeter quoted near the end of his life: "Mundus regitur parva sapientia" (With how little wisdom the world is governed!) (1950a, 376).[17]

A changing power distribution

This chapter on the sociology of science cannot close without mention of a well-thumbed topic: why there was no Schumpeter school of economics. The explanation that has been regarded as the most plausible is the one given by Schumpeter himself, that since economics is not a philosophy but a science, there should be no schools in economics.[18]

Although this explanation is consistent with Schumpeter's thought on the ideal of science, it does not do justice to his sociological view of schools, leadership, and innovation. Moreover, it contradicts his personal portrait. Whether or not the academic success would result in the formation of a school, no one would deny the desire to win a reputation. The conventional view, which was probably forged in the heyday of the logical positivist philosophy of science, seems to commit the error of explaining sociological phenomena of science by a normative proposition of the philosophy of science. The question of why there is no Schumpeter school seems to presuppose a kind of valuation that he deserved to have a school. The conventional answer rests on Schumpeter's ostensibly negative attitude toward schools, but the formation of schools is an objective fact that is related not only to a scientific appraisal but also to a highly sociological phenomenon. Therefore, it is important to ask why Schumpeter could not dominate the academic field, independently from his positive or negative attitude toward schools. To this question the existence of Keynes is crucially important.

The Keynesian Revolution in terms of science and ideology was complete; the loyalty test for the Keynesians was a denial of Say's law. From the 1930s to the 1960s, however, the general equilibrium theory, detached from the problem of reality, was concerned with the mathematical inquiry into the existence, uniqueness, and stability of equilibrium in order to harden its "hard core." Despite Schumpeter's interest in general equilibrium analysis, he had nothing to do with this development.

Of course, this does not mean that there were no inherent reasons why Schumpeter could not have had a school. One point relating to his ideology should be raised here. Although mathematical economics made progress during the period under study, Schumpeter could not lead it in the direction of his vision of economic and social development. Mathematical economics and econometrics developed along the track of Keynesian macrodynamics. Schumpeter's failure to attract this emerging potentiality of economic analysis was due not only to his lack of a mathematical orientation but also to the unamenability of his vision of dynamics to mathematical manipulation.

Furthermore, another sociological factor was that Schumpeter was not blessed with the opportunity for long-standing positions in academic centers. In the first half of his life he was not accepted by the Austrian and German academic establishment. Czernovitz, Graz, and Bonn were just provincial universities; his work in government and banking was a digression from this point of view. He was a gipsy economist.[19] In the second half of his life he stayed at Harvard for seventeen years; it was a chance. But, except for having some influence on studies of entrepreneurial history, he could not form a school at Harvard, which after 1936, experienced a wave of the Keynesian Revolution. Moreover, his aversion to the tradition of American Institutionalism and the technocracy of the New Deal much weakened his impact in the United States.

After Keynesian economics was established as a new orthodoxy, all the claims arising from theoretical and political issues were heaped upon it. The practical problems of an economy that could not be solved by Keynesian economics were pointed out one after the other: cost inflation instead of demand inflation, rigidity in fiscal policy operation under democracy instead of functional finance, economic development instead of economic stability, and so forth. In the meantime, neoclassical economics regained its strength through a series of objections to Keynesian economics: neoclassical synthesis, monetarism, libertarianism, new Austrian economics, rational expectation, supply-side economics – all of these movements were reactions to Keynesian economics.

After Keynesian economics was properly stored in the toolbox of economics, changes in the distribution of power in the economics field brought about the restoration of Keynes's two former rivals: Friedrich von Hayek and Schumpeter. In the case of Hayek, freedom was emphasized instead of Keynesian government intervention; in the case of Schumpeter, economic development and technological innovation were stressed instead of the Keynesian preoccupation with short-term economic stability. In 1986 the International Schumpeter Society was established by a group of scholars who shared Schumpeter's vision of development. Whether or not this can be properly called the formation of a school, a change in the distribution of power occurred in the intellectual field after the enthusiasm for the Keynesian Revolution had run its course.[20] The fourth quarter of the twentieth century may be called the age of Schumpeter (Giersch 1984, 103). Obviously, it would have been more agreeable to Schumpeter to say that his theories had belonged to the filiation of economic ideas than to say that a Schumpeter school was emerging.

CHAPTER 5

The economic methodology of instrumentalism

Schumpeter's first book, *Das Wesen und der Hauptinhalt der theoretischen Nationalö-konomie*, published in 1908 when he was twenty-five, was one of the earliest attempts to give neoclassical economics a methodological foundation.[1] His approach was influenced by the precursors of logical positivism, such as Ernst Mach, Henri Poincaré, and Pierre Duhem.[2] In a historical survey of nineteenth-century positivism David Oldroyd observes:

> Between them [logical positivists] and Comte we have a number of moderately distinct schools or "isms," such as pragmatism, conventionalism and instrumentalism, which may nonetheless be classified more or less satisfactorily as different manifestations of positivism. (Oldroyd 1986, 168)

It was these "isms" that influenced Schumpeter's economic methodology. My argument in this chapter is that Schumpeter's methodology in *Wesen* can best be interpreted as instrumentalism, that is, the view that theories are not descriptions but instruments for deriving useful results and are neither true nor false. Instrumentalism is the opposite of scientific realism, which asserts that the object of science exists; theory describes it, and therefore it is possible to ask whether a theory is true or false.

A lacuna in the history of economic methodology

Schumpeter's contribution to economic methodology has not received the attention it deserves. There are several reasons for this.

Why his methodology was neglected

First, economists have been readily misled by Schumpeter's comments on the sterility of the *Methodenstreit* (the dispute over methods between Menger and Schmoller), of philosophical speculation, and of the conflicts between schools and have thus neglected the importance of his methodological work. In evaluating Schumpeter's early German works, Erich Schneider concluded:

"His greatest loathing was reserved for methodological controversy, which he regarded not only as sterile, but as a direct obstacle to the progress of our discipline" (Schneider 1951, 58). This assertion should not be interpreted as meaning that Schumpeter actually claimed that *methodology* was sterile; rather, it refers to the sterility of *disputes on methods*. In fact, Schumpeter advocated a methodology that would make any controversy on methods superfluous.

Second, because *Wesen* was not reprinted until 1970 and has not yet been translated into English, it has not been widely read.[3] There is little doubt, however, that the book had a strong impact on a portion of the German-speaking academic field. As Oskar Morgenstern observed:

The work was read avidly in Vienna even long after the First World War, and its youthful freshness and vigor appealed to the young students. I myself remember what sort of revelation it was to me when I first laid hands on it and, like many others of my generation, I resolved to read everything Schumpeter had written and would ever write. (Morgenstern 1951, 198)

Third, because Schumpeter's primary contribution was to economic dynamics rather than to economic statics, *Wesen*, which was concerned exclusively with static theory, has naturally attracted little attention, even among his admirers. Paul Samuelson correctly pointed out, however, that "Schumpeter's most theoretical work was his first German book of 1908 – *Das Wesen und [der] Hauptinhalt der theoretischen Nationalökonomie*" (Samuelson 1982, 3). Only on rare occasions was such an appropriate reference made to *Wesen*, but its contents were never subjected to any serious scrutiny. As this chapter will demonstrate, *Wesen* was a theoretical work that was also uniquely constructed as a methodological work.

The literature on economic methodology has often maintained that the nineteenth-century methodologists, such as Nassau Senior, John Stuart Mill, John Elliott Cairnes, and John Neville Keynes, were directly followed by Lionel Robbins in the 1930s, and has made no reference to the early part of the twentieth century, by which time neoclassical economics had been essentially established. Moreover, Robbins's methodology in *An Essay on the Nature and Significance of Economic Science* (Robbins 1932), though representing only one among competing positions, has been treated as the primary authority and has won universal acceptance in modern economic theory. Robbins's dominance might be attributed to the wide agreement with the definition of economics in his book.[4] Recently this situation has changed: in accordance with an increasing plurality in the philosophy of science and a growing interest in the history of methodology as a result of the decline in the influence of logical positivism, different approaches to economic methodology, such as those of Robbins, Terence Hutchison, Fritz Machlup, Milton

Friedman, and Samuelson, are now recognized.[5] Nevertheless, Schumpeter's methodology is still overlooked in the literature.

By clarifying the origin and nature of Schumpeter's methodology in *Wesen*, this chapter helps fill a lacuna in the history of economic methodology. Moreover, through this inquiry we can discuss its relationship to Friedman's methodology. Although in the current literature on economic methodology Friedman's essay "The Methodology of Positive Economics" (1953) has been viewed as typical of the instrumentalist position, Schumpeter's instrumentalist methodology, described forty-five years before Friedman's, is noteworthy because it is explicitly and completely framed in methodological terms and has a clear source in nineteenth-century positivism. Finally, this chapter confirms in a concrete form that methodological thought underlay Schumpeter's substantive economic inquiry.

Das Wesen und der Hauptinhalt der theoretischen Nationalökonomie

Before making the case that Schumpeter's *Wesen* is a clear statement of instrumentalist economic methodology, it is first necessary to provide some background information. This section explains Schumpeter's purpose in writing *Wesen* and presents his views on the method and methodology by which this purpose was to be realized. The next section outlines the currently accepted view of instrumentalism in order to compare it with Schumpeter's version.

Purposes

What were the intentions of *Wesen*, a book of more than six hundred pages? As is clear from the title, *The Nature and Substance of Theoretical Economics*,[6] the author was attempting to present a fundamental and systematic treatment of theoretical economics. Schumpeter understood "theoretical (or pure) economics" to be the "exact theory of economics," or what is known today as neoclassical static theory.[7] In his view, although dynamics should belong to economics, it did not yet constitute a part of theoretical economics because it was far less developed. Schumpeter saw the task of *Wesen* as follows: "The following description ... tries to examine as correctly as possible the foundation, methods, and main results of pure economics with reference to its nature, its significance, and its development possibilities" (1908, 20). He referred to the task of *Wesen* as writing the epistemology, or methodology, of economics.

There were two reasons why Schumpeter wanted to write a book on methodology. First, he deplored the confusion in economics around the turn of the century, as reflected in the conflicts between schools, disputes over methods, and futile controversies. He believed that this confusion was due to the lack of a clear understanding regarding the foundation, nature, and significance of economics. The Marginal Revolution by William Stanley Jevons, Carl Menger, and Léon Walras had already occurred, but British classical economics still dominated thinking in Britain and the United States. The German Historical School was steadily expanding, and the Marxists were gaining strength. At this time the intellectual field of economics was turbulent, compared with the century after Adam Smith, during which the British Classical School maintained an almost monopolistic position. The situation was as chaotic as a political struggle; indeed, there were elements of political confrontation in the disputes within economics. Knut Wicksell in Sweden also denounced the state of the economics field of that period: "[In economics] no generally recognized result is to be found, as is also the case with theology, and for roughly the same reasons; there is no single doctrine taken to be a scientific truth without the diametrically opposed view being similarly upheld by authors of high repute" (Wicksell [1904] 1958, 51). Wicksell observed that the cause of the split was not so much due to conflicting methods in economics as it was to the confrontation between political and social viewpoints.

In *Wesen* Schumpeter did not attempt to provide a textbook description of economics but rather sought to interpret and evaluate the procedures in economics from a methodological standpoint in order to rid the field of the confusion surrounding it. Economics as a self-contained or "autonomous science" was at the heart of his interpretation and evaluation, and he believed that it must not seek help from other disciplines but explain the economic world from its own perspective. He proposed how to establish the foundation to enable economics to do so.

Second, Schumpeter hoped to familiarize German economists with theoretical economics, especially Walrasian economics, because, in his view, theoretical development had not been pursued satisfactorily in Germany, where social policy and history research wielded power.[8] He tried to acquaint them with economic theory through a methodological orientation rather than through its direct presentation in a mathematical form. This roundabout approach was perhaps thought to be more suitable for German economists, who were accustomed to philosophical and methodological speculation. Schumpeter frankly notes:

One of my purposes is to familiarize the German public with many things – concepts, propositions, and approaches – which have so far remained unknown to them because the development of theories has not been adequately pursued. German economists often have very little idea of what "pure" theorists are really concerned with. Thus, even if the knowledge of theories is taken for granted, much can be done in order to bring the theories of foreign countries closer to the German discipline. (1908, xxi)

In view of the intellectual field in Germany at that time, such a goal was quite outrageous and can only be understood in terms of his self-assurance and high spirits in wishing to conquer the field of economics.

Method and methodology

What then is methodology? Following Machlup, I understand methodology to be the study of reasons behind the rules or principles of scientific procedure (i.e., methods), on the basis of which certain propositions in science are accepted or rejected (Machlup 1978, 54–56). In this sense methodology is a branch of philosophy or logic. On the other hand, methods or techniques in any field of science, which should be distinguished from methodology, relate to the prescribed rules or principles of scientific procedure, including constructing concepts, making assumptions, building models, formulating hypotheses, observing facts, and testing theories.

There is no doubt that in *Wesen* Schumpeter correctly distinguished between method and methodology. In his academic life he occasionally discussed the significance of various methods of research in economics, that is, theoretical and historical, static and dynamic, mathematical and statistical, micro and macro, and economic and sociocultural. Although he briefly touched on the subject of methodology again in the introduction to his posthumous book, *History of Economic Analysis*, it was only once in *Wesen* that he intensively analyzed the methodology of economics. He refers to *Wesen* as a study of methodology or epistemology, but he does not give any specific definition of the two terms. As is often found in most authors of methodology, the distinction between methodology and epistemology is neither definite nor essential in Schumpeter's thought. Considering the ideas of the time, however, it would be safe to assume that he regarded epistemology as an inquiry into the nature and basis of knowledge.

The *Methodenstreit* was a conflict between the uses of historical and theoretical methods in economics and served as a stimulus for Schumpeter to embark on a study of methodology. In *Wesen* he hoped to clarify the rules of procedure in neoclassical economics and to propose reasons justifying such rules. For this purpose he adopted a particular approach to methodology. I have referred to *Wesen* as a fundamental and systematic treatment of theoretical economics, but the book is quite different from those usually entitled *Principles of Economics*; it is so concerned with methodology that beginners would be unable to learn economics from it. *Wesen* clearly presupposes that the reader has a sufficient knowledge of economics. The book is also different from methodological works often entitled *The Scope and Method of Political Economy*; it is so concerned with specific theoretical problems in economics that those who expect a philosophical analysis of general ideas will be puzzled. *Wesen* is unique: it is not a mere presentation of theoretical "substance" or of the epistemological "nature" of economics, nor does it attempt to display the two separate approaches taken by economic theory and economic methodology. A fundamental characteristic of *Wesen* is that it discusses both the nature and substance simultaneously. Schumpeter addresses methodological issues in the context of every detail of economic principles and hypotheses. The title, *Wesen und Hauptinhalt* (Nature and Substance), indicates, as it were, a synthesis of economic methodology and economic theory, namely that of a metatheory and a substantive theory.[9]

Schumpeter expresses his basic approach to methodology as follows:

> In *our* view, one should not construct a methodological viewpoint a priori but adopt what leads us furthest in each case without being affected by any preconception. In particular, one should not mark off a priori the field of economics. We should instead innocently approach the problems that interest us and try to elucidate them. The method found useful, however, need not be universal for that reason ... One cannot separate the study of methods from the study of concrete problems. Only in relation to the latter has the former any meaning. (1908, xiii–xiv)

His claim concerning so-called methodological tolerance follows from the recognition of the dependence of methods on problems.[10] He explains:

> Like many specialists [of the natural sciences] in our time, I am convinced that the contentions of almost all "schools" and of all individual authors are *correct*; most contentions are *true in ways* for which they are meant and *for the purposes intended* (1908, vi).

> Each method has its concrete areas of application, and it is useless to struggle for its universal validity. We shall emphasize over and over again that a discussion of methods has meaning only in relation to practical scientific works. (1908, 7)

Although Schumpeter refers to his particular methodological position of allowing methodical diversity as simply being "pragmatic" (1908, xvi), I propose that it is fundamentally "instrumentalist." Concerning the fact that Schumpeter did not take one side or the other in regard to the *Methodenstreit*, Samuelson observes that "his methodology took the eclectic road of good sense" and calls him an "eclectic methodologist" (Samuelson 1982, 4). Schumpeter's position, however, is actually more sophisticated than this. Before I proceed to an interpretation of his methodology, it is necessary and useful to comment on the current conception of instrumentalism.

The conceptions of instrumentalism

The central claims of instrumentalism: strong and weak forms

The currently accepted view of instrumentalism is articulated by Karl Popper, one of its leading critics. Popper refers to physicists such as Ernst Mach,

Gustav Kirchhoff, Heinrich Hertz, Pierre Duhem, Henri Poincaré, Percy W. Bridgman, and Arthur S. Eddington as instrumentalists (Popper 1963, 99), and he also calls Duhem and Poincaré conventionalists (1983, 112). Popper defines instrumentalism as follows:

By instrumentalism I mean the doctrine that a scientific theory ... should be interpreted as an instrument, *and nothing but an instrument*, for the deduction of predictions of future events (especially measurements) and for other practical applications; and more specifically, that a scientific theory should not be interpreted as a genuine conjecture about the structure of the world, or as a genuine attempt to describe certain aspects of our world. The instrumentalist doctrine implies that scientific theories can be more or less useful, and more or less efficient; but it denies that they can, like descriptive statements, be true or false. (Popper 1983, 111–12)

Paul Feyerabend, also a critic of instrumentalism, succinctly describes it as "the view that scientific theories are instruments of prediction which do not possess any descriptive meaning" (Feyerabend 1981, 17). Lawrence Boland, who interpreted Friedman's 1953 essay as instrumentalist economic methodology, relied on a similar characterization of instrumentalism:

It [instrumentalism] says that theories are convenient and useful ways of (logically) generating what have turned out to be true (or successful) predictions or conclusions ... Thus, theories do not have to be considered true statements about the nature of the world, but only convenient ways of systematically generating the already known "true" conclusions. (Boland 1979, 508–9)

In these three quotations two aspects of theories are specified: the role of theories (they are merely tools for generating prediction) and the cognitive status of theories (they are regarded as neither true nor false). Today the instrumentalist position is often defined along these lines. However, because this formulation limits the role of theories to prediction, it has given rise to the criticism that instrumentalism does not accept explanation as a role of theories. Popper's version of instrumentalism is an extreme one in which scientific theories are nothing but computational rules for prediction. But original instrumentalists did not view the role of theories in such a narrow way. If there was any reason to deny "explanation" in the original instrumentalist view of the role of scientific theories, it would be found in the special sense of the term used by the positivist schools, including the instrumentalists themselves, namely "metaphysical explanation." Thus when Duhem said that a physical theory is not an explanation, he meant by "explanation" a metaphysical or ultimate explanation that describes the reality behind the appearance.[11]

Among the current philosophers of science, Ernst Nagel gives a moderate definition regarding the role of theories in instrumentalism. He views instrumentalism in a much broader light, one that does not limit the role of theories to prediction alone:

[Instrumentalism] maintains that theories are primarily logical instruments for organizing our experience and for ordering experimental laws. Although some theories are
more effective than others for attaining these ends, theories are not statements, and
belong to a different category of linguistic expressions than do statements ... They
cannot therefore be usefully characterized as either true or false. (Nagel 1961, 118)

Sidney Morgenbesser, too, accepts explanation and prediction as the roles of
theories in the instrumentalist view and calls this position weak noncognitivist
instrumentalism, in contrast to strong noncognitivist instrumentalism; in the
latter version, theories are construed as having only predictive use (Morgenbesser 1969, 202). Noncognitive means that it is impossible to identify the
truth or falsity of statements. While the instrumentalist view on the cognitive
status of theories is always noncognitive, there are different views on the role
of theories among instrumentalists. Thus instrumentalists can hold the
broader view that theories are rules or devices for classifying, organizing,
explaining, and predicting observable phenomena and for serving as guides
for action, although the current critics of instrumentalism insist that theories
that are not statements cannot lead to explanation.

Although a fundamental assertion of original instrumentalism has been that
serious problems of truth value associated with the method of induction must
be avoided, instrumentalism need not be characterized, in the minds of
original instrumentalists, by the view that theories are tools for prediction
alone. What is essential is its claim concerning the instrumentality of theories
for any purpose. By examining the original instrumentalist authors, Jerzy
Giedymin demonstrated that they did not hold such extreme views as
interpreted by contemporary philosophers, especially Popper, and instead
proposed that these earlier writers offered a more moderate interpretation of
instrumentalism (Giedymin 1976).

Instead of using the modern, narrow conception of instrumentalism as a
Procrustean bed to which Schumpeter's methodological position must be
adapted by force, it is more appropriate to interpret his point of view in light
of the broad conception of instrumentalist philosophy that was held by his
contemporaries and by which he was actually affected. Hence we should
understand the *central* claims of instrumentalism as the belief that, first, with
regard to the role of theories, they are merely tools, and second, with regard
to the cognitive status of theories, they are neither true nor false.

The subsidiary claims of instrumentalism

In addition to these two central claims, instrumentalism often makes three
salient, closely related claims. A discussion of these claims is necessary both to
clarify the epistemological implications and, more important, to give a
broader perspective of the instrumentalist view. But since these claims are also

made by noninstrumentalists, and, further, since all instrumentalists do not necessarily support them, one should carefully differentiate them from the central or distinguishing claims of instrumentalism. Let us refer to them as the *subsidiary* claims of instrumentalism.

The first subsidiary claim is that instrumentalism is a response to the "problem of induction." As is well known, whereas *inductivism* asserts that knowledge must be judged on the basis of observations (Boland 1982, 14), it is impossible to argue inductively from the truth of the particulars to a general truth. Moreover, any given set of empirical phenomena can be explained by an infinite number of mutually incompatible hypotheses, so that it is impossible to find a true theory by observational methods. Instrumentalism dismisses the problem of induction by directing sole attention to the usefulness of theories, not to their truth.

Second, instrumentalism is opposed to *essentialism*, which holds that theories describe the essences of phenomena or the realities that lie behind observable phenomena (Popper 1963, 103–7). As explained above in relation to the special usage of the term *explanation*, namely metaphysical explanation, instrumentalism denies ultimate causes and ultimate explanations. The opposition to inductivism and essentialism is shared with realism, as is demonstrated by Popper (Popper 1963, 103–5).

Third, instrumentalism is generally taken to be opposed to *realism*. The central theses of realism may be articulated in the following manner: "Theoretical statements, read literally, possess definitive truth values, and, if true, the objects they postulate are on a par ontologically with ordinary objects of perception" (Levin 1984, 124).[12] Instrumentalism claims that the theoretical (nonobservational) terms of science are not really assertions about the world but nonreferring symbolic devices for permitting the derivation of statements about observable phenomena. Thus it denies ontological status to theoretical entities and structures. But some instrumentalists, still holding the thesis that theories are neither true nor false, admit that some theoretical entities are real.[13] This is the reason why the difference between instrumentalism and realism is sometimes viewed as blurred; moreover, it is also why I regard the response to realism as a subsidiary claim of instrumentalism.

The influence of Mach and Poincaré

A passage in the preface to *Wesen* indicates the source of Schumpeter's methodological ideas:

This approach to our problems [the pragmatic approach of searching for the usefulness rather than the truthfulness of theories] might appear strange. But it coincides with the line of modern epistemology that has grown out of practical works in the exact natural sciences. We will not and cannot discuss this point here; rather, we would like to be careful lest our arguments appear to depend on the acceptance of that line of thought. Our arguments should be understood straightforwardly and unbiasedly in the same way as they were written, without being biased by any superior principle. I would only like to mention that I am not alone in my epistemological view, so that many expressions and remarks in this regard would not strike one as strange. (1908, xvi)

This statement clearly shows that Schumpeter was familiar with the contemporary philosophy of the natural sciences. Although he agreed with its views, he seemed to be rather reluctant to express his uncritical acceptance of them. In view of the antitheoretical atmosphere in German academism at the time, he was probably worried about being accused of imitating the natural sciences. Nevertheless, near the end of the book Schumpeter dared to say that "pure economics would be a 'natural science' in terms of its methodological and epistemological nature" (1908, 536). Further discussion in this section will illuminate Schumpeter's indebtedness to the contemporary philosophy of the natural sciences. However gifted he might have been, the young man just twenty-four or twenty-five years old could not have proposed a completely new methodology. The fact was that Schumpeter borrowed the methodology of natural scientists and applied it to economics; but his ways of borrowing and application were ingenious.

Mach

Ernst Mach (1838–1916), an Austrian physicist, was a professor of the "History and Theory of Inductive Science" at the University of Vienna from 1895 to 1901, after teaching at Graz and Prague. Along with Richard Avenarius he established what is known as empirico-criticism, a forerunner of logical positivism. His thought dominated much of the intellectual field of the Austro-German world at the turn of the century. My contention is that young Schumpeter was greatly influenced by Mach and adapted Mach's methodological approach to economics. Mach's philosophy of science is usually characterized by (1) the view that the aim of science is economy of thought, (2) phenomenalist epistemology, (3) instrumentalist methodology, and (4) the biological theory of knowledge.[14]

First, Mach held that scientific theories are devices for effecting the economy of thought (Mach 1882, 1883). According to him, the aim of scientific theories is to describe the world as economically as possible; in other words, it is to eliminate the need to know mere individual facts or to "save the phenomena." Mach himself noted that his view was similar to that of Kirchhoff, W. K. Clifford, and Avenarius (Mach [1883] 1960, 592). It suffices here to refer to Gustav Kirchhoff, a German physicist, whose definition of mechanics had an significant impact on the philosophy of science:

I maintain that the proper task of mechanics is to *describe* the motion which we observe in nature, and of course to make this description as complete as possible and to make it in the simplest possible way. By that I mean that we are concerned here with declaring *what* are the phenomena that occur, and not with ascertaining their *causes*. (Kirchhoff 1876, 1)[15]

Although in *Wesen* Schumpeter makes no explicit reference to Mach as the source of the economy of thought principle,[16] he does mention Kirchhoff's definition of mechanics as the clearest expression of the task of exact science (1908, 38), and writes: "A theory constructs a scheme for facts; its aim is to give a brief representation to an immense amount of facts and to achieve as simply and completely as possible what we call understanding" (1908, 42).

Second, not only did Schumpeter accept Mach's general view of the aim of scientific theories, but also, and more importantly, in the hope of eliminating metaphysical speculation from economics, he attempted to apply to economics Mach's specific epistemological approach to physics. Mach's approach, which he himself called "phenomenological physics," rejected the assumption that essence and causal relations were behind phenomena and confined the task of physics to a concise description of functional relations between "elements" known to us only through sense experience. Mach's phenomenalism has also been referred to as physicalism or sensationalism. Schumpeter explicitly states:

I would like to mention that in exact reasoning we avoid the concepts of "cause" and "effect" whenever practicable and replace them with the more satisfactory concept of function. (1908, xvi)

I want to talk not about the "cause" of phenomena, but only about functional relations between them. This brings greater precision. The concept of function is carefully elaborated by mathematics and has clear, unquestionable contents, but that is not the case with the concept of cause. (1908, 47)

Schumpeter found in Walras an ideal application of Mach's phenomenalism to economics. He favored the Walrasian version of neoclassical economics – general equilibrium theory – because, on the basis of Mach's view, he believed that economic science should be constructed on the conception of a general interdependence of such observable economic variables as the price and quantity of goods and factors of production. Walras's general equilibrium theory was a perfect object to which Mach's idea could be applied. In *Wesen* we find the following remarkable account of phenomenalism applied to the foundation of economics:

In our view, the objects of our inquiry are *certain dependent relations or functional relations*. The fact that economic quantities have such an interdependent relationship warrants a separate treatment of them if they are uniquely determined. The unique determinate-ness of the system of quantities is a scientific fact of the greatest importance. It means that when certain *data* are given, we have together all the necessary elements to *"understand"* the magnitude and movement of these quantities. In that case a separate, independent science about such phenomena is possible, and this is what we must establish above all. Even if an equation system shows nothing more than a proof of uniquely determined interdependence, that is in itself a great deal: that is the foundation of a scientific structure. (1908, 33–34)

Walras and the members of the Lausanne School, except Vilfredo Pareto,[17] had less interest in methodology than the Austrians. In this context Schumpeter's *Wesen* can be interpreted as the first epistemological work which was devoted to a clarification of general equilibrium theory on the basis of Mach's phenomenalist view of science.

Another statement of Schumpeter's summarizes Mach's influence with regard to economy of thought and phenomenalism: "The explanation rendered by our theory is therefore a description of the functional relations between elements of our system with the help of formulas that are as concise and generally valid as possible. *These formulas we now call 'laws'"* (1908, 43).

Third, Schumpeter's most characteristic methodological position in *Wesen* is also pure Mach instrumentalism. Although Mach's phenomenalist position was that scientific theories only make existential claims about those entities that are observable, he did not argue against the use of theoretical, unobservable entities as useful fictions, provided that they led to the discovery of new empirically testable relations between observables. This is an assertion of instrumentalist methodology and does not contradict phenomenalist epistemology. In fact, Mach's critique of atomic and molecular theories was based not on his phenomenalism or sensationalism, but rather on his instrumentalism, that is, on his view that they had long since outlived their heuristic usefulness.[18] Nothing shows more revealingly Mach's position on the relationship between epistemology and methodology than the following passage: "It should be emphasized that a hypothesis can have great heuristic value as a working hypothesis, and at the same time be of very dubious epistemological value" (Mach 1896b, 430).[19] Schumpeter's attitude toward psychologism (the use of psychological hypotheses in economics) is in line with Mach's attitude toward atomism and therefore different from the Austrian approach.

Fourth, on the basis of the Darwinian theory of evolution by natural selection, Mach talked about a kind of biological adaptation of thoughts or scientific hypotheses to facts. The cognitive functions of the human mind, he believed, are subject to gradual growth, and when thoughts as creations of the human mind are well adapted to facts, we have a successful theory. Hence theories evolve as a consequence of the biological survival of thoughts. Mach's biological epistemology can be seen as an account of the historical process of scientific activity, in which science, conceived in terms of phenomenalism and instrumentalism, is really a result of natural selection or the adaptation to facts. Since Schumpeter in *Wesen* is not concerned with the history of economics, the book reveals little influence of Mach's biologism. But the history of economics was a major concern of Schumpeter's, and his subsequent works on the subject, I suggest here, indicate the influence of Mach and, in particular, of Poincaré, another proponent of biologically oriented epistemology.

Poincaré

Closely related to instrumentalism is conventionalism, and Henri Poincaré (1854–1912) is best known as a conventionalist.[20] Conventionalism is the view that hypotheses in science are conventions or definitions, that depend on free creations of the human mind and are not subject to empirical testing. They might or might not be useful in understanding the real world, but in themselves they cannot be said to be true or false. While conventionalism stresses that theories are arbitrary constructs based on conventional criteria, the same view can be called instrumentalism when a focus is placed on the instrumentality of theories in attaining their goals. In this sense, conventionalism and instrumentalism are often viewed interchangeably. Both deny a truth status to theories.

An alternative to the two is pragmatism, a movement of American origin, which stresses practical success as a sufficient criterion of the truth of theories. Although pragmatism is similar to instrumentalism, which characteristically emphasizes the practical usefulness of theories for any prescribed purpose, instrumentalism, unlike pragmatism, does not claim that a useful theory is a "true" theory. And although pragmatism is also similar to conventionalism, which provides the conventional criteria of theory choice, conventionalism, unlike pragmatism, does not claim that they are the criteria of truth.[21] But the three views are similar in that they are all antirealist, denying an ontological status to theoretical entities insofar as they are unobservable in principle.

In discussing the relationship between theory choice and empirical evidence, Schumpeter articulates an important conventionalist and antirealist view with an analogy:

Pure static economics is nothing but an abstract picture of certain economic facts, i.e., *a schema that should serve as a description about them.* It depends on certain assumptions, and *in this respect* it is a *creation of our arbitrariness,* just as every exact science is. If, therefore, a historian says that our theory is a product of our fancy, he is right *in a sense.* Indeed, in the phenomenal world neither our "assumptions" nor our "laws" as such exist. But from this there follows no objection against them. For this does not prevent theories from *fitting* the facts. Where then does this come from? The reason is simply that we work arbitrarily but rationally in the construction of our schema and *design it in view of the facts*. To use the analogy of a deep thinker: when a tailor makes a jacket, it is a product of his arbitrariness in the sense that he could cut it out differently. Nevertheless, we expect that a jacket will fit us, and we are not at all surprised when it does. This is because he makes it to order ... We do not always make research "to order," but hope that our schema will also fit the facts which we have not observed. Like a tailor who keeps ready-made jackets in stock, we expect that our products will fit a sufficient number of customers. (1908, 527–28)[22]

In his *History of Economic Analysis* Schumpeter again refers to this analogy of the tailor, but this time he explicitly states that its source was Poincaré (Schumpeter 1954a, 15). In Poincaré's trilogy on the philosophy of science is found the following description:

This frame into which we wish to force everything is one of our own construction; but we have not made it at random. We have made it, so to speak, by measure and therefore we can make facts fit into it without changing what is essential in them. (Poincaré [1902] 1913, 29)

Schumpeter's connection with Poincaré was not confined to the casual quotation of the above metaphor; they shared common views on the philosophy of science, that is, conventionalism and biologism. However, their biological epistemology mainly relates to the process of scientific progress, a subject outside the scope of *Wesen*.

Schumpeter's instrumentalism

On the basis of Mach's notion of economy of thought, Schumpeter's view of scientific theories was that they were to describe facts not individually but "schematically." What he called a "schema," "scheme," "formula," or "law" is simply a "model" in our current usage. I shall now reconstruct his economic methodology by specifying a set of key propositions that concern the conceptions of, and relations between, theory, hypothesis, and fact. By this it will be shown that his methodology was clearly instrumentalist.

Schumpeter's propositions of instrumentalism

The following two passages from *Wesen* provide us with an important clue to my task:

The hypotheses we make are in themselves artificial, just as definitions are. Indeed, we are *induced* by facts to make hypotheses, but in principle we create them on our own authority. Their apparent certainty is due only to this circumstance, again as in the case of definitions. However, we must *claim* in hypotheses *as little as possible*, and even this little is presented not in the least as a *cognition*, but merely as *an auxiliary means for description*. (1908, 46)

Whatever sophistication we may use in order to make the hypotheses appear justified or to disguise their hypothetical character, all this is meaningless to pure economics; and all metaphysical arguments or whatever on behalf of our hypotheses cannot help them if their application leads to results contradicting reality. It is the sole purpose of hypotheses to produce a schema fit for economic reality; the merit of hypotheses can lie only in this purpose; it is irrelevant to this purpose to discuss where hypotheses originate and how they are embellished. (1908, 68)

In *Wesen* Schumpeter repeatedly emphasizes the importance of the ideas expressed in these two passages. The following statement summarizes them:

The crucial point, upon which everything depends, lies in the distinction between two different aspects of the matter: on the one hand, we have the fundamental arbitrariness of theories, on which their system, rigor, and exactness are based; on the other hand, we have the conformity of theories to, and their dependence on, phenomena, and this alone gives content and significance to theories. If one distinguishes between these concerns and places them in a proper relationship with each other, a clear interpretation will follow, and thus the difficulties and doubts that we come across in the usual discussions of these questions will be effectively overcome. (1908, 533)

The first passage is concerned with the arbitrariness of theories and is reminiscent of the conventionalism of Poincaré and the fictionalism of H. Vaihinger. This statement can be broken down into four distinct propositions:

S_1: Hypotheses, rather than being ontologically real, are artificial creations of the human mind.

S_2: Theories are not descriptive statements of the real world, and therefore they cannot be judged for their truth or falsity.

S_3: Theories are merely instruments for the purpose of description.

S_4: Theories should describe facts as simply and as completely as possible.

Similarly, the second passage, concerning the empirical relevance of theories, can be divided into two propositions:

S_5: It is not necessary to seek to justify hypotheses as such in order to establish their truth.

S_6: The purpose of hypotheses is to produce a theory suitable for facts, and thus they are evaluated by their practical success.

In order to interpret Schumpeter's methodology and assess its implications, it will be useful to create a structure of thought by using propositions S_1–S_6 as building blocks. (S_7 will be added later.) The kind of model of economic

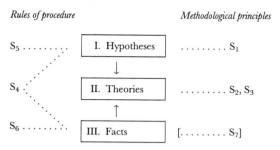

Figure 5   *The structure of Schumpeter's instrumentalism*

methodology that Schumpeter appears to have had in mind is represented in Figure 5.

"Hypotheses" at level I on the Figure may also be called axioms, postulates, or assumptions. "Theories" at level II, that is, the conclusions derived by a certain procedure from "hypotheses," may be called laws, principles, or theorems. "Facts" at level III are observations, data, or phenomena.

S_1 expresses the conventionalist view regarding the nature of hypotheses and is found at level I. S_2 specifies the cognitive status of theories and denies them any truth status; S_3 specifies the instrumental role of theories. S_2 and S_3 are properly located at level II and have been previously identified as propositions concerning the central claims of instrumentalism. Description, conceived as the comprehensive role of theories by Schumpeter in S_3, is explicated as follows:

We have identified as the task of our science *the description of interdependent relationships of elements within our system for the purpose of successively reducing different situations to one another.* We have said that we understand just such a description under *the concept of the scientific explanation of phenomena* with which we are concerned. Accordingly, *the expressions "explanation" and "description" are generally synonymous for us,* or in other words, *we do not want and cannot contribute anything other than description to the explanation and understanding of economic facts.* (1908, 37)

The instrumentality of theories for explanation, description, understanding, and the like was fundamentally important to Schumpeter. It should be noted that although he did not regard theories as strictly the instrument of prediction, he did not reject their predictive role in the sense of stating the essential tendencies of history.

As S_2 and S_3 form the core of instrumentalist methodology, it is useful to quote Schumpeter's own remarks to this effect:

The absolute truth of our hypotheses does not matter. Hypotheses are not a part of the results we have to defend, but are simply auxiliary methodological means whose value can only be judged by their fruitfulness. The role of hypotheses is merely *formal*; even if it were proved that they were in themselves true, nothing would be gained from it in support of our laws. (1908, 64)

For a proper understanding of our theory and, eventually, every theory, it is extremely important to be aware of this arbitrary character of a theory and not to seek from it an expression of some "absolute" truth. It is a method for description and nothing more, and as such it must be judged and organized for good or evil ... *A theory consists only of a measure* that simplifies description and prevents it from becoming hopelessly complicated ... If one realizes that only the goal justifies a theory, namely that only the result warrants it, then many objections and claims blocking our path will be removed. (1908, 528–29)

Whereas S_1–S_3 are methodological principles, S_4–S_6 are concerned with the rules of procedure for the formulation and evaluation of hypotheses and theories. It is logical to explain S_5 and S_6 before S_4. S_5 simply denies that a direct and independent justification of hypotheses should be made at level I alone. S_6 prescribes that theories, as the conclusions reached from hypotheses, should fit observations at level III. In accordance with the methodological proposition concerning the role of theories (S_3), the fitness of theories to facts means that theories should describe the important aspects of facts. In *Wesen* Schumpeter does not discuss at length the problem of empirical fitting or testing. But it is clear that by fitness to facts he does not mean that a theory should make an unconditional forecast for an actual course of events. Although in *Wesen* he is concerned with static, abstract theory, which obviously cannot explain all economic phenomena, he still emphasizes that it can fit the important, basic, and universal aspects of an economy. Since in static theory all unessential factors that are unrelated to the formation of equilibrium in a market are grouped as exogenous data, a static explanation will succeed if the results of static theory agree with those facts that are similarly elaborated in accordance with the abstraction on the theoretical side. This is not a problem of unconditional prediction.

S_4 is synonymous with Mach's principle of economy of thought and gives the criterion for the efficiency of hypotheses: deriving a theory that will subsume a large number of observations by a small number of simple hypotheses. It is thus concerned with the relationship between level I and level III and in fact integrates Schumpeter's two key passages and, more specifically, it integrates two procedural rules, S_5 and S_6. In other words, S_4 chooses among the theories that, starting from different arbitrary hypotheses, equally satisfy the requirement S_6. Schumpeter clearly states the relationship between the two requirements S_6 and S_4, namely, between the fitness (capacity for explanation or description) and the usefulness (efficiency) of theories:

Let us remind ourselves what we mean by "explanation." It is nothing but a specification of the uniquely determined magnitude of the unknowns and of the laws of their motion. Every theoretical construction that achieves it is "right" for us, and one that achieves it most simply and best we call the "most useful." (1908, 340–41)

In regard to testing, it is interesting to note in Figure 5 that Schumpeter does not comment on the epistemological nature of "facts," which could be placed at level III and named S_7. Do facts exist independently of theories? Or are they based on the acceptance of any theory? Schumpeter does not make his views on this question explicit, nor does he seem to be aware of it at all. Yet he does not assert in *Wesen* the so-called theory-ladenness thesis. This suggests that he was not an extreme conventionalist, one who contends that not only theories but also facts are conventions created by scientists. (It was on this point that Poincaré criticized E. LeRoy.) Schumpeter seems to have had what would today be called a naive positivist view that objective facts exist independently of theories. We can argue that he implicitly believed that there is a distinction between theory and observation. That is how he made economics safe from the ravages of metaphysics. In fact, whether the observations are theory-dependent or not has little to do with the instrumentalist or realist standpoint.[23]

As will be suggested from his discussion of alternative theories of value, Schumpeter also held the view that conceptually different theories might be observationally equivalent. In that case it would be impossible to provide an inductive proof of a theory. This position was originally one of the basic sources of instrumentalism. We may, therefore, add the following to Schumpeter's set of propositions:

S_7:   Observational facts exist independently of theories, but for any set of observed facts there might be several different theories.

In light of a set of these propositions, I hope to have shown that Schumpeter's methodological standpoint can best be construed as instrumentalist. One may interpret his proposition S_1 as conventionalist and S_3 and S_6 as pragmatist, but as a whole his system appears to be instrumentalist because S_2 and S_3 point clearly in that direction.

A comparison with Friedman

In light of this framework it is appropriate to mention Friedman's 1953 essay, which, after Stanley Wong's and Lawrence Boland's interpretation that it offers an instrumentalist perspective, has provoked much discussion in economic methodology.[24] Surprisingly enough, there is no commentary in Friedman's essay about the two *central* claims of instrumentalism, which I have identified through the examination of philosophers' views. This seems so because his essay lacks a philosophical analysis. Instead, the article properly regards the following four points as the building blocks of his system:

(1) The realism of assumption does not matter.
(2) The validity of theories is to be judged by their predictive ability.
(3) Observations cannot prove theories, only falsify them.
(4) The choice of theory depends on supplementary criteria such as the generality or fruitfulness of theories.

Can one interpret this system as instrumentalist, without introducing other elements, by hazarding a guess? We can say that (1) is synonymous with antirealism, and (3) is synonymous with anti-inductivism, and that both are responses to the subsidiary claims of instrumentalism. But (1) still allows different positions other than instrumentalism; (3) is the falsification thesis of Popper, an anti-instrumentalist; and (4) is not directly relevant to instrumentalism. Apparently only (2) is likely to be taken as the crucial element of instrumentalism, if one follows its current narrow version. But (2) does not necessarily mean that theories are merely instruments. More important, Friedman does not say that theories are neither true nor false. When he states that "to be important, therefore, a hypothesis must be descriptively false in its assumptions" (Friedman 1953, 14), he seems to be admitting that the assumptions of a theory are judged to be true or false. Friedman's essay thus does not include the necessary definitional elements of instrumentalism as formulated by its central claims, namely the propositions of the instrumentality and the noncognitive status of theories.

The current interpretation of Friedman as an instrumentalist is based on a dubious inference from (1) and (2). The typical inference is this: "Friedman's most controversial statements, that the purpose of science is prediction and that the realism of assumptions does not matter, are instrumentalist" (Caldwell 1982, 178).[25] Theses (1) and (2), which provide the basis of the current interpretation of Friedman as an instrumentalist, correspond to Schumpeter's theses S_5 and S_6, respectively; but (1) and (2) are not the same as S_2 and S_3. What should correspond to S_2 and S_3 are missing in Friedman. If Friedman were an instrumentalist, he might hold views (1) and (2). But the converse is not true.

Friedman's point (4), if elaborated upon and integrated in some way, will correspond to Schumpeter's efficiency criterion S_4. In our framework (1), (2), and (4) – or, alternatively, S_5, S_6, and S_4 – are regarded as "rules of procedure," practical prescriptions for scientific activity. Friedman's element (3) accords with Schumpeter's S_7 and belongs to the category of "methodological principles." As regards S_1, another missing element in Friedman, Friedman might be interpreted as implicitly holding such a conventionalist view, but this is not certain.

At any rate, because of the crucial lack of the instrumentalist "methodological principles" S_2 and S_3, Friedman's essay is an insufficient basis on which to interpret him as an instrumentalist. As stated above, methodology is a philosophical study of the procedural rules governing scientific activity; it argues the reasons or logic justifying such rules. Friedman's essay provides only the "procedural rules" in positive economics, not the instrumentalist "methodological principles."

Instrumentalism in the context of economics

I have discussed Schumpeter's instrumentalist position in terms of general propositions, but his methodology was actually developed in the practical context of economic research. Thus, to do justice to his methodology, it is useful to examine the circumstances that led him to the instrumentalist point of view in the context of neoclassical theory. He resorted to this position in order to overcome the practical difficulties that surrounded the economics of the time. He believed that methodological clarification was required to elucidate what economists should not be concerned with and how economics should be constructed and appraised. Instrumentalism gave him an appropriate tool for this task.

For Schumpeter, the difficulties were the result of at least three kinds of useless controversies in economics, apart from the intrusion of political beliefs into economic discussions: (1) the conflict between theoretical and historical methods (Menger versus Schmoller), (2) the controversy over value theory (classical versus neoclassical versus Marxian theories), and (3) the conflict between causal and functional approaches in neoclassical economics (Menger versus Walras). Schumpeter relied on instrumentalism to cope with these issues. They were, he argued, not a challenge but an obstacle to the development of economics; it was necessary to devise methodological rules that would enable economists to dismiss them. Schumpeter's argument also fulfilled the subsidiary claims for an instrumentalist approach, because his case for instrumentalism included criticism of three views of knowledge in economics: essentialism, inductivism, and realism.

The separation of historicism

The first controversial issue confronting Schumpeter was the *Methodenstreit* between theory and history. Although the doctrine of instrumentalism generally relates to the role and status of theoretical methods, not those of historical methods, Schumpeter undoubtedly developed his argument for instrumentalism at least partly for the purpose of making a distinction and a separation between theoretical and historical methods.

One of the claims of early instrumentalists in natural science was to oppose essentialism, according to which science can establish the truth of theories and true scientific theories describe the essence of things, namely the reality behind the phenomena (Popper 1963, 104–5). In other words, the essence of things means the ultimate cause of things. As we shall see, one of the reasons why Schumpeter claimed to pursue not causal relations but functional relations as the task of economic theory was to deny the essentialist ultimate explanation by means of instrumentalist methodology. But Schumpeter had more tasks to do with instrumentalism.

Suppose, according to essentialism, that we can distinguish between three universes: essence, fact, and theory. Because Schumpeter denied the universe of essential reality (*essence*) by rejecting essentialism, there remain for him the universe of observable phenomena (*fact*) and that of descriptive language or symbolic representation (*theory*). He accepted the instrumentalist position not only to deny the universe of essential reality, just as the instrumentalist natural scientists did, but also to specify various possible relationships between the universe of observable phenomena and that of symbolic representation. Scientific hypotheses enable certain conceptual manipulations and calculations to take place within the universe of symbolic representation, but they do not have corresponding observable phenomena within their own universe: "In the universe of phenomena as such, neither our 'hypotheses' nor our 'laws' exist by themselves" (1908, 527) because they are arbitrarily constructed. The function of theoretical hypotheses is not to record events in the universe of observable phenomena, but rather to make it possible to infer from some symbols to other symbols in the universe of symbolic language. In order to consider the relationship between the universe of fact and that of theory in the social sciences, it is necessary, unlike in natural science, to take into account two approaches to fact: the theoretical method and the historical method.[26]

While the *Methodenstreit* was concerned with the dispute between these two methods, Schumpeter denies in *Wesen* that in principle any contradiction exists between theory and history, because "even 'descriptive' economists or historians do not undertake an impossible attempt to describe *all* facts that fall strictly into their themes, everything that are found in their material" (1908, 41); they must select and transform the facts. He explains the difference between theory and history in terms of the different concerns of theorists and historians with regard to which problems they are going to solve and how they are going to select facts. He contends that the number of facts needed by observers varies with their objectives and that

there is the highest yield of knowledge for every purpose and for every observer under a given amount of phenomena, just as an appreciation of artistic objects requires the best distance from observers according to their purposes. (1908, 41)

Schumpeter then compares the theoretical method with the historical method:

While [historical] description does no more than make a catalogue of facts, a theory undertakes the transformation of facts, not for any far-reaching or mysterious purpose but for a better summary of facts. *A theory constructs a scheme for facts; its aim is to give a brief representation to an immense amount of facts and to achieve as simply and completely as possible what we call understanding.* (1908, 42)

As shown above in proposition S_4, this is how Schumpeter defines a theory with Mach's economy-of-thought thesis in mind. I emphasize that he discusses the thesis not only generally but also to determine a practical solution of the *Methodenstreit* and that he generalizes the thesis in order to cover history as well as theory, so that economy of thought should be interpreted as a relative concept based on the purposes of the inquiry. In his *History of Economic Analysis* Schumpeter, now explicitly referring to Mach's principle of economy of thought, compares theories or general "simplifying schemata or models" with history or *ad hoc* "explanatory hypotheses" about facts (1954a, 14–15). He holds that the difference between theory and history does not mean a conflict between incommensurable procedural rules but rather different degrees of abstraction in different hypotheses framed for different purposes.

Specifically, Schumpeter distinguished between the two types of hypotheses as follows (1908, 531–32). (1) Historical hypotheses can describe phenomena in the universe of observables; theoretical hypotheses, on the other hand, are formal assumptions and need not have corresponding phenomena in that universe. (2) Historical hypotheses are attempts to reconstruct facts that are beyond observation and need verification by empirical testing; theoretical hypotheses are artificial constructs and need not be true in themselves. (3) Historical hypotheses represent a cognition; theoretical hypotheses are mere methodological tools and do not mean anything real in themselves. (4) Historical hypotheses must be grounded in facts; theoretical hypotheses can be unrealistic. (5) Historical hypotheses can be matters on which opinions differ; for theoretical hypotheses realism does not matter, only expediency does.

In sum, Schumpeter applied his instrumentalism to the differentiation between theoretical and historical hypotheses. If we follow the common practice in labeling as "historicism" an approach which emphasizes the historical method in economics,[27] we can argue that his instrumentalism excludes historicism from static economics. Considering that the instrumentalist position was mainly taken by natural scientists, Schumpeter's unique contribution was to introduce instrumentalism to economics and to pay attention to the differences between theoretical and historical hypotheses. To avoid misunderstanding, it should be noted that he never rejected historicism but only separated it from the domain of static economic theory. The separation of theory and history on the basis of instrumentalism was his own methodological solution to the *Methodenstreit*. Moreover, his economic sociology is not a historical hypothesis but a theoretical hypothesis, although the distance between observers and facts is shorter than in economic theory, as shown in chapter 8.

The choice of value theory

The second controversy in economics concerned the general principle of value in economics. Schumpeter asked which principle was superior as a means of describing exchange relations, the main theme of static economics: the cost theory of value in the classical school, Marx's labor theory of value, or the subjective theory of value in the neoclassical school (1908, 55–68). Contrasting the truthfulness with the usefulness of theories as a criterion of theory choice, he adopted the last approach. Schumpeter refused to discuss the truth and falsity of theories and was concerned with the competition of theories in producing "results." He concluded:

We shall use the [subjective] value theory, not because we regard it as the only correct view, but because it is the most practical in obtaining our results and because we can go the furthest with it. But we shall not contend that all other views are "false" and cannot bring useful results, as is often said. (1908, 57)

In his early work on the history of economics Schumpeter summarized the reasons why the subjective value theory should be accepted: "This shifting of emphasis to the doctrine of 'subjective values' in economics produced four advantages. It is more correct ... It is simpler ... It is more general ... Finally, the theory of marginal utility makes economic conclusions more relevant" ([1914a] 1954c, 189–90).

In *Wesen* Schumpeter repeatedly speaks of the "results" of hypotheses and theories; hypotheses and theories are to be assessed by their usefulness in producing results. What, then, are results? He asserts that fitness to reality is a necessary condition for a theory to be useful. The fitness of theories to reality refers to the ability of theories to describe, predict, and explain phenomena. In this regard, proposition S_6 gives a rule of procedure advocated by instrumentalist methodology. The condition that theories fit or be consistent with observable facts, however, cannot be the exclusive criterion for ascertaining the usefulness of theories; it is also important to see how consistent they are with facts, because, as proposition S_7 asserts, facts allow an infinite number of mutually incompatible theories. Other criteria must be invoked, therefore, to choose among theories that are more or less consistent with facts. One may bring in additional criteria such as simplicity, generality, and the like. But Schumpeter is consistent in defining the usefulness of hypotheses and theories by applying Mach's principle of economy of thought (S_4) to the appraisal of theories that are all equally regarded as fitting the facts.

From Mach's thesis it follows naturally, in Schumpeter, that theories should be judged by their efficiency in attaining economy of thought. Efficiency is a relational concept between means and ends. Given the ends, it is more efficient for a theory to have simpler assumptions; given the means, it is more efficient for a theory to have more general or wider applicability. By applicability of theories, Schumpeter meant not only their fitness to a wide range of facts, but also the inclusiveness of a coherent theoretical system. For him the subjective theory of value explained a wider range of phenomena, including consumption, production, distribution, and money, with the minimum principle of utility. Thus the criterion of economy of thought could comprise a variety of attributes of hypotheses and theories. Schumpeter, unlike Friedman, did not need to supplement the criterion of the predictive ability of theories with additional criteria (such as simplicity and fruitfulness); proposition S_4 is a single criterion for the choice among hypotheses and theories that are equally consistent with observable facts.

In relation to fitness to facts Schumpeter took into account verification and falsification, which play crucial roles in determining the truth of theories in the doctrines of logical positivism and falsificationism. He did not believe, however, that truth or falsity could be settled in this way and was more concerned with the expediency of theories. Schumpeter provided an interesting discussion of verification and falsification in relation to the different theories of value indicated above (1908, 59–60). He argued that if one adopted the cost theory, the reproduction theory of wages (the doctrine that regards wages as the reproduction cost of labor) would be derived as its necessary corollary, and that the cost theory as a hypothesis would only require that its derived theory of wages not be falsified by experience. On the other hand, if one adopted the subjective theory, one would not deduce the reproduction theory of wages from it. Thus, in order to incorporate this kind of wage theory into the subjective theory of value, it should be recognized positively as an undeniable fact. In that case, the reproduction theory of wages would serve as an *ad hoc* hypothesis auxiliary to the subjective theory of value.

In this argument it is assumed that in both the cost theory and the subjective theory, the idea of reproduction wages is supported by, or at least not falsified by, facts. Two different theories are thus available to explain or predict the same fact about wages, so that it is not possible for the fact to give an inductive proof for any true theory. In order to avoid this difficulty, instrumentalism is concerned with only the usefulness of theories, without reference to their truth or falsity. As a matter of fact, however, Schumpeter denied the idea of reproduction wages on the grounds that it was not verified. And he regarded the labor force as exogenously given in the subjective theory of value, for it could not explain the supply of labor.

If verification were actually unable to perform the justification of hypotheses, then even falsification would not necessarily proclaim the sudden death of hypotheses. Schumpeter argued that even if the consequences of a hypothesis were denied by experience, that would not compel one to discard the hypothesis entirely:

> In general we do not abandon a system only because it fails on one point ... If, for several reasons, we are induced to stay in the system in question, we will do so with the aid of auxiliary hypotheses. (1908, 60)

Whereas Popper asserts that a theory is simply discarded by an act of falsification, Lakatos indicates that if the concept of a "protective belt" is introduced, there exists the possibility that a theory can survive tenaciously even when it is falsified (Lakatos [1970] 1978, 48). What Schumpeter called an auxiliary hypothesis was Lakatos's "protective belt"; it is because of its productivity and usefulness in all other respects that a theory is supported and reinforced by this means.

The criticism of psychologism

Among the champions of the Marginal Revolution Carl Menger was unique in maintaining that scientists should aim at the essence of economic phenomena in order to "explain" them, and that theories are not creations of the human mind but descriptions of eternal structures in the economic world. Emil Kauder calls this view philosophical realism (Kauder 1957, 414); Terence Hutchison, following Popper, considers it to be methodological essentialism (Hutchison 1981, 178). The dual characteristics of Menger's thought, realism and essentialism, essentially apply to the psychologism of the Austrian School.

Austrian psychologism held that economics should be rooted in psychological facts as the ultimate explanatory basis. The Austrian School found the essence of economic behavior to be the satisfaction of wants; the fundamental principles in psychologism were the maximization principle and the law of diminishing marginal utility. Insofar as psychologism asserted an ultimate explanation of economic value based on the essences of phenomena, that is, on such psychological factors as need, want, satisfaction, and the like, its epistemological position was essentialism. At the same time, psychologism also claimed that these theoretical entities, structures, and processes really did exist. In this respect, it was identified with realism.

Schumpeter opposed any attempt to provide a justified basis for hypotheses on instrumentalist grounds. Specifically, he was against Austrian psychologism:

An attempt to ground [subjective] value hypotheses leads us to fields that are unrelated to economists, namely psychology and physiology. [According to psychologism] one starts from wants and defines economic goods as objects in the outer world, which are causally connected to want satisfaction. From the relative intensity of the want impulse of economic agents making an exchange, one derives exchange relations, and for this purpose the laws of valuation are established on the ground of psychological observation. One says, for example, that as saturation increases the demand for further food will decline, and, as a result, a saturated individual is only willing to pay a decreasing price for every additional quantity ... Why is such an explanation given? The fact we see is only that the individual offers a decreasing price. *Why* he does so is not interesting from the standpoint of economics. Moreover, we see only from the behavior of the individual that he is actually saturated. (1908, 64)

It is clear that when Schumpeter said this he had Menger in mind. Menger wrote in *Grundsätze der Volkswirtschaftslehre*: "the requirement for the acquisition of goods-character is the existence of some causal connection ... between things and the satisfaction of needs" (Menger [1871] 1923, 57). Although he revised the expression "causal connection" to "teleological connection" in the second edition of *Grundsätze* (Menger [1871] 1923, 23), it does not change the nature of his basic approach, because teleology is based on causality. The main reason for Schumpeter's opposition to psychologism was twofold: he objected to both its causal approach and its realist approach to value theory.

Within the framework of general equilibrium analysis, it is meaningless to offer a causal explanation of economic phenomena based on psychological factors. Both the cost theory and the labor theory of value had cut the chains of general economic interdependence at arbitrary points and tried to establish a causal explanation of value by a single factor, namely the costs of production or the amount of labor. In the early stage of the Marginal Revolution, marginal utility theorists, represented by Menger, had tried to provide a similar causal explanation based on their concept of marginal utility. Such an attempt, Schumpeter argued, should be replaced by general equilibrium theory, in which psychological factors are no longer the ultimate cause of value phenomena but are revealed as an interdependent solution as the economic system as a whole works itself out. Marginal utility, which is assumed to be the function of the quantity of goods in question, does not causally determine prices but is only related to prices in some specific way in an equilibrium.

Most of the differences between Menger and Walras, between the Austrian School and the Lausanne School, and between the causal approach and the functional approach to the theory of value is well known.[28] This is the third dispute Schumpeter identified, and he was directly involved in it. Although

Schumpeter favored Walras's position in this internal conflict of neoclassical economics, he did not simply take sides – that would not have contributed to a solution of the antithesis. He first contrasted Austrian essentialism and Lausanne phenomenalism and then resorted to instrumentalism in order to provide a kind of compromise between them. If the instrumentality of theories and hypotheses is accepted, then a disagreement over the ontological nature of theoretical entities can be replaced by a rivalry over the practical success of theories.

Although Schumpeter accepted that the psychological hypotheses concerning the utility function were central to the subjective theory of value, he maintained that economists should not adduce human psychology, desires, interests, and motives in order to justify psychological hypotheses. How was it possible, then, for economists to refrain from justifying psychological hypotheses when hypotheses such as diminishing marginal utility and the maximization of satisfaction still constituted the basis of economics?

If psychological hypotheses in economics are no more than instruments for practical purposes, Schumpeter asserts in *Wesen*, then it is unnecessary to ask psychologists to justify these hypotheses. The dependence of economics on psychology for judging the truth or falsity of hypotheses would deprive economics of scientific autonomy. Assumptions in economics can prove adequate only insofar as they are useful to given tasks, irrespective of whether they are true or not. The major consequence of psychological hypotheses in economics is that they make it possible to describe and understand an exchange equilibrium in markets in terms of the maximization of human satisfaction. Schumpeter's instrumentalist, nonrealist characterization of psychological hypotheses is most clearly pronounced in the following remark: "The economic facts, not the psychological facts, induce us to make those [psychological] assumptions" (1908, 542).

Schumpeter's criticism of psychologism was naturally unpopular among the Austrian theorists. In a long review article Friedrich von Wieser attacked *Wesen*, focusing on the role of psychologism (Wieser [1911] 1929).[29] Wieser objected to Schumpeter's rejection of the psychological approach on two grounds. First, whereas Schumpeter had imitated the methods of the natural sciences and confined himself to external observation, it was nevertheless possible to observe human beings from within and to learn much more than from outside, because economics is concerned with conscious human beings. Therefore, Wieser asserted, there was no reason to abandon the psychological approach in economics. Second, whereas Schumpeter emphasized the arbitrariness of hypotheses, psychological or nonpsychological, Wieser contended that all hypotheses should be real and be based directly on empirical facts; the psychological method, placing emphasis on inner observation, could derive empirically confirmed psychological statements.

Wieser's first point did not constitute a basic area of dispute, because Schumpeter admitted that one could start from any hypothesis. The second point represented a more substantive confrontation between their views, as they were divided on the cognitive status of psychological hypotheses. The following passage from Wieser indicates the difference between the two economists on this point:

In contrast to Schumpeter, the assumptions used by the psychological school are all empirical. No matter how many assumptions there may be, they must all be founded on facts ... If theories are to retain their empirical character, all assumptions must be taken from experience. Not only must assumptions not be hypothetical, but also they must not be arbitrary and formal. Their usefulness or expediency depends on their truth ... The facts taken from experience are observed in isolation or transformed ideally as far as necessary; they provide the psychological method with the substance of its assumptions. The psychological method builds these assumptions by steps so as to construct a system that is wide enough to absorb a great variety of common economic experience. It has been made clear, I believe, that Schumpeter erred when he tried to use hypotheses in our theory. Hypotheses are assumptions about unknowns; on the contrary, our idealizing assumptions are conscious transformations of knowns. Now with greater emphasis I can repeat the contention given above, that this whole system of assumptions must be based on facts and that in this system there is no room for hypotheses. The psychological method does not permit hypotheses. (Wieser 1911, 406–9)

Schumpeter, on the contrary, thought that the Austrians were mistaken in believing that their psychological hypotheses originated in empirical statements. We find his position best expressed in his ingenious remark that "the utility theory of value has much better claim to being called a logic than a psychology of values" (1954a, 1058). This idea corresponds to what Schumpeter had in mind in *Wesen* when he called static theory a "logic of economic matters" (1908, 134). This means that neoclassical theory is a logical system deduced from arbitrary assumptions, while it can still hope to fit economic facts.

Robbins, Hutchison, and Machlup

For a better understanding of Schumpeter's instrumentalist position in light of the current field of economic methodology, it is illuminating to refer to the subsequent controversy over verification among Robbins, Hutchison, and Machlup. In the 1930s two books of economic methodology belonging to different positions were published. One was the work of Robbins based on Austrian apriorism, and the other was that of Hutchison based on Popper's falsificationism.[30]

Robbins (1932) asserts that the fundamental assumptions in economics are simple and doubtless empirical facts and include the scarcity of goods, individual economic valuations, and so forth. Economics is constructed deductively from these and other subsidiary empirical assumptions. Empirical studies in economics are concerned only with discovering subsidiary empirical assumptions and with ascertaining the scope of application of theories; there is no need to test economic propositions empirically. Empiricity alleged as the characteristic of the fundamental assumptions indicates ordinary, empirical self-evidence; rather, it is "a priori" or "a priori synthetic" in the Kantian sense. Austrian apriorism, in its extreme form, is the basis of Mises's praxeology as the science of human action. Although psychologism or subjectivism in the Austrian School, including that of Wieser, emphasizes the empirical nature of introspection, introspection is regarded as nothing more than intuitive, a priori self-evidence. Praxeology is in fact a priori science. Hutchison is correct in describing Mises, a pupil of Wieser, as having taken over and expanded Wieser's methodological claim concerning the reliability of introspection (Hutchison 1981, 208).

The basic assumptions in psychologism consist of the maximization principle and diminishing marginal utility, and these are conceived not as mere assumptions but, by means of the intuitive method of introspection, as the self-evident truth. Thus the fundamental postulate in praxeology is that all human actions are objective-oriented and rational by definition.

In contrast, Hutchison, a Popperian, contends that whereas the fundamental assumptions in economics are analytic and do not have empirical contents, all propositions other than analytic ones must be testable by empirical observation or be reducible to testable propositions (Hutchison 1938). He is regarded as the first person to introduce logical positivism to economics. With regard to psychological method, he thinks that it can suggest or discover hypotheses but cannot justify them.

In short, there is a difference in the basis of justification between Austrian apriorism and Hutchison's positivism (or falsificationism). Whereas the former depends on the intuitive self-evidence of assumptions, the latter relies on the empirical confirmation of deduced results. Although Austrian apriorism does not accept the positivist distinction between the analytic and the synthetic and stands on a different epistemological foundation, the two positions agree on cognitivism, that is, that it is possible to judge the truth or falsity of assumptions.

Machlup, a member of the positivist camp, argues that assumptions in economics are neither true nor false but merely rules of procedure (Machlup 1955). This is an instrumentalist assertion. He criticizes Hutchison's extreme positivism and maintains that all propositions do not need to be tested individually but only the results of theories as a whole have to be tested empirically. For all elements in the hypothetical deductive system cannot have their empirical counterparts. On the other hand, he was not an apriorist.

Machlup stands between ultra-empiricism and ultra-apriorism. Although there is a wide range for the middle position, he refers to Friedman's view that emphasizes the usefulness of a theory as the criterion of theory acceptance. Schumpeter's view anticipated Machlup's position, and the confrontation between Schumpeter and Wieser on psychologism was replaced by the confrontation between Machlup and the Austrian School (or Robbins). Thus Schumpeter's position on the philosophy of science was different from Austrian apriorism and from logical positivism (and falsificationism).

Prediction or understanding?

In concluding this interpretation of Schumpeter's methodology, I must try to eliminate any doubt that he was an instrumentalist. Machlup's essay on Schumpeter, one of few works dealing with Schumpeter's methodology, might suggest such a doubt (Machlup 1951). His examination is not confined to *Wesen*, but here I shall discuss only his treatment of Schumpeter in relation to instrumentalism. Although Machlup does not use the term *instrumentalism*, he admits in a footnote that "it is noteworthy how closely these formulations – published in 1908 – correspond to the most recent statements with respect to the methodology of physics" (Machlup 1951, 98). Nevertheless, part of his argument in that essay might give the impression that Schumpeter was not an instrumentalist, because he argues that Schumpeter would reject "the old dictum that correct prediction is the best or only test of whether a science has achieved its purposes" (Machlup 1951, 101). Schumpeter was against the hasty application of economic theory to policies; this stance is quite explicit in *Wesen*. As policy discussions must presuppose predictions of the effects of policy, it is reasonable to expect that he would oppose prediction in the real world as the test of economic theory. Machlup quotes from Schumpeter's *Business Cycles*:

It is as unreasonable to expect the economist to forecast correctly what will actually happen as it would be to expect a doctor to prognosticate when his patient will be the victim of a railroad accident and how this will affect his state of health. (Schumpeter 1939, 1, 13)

Does this view contradict Schumpeter's instrumentalist position as I have described it? I believe it does not; rather, it attests to Schumpeter's moderate form of instrumentalism, which I have tried to differentiate from its modern, narrow version.

The meaning of verification

Despite his explicit statement about achieving fitness to facts as the goal of hypotheses and theories, *Wesen* offers no thorough consideration of the relationship between theory and fact and of the empirical testing of theory. When we leave *Wesen* and come to dynamic theory and the analysis of historical development in Schumpeter's subsequent works, we find him dealing with facts explicitly in terms of statistical and historical concepts. It was not until this stage that he became strongly conscious of the problem of testing a theory. But this neither meant, nor was there a reason, that he had to change his instrumentalist view. Instead, he actually practiced instrumentalist methodology during this period of his empirical economic research. In 1935, when he was working on *Business Cycles*, he wrote on the meaning of verification in his preface to the fourth German edition of *Theorie der wirtschaftlichen Entwicklung*.[31] The following passage clearly shows that he had maintained the basic position of instrumentalism:

What is important to the practice of scientific work is not some "truth" but methods with which one can operate and – to put it simply – deal with data so that something may emerge corresponding to observed facts. From this viewpoint the words "true" or "false" will be used; and if one is conscious of his pragmatism, which must offend the philosophically minded, he may use those words. (1935a, xv)

What he calls pragmatism is the same as our instrumentalism; he says here that one may use the words truth or falsity if they mean instrumental usefulness.

Then, he discusses the practical goal of testing the fitness of theories to facts:

We must first agree on what we mean by "verification." Any situation that is not analyzed and *elaborated* cannot actually prove the truth or falsity of a theoretical statement. It would not even be true that observations of *statistical or historical* facts could show us whether or not a specific theory is consistent with them. For a very real relationship may be so concealed by other factors that we can understand nothing about it *without an analysis that digs deeply* into the situation itself. Therefore only a more modest goal can be attained – namely, to ascertain how the relationships asserted by a theory are *perceptible*, or to put it differently, how much a theory contributes to an understanding of the situation. (1935a, xiv)

Owing to the inevitable assumptions of *ceteris paribus* in the social sciences and to the disturbing factors included in the observation of social phenomena, Schumpeter says, a prediction or forecast that foretells an actual course of events is impossible to obtain. In the same place, he argues that the instrumentalist criterion of fitness to facts claims the following: (1) when a theory provides a description that allows quantitative expressions in principle, and when the data required for a test of that description are given, the theory should entail quantitative results that agree with the data; (2) when a theory merely gives a description that does not permit any quantitative expression in principle or because of the limited availability of data, the theory should make us realize that the fact in question is something to be expected by and large on the basis of the theory; (3) when neither is the case, a theory should indicate the concrete circumstances as well as the direction and extent of disturbing factors, so that one can understand the situation by making appropriate modifications (1935a, xv).

In short, the fitness of theories to facts does not mean an easy, successful prediction in the sense that theories should derive deductively what is equivalent to systematized facts that will emerge independently. The instrumental roles of a theory are not confined to prediction in this sense but include organization, classification, reconstruction, and – through all these efforts – the understanding of otherwise chaotic facts. For Schumpeter, the latter roles were much more important than prediction in order that theories might discover and deal with those facts that were not already embodied in existing theories. It was from this standpoint of moderate instrumentalism that Schumpeter opposed the mechanical notion of prediction and the conception of prediction as the ultimate test of a theory. Although in empirical research he became aware of difficult problems concerning the verification of a theory, he always understood the roles of a theory broadly, while upholding the central claims of instrumentalism. His criticism of the view that theories are predictive tools should be interpreted as a rejection of the narrow version of instrumentalism.

Toward a broader perspective

The direct purpose of Schumpeter's instrumentalism in *Wesen* was to rescue economics from a state of confusion and to enable economists to engage in resolving substantive problems in the real world without worrying about problematical issues in economics. Subsequently, he tried to construct a dynamic theory and economic sociology on this basis to achieve a vision of a "universal social science." Insofar as Schumpeter conceived of a consistent scientific theory, instrumentalism as a philosophy of science should be also valid in dynamic theory and economic sociology. This problem will be discussed in chapters 7 and 8, but some points are best made here. In the field beyond statics a closer approximation to reality is attempted, and as a result the problem of verification comes to the fore. In this way theory must get in touch with history and statistics. According to the view presented in chapter 3, theory is related to history through the intermediary of statistics in the field of dynamics, and theory and history are combined through the analysis of institutions in the field of economic sociology. Thus in the fields of dynamics and economic sociology beyond statics the integration of theory and history are conceived as research agenda, whereas in the field of statics theory and history are separate and distinct from one another. Instrumentalism must meet this new task; it is expected to support the effort to formulate historical phenomena by theoretical hypotheses. Although the objects of theories may be large or small, every theory, in Schumpeter's view, is to be interpreted by instrumentalism.

It is the basic contention of Schumpeter's instrumentalism that although assumptions can be made arbitrarily, the consequences of assumptions must fit the facts. Thus the construction of theories ultimately depends on how theorists view fitness to facts. However, there are no fixed rules and simple criteria of that fitness when we must be concerned with various kinds of understanding rather than the mere statistical prediction of facts. According to Schumpeter's later view of science and ideology in the study of the sociology of knowledge, theory construction is preceded by visions that theorists believe are relevant and significant with respect to facts. His sociology of knowledge shed light on the role of visions in bridging the gap between hypotheses and facts.

How did Schumpeter see his first book in later years? Erich Schneider recollects that he suggested to Schumpeter that there be a second printing of *Wesen*, which had become a rarity.[32] Schumpeter did not agree with the proposal, arguing that: "the book was intended for other times and other men. Its message is taken for granted today. If I should write another theoretical work, it will look quite different" (Schneider [1970] 1975, 61).

Ludwig Lachmann remembered a conversation between Schumpeter and Lionel Robbins during a day's excursion on the Thames River; the event was held by the Robbins seminar at the London School of Economics in the summer of 1936. Robbins asked Schumpeter why *Wesen* had not been translated into English. Schumpeter replied, "Because I don't like it ... anymore. It was written with all the arrogance of youth and with a reprehensible pretension to omniscience. There are things in it I no longer believe" (Mittermaier 1992, 11).[33]

Indeed, while the immediate response to *Wesen* in Germany was negative, by the early 1930s the acceptance of neoclassical theory among economists worldwide was indisputable. Hence there was little reason to republish *Wesen* for its substance; in view of the developments in theoretical economics, *Wesen* was already outdated. As far as its methodological passages are concerned, however, instrumentalist methodology should be expounded much more explicitly and developed in light of Schumpeter's efforts regarding the verification and testing of dynamic theory. Thus, after including the methodological argument in his preface to the fourth German edition of *Entwicklung* (1935a), Schumpeter mentioned that he was going to develop this concept in a book entitled *Theoretischer Apparat der Ökonomie*, which would be the second edition of *Wesen*. He also revealed his intentions to the Japanese translators of *Wesen*.[34] But the plan was not realized.

CHAPTER 6

Static economics as an exact science

Following on from Schumpeter's economic methodology, this chapter examines how he dealt with economic theory in *Das Wesen und der Hauptinhalt der theoretischen Nationalökonomie*. By theoretical, pure, or exact economics in *Wesen* Schumpeter meant specifically the system of general equilibrium analysis. His urgent tasks in pure economics were to clarify the logic of economic phenomena, to establish economics as an "autonomous" science, and to confirm its past achievements in order to advance it further. In his view, if economics could properly define the object of study, weed out impurities from its scope, and explain uniquely an equilibrium state of economy given certain data, it would qualify as a self-contained, independent science. He expected that dynamics would be constructed only on the basis of statics.[1] In order to discuss Schumpeter's economic theory, I shall focus on the following problems, keeping in mind his methodological thought explained in the preceding chapter: how he defined the object and scope of statics, how he systematized the achievements of statics, and how he found a key to constructing dynamics on the basis of statics.

The logic of economic phenomena

The autonomy of pure economics

Today the term *autonomous science* is scarcely used in economics because there is no longer any doubt that economics is an autonomous science, equipped with its own logic; in fact, the invasion of economic logic into other fields of the social sciences has even been referred to as "economic imperialism." But at the beginning of the twentieth century, the field of economics as Schumpeter saw it was in danger of losing autonomy. At about the same time, physicist Pierre Duhem warned that if physics sought to explain the essence of empirical laws, it was not an autonomous science but a part of metaphysics (Duhem [1914] 1962, 10). As the situation stood, economics, composed of sundry knowledge, was dependent not only on metaphysics but also on

124

philosophy, psychology, sociology, and other disciplines. Schumpeter's substantive task in *Wesen* was, first of all, to identify the proper scope of economics and exclude irrelevant factors.

At the beginning of the book he took up a series of questions that he called the "grand issues of principle": in particular, the motives of human behavior, the motive power of social phenomena, and the objectives of an economy. Although some practitioners found it necessary to discuss these issues before they could address the concerns appropriate to economics, Schumpeter asked whether economists should settle these matters. He proposed to avoid the "grand issues" and the endless controversies they produced, believing that genuinely valuable inquiry in economics should include no trace of them. Schumpeter maintained that economics should be independent of all metaphysical, psychological, political, social, and historical questions, because they were difficult to solve in the field of science and would sacrifice the clarity of economics. Furthermore, he contended, these problems belonged to other fields of knowledge and would endanger the autonomy of economics. Independence from these issues would thus assure economics "clarity and autonomy" (1908, 23).

What, then, was required for pure economics to become an exact and autonomous science? In *Wesen* Schumpeter defines the domain of pure economics in terms of exchange relations and calls it "catallactics" (theory of exchange) and referred to Richard Whately, an almost unknown nineteenth-century archbishop of Dublin, as the coiner of the word. The word *catallactics* is much narrower and more specific than the meaning of traditional political economy and the moral sciences, where one often indulged in metaphysical speculation as well as political advocacy. Schumpeter's notion of exchange includes all kinds of economic behavior, including production and consumption. Mach would have called this the economy of thought, which assures economics "unity and purity" (Schumpeter 1908, 228).

Exchange relations presuppose a given amount of goods, including factors of production, owned by individuals. These quantities are interdependent in the sense that a change in one will involve a change in the others. General equilibrium is defined as a state in which there will be no further exchange of any kind of goods or services. On the basis of these notions – exchange, the holding of goods, interdependence, and general equilibrium – Schumpeter arrives at his definition of pure economics:

Thus the most exact definition of pure economics in an epistemological sense would be the following: it has to reduce the quantities of goods owned by individual economic agents at a certain point in time to those quantities owned by them a moment before, and yet by the shortest method with reference to formal assumptions. (1908, 143)

He notes that such an intertemporal reduction of phenomena is a fundamental procedure of the natural sciences. This procedure, if applied to economics, makes it possible to determine autonomously (i. e., without the aid of other disciplines) a system of interdependent economic quantities at any point in time.

Here I can demonstrate Schumpeter's characteristic dualism. On the one hand, economists who are fascinated by a high level of abstraction would confine themselves to pure economics and regard it as the most important research area. On the other hand, economists who take seriously those factors excluded from pure economics would be interested in the history and development of society as a whole and neglect the value of pure economics. The discrepancy between theoretical and historical research would ordinarily emerge at this point. Schumpeter, on the contrary, was not biased in either direction and affirmed his interest in both research areas without reservation.

Underlying *Wesen,* given its intention of establishing pure economics as an exact science, is a strong belief in the scientific values of pure economics: exactness, clarity, self-containment, and universality of thought. Schumpeter, however, repeatedly emphasizes that pure economics must abandon all matters of practical interest in exchange for these values:

It [pure economics] is like a hollow skeleton, but it makes the outline of our science all the more clear-cut. (1908, 27)

For the sake of the exact formulation and universal validity of our propositions, we sacrifice all the practical interests that have been raised by the problems of free competition, free trade, laissez-faire, individualism, and so forth. (1908, 52–53)

The most interesting economic facts are their social aspects, power relations, development, and the like, but our theoretical models can contribute nothing to them. (1908, 316)

There is no doubt that compared with phenomena such as the future of nations and the struggles between races, the argument of statics sometimes looks trivial and finicky. (1908, 504)

How poor our models of reality seem compared with the colorful richness of life as we look around us! (1908, 566)

What a miserable figure is our economic agent, who is cautiously seeking for equilibrium without a desire for fame, without entrepreneurship, in short, without power and life! Where are all the resolves and actions that will raise ordinary life out of lethal ash? (1908, 567)

These remarks may appear to be vulgar criticism of pure economics by outsiders. That Schumpeter could not restrain himself from including such apparently antitheoretical evaluations in a book that aimed to lay the foundation for pure economics seems to reveal his peculiar habit of thought:

that of wide-ranging perspective, broad-minded tolerance, and multifaceted curiosity. This habit of thought is likely to give rise to criticism that it is eclectic. For Schumpeter, the basic problems of pure economics, however dull they may be, should be solved before one can proceed to the more attractive fields of social science.

Despite Wieser's relentless critique of one aspect of *Wesen*, noted in the preceding chapter, he highly admired Schumpeter's approach:

He [Schumpeter] shows erudition and versatility far beyond the scope of his subject. The more carefully he tries to guard his own territory, the more clearly one becomes aware that wherever he breaks off inquiries, this man, with rich culture and multifarious training, has reacted to all streams of contemporary ideas without prejudice. And one is tempted to envision that the author will play a similarly conspicuous role in other areas. He has remarkable writing skills, and his descriptions combine scientific rigor and artistic freedom. (Wieser 1911, 396)

This appraisal incisively penetrates the style of thought of the young disciple. Surprisingly, this *enfant terrible*, in his obituary of Wieser, responded to the praise of his former teacher in the following way: "He was deficient in technique and is one of the few examples of clear thinking not implying concise writing" ([1927b] 1951a, 299). Schumpeter repeated the critique in *History*: "he was the worst technician of the three great Austrians" (1954a, 913).[2]

The validity of pure economics

Why does pure economics have values regardless of its inability to analyze important practical problems? Schumpeter's interest in establishing pure economics as an autonomous science meant specifically that he wanted to have a discipline where one could say something definite on the basis of that discipline's own logic, instead of introducing endless controversies in an unlimited area. It does not follow, however, that any hypotheses are acceptable insofar as they lead logically to a self-contained set of economic propositions. As long as economics is an empirical science, Schumpeter argued, we should take into account, as a criterion of theory acceptance, the extent to which a theory can explain the occurrence of economic phenomena. If pure economics is a mere logical construct that has nothing to do with facts or contradicts them, it has no value at all, even thought it may be exact and autonomous (1908, 529).

The point is that Schumpeter regards statics as having wide, practical applicability and relevance (1908, 564–65). He mentions that the facts described by statics are commonplace. Statics is not the representation of phenomena in a vacuum, so to speak, that cannot occur in reality, but the solidification of the universal mechanism of the economy proper. It must be emphasized that this is Schumpeter's conception of statics in *Wesen*.

When and how, then, does the mechanism described by the model of pure economics operate in reality? First, the state of affairs described by static theory is ordinary in real life; economic development and change, however remarkable, are "unusual events" (1908, 568). Most people spend their life in a customary manner over a long period of time. In this sense the base of an equilibrium system is broad, and unusual changes start from the base of a static stationary state or a circular flow.

Second, and more important, the facts described by statics are concerned with an equilibrating mechanism of the economy, which exists even in the process of change and development and absorbs the disturbances of dynamic factors to restore the economic order. As Schumpeter later put it:

The motto of a static system is: "everyone adapts as well as he can under a given circumstance." The contents of statics are composed of the rules of the best adaptation to an enormous amount of data. The essence of statics is ultimately not the givenness of data but the nature of the economic process it describes. (1912, 465)

Although without doubt statics applies in the short run or in a stationary state where data remain constant, the mechanism of equilibrating forces that statics describes is always immanent in an economy. That is the price mechanism, which is concerned with the adjustment of the demand and supply of all economic goods. Schumpeter describes this mechanism:

Price relations ... include all factors necessary to derive a unique state of equilibrium. Under conditions where economic activity is historically conditioned, the significance of this moment will be reduced but not completely eliminated. This does not follow automatically from "historically conditioned facts" such as organizations, environments, and so forth, but follows from the achievements of theories produced by their own power and owned as their own rights. (1908, 562)

The static mechanism works in reality with a high degree of universality; it is an adjustment force inherent in the economy and works in response to disturbing factors in the process of economic and sociocultural development.

In view of this fact, we can say that Schumpeter's efforts to develop the foundation work for statics proved to be useful in building dynamic theory and economic sociology upon it. For him, the price mechanism was a crucial link between statics and its subsidiary structures. Although he claimed that statics could not solve dynamic problems, he needed statics as the basis of dynamic analysis because the static mechanism works in a dynamic process to absorb the impacts of innovations and to bring about a reorganization of the economy. And in the perspective of economic sociology the static mechanism represents the notion of rationality that characterizes the civilization of capitalism, and ultimately determines the destiny of the capitalist economic system. Although pure economics abstracts from dynamic phenomena and is concerned with a limited adaptive economic process, it is all the more universal by its abstract, formal nature. Indicating a nature such as this for pure economics are his notions of "economics as economic logic" (1908, 613) and the "logic of economic phenomena" (1908, 134). For example, the statement that profits of a firm will be maximized when marginal costs are equivalent to marginal revenue is formulated as a proposition in logic (1954a, 17).

Schumpeter summarizes the essential nature of statics by calling it the "dual character of static theory":

It [statics] is general catallactics [theory of exchange], on the one hand, and it is a detailed description of a special type of economic process [adaptation], on the other. (1912, 512)

In a footnote, he explains further:

To put it simply, statics is valid universally as far as it is only the logic of economic behavior. Statics does not apply to a very important case [innovation] as far as it gives the psychology of economic behavior; in this regard, statics is not universally valid. (1912, 512)

As shown in chapter 4 (see pages 72–76), the accepted view of Schumpeter's statics (that it is concerned with the phenomenon of "adaptation," whereas dynamics deals with that of "innovation") has led to a biased interpretation that statics is unrealistic and should be replaced by dynamics. In Schumpeter's view, statics as the "logic of economic phenomena" is universal, and this is the basis of economics as an autonomous science.

The mathematical method

Schumpeter's first serious article was "Über die mathematische Methode der theoretischen Ökonomie." It was published in *Zeitschrift für Volkswirtschaft, Sozialpolitik und Verwaltung* in 1906, when he graduated from the University of Vienna. This journal was founded in 1892 in Vienna with Böhm-Bawerk, Theodor von Inama-Sternegg, and Ernst Plener as editors; after 1904 Eugen von Philippovich and Wieser joined the editorial panel.

How Schumpeter's article anticipated the direction of economics is clearly seen by comparing it with other articles on economics in the same journal.[3] In the early twentieth century, when the weight of neoclassical economics was trifling, especially in Germany and Austria, his article on the mathematical method in economics was without doubt in the advance guard. Here Schumpeter tries to remove prejudice against the mathematical method by showing its usefulness in economics: mathematics is a logical method, and its application to the economic world, whose basic elements are quantitative by nature, will establish the exactness and wide applicability of economic theory. He points out that since pure economics is a hypothetico-deductive system that constructs economic phenomena by abstraction, it needs mathematical method in order to represent assumptions clearly and develop the deductive process correctly; that the interdependent relationship between economic variables can be formulated only by a system of equations; and that economic variables (quantity of production, prices, labor, interest, wage, time, and so on) are quantitative and can be the objects of mathematical manipulation.

In short, Schumpeter was saying that in pure economics "the process of thinking itself takes mathematical forms" (1908, xxii). General criticism that the mathematical method cannot account for the complexity and historical constraint of economic phenomena does not reject the use of the mathematical method in economics because pure economics has scientific value in identifying the universally valid logic in economic phenomena, and the mathematical method is required for this purpose. Schumpeter did not deny the existence of the nonquantitative area and the usefulness of the historical method; he just wanted to exploit the potential of pure economics to its limits. Furthermore, he admitted that the study of pure economics does not lead to practical proposals. To do so, one should not be concerned with economic factors alone, and even those factors should be dealt with in a complex way.

Today the use of the mathematical method is widely accepted in economics, and Schumpeter's attempt at enlightenment appears to have nothing more than a classical meaning. But it is necessary to consider his argument with reference to its methodological perspective. He thought that by using the mathematical method pure economics could be established as an exact science and become similar to natural science. He claimed:

Economics as it is discussed here has methodological similarity with a group of exact natural science rather than moral science. (1906, 36)

According to its methodological and epistemological nature, pure economics is "natural science." (1908, 536)

However he did not believe that pure economics borrowed or even stole the method from natural science because the mathematical method was a universal form of logical thinking.

The method of catallactics (theory of exchange)

In *Wesen* Schumpeter did not present a vast array of mathematical formulations to explain neoclassical theory but depended on only three equations to clarify its basic structure: the maximization condition of the utility function, the budget restraint, and the equality condition of weighted marginal utility. *Wesen* was primarily an attempt to provide methodological interpretation and evaluation of pure economics, with Walras's general equilibrium theory in mind, but at the same time it included some interesting ideas on theoretical substance. Since Walras, the general equilibrium theory has made remarkable progress, especially with regard to the mathematical investigation of the existence and stability of a competitive equilibrium.[4] Nobel Laureates Paul Samuelson, Sir John Hicks, Kenneth Arrow, Wassily Leontief, Tjalling Koopmans, Gérard Debreu, and Maurice Allais are all associated with this tradition, which is now the centerpiece of economics. As several surveys show, the modern tradition of general equilibrium analysis starts from the 1930s with Gustav Cassel, Hicks, Abraham Wald, and John von Neumann, among others.[5] But just as Schumpeter's *Wesen* was neglected by methodologists in economics, so was he ignored by historians of the general equilibrium theory. In order to examine the toolbox of pure economics, this chapter takes up some major interpretations that Schumpeter contributed to the general equilibrium theory. In light of the growing current interest in the Austrian School, Schumpeter's similarity and dissimilarity with the Austrian view in regard to the basic conceptions of economics are still relevant.[6]

Givens and assumptions

Schumpeter defines the object of pure economics as an exchange relationship: "Exchange is, so to speak, a clip which pulls together an economic system … All purely economic things lie within the exchange relationship" (1908, 50).

The exchange relationship refers not only to those exchange phenomena that actually take place between goods and money or between goods and goods, but to the fact that all goods have certain ratios of exchange in relation to one another. In a market economy this relationship appears explicitly as the relations of relative prices, but Schumpeter extends the object of pure economics to a general form because the exchange relationship can be found, for example, both in the case of an isolated economic agent like Robinson Crusoe and in a planned economic system like socialism:

We *interpret all economic acts as an exchange* and assume that even where no exchange actually exists, an economy runs *as if* it did exist. This is not as paradoxical as it looks. One should note that all economic behaviors mean changes in economic quantities. For example, a man who exchanges labor for bread is changing the quantities of two goods in his possession. The same is also true of an isolated man who shoots game, because he diminishes the stock of bullets or labor and increases the stock of foodstuffs. (1908, 50)

To discuss exchange acts we must start from certain stocks of goods owned by individuals. Goods include not only consumer goods but also services of factors of production such as land, labor, and capital. Because exchange means to an economic agent the acquisition of certain goods by reducing his stock of other goods, it changes the quantity of goods that he has on hand. When exchanges no longer take place, a state of equilibrium has been achieved. What will induce people to make an exchange? In order to understand exchange acts we need an assumption of the utility functions of individuals, which Schumpeter calls value functions.[7] People are assumed to maximize utility according to their utility functions, and exchange is considered to be a means of achieving utility maximization.

Various exogenous factors will influence economic activity, including human nature, geographic environment, technology, social organizations, and political conditions. But the data that are explicitly required for pure economics to accomplish the task of describing a state of equilibrium are the quantity of goods owned by individuals and their utility functions. These are the minimum informational bases for deriving an economic equilibrium, and it is the task of equilibrium theory to examine, under these given conditions, an equilibrium of the demand and supply of quantities of goods, the existence of equilibrium prices that make the equilibrium possible, and the stability of the equilibrium. It is to be noted that the production function as a technological constraint is not listed among Schumpeter's givens; as we shall see, it is integrated with the utility function.

By adopting catallactics as the definition of economics, that is, an analysis of the demand and supply of goods in an exchange relationship, Schumpeter rejects various traditional definitions of economics: for example, a science of the means to economic welfare, of want satisfaction, of economic behavior, of economic principles, of individual egoism, and of production, distribution, and consumption. This definition raises the question of which assumptions or hypotheses should serve as the foundation of catallactics. Schumpeter discloses three assumptions as the major postulates of neoclassical theory.

First, in order to justify an economic theory that starts from the goods owned by individuals and their utility functions and concerns their exchange behavior, Schumpeter assumes an atomistic view of society rather than a holistic one. His methodological individualism (see chapter 3) is not a political, ethical, or factual statement.

Second, in order to explain the exchange behavior of individuals, Schumpeter postulates the maximization of want satisfaction by consumers. As explained above, equilibrium is an imaginary state where no further exchange takes place; this is so because the satisfaction of each person's wants is maximized to the extent that there is no further incentive to change the quantity of goods in the hands of individuals. In accordance with the generalized notion of exchange, Schumpeter expands the concept of utility function (or value function) to include the production process and defends this procedure by the Austrian theory of imputation, which derives the value of factors of production from the value of consumer goods.

These two assumptions are combined in the hypothesis of *homo oeconomicus*, which is also not a factual statement. It does not assert that human nature and behavior are exhaustively explained by economic interests, nor does it contend that all economic behavior is explained solely by economic interests.

Third, a hypothesis is required to explain the process toward equilibrium, that is, the assumption of perfect competition (which Schumpeter calls free competition). Again, this hypothesis is neither a normative assertion nor a factual statement. The assumption means that economic agents act by taking prices as given. When Schumpeter describes the scheme of pure economics, he uses the exchange concept as a general one that is independent of institutional conditions. But when he is going to present the achievements of pure economics in terms of price theory, he implicitly assumes a market economy and perfect competition. Finally, he asserts that the principles thus derived will be valid in a nonexchange economy.

The procedure of inference on the basis of the preceding assumptions represents the "methods" of a science as distinguished from the "methodology" of a science. By inquiring more deeply into the meaning of these assumptions, this chapter will clarify Schumpeter's unique position within the basic structure of neoclassical economics. Specifically, it will show how his position with regard to method is supported by his instrumentalist position in methodology. From this viewpoint the following issues are discussed: exchange versus scarcity as the definition of economics, market equilibrium versus utility maximization as the explanatory hypothesis, and market equilibrium versus market process as the theme of inquiry with regard to the assumption of perfect competition. These issues are all related to the differences between Schumpeter and the Austrians.

Exchange versus scarcity

In describing pure economics Schumpeter notes that the ideas of his predecessors Walras and Wieser were closest to his own (1908, ix). Schumpeter extolled Walras, the founder of the Lausanne School, as the greatest theoretical economist for his establishment of the general equilibrium scheme. In *Wesen* Schumpeter does not describe pure Walrasian general equilibrium theory but gives it an Austrian flavor probably inherited from Wieser, one of his teachers at Vienna. Schumpeter introduced the Austrian idea of imputation to the Walrasian system and attempted to provide a unified explanation of economic equilibrium in terms of utility. But he did not adopt all of the characteristics of the Austrian School, deviating from its tradition with regard to his own epistemological and methodological basis, in particular. Let us begin by considering what is involved in the difference between the conceptions of exchange and scarcity as the definition of economics.

In Walras's system, too, the quantity of goods and utility functions were assumed as given, but this assumption was made to treat the phenomenon of exchange as the first step of analysis. His *Eléments d'économie politique pure* (1874) begins from exchange and expands the scope of analysis to production, capital formation, credit, circulation, and money to become closer and closer to reality. Thus Walras's concept of exchange refers to the simplest and most basic aspect of an economic system, whereas Schumpeter's exchange relationship covers all economic activities and his set of assumptions is devised for a unified explanation of production and consumption from the viewpoint of want satisfaction. This approach is essentially Austrian and differs from the Walrasian (and, in this respect, Marshallian) dualistic approach in terms of marginal utility theory and marginal productivity theory.

Despite this difference, both Walras and Schumpeter define economics in terms of the exchange relationship and both differ from Robbins's popular definition in terms of scarcity. Robbins's definition of economics – i.e., "the science which studies human behaviour as a relationship between ends and scarce means which have alternative uses" (Robbins 1935, 16) – follows the Austrian tradition concerning the teleological interpretation of economic phenomena as a relationship between ends (want satisfaction) and means (goods). Menger, who considered an inquiry into the teleological relationship between men's wants and goods as the task of economics, is characteristic of the Austrian School. Just as a teleological relationship amounts to a causal relationship if we look at it from the reverse perspective, want satisfaction occupies the place of cause in explaining the world of goods. In the Lausanne School, on the contrary, the economic world is conceived as an exchange relationship, which is a relationship between goods and goods and denies causal explanations by utility or want satisfaction.

Walras divides economics into three branches: pure economics (science), applied economics (technique), and social economics (morality). Pure economics deals with problems of exchange value, which, according to him, are concerned with natural relationships between goods and goods. Applied economics or the theory of industry deals with the technical relationship between men and goods, social economics or moral science with the ethical relationship between man and man. Although the Lausanne School introduced human want into the theoretical system by assuming utility functions, it did not regard want as a cause that explained the world of goods but aimed at an inquiry of the general interdependence of economic quantities. In this vein Schumpeter explicitly writes: "What we want to observe is not men who act but only quantities they possess" (1908, 86). This is almost equivalent to his breaking off relations with the Austrian School. Mises evaluates Schumpeter from just this point of view:

> Because Austrian economics is a theory of human action, Schumpeter does not belong to the Austrian School. In his first book [*Wesen*] he significantly related himself to Wieser and Walras, but not to Menger and Böhm-Bawerk. Economics, to him, is a theory of "economic quantities," and not of human action. Schumpeter's *Theory of Economic Development* is a typical product of the equilibrium theory. (Mises 1978, 36–37)

Mises is right with regard to *Wesen*, but his view about the *Theory of Economic Development* is not correct, as I argue in chapter 7.

Robbins challenged the Schumpeterian definition in terms of the exchange relationship (Robbins 1935, 16–22). He argued that, under the exchange relationship, there must be a relationship between scarce resources and alternative ends, and the choice behavior of individuals must be explained on this basis. In other words, scarcity must logically precede exchange and explain exchange. Of course, since Schumpeter assumes a utility function, it can be said that Robbins and Schumpeter deal with both sides of the matter. But we should not overlook the difference between their methodological positions. Even if Schumpeter referred to utility, he depended not on the ontological but the instrumental use of the utility concept; moreover, insofar as observable quantities and prices are available in the economic world, there was no reason for him to prefer the utility concept to the exchange concept for he believed in phenomenalism, not essentialism.

Why then did Schumpeter keep the concept of utility and the hypothesis of utility maximization in his system? He recognized the basic differences between natural science and economics: first, that the study of economics does not require laboratory experiments, and second, that it considers the meanings of economic actions (1954a, 16). The second point is relevant here; the study of economics is not confined to the study of objectively observable relations but information about the meanings of economic actions can be used. For Schumpeter, the reference to subjective conditions was an attempt to understand the meaning of exchange acts in terms of the motive of utility maximization. A deeper inquiry into the understanding of meaning will be made in relation to Max Weber in chapter 8.

The exchange approach and the utility approach are sometimes called objectivism and subjectivism respectively, and Schumpeter regarded the dispute between them as meaningless:

> Actually, the "subjective" theory must always appeal to "objective" facts (data) if it is to produce concrete results; and any "objective" theory must always state or imply postulates or propositions about "subjective" factors of behavior. In other words, any

complete subjective theory must be also objective and vice versa, and differences on this score can only be due to differences of emphasis on different parts of the analyst's task. Yet the "issue" was accepted as real and gravely discussed by all scientific parties alike. (1954a, 919)

This comment is typically based on instrumentalism, which outweighs even the conflict between phenomenalism and essentialism.

The word catallactics has been utilized in various contexts in economics. Prior to Schumpeter, Francis Edgeworth used it when referring to the mathematical analysis of a perfectly competitive market by Jevons, Marshall, and Walras (Edgeworth 1881, 30); in this case, the emphasis was not on exchange as the object of study but on a self-contained, special paradigm concerning the exchange relationship.

More recently Mises called economics catallactics because he wanted to distinguish economics from praxeology (Mises 1949, 233–35). He argued that whereas praxeology is a general theory of human action based on choice and preference, economics is concerned with market exchange and therefore only with the economic aspect of human actions. His point is that economics cannot be treated in isolation as a theory of exchange. To Schumpeter, this view would mean that economics should lose autonomy.

With the introduction of subjective elements into economics after the Marginal Revolution, the relationship between economics and psychology became a serious question. Some economists, including Irving Fisher, argued that economics should be confined to catallactics as a theory of market exchange and did not need to consider the psychological motive leading to the exchange (Coats 1976, 47). This is similar to Schumpeter's view.

Recently when Hicks distinguished between neoclassical theory and classical theory, he called them catallactics (theory of exchange) versus plutology (theory of wealth) respectively (Hicks 1976, 212). He probably was not familiar with Schumpeter's discussion of catallactics. Both gave the label "catallactics" to neoclassical economics, but there is a difference. Whereas Hicks, in the Austrian camp, admitted the normative implication of the equilibrium concept that utility is maximized under the scarcity constraint, Schumpeter rejected such a teleological implication and introduced the concept catallactics to avoid such implication. Robbins's "scarcity definition" was derived through his criticism of the "materialistic definition," which was adopted by the classical school to signify its subject matter, that is, the production and distribution of social wealth. Hicks's distinction between catallactics and plutology corresponds with Robbins's distinction between the two definitions of economics; it was not only unnecessary in light of Ockham's razor, a precursor of the idea of thought economy, but also disturbing to Schumpeter's distinction between exchange and scarcity.

Equilibrium versus maximization

The preceding discussion of the definition of economics leads us to the difference in the meanings attributed to the assumptions of utility maximization and the equilibrium state. Schumpeter's central proposition on equilibrium is that "in a state of equilibrium there is no tendency to make further changes" (1908, 199). Two interpretations are possible to account for equilibrium. First, in equilibrium demand and supply are equal and exchange ceases to take place. Second, in equilibrium utility is maximized so that there is no motive for further exchange. Thus Schumpeter writes:

A state of equilibrium can be characterized by either the former moment or the latter moment; in the former case it can be called a state of rest; in the latter case, a state of maximization. Each expression says the same thing; the two are synonyms. This is our principle. (1908, 199)

Whichever characterization one accepts as an interpretation of equilibrium, a state of rest or a state of maximization, is connected with the problem of exchange versus scarcity. Although Schumpeter admits that the two views of equilibrium are not mutually exclusive, he places an emphasis on a state of rest because the maximization interpretation would invoke unnecessary ontological meaning as if a state of maximization really existed. He is opposed to investing any substantive, except logical, meaning on the maximization principle. Current welfare economics calls a state of maximization Pareto optimum and identifies it with a state in which an efficiency criterion is fulfilled. Schumpeter agrees that equilibrium with no incentive for further exchange means tautologically a state of utility maximization, but he refuses to consider equilibrium as desirable in any sense: "We do not give any value judgments to the equilibrium state. Above all, we do not call it 'desirable' or demand that to be realized at all" (1908, 204). The reason why he does not give normative meaning to equilibrium is because, in a state of maximization, "it is certain that maximum satisfaction is achieved, but it is merely satisfaction that is possible under a given condition, namely under the constraints of exogenous factors such as nature, technology, the stock of goods, etc." (1908, 207). By means of exchange man tries to achieve the most favorable ends under a given condition, and the most direct constraint is the quantity of goods owned by individuals before the exchange, namely the distribution of income to individuals. Unless the desirability of the constraint is examined, it is of no use to give normative valuation to equilibrium. Thus Schumpeter remarks: "Pure economics does not 'demand' anything, nor give any criterion to judge the usefulness of organizations" (1908, 193).

On the other hand, the welfare interpretation of the assumption of perfect competition finds significance in an inquiry into a state of welfare maximization rather than a value-free state of rest. Hicks holds that static theory assumes perfect competition not for analytical convenience but for the purpose of studying a perfectly efficient economic system, namely a system of Pareto optimum (Hicks 1959, 160). This interpretation follows directly from the scarcity definition of economics in which the fundamental economic problem is conceived as the efficient allocation of resources in a decentralized system.

Schumpeter's opposition to the normative or welfare interpretation of perfect competition revived in a stronger form when he came to argue the case for competition in a dynamic context in *Capitalism, Socialism and Democracy*. The point, he said, is that "all the essential facts of that process [the process of creative destruction] are absent from the general schema of economic life that yields the traditional propositions about perfect competition" (1950a, 104). In this way, the dynamic aspect of competition comes to the fore in Schumpeter's later work, so that he regards the maximization proposition in static theory as all the more meaningless. The following remark is typical of his later view:

This theorem [maximization theorem], even if we waive the serious objections to speaking of non-observable psychic magnitudes, is readily seen to boiled down to the triviality that, whatever the data and in particular the institutional arrangements of a society may be, human action, as far as it is rational, will always try to make the best of any given situation. (1950a, 77)

I do not mean that his view of equilibrium analysis changed from *Wesen* to *Capitalism*; he had already stressed in *Wesen* that pure economics excludes all the interesting factors in a capitalist process and consists of, so to speak, formal logic. Therefore it was his immutable view that the tautological maximization theorem should not be regarded as a normative proposition that has a practical significance.

Market equilibrium versus market process

Another point of dispute involves the assumption of competition within neoclassical economics. Whereas neoclassical theory depends on the concept of utility, different perceptions of the concept give rise to different views of the economic process. The Austrian School emphasized the active aspect of human action under the assumptions of an imperfect market and uncertainty, so that it paid special attention to such factors as information, expectation, and perception in markets. As a result, it was much more concerned with the process of price formation in markets through human action rather than the determination of equilibrium prices at the end of the process. Hayek's view that market competition is a procedure for the discovery and utilization of information is a typical product of the Austrian tradition (Hayek 1937). In other neoclassical theories and in general equilibrium analysis in particular, those factors that must be discovered in an economic process are simply assumed as given in the form of utility functions and production functions at the outset of analysis. Utility maximization under given data is treated as the mathematical conditions required to find an equilibrium solution, and the determination of the equilibrium values of economic variables is a central concern. Therefore, in this approach, the assumption of well-organized, perfect markets is essential. The issue was recognized in recent studies of the Austrian School as contrasting subject matters, that is, market equilibrium of the Lausanne School versus market process of the Austrian School (Lachmann 1986). With regard to contrasting positions in subjectivism, one may distinguish between Lausanne static subjectivism and Austrian dynamic subjectivism (O'Driscoll and Rizzo 1985).

In light of the contemporary studies of neoclassical theory, it is obvious that Schumpeter's pure economics was concerned with market equilibrium along the lines of the Lausanne School, and his assumption of perfect competition was conceived in that vein. For him, the assumption of perfect competition was not a description of the actual market form, nor was it a criterion of desirable policy. Rather it was a mathematical condition, a supplementary means for solving the equilibrium value of an economic system. On the role of the hypothesis of free competition, he wrote:

The role of this principle is mainly negative; it neither claims nor demands anything. It excludes only what does not belong to pure theory. In this sense this principle is, so to speak, merely a separation apparatus, and this will be the only significance conferred on this principle in the future. (1908, 196)

The assumption that perfect competition separates and excludes some influences means that prices are determined exclusively by given quantities of goods and utility functions.

The central task of pure economics is to clarify how an economy can create an order through the adjustment role of the price system. For Schumpeter, this order was described by general equilibrium, and the hypothetical schema that proved most efficiently the process of order-making was the model of perfect competition. Mach's thought economy was practiced on the assumption of perfect competition as a separation apparatus. Given the demand for the establishment of an autonomous science, Schumpeter's task was to deal with market equilibrium rather than market process.

We can argue, however, that the problems of entrepreneurial activity in Schumpeter's *Entwicklung* are concerned with aspects of the market process from the Austrian School's perspective. Innovation is the creation of new information, and competition in a dynamic world is naturally imperfect. Schumpeter's criticism, in *Capitalism*, of the concept of competition is directed to the role of the assumption in statics, which is merely a mathematical condition for maximization, and suggests that the market process should matter in a dynamic world.

Methodological individualism versus holism

Pure economics is based on methodological individualism, which holds that all social phenomena must be explained by the aims, behaviors, propensities, and beliefs of individuals. Pure economics accounts for the ways in which the allocation of economic resources is determined through the behavior of individuals in markets and their interactions. Methodological holism, on the contrary, claims that society is the whole that is more than its parts and that it is governed by its own rules and forces. The holist retorts to the individualist that society affects the individual's aims and constrains his behavior. For Schumpeter, the instrumentalist, the issue of methodological individualism versus holism was not that of ideals or facts but that of usefulness for analytic purposes.

In his article "On the Concept of Social Value" (1909), published after *Wesen*, Schumpeter maintained from the position of methodological individualism that insofar as the problem of resource allocation in a noncommunistic society is concerned, social wants, social values, and social utility do not exist except for individual wants, individual values, and individual utility. When prices and the distribution of income are determined, the social valuation is only an aggregate result of individual interactions.

At the same time, Schumpeter commented on the limits of methodological individualism:

> We already saw that it [methodological individualism] does not include any practical demands and moral and other evaluations of different forms of organization in an economy, nor does it meet with objections of this type. We now see that it does not invoke any statement of fact because we do not say what determines the behavior of individuals ... We mean only that the individualistic method of observation brings about remarkably useful results quickly and expediently and that within a pure theory the collective method of observation does not give us an essential advantage and therefore is useless. It is true that as soon as we go beyond the limits of a pure theory, the situation changes. In organization theory as well as sociology, one cannot get along with individualism. (1908, 94–95)

Comparing economics and economic sociology, Schumpeter later observed: "economic analysis deals with the questions how people behave at any time and what the economic effects are they produce by so behaving; economic sociology deals with the question how they became to behave as they do" (1954a, 21). Since economic sociology discusses, according to him, the influences of social institutions on individuals, methodological holism is effective for this purpose.

As a result of the fact that pure economics has logical rigor as well as practical validity, it entails various consequences in explaining economic phenomena. In *Wesen*, Schumpeter remarks:

> It [pure economics] allows various applications and yields results whose values cannot be denied. The theory of money, the theory of distribution, and the laws of price changes are important examples. It can be argued that in discussions of these problems the contribution of theories is essential, and the lack of knowledge in many areas will pose a serious impediment to clear understanding. (1908, 563)

The next three sections demonstrate how Schumpeter viewed the achievements of pure economics in relation to the theories of distribution, interest, and money. In all these areas his originality was distinct.

Income distribution and the theory of imputation

The Austrian idea

In the subjective theory of value, consumption goods as the explanatory variables in utility functions yield utility and are directly evaluated by consumers. The level of utility that determines the value of a certain amount of a good is the lowest level of utility attainable by that amount of the good. However, this principle is not immediately applicable to factors of production or producer goods that do not by themselves satisfy the wants of consumers but are devoted to the production of consumer goods or producer goods. In order to make the subjective theory of value consistent in the context of a complete system of economic theory, it is possible to impute the value of consumption goods that are produced by producer goods to the value of the producer goods in question. This is the idea of the imputation theory (*Zurechnungstheorie*). The solution of the imputation problem makes possible a uniform explanation of the values of all goods and services as well as of income distribution based on the pricing of factors of production. Thus the subjective theory of value is regarded as comprehensive in explaining value and distribution.

The imputation theory is characteristic of the Austrian School, and Menger's concepts of goods of higher and lower orders are the sources of the idea. In the hierarchy of goods, which represents the economy's capital structure, whereas lower-order goods (consumer goods) receive values directly from the satisfaction of human wants, higher-order goods (producer goods or capital goods) receive values indirectly in proportion to their contribution to the production of consumer goods. Wieser and Böhm-Bawerk formulated this idea; the word *imputation* is credited to Wieser's knowledge of jurisprudence.

According to Wieser, in the subjective theory of value the relationship between the value of consumer goods and that of producer goods is that "the former is a determining factor and the latter is a determined factor" (Wieser 1889, 69), contrary to the view of the classical school. The concept of imputation means a causal explanation that attributes results to causes (Wieser 1889, 87–89). Although Wieser's quotation might sound as if the value of consumer goods is the cause of the value of producer goods, producer goods are in fact the cause of consumer goods; the concept of imputation involves a consequentialist view that a cause is valued by the value of results.

The theory of imputation, however, was soon removed from the system of economics because, in the development of neoclassical economics, production was treated on the basis of the marginal productivity theory under the explicit assumption of the production function. Except for some current successors to the Austrian School who uphold the imputation theory as part of the subjectivist framework, it has lost significance. But Schumpeter's acceptance of the imputation theory was an obvious reflection of his methodological standpoint. He is often seen as having adopted the Austrian position by accepting the imputation theory, but this is not so. His imputation theory was not intended to offer a causal explanation of value, as the Austrians did; rather, it was an application of Mach's idea of thought economy to the subjective theory of value.

Schumpeter's idea

For Schumpeter, the world of pure economics is that of exchange. Exchange is the act of acquiring one value in exchange for another value. He regards the following equality of weighted marginal utility as the essence of pure economics:

$$U_a/P_a = U_b/P_b.$$

U_a and U_b are the marginal utility of goods A and goods B respectively; P_a and P_b are the price of goods A and goods B. This equation describes an equilibrium situation in which the exchange between A and B ceases and can be rewritten as:

$$U_a = U_b \cdot P_a/P_b.$$

Since the relative price P_a / P_b indicates the units of goods B that are to be sacrificed in order to acquire one unit of goods A, the right side of the second equation shows, in terms of the utility of goods B, the costs that are to be sacrificed in order to acquire one unit of goods A. Therefore, the second equation represents the marginal utility of goods A (left side) = marginal cost of goods A (right side). The basic idea of imputation in Schumpeter is that first, the above equality holds in consumption as well as in production (by imputation), and second, the above equality indicates not a causal relationship but an equilibrium relationship.

Let us now consider how a supply curve can be derived corresponding to a demand curve. Schumpeter argues that a supply curve is an "inverted value curve" (1908, 226). The value curve (or function) here means the marginal utility curve (or function). This view differs from today's view of price theory, which rests on the dualism of attributing demand to utility and supply to cost. In contrast, Schumpeter attributes supply to utility too; supply does not have an independent meaning.

According to Schumpeter, all producer goods are potential consumer goods. A process in producing consumer goods is an exchange between producer goods and consumer goods produced by the former. Let us suppose that consumer goods A and B are produced by certain producer goods. When A is not produced, B will be produced by the unused amount of producer goods. The production process of A means the acquisition of A at the sacrifice of B which could potentially be produced, so that it can be seen as an exchange of actual goods A with potential goods B. This idea is nothing more than a conception of opportunity cost,[8] and based on this notion a supply function of A is expressed by the utility function of B which is sacrificed by the choice of producing A. In other words, the problems of cost and distribution involved in the supply function are reduced to the problems of exchange based on the utility function. Thus one can explain the supply-side problems without recourse to hypotheses other than the utility function, such as productivity or disutility. Schumpeter asserts:

> This view not only includes the cases of exchange and production at the same time but also has another advantage. If it is possible to relate a supply curve conceived as a value function to the value functions of consumer goods, so that one may derive the former from the latter, then there is a possibility of substantially reducing the number of our fundamental assumptions. Then one has only to "ask" individuals about the *value functions of consumer goods*; all the rest will be obtained from them. (1908, 226–27)

Thus, Schumpeter argues, the distribution problem is reduced to an exchange problem, and the system of pure economics acquires "marvelous unity and purity" (1908, 228) based on the principle of thought economy. For him, the question of imputation was not a trivial, technical problem: if the value of producer goods is explained by the imputation theory, then "the whole of the organ of pure economics thus finds itself unified in the light of a single principle – in a sense in which it never had been before" (1954a, 914).

Against the dualism of demand and supply

In Schumpeter's system of pure economics the quantity of goods and utility functions were assumed as given. Since, in his definition, factors of production are included in the category of goods, the application of the imputation theory seems to make these given data sufficient as the informational basis for the microeconomic analysis of an economy. However, I would argue that Schumpeter's interpretation of the imputation theory was not based exclusively on the methodological consideration of thought economy but contained a substantive claim against the traditional dualism of demand and supply in the exposition of economic equilibrium. He notes that:

Despite widespread recognition that the old approach is imperfect, one still holds fast to the dualism of demand and supply, and despite the acknowledgment that one cannot attribute demand to value and supply to cost alone, which we find among progressive-minded scholars, everything remains the same. (1908, 236)

He asks whether a supply curve should be based on an independent principle:

Indeed, one can explain the shape of a supply curve in different ways. This is not surprising because we know and need to know very little about the general characteristics of a supply curve. But it is redundant to resort to other hypotheses. (1908, 227)

It is wrong to say that one can derive the value of factors of production only from the value of products. For the value of products is determined by the scarcity imposed by the quantity of factors of production and technology in addition to individual preference. Similarly, it is wrong to say that one can derive the value of products only from the value of the factors of production independently of the preference conditions of individuals. Hence we need a scheme in which the demand and supply of factors of production as well as products are simultaneously determined. What Schumpeter tried to offer under the imputation theory must be the components of this scheme.

According to the dualism of demand and supply, the demand for goods and the supply of factors of production are explained by the marginal utility theory, and the demand for factors of production and the supply of goods are explained by the marginal productivity theory. Since Schumpeter regarded a supply curve of goods as an inverted marginal utility curve, he believed that he did not need an explicit assumption about marginal productivity; the necessary and sufficient conditions for him were the quantity of goods and the utility function. In his case, the production of goods by factors of production was conceptually included in the exchange between goods, so that information about the technological production function and marginal productivity was only implicitly involved in the evaluation of potential products. This information cannot be derived from the ordinary utility function. But it was Schumpeter's judgment that this information was unnecessary. What did he mean?

Behind the given conditions of the quantity of goods and the utility function there are groups of noneconomic data that include nature, technology, organization, human nature, and so forth. In pure economics all of these factors are treated as given. For Schumpeter the information on the production function and the marginal productivity derived from it was pushed into the background together with other given factors because technology is constant in statics. Relating to the rent theory, Schumpeter says:

We no longer need the law of decreasing returns ... It no longer constitutes a component of our scientific arsenal ... For us it is merely a *technical fact*, which is naturally very important in practice but no longer interesting for pure theory. (1908, 379)

From the standpoint of the formal dualism of demand and supply Schumpeter might seem to have brandished Ockham's razor too much in order to achieve an economy of thought. But he was convinced that so far as assumptions are arbitrary in nature, useless things should be jettisoned. It is interesting to observe that in dynamic theory he emphasized the supply side and found the source of innovation in technical facts in contrast to what he had said about statics. It is the supply side that dominates the dynamic world.

Schumpeter did not deny the concept of marginal productivity in statics; in *Entwicklung* he states that corresponding to the marginal utility of consumer goods, producer goods or productive services get "marginal utility of productivity" (*Produktivitätgrenznutzen*) or marginal productivity (1926a, 31). To be exact, this is marginal value (or utility) productivity, which factors of production receive from consumer goods according to the theory of imputation. In this context he refers to "the law of decreasing returns":

We can speak here of the law of decreasing returns in production. This has, however, a completely different meaning from the law of the decreasing physical product. What matters here is decreasing returns in the sense of *utility per unit of product*, which is entirely different from the former. The validity of this proposition has nothing to do with the law of decreasing physical returns. (1926a, 35)

What he meant by the law of decreasing returns is expressed in terms of utility and is different from our contemporary concept of the law of decreasing value returns, which consists of decreasing marginal physical productivity multiplied by the constant product price.[9] For him, technological conditions were always behind the scenes as long as he was working in statics.

Capital interest and the dynamic theory

Statics is concerned with the static equilibrium that is attained under given data, but it must also answer the question: "Given some state of an economy in equilibrium and certain causes of disturbance, how will prices and income change?" (1908, 446). This is the problem to which Schumpeter's "variation method" (today it is called comparative statics) in *Wesen* should be applied. Whereas both statics and comparative statics are concerned with equilibrium analysis and constitute pure economics, dynamics is an entirely different theory. The central problem of statics and comparative statics is equilibrium, whereas the focus of dynamics is development:

Statics is not accessible to all that is related to the phenomena of *development*. Yes – development and what belongs to it are beyond our investigation. The system of pure economics is essentially devoid of development. (1908, 186)

A dynamic element in Wesen

In *Wesen* there is no analysis of development. Development is the subject of Schumpeter's next book, *Theorie der wirtschaftlichen Entwicklung* (1912). But in *Wesen* there is one argument that presupposes a dynamic standpoint; that is the issue of capital interest. Through this topic Schumpeter's statics and dynamics are internally linked.

As mentioned in the preceding section, the theory of income distribution in pure economics is based on the imputation theory. When Schumpeter examined three categories of income, wages, rents, and interest, he criticized Böhm-Bawerk's theory of interest because it was not consistent with static theory. In *Wesen* Schumpeter contends that interest is not a static phenomenon, an argument that leads to a logical leap into dynamics.

According to Schumpeter, the analytic task of income formation in pure economics is to explain the process of income distribution in terms of the price formation of factors of production. Income that cannot be accounted for in this way does not belong to the system of pure economics; thus the profits of the entrepreneur and capital interest are regarded as income that cannot be explained by statics. For Schumpeter the principle of price formation for factors of production is the imputation theory, and its greatest insight is

the recognition that the categories of income that appear in statics as we have limited them are *equal in nature*; that is, they depend on the same methods and are explained in the same way. This result is very important and gives our system the unity that must be characterized as demonstrating great progress compared with the old system. (1908, 326)

He argues from the perspective that whereas wages for labor and rents for land are paid because these services are useful, and belong to the static income categories, interest on capital cannot be treated similarly. In other words, capital interest, usually regarded as the third income category, cannot be explained by static economics.

When wages and rents are established as income for labor and land respectively, what will be established as income for capital? The values of what Schumpeter calls "tools and materials" – that is, fixed capital and liquid capital – are the total values of these capital services and equal to the values of the products imputed to capital. However, from the point of view of the commodity hierarchy the capital as the produced means of production is decomposed into labor and land at a higher level, and the values of capital services are still regarded as a transitional item, that is, as the costs of intermediate goods. Therefore no surplus exists that is not imputed to the original means of production, labor and land. The price of capital services is not called interest. The income that represents the net of the costs of intermediate products includes only wages and rents. As we shall see, Schumpeter excludes the productivity of capital and time preference as the cause of capital interest. Then he distinguishes between capital goods and capital as a sum of money in order to seek the cause of interest in money capital.

Now the question is, how can one explain the phenomenon of interest? First, Schumpeter identified the core of the interest phenomenon in "industrial interest":

The essential thing is the interest on lending that is used for the creation of new industries, new forms of organization, new technologies, and new consumer goods, and with this half of the crucial points are described. (1908, 417)

The new activities described here are what Schumpeter calls the phenomena of economic development.

Second, he identified the source of lending in the money market, stating that "the heart of the phenomena beats in the money market" (1908, 418). Although the phenomenon of money credit appears in the static system, what is essential to credit is credit creation.

Thus it follows that "in *development and credit* lies the source of the interest phenomenon, and its explanation must be sought here" (1908, 420). We should note that the essential relationship between development and credit later developed in *Entwicklung* is already present in *Wesen*. New purchasing power created by credit "provides the biggest spurs to get rid of the equilibrium state and make an *unusual endeavor*" (1908, 420).

Interest is explained by the fact that entrepreneurial profits emerge as a special surplus produced by the activities of the entrepreneur who carries out economic development. Schumpeter asserts:

The supply and demand for these services [entrepreneurial activities] do not exist in markets, like other labor – they are not *separately* bought and sold. (1908, 367)

What the entrepreneur gets is not determined definitely and may be larger or smaller than the "value" of his services for somebody. Furthermore, it cannot be a price because no value functions exist for these "goods." (1908, 434)

Thus entrepreneurial profits are not subject to the imputation theory. This is the core of Schumpeter's theory. Static theory deals with the economic order established under certain value functions, and the imputation theory prescribes the value relationship among the production, distribution, and expenditure of products under the static order. Want satisfaction attributes values to production and distribution. Dynamic theory, however, is concerned with the process in which the static order prescribed by the imputation theory is destroyed and is reestablished later on new ground. This process is initiated by innovation in production, and a deviation from the old order yields entrepreneurial profits.

Schumpeter also emphasizes that worn-out capital is not made good automatically because the maintenance of capital, as well as the provision of capital, is not a static process. Both are gross investment. It follows that it is a fiction to regard capital as a perpetual source of income and to assume that capital yields interest as a cherry tree bears cherries. Capital stock, as one of physical goods, does not have value by itself but has value only if it is a useful means of production. Often physically workable capital becomes economically obsolete. Therefore whether or not capital endures as a perpetual source of income depends on dynamic conditions. Even the maintenance of capital requires "endeavor" (1908, 421). In a dynamic economy old capital dies out, new capital appears, and thus the content of capital changes.

In this connection, Schumpeter criticized Böhm-Bawerk's theory of capital.[10] Böhm-Bawerk had argued three reasons for a positive rate of interest. First, present goods are preferred to future goods because of higher expected incomes in the future. Second, present goods are preferred to future goods because of uncertainties such as the finiteness of life. Third, by investing present goods in production, the advantage of roundabout production is obtained. The first and second reasons are related to time preference, the third to the marginal productivity of capital. Schumpeter's criticism was that, first, capital *qua* capital does not yield interest; a positive rate of interest requires a dynamic condition. Second, interest does not flow from capital stock as a perpetual source of income, but rather from credit creation. In short, interest is a dynamic and monetary phenomenon, although economic statics does not accept this function of money.

The zero-interest-rate theory

How is Schumpeter's zero-interest-rate theory to be evaluated? Gottfried Haberler thinks that it is necessary to distinguish between the extreme view and the moderate view in interpreting this theory (Haberler 1951a, 72). The extreme view is that interest does not exist in a static economy, whereas the moderate view admits a positive interest in a static economy but a qualitatively distinct interest in a dynamic economy.

Two conditions lead to a zero interest. First, time preference does not exist in the sense that future goods are not less evaluated than present goods. Second, the marginal productivity of capital is zero in the sense that the abstinence of present goods does not yield larger future goods. In other words, when both the marginal rate of substitution in consumption and the marginal rate of transformation in production between present goods and future goods equal zero, the rate of interest is zero and the economy is stationary. Schumpeter maintained that in a static state or circular flow these two conditions must hold (1926a, 43–49). As Samuelson says, Schumpeter was wrong on this point as he thought that these premises leading to a zero interest rate were the result of circular flow (Samuelson 1982, 21).[11]

In conclusion, let us suppose that when there is no technical innovation and no time preference, and if investment is a function of a positive rate of interest, capital investment will continue to a point where the marginal productivity of capital is zero. Then, in a subsequent stationary world a zero interest rate will hold. This was the case for Schumpeter; this case is logically possible but not inevitable, as Samuelson says. For because of technological conditions, it is possible that the marginal productivity of capital will be zero given an infinite amount of capital. Furthermore, when a time preference exists, capital investment will continue to a point where a rate of interest is equal to a positive rate of time preference, provided investment is a function of the difference between the rate of interest and the rate of time preference. In a stationary state, the rate of interest will be equal to the rate of time preference. Insofar as a lifetime is limited, a time preference will always exist.

Thus we are led to the moderate view that admits a positive rate of interest corresponding to the positive time preference and the positive marginal productivity of capital in a stationary state as well as in a period of steady growth where an economy expands only in scale. In either view, Schumpeter's point is that profits created by entrepreneurial innovation are a source of dynamic interest that is distinct from a static phenomenon. The difference between the extreme and moderate views is not essential because it depends on whether one adopts a model of the static state in the narrow or wider sense. The weight of his argument is that in economic development dynamic interest will emerge, which is categorically different from static interest based on the marginal productivity under constant technology and on the time preference, rather than that there is a zero rate of interest in a static economy.

Evaluation of the quantity theory of money

What is the place of monetary theory in pure economics? The central component of pure economics is exchange. Exchange in markets actually takes the form of indirect exchange, that is, an exchange between money and goods. Money always intervenes in acts of exchange between goods; this is the function of money as a medium of exchange. Money also functions as a measure of account. A price system that is created by a network of exchange actually depends on money's measure of account.

Preconceptions on the theory of money

While maintaining that a satisfactory theory of money did not then exist, Schumpeter wrote about the quantity theory of money:

It builds the only component of the theory of money, which is – true or untrue – quite important. No one has been able to disprove this theory. Although the grounds for and against it have been accumulating, no one has yet succeeded in solving the problems it has raised and, in particular, in constructing a new theory that could replace it ... No one is satisfied with the present situation, but no one knows how to improve it, and a discussion whose defects everyone has seen all along drags on endlessly. (1908, 285)

Thus Schumpeter briefly discussed the quantity theory in *Wesen* but made no serious attempt to deal with it.

Schumpeter had two preconceptions about the theory of money. First, he was aware that the theory of money should be treated as an integral part of value and price theory. According to him, however, the customary approach treated the theory of money as separate from a body of theory dealing with the real side of an economy and aimed to look at the workings of the real economy behind the veil of money that covered economic phenomena. Thus the conventional approach represented by the quantity theory of money regarded money as merely an expedient for exchange. But Schumpeter believed:

What is important is not mere *end-and-means rationality* but the *indispensability* of money to the market mechanism, and this is the key to understanding the theory of money ... This important point, which is also very interesting epistemologically and places the theory of money in a uniquely correct relation to price theory, is always missing to my knowledge. (1908, 282)

In other words, he searched for an "anchor that fastens the theory of money to price theory" (1908, 281). John Maynard Keynes, who had been working in the same vein, established the liquidity preference theory in his *General Theory* and finally proved to be the winner in this treasure hunt. But the development of monetary theory was not limited to Keynes's approach; Schumpeter went in a different direction.

Second, Schumpeter criticized the conventional approach to money because proponents were absorbed in the technical exposition of the physical materials of money, such as gold and silver, and in historical explanations of the development of money in human history in order to conceal the poverty of their theoretical content. According to him, these explanations had nothing to do with theory and offered no value at all, apart from contributing to cultural history. Specifically, he sneered at descriptions of the materials of money, saying that one could similarly argue in economic theory about the nature of foods and their merits and demerits. As for a common argument about the importance of precious metals as the material of money, he declared: "I don't hear or read about it without an acute feeling of humiliation" (1908, 283).

I mention these two points because they are of interest in light of the later development of Schumpeter's thought. Regarding the first point, the relationship between Schumpeter and the quantity theory of money is significant. He criticized conventional theories for their veiled view of money. It should be noted that the theory of money he wanted to describe as a component of pure economics was already oriented to overcome the veiled view of money. The need to reject the veil of money did not occur to him until he launched into a theory of economic development. The second point is concerned with the problem of the autonomy of pure economics. In *Wesen* Schumpeter limited himself to the viewpoint of pure economics, but after confirming the basis of economics he began to observe broader social phenomena. This was true of the theory of money, too. Although he had almost completed his theory of money by the 1930s, he gave up the idea of publishing it. His posthumous book, *Das Wesen des Geldes* (1970), not only includes a pure economic analysis of money but also deals with monetary phenomena against a historical, political, institutional, and sociological background.

A deviation from the quantity theory

As a component of pure economics, Schumpeter's monetary theory was described in the first chapter of *Entwicklung* in the discussion of a circular flow; this description was then developed in a long article entitled "Das Sozialprodukt und die Rechenpfennige. Glossen und Beiträge zur Geldtheorie von heute" (1917–18). His theory had three essential elements.

First, the introduction of money into a circular flow that is the object of pure economics makes possible a sort of social accounting framework. In real terms, an economy is the exchange of services of factors of production (X) and consumer goods (Y) taking place between firms and households. On the basis of his theory of interest, Schumpeter regarded X as the services of labor and land. Y represented the social product. The introduction of money split this exchange into two: first, in the market of factor services, households offer factor services (X) to firms in exchange for money (X'). Second, in the market of consumer goods, firms offer consumer goods (Y) in exchange for money (Y'). Since households spend all earned income on consumer goods, X' is equal to Y'. As the imputation theory maintains, the value of factor services X is the imputed value of consumer goods Y. By the introduction of money, we find not only that the direct exchange of X and Y is split into the exchange of X and X' and of Y and Y', but also that the two exchanges are equal in monetary terms. With regard to the circulation of money, Schumpeter arrived at the following proposition: "Given stationary equilibrium, the money value of all consumer goods should equal the money value of all producer goods [factor services], and both identically equal the sum of all money incomes" ([1917–18] 1956, 153). In symbolic terms this statement means that the value of Y is equal to the value of X and that they are both equal to X'. In our contemporary terminology this is the proposition of the equality of the three aspects of national income: production, distribution and expenditure.

Arthur Marget argues that Schumpeter's theory of the economic process in terms of money flow constitutes his central contribution to monetary theory (Marget 1951, 63). Indeed, this scheme gives a basic perspective that makes possible both theoretical analysis and quantitative measurement of a total economy. But Schumpeter's contribution went further than this.

Second, on the basis of the correspondence between money flow and real flow Schumpeter adopted Friedrich Bendixen's view that money is a "claim ticket to goods." Thus the value of money or the purchasing power of money is the quantity of goods that money can dispose of or control. According to Schumpeter's metaphor, money is an entrance ticket to a theater and the total goods are represented by the space inside. The purchasing power of money, then, is the space each audience can occupy in the theater. The number of tickets is crucial to the size of the purchasing power. This corresponds with the fundamental idea of the quantity theory of money. The claim theory of money seems self-evident, but it is meaningful because there was still a view that based purchasing power on the material value of money.

Corresponding with the general purchasing power of money is the concept of general price level. This concept must be devised to reflect only monetary influences. But since the general price index ordinarily reflects the influences of nonmonetary factors or of individual prices, it is not useful as a measure of purchasing power. Schumpeter then attempted to argue that the purchasing power of money was determined by the following scheme. His "fundamental equation of monetary theory" ([1917–18] 1956, 182) is written as:

$$E = M \cdot U = p_1 m_1 + p_2 m_2 + \ldots + p_n m_n.$$

E is the sum of incomes in an economy, M is the quantity of money in circulation, U is the velocity of money, p_i $(i = 1, 2, \ldots, n)$ is the price of consumer goods i, and m_i $(i = 1, 2, \ldots, n)$ is its quantity. The equation differs from the ordinary version of the quantity theory in that the right side is not the product of the general price level and total real income but the sum of the products of individual prices and quantities, and this difference involves an important claim. Thus Schumpeter argued:

In the absence of simultaneous or prior changes in $M \cdot U$, therefore, movements of all prices in the same direction must be offset by corresponding changes in the quantities of commodities, and *vice versa*. General price changes which are not offset in this way can originate only from a monetary impulse and never from the commodity side. The direct influence of the commodity side always results in a shift in the relation of prices to each other; uniform price movements which do not affect this relation can have as their cause only the purely external play of the accounting mechanism of the economy. ([1917–18] 1956, 187)

Here he accepted the quantity theory of money in that insofar as all prices change uniformly, general purchasing power depends on the quantity of money. But this does not mean that Schumpeter supported the quantity theory. Instead, he remarked: "it must be emphasized that it is in no way my purpose to defend the quantity theory as such" ([1917–18] 1956, 163).

Third, money in the preceding scheme is limited in nature; it is part of total money. According to Schumpeter, total money is distributed over three spheres: the sphere of circulation, the sphere of hoards and reserves, and the sphere of capital. Money in the sphere of capital refers to money in the markets of assets such as real estate, mortgage, and stock. Money circulation corresponding to commodity circulation is carried out by money in the sphere of circulation, where it functions only as a medium of exchange.

Money in a circular flow has the nature not only of a claim ticket but also of a certificate of productive services. In other words, money is not only a ticket for buying commodities in the future but also a certificate of having rendered productive services in the past. As a result, distribution income and expenditure income are in balance at certain fixed prices in a circular flow. However, newly created bank credit is a claim ticket for commodities but not a certificate of past services. Consequently, when new credit is directed to demand productive services, the prices of these services will rise, the income of those offering the services will rise, and consumer prices will rise by an increase in expenditures. Forced saving caused by price increases acts as a lever to achieve a shift in the productive services required by economic development. Thus credit creation gives "a scope to the *capitalistic function of* money, as opposed to its exchange-economy function" ([1917–18] 1956, 206). This can be called a development function of money. For Schumpeter, an inquiry into monetary theory, together with a discussion of interest theory, opened the way to dynamic theory.

It should be emphasized that Schumpeter's fundamental equation does not mean the same thing as the quantity theory. The quantity theory asserts a causal relationship with the quantity of money as the *explanans* and the general price level as the *explanandum*. He did not believe that an increase in the quantity of money occurs uniformly with respect to all economic agents and that prices increase uniformly with respect to all commodities so that a price increase remains nominal. He also insisted that it could not be assumed that the velocity remained constant.

In an exposition of the quantity theory of money, Milton Friedman assumes that in a stationary economy when a helicopter scatters additional money in the air, everyone holds twice as much money as before (Friedman 1969, 4–5). Schumpeter criticized this sort of assumption. Indeed, if money doubled suddenly in a given place and every transaction involved twice as much money, all prices would double. But, he said:

Increases in the quantity of money never occur uniformly for all people ... Prices never rise uniformly – neither the prices for consumer goods relative to each other nor the prices of consumer goods relative to those of the means of production. Thereby the price rise ceases to be merely nominal. It means a real shift of wealth on the market for consumer goods and a real shift of power on the market for the means of production, and it affects the quantities of commodities and the whole productive process. ([1917–18] 1956, 191)

Instead of the aggregative expression of the quantity theory $MV = PY$, Schumpeter gave the right side of the equation as the sum total of the values of each product $p_i m_i$ because he acknowledged the influence of money on the microeconomic structure of an economy. Hence "it is decisive for these effects where, in the body economic, the increase of money appears" ([1917–18] 1956, 192). In short, Schumpeter was not content with the thinking behind the quantity theory even in the static system; rather, he assumed that the monetary impact would cause changes in the real economy. An inquiry into the total process of the monetary impact, he said, was the task of a theory of economic development and fluctuation.

Acceptance and refutation

Several years after the publication of *Wesen*, the leading economics journals worldwide published book reviews by more than a dozen scholars, which amounted to a volume exceeding 150 pages. At that time *Wesen* was not well received except in countries where the mathematical approach in economics had more or less taken root.[12] While most reviews in the non-German journals were brief, taking up only a few pages, the German journals contained serious, generally negative appraisals extending to twenty or thirty pages. These responses, although mostly critical, seem to reflect the extent to which the first book of the young, unknown scholar had attracted academic attention.

The German atmosphere

The central themes of *Wesen* were the formulation of methodological instrumentalism and the limitation of pure economics to the static general equilibrium system and were discussed in general terms (apart from the German context), although they challenged the most generally accepted views. Thus, John Bates Clark in the United States, from the standpoint of a third party, gave a favorable evaluation of Schumpeter's book:

This book is both critical and constructive, and in each direction it contributes distinctly to the progress of economic science. One of its purposes is to indicate the weak points in current theories, and to this extent it is controversial; but it aims to reduce the amount of controversy in progress rather than to increase it, and the candor with which it treats other men's work gives ground for hoping that this end may be attained. The work holds aloof from entangling controversies as to method and uses whatever method is best adapted to the purpose at any time in view. (Clark 1909, 721)

But *Wesen* was in fact addressed to German and Austrian economists in the context of the *Methodenstreit*, and although it took neither side of the dispute, it was openly critical of the foundation of the Austrian School. Therefore it evoked critiques from both theoretical and nontheoretical economists in Germany and Austria.

Friedrich von Wieser, as we have seen, praised Schumpeter for the way in which *Wesen* achieved the task of introducing the main substance of neoclassical economic theory to German scholars, but he criticized Schumpeter for applying the natural scientific method to economics in another task inquiring into the nature of theoretical economics. Although Wieser was mentioned in *Wesen* as one of the authors (besides Walras) closest to Schumpeter, he confirmed that Schumpeter was in accord only with the outcome of the Austrian School but denied its psychological method. Those who agreed with its outcome, he asserted, must accept its method because outcome and method were inseparable; Schumpeter's inappropriate application of the natural scientific method to economics violated that discipline. Thus he concluded that: "I believe that Schumpeter would have portrayed the essence of theoretical economics more perfectly and more simply if he had not wanted to characterize its nature by his method" (Wieser 1911, 416).

It is interesting to consider the book reviews of two contrasting scholars, Othmar Spann and Hans Mayer, who would be appointed professors at the University of Vienna after World War I.[13] Spann, a unique proponent of universalism, found in *Wesen* a pertinent instance of criticism from the same viewpoint that he had just expressed in his long article, "Der logische Aufbau der Nationalökonomie und ihr Verhältniss zu Psychologie und zu Naturwissenschaften" (Spann 1908); his review of *Wesen* was entitled "Die mechanisch-mathematische Analogie in der Volkswirtschaftslehre" (Spann 1910). Spann believed that economic phenomena essentially consisted of the relationship of human behavior, which was characterized by the system of means to the achievement of economic ends. He called this relationship the functional character of economic phenomena, in contrast to the material character. According to him, true social scientific concepts must be functional ones; material concepts that were, for example, psychological, physical, and biological had nothing to do with economic thought. As a result, economics could not be based on psychology, on the one hand (in this regard, Spann differed from the Austrian School), and on mechanics, biology, and other natural sciences, on the other.

As we know, Schumpeter rejected the attempt to base economics on other disciplines and advocated the autonomy of economics. But Spann criticized *Wesen*'s central idea that the object of pure economics was the relationship among the quantities of goods and could be rigorously analyzed by a mathematical method. For Spann, the idea of a general economic equilibrium, expressed by a system of quantities of goods on the basis of the mechanical analogy, did not provide a rigorous definition of economic phenomena. Phenomena relating to the quantities of goods, he contended, are only incidental to human behavior and, so to speak, their shadowgraphs; in other words, quantities of goods do not constitute automatically and directly any interdependent relationship independently of a whole complex structure of human behavior. Goods become economic phenomena only if they are functionally (as a means to economic ends) integrated into the system of human behavior. Spann argued that applying a mathematical method to the quantity dimension of economics was a fruitless game.

Spann's critique represented the most stereotypical response to neoclassical economics among German economists; based on the neo-Kantian dichotomy between social science and natural science, he claimed that different objects in different sciences should require epistemologically different methods. With regard to methodology, Spann did not grasp Schumpeter's basic position as instrumentalism but merely considered his apparent methodological tolerance to be terrible nihilism and relativism; he also scoffed at Schumpeter's attempt to reconcile theory to history as philosophical quixotism.

Mayer was a follower of the Austrian School, and his critique of *Wesen* basically coincided with Wieser's (Mayer 1911). He maintained that the general equilibrium system did not concern anything found in reality; it was neither an assumption nor a hypothesis but merely a fiction. According to Mayer, it was a fundamental error for Schumpeter to build economic theory on the basis of a fiction. In order to use the concept of subjective value, he argued, one must give it empirical substance; this was only possible by the method of psychological analysis, which Schumpeter evaded.

A more unfriendly comment came from Ludwig Pohle, a professor at Frankfurt. In his banal criticism of *Wesen*, Pohle wrote that it was totally unrealistic and devoid of substance: "The mill rattles very noisily, but produces only a little flour" (Pohle 1909, 337). He found the greatest defect of Schumpeter's work in his confinement of economics to the analysis of static equilibrium; Pohle contended that the proper goal of economics was not to study the static situation, which did not exist, but the dynamic situation in the real world, that is, economic development, changes in social organizations, and business cycles. He concluded: "In sum, we can view Schumpeter's book only as a failure. It will retard rather than promote the progress of theoretical inquiry" (Pohle 1909, 358). It is interesting that the editor of *Zeitschrift für Sozialwissenschaft*, in which Pohle's article was published, added a footnote at the end of his article saying that the editor did not fully share Pohle's evaluation of Schumpeter's work because his critique would also apply to the Austrian School and mathematical economics.

Schmoller's appraisal of Schumpeter

In view of the state of economics of Germany at that time, perhaps the most authoritative appraisal of *Wesen* was that of Gustav von Schmoller. In his long article, "Volkswirtschaft, Volkswirtschaftslehre und -methode" in *Handwörterbuch der Staatswissenschaften*, Schmoller discussed Schumpeter's work in relation to contemporary German economics (Schmoller 1911). It is worthwhile quoting his sometimes ironical comment:

Lately a young, very fine, and almost too brilliant mind, Joseph Schumpeter, has tried to grasp "the nature of theoretical economics" by the abstract, purely natural scientific method. His substantive thought is much the same as that of his masters, mainly Walras and Wieser. But he basically rejects all psychological foundations as suspicious and permeated with a metaphysical flavor. He also does not want to know anything about causal inquiry but only the functional relations of economic quantities. He rises to the height of abstract thought when he says that "the substance of economy is indifferent to economics." He plans, so to speak, a bargain sale of many chapters of our discipline; he wants to sell them off to neighboring disciplines; man and nature, labor and capital, population, economic organizations, power, and all questions of social policy do not belong to pure theory. Realistic and historical economics is taught by this young man half politely and half obtrusively; he says that it is about the commonplace and generally not scientific. In any case, the book is extraordinarily attractive and instructive. I have never read anything more objective in our discipline. The book admits that the classical system of economics lies in ruins; hence new methods should be sought from every quarter. The author is indeed right in that most of the modern methodological controversies were futile. But it is doubtful whether he has found a philosopher's stone by limiting himself to the narrowest area. His pure theory has only the task of comprehending the equilibrium state of economic quantities in an interdependent condition in markets that are not subject to significant change. He does not want to study men and behavior but the value relations of goods; he overlooks the fact that goods and the value of goods are interrelated only through men, their behavior, and their value judgments. Every few pages he must reuse the psychology that he has done away with. Of his masters, Walras and Wieser, the latter, who is still alive, rejects on principle Schumpeter's positions. The neo-Kantians in the Austrian School, like Gottl, will do the same because they abhor excessively the natural scientific method. A malicious critic would ask Schumpeter if he wanted to apply in his book *reductio ad absurdum* to the natural scientific method of economics. On the contrary, I would like to say that he shows a partial justification of this method for certain narrow problems but at the same time he reveals a dark side of this procedure: a large number of scholars and readers either do not understand such an inquiry at all, or, insofar as they are concerned with it, they reduce their ability to judge political and social problems. Those readers who agree with him regard abstract theses as directly applicable to reality; they forget that these are theses of an economy on other planet. This is wrong, because all the practical progress in the life of a state, society, and economy today basically depends on the increasing ability of the groups of people who study at universities and read books on economic, social, and political questions. (Schmoller 1911, 449–50)

As the reviews demonstrate, Schumpeter did not win the highest or universal praise when he made his debut as the author of *Wesen*. The book was not successful, especially among the group of German economists it addressed. Of course, one cannot deny that, as Oskar Morgenstern recollected (see page 92), *Wesen* was accepted enthusiastically by the younger generation of economists in Vienna who held the future of theoretical economics in their hands. But the first half of the twentieth century saw a revival of historicism, idealism, and holism – versus empiricism and positivism – in the social sciences in Germany. During this trend Spann could remark that Schumpeter's work was a reversion to unsophisticated, radical empiricism and positivism (Spann 1910, 787). Schumpeter had to swim against the stream.

Just at that time, Schumpeter contributed a long survey article, "Die neuere Wirtschaftstheorie in den Vereinigten Staaten" (1910a), to the journal edited by Schmoller. This article was a detailed examination of the state of economic theory in relation to various branches of neoclassical economics in the United States. Schumpeter referred to Irving Fisher, J. B. Clark, Frank

Taussig, Frank Fetter, and others and praised their theoretical achievements. Schmoller, who as the editor might have been embarrassed by the article, added a footnote to the first page saying that although a survey of American economic literature by a distinguished scholar like Schumpeter was valuable, whether or not his evaluation of American neoclassical economics was too favorable must be left to the judgment of the future generation.

CHAPTER 7

The theory of economic development as a midpoint

In *Theorie der wirtschaftlichen Entwicklung* (1912) Schumpeter wrote that "the armor of methodological commentaries I renounce completely" (1934, 4) and referred the reader to his previous book, *Wesen*, for methodology. Nevertheless, this chapter will examine not only the substance of his dynamic theory but also its methodological nature.

The nature and substance of *Theorie der wirtschaftlichen Entwicklung*

Schumpeter began to study economic crises in 1905, but he soon realized that the problems of economic crises were related to the total problems of capitalist economic development and therefore to the entire field of economic theory (1912, viii). As an introduction to *Entwicklung*, it is useful to consider his article on "Über das Wesen der Wirtschaftskrisen" (1910b), written just before the publication of *Entwicklung*. This essay is a summary of well-developed thought claiming nine propositions:[1]

1. Economic phenomena are classified into two distinct categories: static phenomena and dynamic phenomena.
2. Dynamic phenomena relate to purely economic development, the changes in an economy that originate from within the economy and are generated by the creation of new combinations (innovations) by entrepreneurs with uncommon talents and energy.
3. Economic development is essentially the disturbance of a static economic equilibrium.
4. This disturbance evokes reactions that eventually lead the economy to a new equilibrium.
5. The process toward equilibrium terminates the development phenomena and brings about the liquidation and reconstruction of the value and price system of the economy.
6. As a result, there are alternating booms and depressions.

7. In the process toward equilibrium an economic crisis can easily, though not necessarily, take place.
8. Even a static economy is exposed to accidental disturbances leading to economic crises.
9. Disturbances are not uniform phenomena, nor are they characterized by common features.

The 1910 article, though focusing on economic crises, is based on the dichotomy between statics and dynamics and contains the basic idea that economic crises are a part of the business cycle and are necessarily caused by economic development. For Schumpeter, the goal of dynamic theory was an autonomous theory that would explain endogenously the dynamic mechanism of a capitalist economy in a similar way to which the static theory endogenously explains the working of a static economy. In his view, economic problems other than value and distribution in static equilibrium – such as capital formation, capital interest, entrepreneurial profit, and crises – had been given only historical description or treated theoretically in a wrong way. Whereas in *Wesen* Schumpeter had called these issues "economic problems outside of our theoretical system" (1908, 614), it was now the task of dynamic theory to incorporate them into economic theory.

The endogenous explanation of dynamic phenomena

It is illuminating to describe metaphorically what is meant by the endogenous explanation of dynamic phenomena. Suppose that a pendulum is swinging back and forth in the air. Over time, it will cease to swing. The concept of economic equilibrium, which was an adaptation of a physical phenomenon, corresponds to the pendulum at rest; it is the state where the demand and supply of goods and services are in equilibrium and exchange no longer takes place. This framework is indeed useful in clarifying the equilibrating mechanism inherent in an economy, but the idea of equilibrium in a state of rest is hard to apply to an economy. For this reason, Schumpeter, in the first chapter of *Entwicklung*, devised the concept of circular flow, in which an economy repeats itself on the same scale year in and year out by introducing time into the concept of equilibrium. This is a stationary process to which the static equilibrium theory is applicable.[2]

If force is added to the stationary pendulum, it begins to move again. To Schumpeter, this was not a dynamic phenomenon but passive adaptation to a change in exogenously given conditions. In the case of an economy, the passive adaptation is treated in one of two ways. First, if social, political, and cultural circumstances change, an economy will respond to them and change accordingly. Schumpeter called an approach dealing with such changes a "milieu theory" (1912, 469), which should fall into the category of static theory. Second, the common view of classical economics, which was then represented by the distinction between statics and dynamics in John Bates Clark, identified five factors causing dynamics: the increase of population, the increase of capital, progress in the method of production, progress in the method of economic organization, and the development of wants (Clark 1907). These changes, Schumpeter believed, do not bring about qualitatively new phenomena but merely indicate a response to changes in data. He called an approach concerning these changes a "theory of organic growth" (1912, 474) and regarded it also as a part of the static theory.

Of Clark's five factors, progress in the method of production and progress in economic organization appear among Schumpeter's criteria for innovation. According to Schumpeter, however, these factors do not work automatically but only through the hand of an entrepreneur. He found that the cause of changes in techniques and organization involved more than mere disturbances and arrived at the idea of a dynamic theory by emphasizing the agents of these changes.

Thus, suppose that the stationary pendulum suddenly begins to swing by itself. Metaphorically this corresponds to Schumpeter's dynamic phenomenon, in which changes emerge from within an economy. He called the phenomena resulting from the creative activities of entrepreneurs "development of economy from within" (1912, 471). In this example, a mechanical analogy no longer applies. In his preface to the English edition of *Entwicklung*, Schumpeter suggested that in view of the history of the terms "static" and "dynamic" in economics, one should speak of a zoological analogy instead of a mechanical analogy, for these terms were introduced into economics by John Stuart Mill, who took them from Auguste Comte; Comte, in turn, borrowed from the zoologist Henri de Blainville (1934, xi).[3] Schumpeter meant that if a study of the organism of a dog is comparable to statics, research on how dogs have come to exist at all in terms of concepts such as selection, mutation, or evolution would be analogous to dynamics (1939, 1, 36–37).

Economic development, in the above sense, is a unique process of evolution that has emerged from within the economic system and requires a unique theoretical apparatus. Looking back over his *Entwicklung* of a quarter of a century earlier, Schumpeter said that "I was trying to construct a theoretical model of the process of economic change in time, or perhaps more clearly, to answer the question how the economic system generates the force which incessantly transforms it" (1937, 1–2).

Three elements in economic development

In Schumpeter's theory of economic development, three key words concern economic development. The first is *innovation*, the cause of economic development. Innovation covers the introduction of a new product or a new method of production, the opening of a new market, the acquisition of a new source of supply, and the reorganization of an existing industry. With the introduction of these new elements into an economy, the traditional channels of the economy have to be changed. Innovation destroys old things and creates new ones and is thus called creative destruction.

The second key word is *entrepreneur*, the subject of economic development or the agent of innovation. Schumpeter's entrepreneur is not a business manager himself. In contrast to a manager, who depends on existing goods and existing methods of production, the entrepreneur carries out new and creative projects. When one attempts to initiate new things, he is confronted with various kinds of risk, resistance, and hesitation. Those who are able to prevail are scarce, for innovation requires foresight and originality, resolution and action. If one succeeds in introducing a change, he can get entrepreneurial profits.

The third element is *bank credit*, the means by which the entrepreneur accomplishes innovation. If one wants to undertake innovative activities, one must have control over productive resources. When an economy is in a static state with full employment, the utilization of productive resources for new activities requires the forced withdrawal of the resources from existing uses. The entrepreneur acquires new credit from capitalists or banks and by means of the newly created purchasing power, pays higher prices than before for the needed resources. He is typically a debtor and repays what he owes out of entrepreneurial profits.

As the implementation of new combinations – defined by innovation (cause), entrepreneur (subject), and bank credit (means) – proceeds, a series of changes including those in the business cycle will occur in the economic process; in its totality such transformation is called *economic development*. Economic development presupposes capitalism as an institution. Although capitalism is ordinarily defined in terms of private ownership and profit incentives through market mechanisms, Schumpeter stipulated bank credit as essential to the functioning of capitalism (1939, 1, 223). He called a society with private ownership and the profit incentive a commercial society (1943, 113). In capitalism, by contrast, entrepreneurs demanding finance and capitalists supplying finance are linked through innovation, and profit and interest are related for the same reason. Schumpeter claimed that interest does not exist in a static state; rather, the source of interest is found in economic development and profit. On the other hand, innovations and entrepreneurs are not confined to capitalist societies, because insofar as economic leadership exists, even a tribal society or a socialist society can have an entrepreneurial function.

In *Entwicklung* Schumpeter wanted to present not a historical description but a theoretical explanation of economic development. In the economics of the early twentieth century, economic development meant the historical process of an economy, and his book was misunderstood as a work in economic history. In the preface to the second German edition, Schumpeter noted that the title of *Entwicklung* was misleading. In order to eliminate any confusion, he subtitled the second edition "An Inquiry into Profits, Capital, Credit, Interest, and the Business Cycle," omitted chapter 7, which included important sociological ideas, and rewrote chapters 2 and 6. His theory of economic development, like that of static pure economics, aimed at providing a general, idealistic picture, not a description of specific facts (1912, 488).

This chapter will examine first the concept of the entrepreneur as it constitutes the ultimate element of economic development from within. After the publication of *Entwicklung*, Schumpeter's efforts at elaboration were directed to theories of business cycles and money. The results of his long, ardous labors were *Business Cycles* (1939) and *Das Wesen des Geldes* (posthumous publication, 1970).

Hypotheses non fingo

It is little known that in the title page of the first edition of *Entwicklung*, Schumpeter quoted the Latin phrase "Hypotheses non fingo," because he eliminated it in the second edition. This famous maxim of Isaac Newton was introduced in the Scholium Generale of the second edition of *Philosophiae Naturalis Principia Mathematica* (Newton 1713). In 1729, after Newton's death, it was translated into English as "I frame no hypotheses," which prevailed for more than two hundred years. In 1956, however, Alexandre Koyré, the French Newtonian scholar, argued that the phrase should be read as "I feign no hypotheses" (Koyré 1956). Because Newton, in fact, set forth several hypotheses and one cannot, in principle, construct a theory without hypotheses, the translation "I frame no hypotheses" does not make sense. Koyré asserted that what Newton meant by the passage was that he did not make use of fictions; in other words, he did not use false propositions as premises or explanations.

This phrase, one of the most quoted of Newton's writings, first appeared (after several versions of the draft) in the following context: "Indeed, I have not yet been able to deduce the reason of these properties of gravity from phenomena, & I do not feign hypotheses. For whatever is not deduced from phenomena is to be called hypothesis; and Hypotheses of this kind, whether

Metaphysical or Physical or of Occult Qualities or Mechanical, have no place in experimental Philosophy" (Newton [1713] 1971, 241–42). When Newton formulated the law of gravity, he thought that the propositions had to be deduced from phenomena and generalized by induction. To the criticism that he had not shown the cause of gravitation, he replied that he had not feigned unprovable hypotheses that were false.

It is unclear why Schumpeter omitted Newton's passage from the second edition of *Entwicklung*. He might have been embarrassed by his youthful enthusiasm after the publication of the first edition. Or he might have realized that the original meaning was different from the meaning he wanted to convey. There might have been other reasons or perhaps no serious reasons. Apart from probing his subjective rationale, there is every reason to reconsider Schumpeter's position regarding Newton's methodology.

In the *History of Economic Analysis* Schumpeter wrote:

Isaac Newton was a theorist if he was anything. Nevertheless, he displayed a marked hostility toward theory and especially toward [the] framing of causal hypotheses. What he really meant was not theory or [a] hypothesis of our second kind [theoretical hypothesis] but just inadequately substantiated speculation. Perhaps there was something else in this hostility, namely the aversion of the truly scientific mind to the use of the word "cause" that carries a metaphysical flavor. Newton's example may also be appealed to in order to illustrate the truth that dislike of the use of metaphysical concepts in the realm of empirical science does not at all imply any dislike of metaphysics itself. (1954a, 20)[4]

Here Schumpeter argues that economics does not consist in framing "unfounded, speculative hypotheses" (1954a, 19). This argument is self-evident in the sense that the whole structure of economics is neither metaphysical nor ideological, but the nature of individual hypotheses in the structure is subject to different interpretations. In *Wesen*, Schumpeter, responding to a rebuke that pure economics rested on "unprovable hypotheses" (1908, 45), argued, from the standpoint of thought economy and instrumentalism, that hypotheses were indeed arbitrary and required no factual justification, although their usefulness was in matching their results to facts. "We try," he wrote, "to claim as little as possible in hypotheses, and even these little claims are used only as a means of description and never presented as recognition. These two points distinguish our hypotheses from a priori speculation and are, in my view, enough to silence all objections" (1908, 46).

According to Schumpeter's instrumentalism, to follow the scientific logic and procedure of verification does not necessarily mean to exclude inferences concerning all objects other than verifiable facts. He once stated: "Aversion to introducing any entities that cannot be observed or experimentally produced is part of the scientific attitude only so far as it is based on the principle of economy in description. If the hypothesis that planets are moved by angels opened the shortest way to describing their motion, there could be no objection to it on grounds of scientific rationality" ([1940] 1991, 316–17).

The propositions relating to economic development presented in *Entwicklung* had to be tested empirically. Schumpeter tried to accomplish this task through a historical and statistical inquiry in *Business Cycles*. In 1912, in anticipation of this work, he would have expressed, by referring to Newton's passage, confidence that his theory was not based on feigned hypotheses because economic development was a fact. And, keeping in mind Wieser's critique of *Wesen* regarding its use of hypotheses (see pages 117–18), Schumpeter might have wanted to show that his theory would not remain as an arbitrary hypothesis.

It is a mistake to regard Newton as a mere positivist. For him the existence of God was certain by induction from the order and beauty in nature, and this recognition had nothing to do with natural science based on scientific proof. Thus Schumpeter did not deny Newton's belief in metaphysics. But, insofar as scientific hypotheses were concerned, Newton did not accept instrumentalism. This is the biggest difference between the two men, and, objectively speaking, may be the reason for Schumpeter's omission of Newton's passage in the second edition of *Entwicklung*.

Leaders and innovation

Schumpeter's central notion of economic development was the concept of entrepreneurs, not the concept of innovation detached from the entrepreneurial personality. Those who carry out innovation are defined as entrepreneurs. Changes in technological and organizational conditions that are stimulated by innovation are, in themselves, only changes in data. Schumpeter defined entrepreneurial activity as the "fundamental phenomenon of economic development" (1926a, 110).

Did Schumpeter change his mind?

When Schumpeter was concerned with pure economics in *Wesen*, he thought that there was no need to deal with man's behavior in the static world of economy, the logic of which was described adequately by the system of the quantity of commodities. As observed in the previous methodological discussion, Schumpeter denied psychologism from the standpoint of instrumentalism and general equilibrium theory (see pages 115–17). Austrian psychologism attempted to found basic propositions of economics on psychology. Also explained in the discussion of concrete methods of neoclassical economics was the reason why Schumpeter had accepted the concepts of marginal utility and want satisfaction, although he claimed that economic theory did not need to consider human psychology, wants, and motives (see page 135). He was sharply criticized for contemplating an economics in which man did not appear. In *Entwicklung*, in contrast, men are the heroes. The contrast between *Entwicklung* and *Wesen* is obvious.

About this point a methodological note is necessary. Fritz Machlup argued that Schumpeter abandoned his earlier view that it was unnecessary and wrong for economists to deal with psychology and human motivation and introduced the concept of entrepreneurs in *Entwicklung* (Machlup 1951, 97). Haberler also believed this (Haberler 1951a, 30). However, there is some doubt as to whether Schumpeter had changed his mind. As he mentioned, because it is possible for a static theory to describe the system of the quantity of commodities without regard to human motives, it is unnecessary to investigate specific human types in a static economy (1926a, 132). In a dynamic world, however, it is essential to be concerned with behavioral patterns of the various types of man, because innovation without the personality of an entrepreneur merely changes data and does not invoke a genuine dynamic theory. It was necessary for Schumpeter to resort to assumptions about human types and motives in order to explain, by the most expeditious method, economic development that emerged from within an economic system. For this reason, the shift of his inquiry from commodities to man entailed lengthening the distance to causal factors in comparison with the static case, but this was due to the nature of the problems and objectives in question. If dynamic man is defined, static man can be conveniently defined for a comparison. Schumpeter called the former "energisch" and the latter "hedonisch" (1912, 128). These are instrumental assumptions that do not require psychological or other justification; they are heuristic means to describe and analyze visible economic behavior. Furthermore, it is important to recognize that the concept of entrepreneurs, the core of the assumptions, does not denote specific persons or classes but the function of entrepreneurship or, more generally, of leadership.

Types of behavior and motives

In *Entwicklung* the description of entrepreneurs in chapter 2 ("The Fundamental Phenomenon of Economic Development") stands out the most. Chapter 2 was completely rewritten for the second edition, and the method of description was also changed. The description in the first edition is worth considering in order to see Schumpeter's original idea.

In chapter 2 of the second edition, Schumpeter propounded the object of investigation:

Our problem is as follows. The theory of the first chapter describes economic life from the standpoint of a "circular flow," running on in channels essentially the same year after year – similar to the circulation of the blood in an animal organism. Now this circular flow and its channels do alter in time and here we abandon the analogy with the circulation of the blood. For although the latter also changes in the course of the growth and decline of the organism, yet it only does so continuously, that is by steps which one can choose smaller than any assignable quantity, however small, and always within the same framework. Economic life experiences such changes too, but it also experiences others which do not appear continuously and which change the frame-work, the traditional course itself.[5] They cannot be understood by means of any analysis of the circular flow, although they are purely economic and although their explanation is obviously among the tasks of pure theory. Now such changes and the phenomena which appear in their train are the object of our investigation. (1934, 61–62)

After defining the object of investigation, Schumpeter proceeded to explain the three elements of economic development in the following order: innova-tion, bank credit, and entrepreneurs. Thus entrepreneurs appeared last.

By contrast, the object of study in the first edition was defined in this way:

We have so far described the economic process conditioned by data; that is to say, we have made it clear how men's economic behavior appears when they pursue results in order to attain the maximum satisfaction of wants under given conditions ... Now I will present the second type of economic behavior, one that represents a new and independent factor in an economy, namely a creative form in the economic area. The adaptive "pursuit of results" is not the only possible economic behavior. For one can attempt to change existing conditions. (1912, 104)

Here the starting point was dynamic man in general. After giving an overall picture of such a dynamic human type, as compared with the static type, not only in the area of the economy but also in the areas of art, politics, science, and others, Schumpeter spotlighted the entrepreneur as the dynamic man in the economy. Then, he introduced new combinations or innovations as external forms of economic development carried out by entrepreneurs, and finally, bank credit as the means of creating new combinations.

"The Fundamental Phenomenon of Economic Development," the title of chapter 2, represents neither innovation nor bank credit, but entrepreneur. The fact that in the first edition the discovery of the entrepreneur as the dynamic agent was located first is important because it suggests the order of thought in the formulation of theory. In the second edition, the argument was reshuffled in a fashion that apparently reduces the importance of the entrepreneur. This might have been the result of the criticism that Schump-eter glorified the entrepreneurial type. In any case, this change diminishes the importance of human factors in Schumpeter's idea of economic development and therefore lessens its appeal. As a result, there has been a tendency to interpret the analysis of external forms such as technical progress as the essence of his economics. According to this interpretation, insofar as technical change takes place, economic development continues, contrary to Schumpeter's later view in *Capitalism, Socialism and Democracy*.

Then, what is the dynamic human type he described as energetic and nonhedonistic? Their essential nature lies in energetic behavior and in specific motivations.

First, regarding behavior, there are a large number of people in a society who act conventionally, and at the same time there are a relatively small number of men who try to change customary practices and introduce new things. In the first edition of *Entwicklung*, Schumpeter called the latter "Mann der Tat" (man of action) (1912, 132). Although this type of person encounters uncertainty or resistance as he attempts to change existing situations, he has enough energy and will, foresight and creativity to overcome difficulties and introduce innovations. If successful, he establishes the direction in which many people will go. Innovation leads to imitation. In this sense, the performance of the dynamic type of man is that of a leader. Leading is not working *per se* but influencing others through work. Leaders are energetic in their actions, not in their thought. They are distinctive in will, not in intelligence. They need not invent or create new possibilities; the activity of leaders consists in combining existing possibilities in a new way. In *Entwicklung* Schumpeter called innovations "new combinations" in the broader sense of rearranging existing possibilities, not in the narrow meaning of changing the combinations of productive resources.[6]

Second, with regard to the types of motivations, hedonism and nonhedonism are distinguished. Hedonism holds that under a given circumstance, pleasure and pleasure alone is the desired end; more exactly, the balance of pleasure and pain is the standard of human behavior. In fact, economics has interpreted hedonism as the principle of the rational economic man. Hedonism appears to apply not only to economic behavior but also to human behavior in general, because it is asserted as the only rational criterion. However, Schumpeter argued that although this may explain human behavior in a static state, it does not fit the behavior of entrepreneurs:

In *all* cases, the *meaning* of economic action is the satisfaction of wants in the sense that there would be no economic action if there were no wants. In the case of the circular flow, we may also think of satisfaction of wants as the normal *motive*. The latter is not true for our type [entrepreneur]. In one sense, he may indeed be called the most rational and the most egoistical of all. For, as we have seen, conscious rationality enters much more into the carrying out of new plans, which themselves have to be worked out before they can be acted upon, than into the mere running of an established business, which is largely a matter of routine ... But his conduct and his motive are "rational" in no other sense. And in *no* sense is his characteristic motivation of the hedonist kind ... If we wish to give it [a hedonistic motive] meaning, we must restrict it to such wants as are capable of being satisfied by the consumption of goods, and to that kind of satisfaction which is expected from it. Then it is no longer true that our type is acting on a wish to satisfy his wants. (1934, 91–92)

Schumpeter called the behavior of entrepreneurs irrational and nonhedonistic, regarded it at least as a fundamentally different kind of rationalism (1926a, 134), and concluded that it had three types of motivation: "the dream and the will to found a private kingdom, usually, though not necessarily, also a dynasty"; "the will to conquer: the impulse to fight, to prove oneself superior to others, to succeed for the sake, not of the fruits of success, but of success itself"; and "the joy of creating, of getting things done, or simply of exercising one's energy and ingenuity" (1934, 93).

The task of *Entwicklung* is to identify the type of entrepreneur with the endogenous element of economic development and to describe the concomitant phenomena of entrepreneurial activity as the process of economic development. One may agree with Schumpeter that the entrepreneur is endogenous in the sense that the person belongs to the economic area, but he must be interpreted as exogenous in the sense that, for Schumpeter, he represents an ultimate factor further causes of which cannot be found in an economy. The entrepreneur is, so to speak, an exogenous element within the economic system. Schumpeter's own rule of procedure in this respect was that "When we succeed in finding a definite causal relation between two phenomena, our problem is solved if the one which plays the 'causal' role is non-economic ... If, on the other hand, the causal factor is itself economic in nature, we must continue our explanatory efforts until we ground upon non-economic bottom" (1934, 4–5). Schumpeter's concept of the entrepreneur with which he explained economic development from within an economy was an exogenous factor to his system of dynamic theory, although he emphasized rhetorically the endogeneity of the concept.

According to the method of policy analysis, policy variables at the command of a government are usually treated as exogenous variables. Thus, in Keynes's *General Theory* the quantity of money is a policy variable as well as an ultimate causal factor in his macroeconomic system.[7] Although Schumpeter's entrepreneur occupies a similar strategic place in his system, it is not a policy variable but a link combining the dynamic economic theory with broader economic sociology. Each area of social life, including the economy, has its own type of leader and contributes to the formation of social classes as a whole. Schumpeter's theory of social classes is different from Marx's, but it occupies no less an important position in the understanding of society as a whole. (This issue will be discussed on pages 229–30). In another comparison with Keynes, in Schumpeter's theory money is the essential means of entrepreneurial activity, but he thought that where there is enterprise, there is always finance.

The sources of the concept of entrepreneur

Chapter 6 (page 146) touched on the dynamic elements dispersed in *Wesen*. There Schumpeter argued that interest as a component of income does not exist in the static economy but emerges from entrepreneurial profits in the dynamic economy. He explained where interest should be sought: "The interest on loans is essential; loans are used for the creation of new industries, new forms of organization, new techniques, and new commodities ... The source of interest lies in development and credit, and the source of its definition should be sought there" (1908, 417, 420). As this short quotation makes clear, innovation and credit – among the three elements of economic development – had already been recognized in *Wesen*. But the concept of entrepreneur as the carrier of innovation was not there. In *Wesen*, Schumpeter dealt with a theory that regarded entrepreneurial profits as the reward for entrepreneurial activity (which consisted of a combination of productive factors), but he regarded this theory as defective because it admitted profits and interest in the static economy.

The question arises, then, how did the concept of dynamic entrepreneurship occur to Schumpeter after *Wesen*? He never made any mention of this, but I suggest that with regard to his starting point for developing the whole idea, there are three possibilities: the dynamic concept of entrepreneurs as distinguished from the static concept of managers; the dichotomy of statics and dynamics; and the dichotomy of human type. Although Schumpeter's theory of economic development, once constructed, contains all three sets of ideas, is it possible to infer which idea came first in the process of theory construction?

Did Schumpeter derive the concept of a dynamic entrepreneur from any past writers? Naturally in economics and economic history entrepreneurs in the capacity of producers had been discussed frequently. But the descriptions of entrepreneurs in the writings of his predecessors were not necessarily accompanied by a framework of dynamic theory that would appeal to Schumpeter. In examining the history of the concept of entrepreneurs, he declared that previous writers "in fact almost accomplished what I have described as an impossible feat, namely, the exclusion of the figure of the entrepreneur completely" (1954a, 556); this he said after he had formed the idea of a dynamic theory. In *Wesen* he presented a picture of static entrepreneurs in terms of Walras's phrase: "entrepreneur faisant ni benefice ni perte" (1908, 438), but he did not define it specifically as an agent engaged in an ordinary business as distinct from the planning of a new business. When he wanted to construct dynamic theory on the basis of static theory, it might not have been immediately clear which idea should be the leverage. It is hardly conceivable that Schumpeter hit on the idea of the entrepreneur engaged in unordinary business as the leverage for constructing a dynamic theory from the traditional descriptions of the entrepreneur in economics. Even if some earlier economists had suggested the dynamic function of the entrepreneur as stressed by Schumpeter, it is not appropriate to regard them as the sources of his idea. Interestingly, he made the following comment about the utilitarian philosopher Jeremy Bentham, the object of his contempt and antipathy: "Still more clearly the nature and importance of entrepreneurship were perceived by Jeremy Bentham. It is a curious fact (curious, that is, considering the tremendous influence that Bentham exerted in other respects) that his views on this subject – which were not fully given to the public until the posthumous publication of his collected works – remained almost unnoticed by professional economists" ([1949d] 1951c, 249).[8]

In view of the fact that the dichotomy of statics and dynamics had been explicitly introduced into economics by John Stuart Mill, did Schumpeter derive the idea from this stream of thought? Schumpeter paid attention to a zoological analogy along the lines of Blainville, Comte, and Mill concerning the statics–dynamics dichotomy. As seen in his criticism of John Bates Clark, who had understood changes in the five types of data as the causes of dynamics, it is important to realize what is perceived as the core factor relevant to a zoological analogy in place of changes in data. Schumpeter's idea that the concept of entrepreneur would fit a zoological analogy did not emerge from the context of the statics–dynamics dichotomy alone.

The dichotomy of the human type as static man and dynamic man, or as follower and leader, is a concept not of economics but of sociology. My reasoning is that this dichotomy was first adopted by Schumpeter and then interpreted as the foundation of the statics–dynamics dichotomy, which was generally applicable to each area of social life; finally, the dichotomy of entrepreneurs and mere producers in the economic area was established as a special case. Only when the general counter-concepts of the human type occurred to Schumpeter did they prove to be the key to constructing a theory of economic development; they were combined with the idea of the statics–dynamics dichotomy in social life and extended to the concept of entrepreneur.

In those days, several thinkers were discussing the sociology of leadership; the closest to Schumpeter was his teacher Friedrich von Wieser, who advocated the "law of the small number"; that is, in every social group there are a small number of people who function as the leaders of others. In his *Recht und Macht* (1910), *Theorie der gesellschaftlichen Wirtschaft* (1914), and *Das Gesetz der Macht* (1926), Wieser distinguished between leaders and the masses and regarded success in the various areas of social life as the source of leaders' power. Erich Streissler (1982, 1986) and Warren Samuels (1983) are correct in pointing out that Wieser influenced Schumpeter with regard to the idea of leaders.

Viewed in a broader perspective, Schumpeter's dichotomy of the human type reflected the philosophical thought of his age. In the *History of Economic Analysis* he described the background to the period 1870–1914 and referred to the current of thought that was "contemptuously hostile to bourgeois civilization" (1954a, 774). It ran against the bourgeoisie's cult of utilitarianism and the liberal belief in rationality and progress and was called anti-democratic and anti-intellectualist. Schumpeter treated Friedrich Nietzsche, Henri Bergson, and Georges Sorel as the representatives of the current thought. Nietzsche's superman, Bergson's *élan vital*, Pareto's circulation of elites, Tarde's imitation, Weber's charisma, and Ortega's life philosophy were all variants of the human type of that age. Some investigations have been devoted to the influence of these ideas on Schumpeter's, or at least, to their similarity with his ideas; the general findings sound reasonable unless they restrict the source of Schumpeter's ideas to any specific thought within the current.[9]

Despite such influences and similarities, Schumpeter's originality is not lost. It lies in the application of the sociological dichotomy of the human type to the economic dichotomy of statics and dynamics in order to derive the distinction between entrepreneurs and mere managers and the solution of interdependence among the three possibilities. In other words, he presented a new combination of the three sets of concepts.

Is a leader an exemplar?

In analyzing Schumpeter's concept of entrepreneurs, let us take a step forward by focusing on the question of whether it is a functional concept or a value concept. The title of this section is based on Max Scheler's posthumously published manuscript "Vorbild und Führer" (Scheler 1957), which was written in 1912–14. In this work Scheler developed a typology of leaders; he defined the leaders (*Führer*) as a value-free sociological concept, while he kept the concept of the exemplars (*Vorbild*) as a normative ideal. Personal exemplars are shown as five models of persons corresponding to the five highest categories of values: the idea of the holy, of mental values, of nobleness, of the useful, and of the pleasant. The models of personal exemplars are, correspondingly, the saint, the genius, the hero, the leader of civilization, and the master in the art of living. Whereas the leaders are characterized by their actions, the exemplars are differentiated by their existence. Because an act follows only from existence, the leaders can be exemplars.

Scheler assumed a hierarchical order of values from the holy to the pleasant, but that is not our concern. An important point for us is that there are different categories of exemplars that realize different categories of values and that Schumpeter's concept of entrepreneurs can be identified as one of the exemplars. Of the five categories of person, Scheler defined the entrepreneur as possessing one of the leading minds of civilized life who belonged to the sphere of the technical and social values of civilization. Entrepreneurs may share the elements of the genius and the hero in that they possess originality, determination, and courage, but their functions have nothing to do with the spheres of spiritual and noble values; they are leaders because of their actions and accomplishments. Scheler wrote:

A leader of economy is he who finds new ways and forms that are beyond economic needs, and who stimulates new needs through production. In the age of capitalism an outstanding leader of economy – he who has the nature of the entrepreneur – is, in contrast to a bourgeois, never a hedonist or egoist. He resembles large amounts of energy seeking their effects in profit, and seeking power, and not domination, in the controls of an economy. (Scheler [1957] 1987, 196)

This characterization of entrepreneurs is not different from Schumpeter's description that emphasizes the aspect of the "man of action" in entrepreneurs. Possessed of an insatiable impulse to act, defiance of ordinariness and utility, and a challenge to innovations, the entrepreneurs thus characterized are a personal exemplar in the Schelerian sense.

If this interpretation is acceptable, several implications of Schumpeter's thought can be derived from it. First, Schumpeter distinguished the areas of social life, assumed that there were generally leaders and followers in each area, and illustrated statics and dynamics in each area (see pages 37–38). He pointed out analogies between leaders in the military, in art and science, and in the economy. But, in light of Scheler's typology, the leaders in each area of society represented qualitatively different exemplars. The dynamics of the social classes constructed by social areas must be understood in terms of such a multilayered value framework. The structure of values changes over time; so does the social status enjoyed by entrepreneurs and bourgeois in comparison with the saint, the genius, and the hero. This is the viewpoint that will disclose the core of Schumpeter's argument about the transformation of capitalism. In fact, he used to mention the dissimilarities of entrepreneurs from other categories of leaders: they are devoid of romance and charm; intelligence is of little importance to them; they are not the object of hero worship and admiration. He wrote that "any craving for personal hero-worship can hardly hope for satisfaction where, among, to be sure, other types, we meet with slave-trading and brandy-producing puritans at the historic threshold of the subject" (1928, 379).

Second, Schumpeter's invariable antipathy to and contempt for utilitarianism is interpreted as the opposite of his enthusiasm for the idea of leadership in pursuit of distinction. As Scheler aptly said, entrepreneurs are the leaders of civilization. The channels of civilization they have opened are actually followed by people. In order to understand the force of motives and the working of history, one must pay attention to the leaders of civilization, not because their products are ethically and aesthetically good, but because they are the movers of civilization for good or evil. Utilitarian thought, which simply aggregates all kinds of wants without differentiation and takes no account of desires to change the social framework, does not give an accurate picture of society. Schumpeter asserted:

A new and another kind of effort of will is therefore necessary in order to wrest, amidst the work and care of the daily round, scope and time for conceiving and working out the new combination and to bring oneself to look upon it as a real possibility and not merely as a day-dream. This mental freedom presupposes a great surplus force over the everyday demand and is something peculiar and by nature rare. (1934, 86)

Third, Schumpeter mentioned three essential characteristics of creative activity as opposed to an adaptive one (1947, 150). This explanation sheds light on the peculiar impact of creative activity on the observation and recognition of mind and society. In the first place, creative activity cannot be predicted by applying the ordinary rules of inference from preexisting facts. It is so unique that the mechanism or the *modus operandi* must be examined on a case-by-case basis. Second, creative activity shapes the whole course of subsequent events and their long-term outcome, and causes discontinuity from preceding situations. Third, creative activity is an enigma of human beings and has something to do with the distribution of talent and therefore with the phenomenon of leadership. Considerations of these features led Schumpeter to forge unique techniques for analyzing the process of innovations, especially business cycles.

A theory of money and credit

Schumpeter's basic vision of money and credit was to regard credit creation as the means of carrying out innovations. Credit creation is the establishment of purchasing power given by capitalists or bankers to entrepreneurs, who thereby wrest the means of production required for innovations from an accustomed channel of an economy. Simple as this vision was, it demanded a new construction of economic theory because of its profound implications.

A theory of monetary economy

According to Schumpeter, innovative investment is financed not by savings but by credit creation; savings are the result of development. Interest is not concerned with a real economy; it is not an intermediary between savings and investment. Interest is a monetary and dynamic phenomenon; it is paid, in compensation for credit creation, out of profits obtained as the result of innovation. The view of money as a veil covering the exterior of a real economy, which has traditionally been inherent in the quantity theory of money, must be rejected because in the world of economic development, money in the form of credit creation intervenes in a real economy. An increase in the quantity of money does not give rise to an increase in general prices under the constant relative prices of commodities, but shakes the structure of production through the introduction of innovations and creates business cycles. Schumpeter's vision of the role of money in economic development recognized an economy as a monetary economy. He shared this view with Keynes in *General Theory*; both economists attempted to get rid of the quantity theory of money.[10]

This, however, does not mean that Schumpeter's dynamic theory should be categorized as a monetary theory of business cycles. He explicitly denied this (1939, 1, 142). For him, the independent variable was the innovation of entrepreneurs, not the money supply; on the contrary, the latter depends on innovative activity. In examining theories of money, credit, and business cycles during the period of 1870–1914 in the *History of Economic Analysis*, he distinguished between monetary theories and nonmonetary theories of business cycles. Although, as usual, his theory does not appear in the history of economics, it is, without doubt, a nonmonetary theory, because it emphasizes the real factor of innovations. When he pointed out in *History* the defects of most nonmonetary theories of cycles that did not recognize business cycles as the essential form of the capitalist economy, Elizabeth B. Schumpeter (as the editor of the book) observed in an footnote that it was, of course, Schumpeter who attempted to construct a theory on the basis of such a recognition (1954a, 1135).

We saw that Schumpeter, in a jump from statics to dynamics, outlined a new monetary theory in order to escape from the quantity theory of money (see page 151). This was the frontier he had arrived at through *Entwicklung* and "Das Sozialprodukt und die Rechenpfennige" (1917–18). It will be recalled that after World War I Schumpeter worked outside academe for a time and did not resume his study of monetary theory until 1925, when he was appointed at the University of Bonn. After some years, he gave up the project – reportedly because he was dispirited at the appearance of Keynes's *A Treatise on Money* (1930).[11] After Schumpeter's death this unfinished manuscript was published as *Das Wesen des Geldes* (1970) by Fritz Karl Mann.[12] The following discussion focuses on the new monetary theory presented in that book.

The sociology of money

Das Wesen des Geldes has a chapter entitled "Toward a Sociology of Money," which precedes the chapters on the economic theory of money. The major feature of Schumpeter's definition of capitalism was that it was equipped with the machinery of credit creation. This view entails the idea of money as an institution that determines economic activities and demands inquiries into not only the theoretical and historical but also the institutional and sociological aspects of money and monetary systems. For Schumpeter these inquiries are nothing more than a sociology of money. His chapter on the sociology of money deals with the origin of money; his argument includes an epistemological problem on the relationship between the historical origins and the logical nature of a phenomenon. Schumpeter's basic contention was that the historical origins of a phenomenon do not show its logical nature in a pure form; in other words, the former explains how money has developed as a cultural phenomenon but not the reason why money exists in the economic world. Of course, he did not mean that either direction of research is useless but that existing monetary theories confused the two.

Specifically, in *Das Wesen des Geldes* Schumpeter discusses the historical origins of the four well-known functions of money (that is, medium of exchange, measure of value, standard of deferred payments, and store of value). Money was established as a medium of exchange because of its usefulness; this is the *raison d'être* of money usually explained in economics. But this argument does not tell how the medium actually came into being. The historical process of the establishment of money was spontaneous and not invented on the basis of advantages known in advance. Those commodities that had a high degree of salability or marketability became the means of intermediate exchange. Money is the most marketable of all commodities. The concept of marketability was developed by Carl Menger, who defined it as the greater or lesser facility with which commodities are disposed of in a market to obtain other commodities. Highly marketable commodities are those that people are willing to hold and can be easily exchanged for any other goods. Historically, several kinds of commodities became a medium of exchange not because of their fulfillment of that function of money but because of their significance as commodities.

We need not follow Schumpeter's argument for the historical generation of the four functions of money. The basic question here is the relationship between theory and history; analogically speaking, it seems to suggest the difference between the economics of economic development and the sociology of the transformation of capitalism. Whereas Schumpeter's theory of economic development deals with the pure logic of the changing economic world, his sociological thesis of capitalism concerns the historical transition of the sociocultural world. Although the logic of capitalism is innovation and subsequent adaptation, the historical and cultural consequences of capitalism amount to the denial of innovation. According to Schumpeter, the historical *origin* of a phenomenon does not show its logical nature in a pure form;

analogically, in his thesis of capitalism, the historical *consequences* of a phenom-enon do not maintain its logical nature for good; this will be discussed more deeply in chapter 9.

Critical numbers of a system

The crucial notion Schumpeter developed in *Das Wesen des Geldes* in conjunction with his 1917–18 article was the concept of "die kritische Ziffer des System" (critical numbers of a system) (1970, 218). In an earlier essay he expressed a version of the quantity theory of money as the "fundamental equation of the monetary theory," and he interpreted the equation as a social accounting process in which the services of the factors of production and consumption are equaled through the medium of money. It was the task of *Das Wesen des Geldes* to examine in detail the idea of monetary machinery as a social clearing system.

As is well known, in a real economic system only relative prices are determined; in order to determine absolute prices, monetary factors must be introduced. According to the quantity theory, it is the quantity of money that determines absolute prices. But, in opposition to the quantity theory, Schumpeter groped for a different approach. He thought that for an economy to have absolute prices, some arbitrarily chosen coefficients, which he called the "critical number," must be introduced. He chose for this number the product of prices and quantities of commodities expressed in the fundamental equation of the monetary theory, that is, the nominal income of an economy. Schumpeter reasoned that the social institution of money provides the methods by which the "critical number" is determined: "These indirect and, in principle, arbitrary methods constitute the nature of a social institution called money. We interpret keeping the critical number constant as a kind of changing of the number based on its own rules, that is, as a kind of continuous fixation that fundamentally gives no consideration to conditions of the commodity world. We now define the monetary method as those methods of social liquidation through which the critical number of an economic system is changed according to its own rules" (1970, 224). Here, the reference to the monetary system's own rules means that the "critical number" depends entirely on how the rules are determined and it is not adjusted automatically by the demands of real economic situations. As a result, problems of inflation and deflation arise.

Schumpeter mentioned two ways of determining the "critical number": the paper standard and the commodity standard. The paper standard determines the nominal quantity of money; the commodity standard fixes the unit of money according to the price of a certain quantity of a specific commodity. In both cases, the credit creation by banks for entrepreneurs breaks down the monetary constraint through an increase in the critical number emerging from within the economic system; conversely, repayment of bank credit after the introduction of innovations decreases the critical number. Thus, in the process of economic development, the inherent forces are operating to change the critical number cyclically. So long as one uses the quantity theory of money or the monetary theories of cycles, business cycles are only explained exogenously through the monetary shocks from outside. Schumpeter wanted to explain an endogenous development of business cycles by combining credit creation and entrepreneurial activity, despite the exogenous nature of the monetary machinery. Herein lies the essence of his monetary theory.

Analysis of business cycles

Schumpeter's *Business Cycles* (1939) aims to analyze empirically the actual process of economic development using historical and statistical material based on the theoretical framework established in *Entwicklung*. Thus the book has an imposing subtitle: "A Theoretical, Historical and Statistical Analysis of the Capitalist Process." What did Schumpeter accomplish in *Business Cycles*? Its task was to integrate theory and history primarily by means of statistics. By primarily I mean that he also introduced the approach of economic sociology in the analysis of institutions and depended on the description of economic history. Schumpeter thought it most important to see the facts of the industrial process behind the statistics. It is because he adopted the method of filling in the statistical contours with detailed industrial history that *Business Cycles* consisted of two huge volumes.

Schumpeter, who had advocated in abstract terms the cooperation of theory and history to resolve the *Methodenstreit*, was now confronted with historical reality and came to grips with tasks of enormous breadth. He was never absorbed by small and fragmented problems; his themes were always grandiose yet basic, and his work cut a royal road to learning. At the beginning of the preface to *Business Cycles*, he declared: "Analyzing business cycles means neither more nor less than analyzing the economic process of the capitalist era. Most of us discover this truth which at once reveals the nature of the task and also its formidable dimensions" (1939, 1, v). Moreover, he always exerted originality, indeed dramatic originality, in attempting to meet a challenge.

Perspectives of business cycle analysis

In addition to his proposition that economic development initiated by the introduction of innovation means essentially the disturbance of, and deviation from, equilibrium, Schumpeter suggested another important concept: that a process following the destruction of equilibrium is not one of dynamic equilibrium but constitutes a series of business cycles. His view was not that economic development is one thing and business cycles quite another; he believed that economic development is synonymous with business cycles.

Schumpeter's unique idea of business cycles in *Entwicklung* was that:

> Economic development is not an organic unity but consists of mutually connected, relatively independent partial developments ... The development of an economy takes place, as it were, in a wavelike form; each of the waves has a life of its own. The level of the economy changes as if by jerks, and the total configuration of the economic development of a nation must be drawn not by a steadily increasing curve that conforms to a uniform law, but by fragments of curves that are linked, each of which has a distinct form even though it entails the overall character of the mechanism of development that is revealed in similar forms of curves. (1912, 490)

In other words, innovations, an ignition point of economic development, are distinctive, partial, and unordered, so that economic development as a whole is no more than an aggregate of its parts, not a unified macro phenomenon. Again in *Business Cycles*, published during the heyday of Keynesian aggregate economics, Schumpeter advocated an anti-aggregate analysis:

> It is, therefore, misleading to reason on aggregative equilibrium as if it displayed the factors which initiate change and as if disturbance in the economic system as a whole could arise only from those aggregates. Such reasoning is at the bottom of much faulty analysis of business cycles. It keeps analysis on the surface of things and prevents it from penetrating into the industrial processes below, which are what really matters. It invites a mechanistic and formalistic treatment of a few isolated contour lines and attributes to aggregates a life of their own and a causal significance that they do not possess. (1939, 1, 43–44)

How then should one approach development phenomena that are an aggregate of diverse parts? It is here that the instrumentalist Schumpeter should get credit for an analysis of complexity. "*Hic Rhodus, hic salta.*" At a glance, Schumpeter's concept of economic development might appear to be a simplistic theory that assigns a single cause of innovations. However, the implications of his theory are far-reaching; in *Entwicklung* as well as *Business Cycles*, Schumpeter seems to have set himself three theoretical tasks for his analysis of economic development.

First, innovations do not emerge evenly in all industrial sectors; rather, they concentrate in particular industries and affect the economy as a whole through the spread of their impact. Therefore, Schumpeter thought that not a macroanalysis but a multisectoral analysis was necessary.

Second, economic development occurs discontinuously and is accompanied by business cycles basically because the possibility of innovation does not spread evenly over time and because, in a competitive market, entrepreneurs are followed by many imitative firms so that innovations tend to cluster. On the introduction of an innovation, a boom begins and entrepreneurs secure profits. Through the bunching of innovations brought about by the clustering of imitators, the supply of commodities will increase and prices will fall; as a result profitability will decrease and a depression will set in. A depression is due not to errors of judgment or excesses of conduct, but to the inevitable consequences of a boom. A theory of economic development must be constructed as a theory of business cycles.

Third, bank credit is required in order to innovate, and an increase in the quantity of money makes the bundling of innovations possible in a limited number of industries and causes changes in the structure of production. Thus changes in the quantity of money affect the real economy and do not remain neutral. From the relationship between the quantity of money and the structure of the real economy, changes in relative prices and business cycles are produced. A monetary theory, not a real theory, of economic development is necessary.

Furthermore, Schumpeter made a methodological claim in asking for the assistance of the equilibrium theory to justify his dynamic theory as a whole (see pages 74–75). Statics is not a fictitious state that is devised only for a comparison with dynamics. The forces of statics as well as of dynamics coexist in an economy; the former brings an economy into equilibrium, whereas the latter destroys the equilibrium and achieves economic development. Static theory is concerned with equilibrium and the process of adaptation, whereas dynamic theory deals with the destruction of equilibrium and the process of innovation. Despite, or rather because of, this contrast, the coordination of statics and dynamics as a system of knowledge requires, in an epistemological sense, the founding of a dynamic theory by a static theory. This task means the elucidation of the process in which the phenomena of equilibrium destruction caused by economic development are absorbed by the equilibrating mechanism of an economy and form a business cycle. Analysis of the relationship between business cycles and equilibrium analysis was expected to result in a solution to the methodological question concerning statics and dynamics. Specifically, Schumpeter interpreted the market mechanism expounded by static theory as the "response apparatus" to innovations and then assumed the "neighborhoods of equilibrium," an actual counterpart of the equilibrium concept, at the midpoint of a business cycle. He thought that after innovations produced a deviation from a neighborhood of equilibrium, the adaptive forces operated through booms and depressions and brought an economy into a new neighborhood of equilibrium.

Schumpeter did not establish satisfactorily a rigid theoretical formulation in response to his theoretical and methodological agenda. The description of a massive industrial history in the two volumes *Business Cycles* did not interest theorists. Theoretical formulation expressed in terms of an equation system was lacking; the methods of statistical manipulation were primitive and did not lead to remarkable theoretical hypotheses from fact-finding. The book was far from a masterpiece. Nevertheless, it covered important issues and presented, as it were, a crucible that would produce something out of a mixture of varied elements, not immediately but over the course of time. In other words, it was a proposal for a progressive research program for economics. In fact, the renaissance of Schumpeter study since the 1980s has focused on empirical research based on his visions of innovation, and research subjects have included the analytic framework of technical innovations, classifications of innovations, the inducement mechanism of innovations, the clustering of innovations, the relationship between market structure and innovation, and long swings.[13]

The three-cycle schema

Schumpeter distinguishes the wavelike fluctuation in economic activity in four phases: prosperity, recession, depression, and recovery. In his conceptual schema, a unit of a business cycle consists of a fluctuation neither from bottom to bottom nor from peak to peak. If, for example, a neighborhood of equilibrium exists at a midpoint in an upward process from the bottom to the peak, the business cycle would start from this benchmark and end at the next neighborhood of equilibrium located in the next upward process. The upward phase from a neighborhood of equilibrium to a peak is called prosperity. Then, a downward process begins from the peak to the bottom, and another neighborhood of equilibrium is marked at a midway point in this process. The process from a peak to a neighborhood of equilibrium is a phase of recession, which is then followed by a phase of depression that indicates the process from a neighborhood of equilibrium to a bottom. Finally, turning upward from the bottom, a phase of revival continues until another neighborhood of equilibrium is reached.

Schumpeter's characteristic view is that the cyclical process of development does not give rise to just one wavelike movement but sets into motion an indefinite number of wavelike fluctuations with different spans and intensities because the locus, scale, gestation period, and absorption period are all different for specific innovations. He concluded that "there is a theoretically indefinite number of fluctuations present in our material at any time" (1939, 1, 168). As a practical approach, he adopted three cycles – the Kondratieff cycle (50–55 years), the Juglar cycle (9–10 years), and the Kitchin cycle (40 months) – on the basis of statistical data generated in England, Germany, and America since the 1780s.[14] This approach, the three-cycle schema, was not derived from his theory but was only a "convenient descriptive device" (1939, 1, 170) suggested from fact-findings. The business cycle research that had thus far been conducted as a mere statistical study was incorporated by Schumpeter into a theoretical framework.

Schumpeter's business cycle analysis was presented within the broadest framework of Kondratieff long-waves. The first wave was the cycle of 1787–1842, characterized by innovations in the Industrial Revolution. The second, the cycle of 1843–97, was related to the age of steam and steel. Schumpeter called the first wave the Industrial Revolution Kondratieff and the second the Bourgeois (or railroads) Kondratieff. The third long-wave of electricity, chemistry, and cars, which he named the Neomercantilist Kondratieff, began in 1898 but was interrupted by World War I and included the world depression after the war.[15]

The framework of the Kondratieffs, by which Schumpeter attempted the periodization of history, served dual purposes. On the one hand, he described the history of industries in several countries, together with the identification of the Juglars and the Kitchins, within each Kondratieff wave. Although this formidable work depended on an enormous amount of historical knowledge, it makes dull reading. This method cannot be said to be successful. On the other hand, as seen from the naming of the Kondratieffs, Schumpeter gave the long-waves the institutional characterization of epochs (about fifty years) and used the long-wave framework as a device with which to clarify the nature of the power, civilization, values, beliefs, and policy of each epoch.[16] Whereas from the standpoint of the theory of economic development he defined capitalism by three factors – private ownership, profit motive, and bank credit – he also took into account the spirit, civilization, and values of epochs when he provided a broader historical perspective (1939, 1, 144–45). The Bourgeois Kondratieff was the epoch in which the interests and attitudes of the industrial and commercial classes dominated the policy, culture, and lifestyle and bourgeois rationalism prevailed. The Neomercantilist Kondratieff, in contrast, saw increasing protectionist policies and social legislation. According to Schumpeter, the contrast between competitive capitalism and trustified capitalism began to appear in the third Kondratieff (1939, 1, 96). He recognized this aspect of capitalism as involving issues of economic sociology, the most significant of which was whether those tendencies were fundamental, whether they grew out of the very logic of capitalist evolution, or whether they were distortions traceable to extracapitalist influences (1939, 1, 399).

In chapters 14 and 15 of *Business Cycles*, which addressed the period after World War I, the situations hostile to capitalism that had emerged as a result of the rationalizing, leveling, mechanizing, and democratizing effects of the capitalist evolution were formulated in four propositions (1939, 2, 697–700).[17] These propositions were concerned with the demise of capitalism, a theme fully developed later in *Capitalism, Socialism and Democracy*. This subject did not attract attention at the time because *Business Cycles* did not appeal to practitioners. Among the book reviews, only that of Oscar Lange was favorable. He considered the work comparable to Marx's *Das Kapital* in terms of its intention and scope and he examined the views of the two authors on the decline of capitalism (Lange 1941, 190).

Of the book reviews dealing with the theoretical and statistical aspects of *Business Cycles*, that of Simon Kuznets seems to be the most scrupulous (Kuznets 1940). His final judgment was that in order to analyze complicated cyclical fluctuations in terms of the primary factors (entrepreneurs, innovations, and equilibrium) emphasized by Schumpeter, it was necessary to identify some theoretical links between these primary factors and statistical observables in cyclical fluctuations. Without the specification of such intermediaries it is not possible to test the relationship between facts and hypotheses. Innovation is not a single factor that operates in historical reality; Kondratieff took into account the causes of the long swings such as technical innovations, new frontiers, war and revolution, gold production (or quantity of money), and agriculture (or resources). Although Schumpeter emphasized that technical innovation was the major driving force, he did not ignore the other causes; in fact, he thought they might play a role in limiting or accelerating the process of economic development. The interrelationship between these factors and endogenous determinants such as prices, income, and employment would constitute what Kuznets called theoretical links which must be formulated as theoretical propositions that go beyond the descriptive level of economic history.

The theory of economic development as a midpoint

Although Schumpeter's theory of economic development set forth a variety of problems with regard to theoretical and empirical research, it was a middle point between economic statics and economic sociology. As we have reached the halfway point of this book, it is useful at this point to outline Schumpeter's later performance.

Schumpeter thought that he had developed an economic theory addressed to pure economic problems by supplementing neoclassical static theory with his dynamic theory. Economic theory consisting of the two structures was self-sufficient as far as the analysis of economic problems was concerned, but he was not content with it. The problems of economic development had already required him to enter the historical arena. Although *Business Cycles* dealt with the integration of history and theory through the medium of statics, it was not well received because of its own defects as well as the popularity of Keynesian economics. Except for a few methodological articles on economic development and business cycles that he wrote after *Business Cycles*, Schumpeter never expanded or elaborated "a theoretical, historical and statistical analysis of the capitalist process." His insight into this field, however, provided a great impetus for theoretical and empirical analysis half a century later. For his part, Schumpeter introduced the prospect of economic sociology, an approach that integrated history and theory, beyond the analysis of business cycles. In this undertaking, one can recognize two paths: the first is the path leading from the concept of entrepreneur, the fundamental phenomenon of economic development, to a theory of social classes that sums up performances in various areas of social life; the second is the path leading from the concept of the Kondratieff waves as the framework of business cycle analysis to the diagnosis of long-term changes in capitalism. To integrate the two paths of thought is the task of economic sociology, examined in chapter 9 of this book.

Business Cycles provides perfect material for analyzing Schumpeter's style of thought. Integrating history and theory through the medium of statistics was the task of the then emerging econometrics. Schumpeter had been active in the Econometric Society since its foundation in 1930. He was vice-president in 1938–39 and president in 1940–41. He understood and aspired to work in the up-to-date science but he was not equipped to undertake it. In Germany, where theoretical studies were backward, his early efforts in abstract static theory gave the impression that he was an *enfant terrible* in avant-garde theory. He wished to impart a rigid formulation to his theory of economic development, but he did not neglect the academic tradition of Germany where he first had become prominent. He enthusiastically absorbed German historicism and advocated the need for the theoretical formulation of history more strongly than any other theorist. But he utilized an old-fashioned historical approach that was not necessarily adequate to the task. Moreover, he felt inferior in mathematics – and for good reason. He said that if he could recommend only one of the three disciplinary tools – history, statistics, or theory – he would choose history (1954a, 12). As far as he was concerned, however, he would have chosen theory (mathematics) if he could start over in economics.

The point here is not only his insufficient competence in mathematics but also the fact that at the time mathematical methods could not cope effectively with his interests and ideas. Although ordinary mathematical economists and econometricians confined themselves to manageable problems, Schumpeter did not hesitate to address imposing and complex problems and, as a leader in his field, cut a path that future economists should follow.

The idea of an evolutionary model

In his review of *Business Cycles* Jacob Marschak criticized Schumpeter for not formulating a precise model, asking whether Schumpeter's model was a closed system that included innovations and credit as endogenous variables, or a system that structured a *deus ex machina* of innovations outside of the model (Marschak 1940, 892–93). Schumpeter, admitting to his regret that he had no exact model, replied in his handwritten comment:

But first I want to explain in what sense my system does, and in what sense it does not, seem to me to be a "closed" one. I think it is closed if "closed" means the same as endogenous. Though I am prepared, in interpreting any given case, to take account of all the outside factors I can see, my theory does not rely on outside factors, that is, on factors outside the logic of the business organism. Enterprise is inside the economic system, an internal, if you so please, source of energy. It is not of the nature of erratic shocks, it is part of a system that could not live without it and the main categories of which are keyed to its occurrence. But my system is not closed, if that means "causal" in the sense of Birkhoff and Lewis. For that source of energy is (it is formal so far) refractory to quantification so that the system subject to this impulse is ex ante indeterminate and in this sense "open." If you will allow me to deviate so far from your severe principles, there is something of *évolution créatrice* about it ... Now this is perhaps the most fundamental reason why I have never attempted to get my system into equations – except for individual bits of mechanism: if you have a system of interdependent quantities you will always be able to describe surface mechanical relations (everything has always also such mechanical effects, e.g. the effects of spending upon prices) ... Therefore I do not feel any contrast between those schemata (Frisch – Tinbergen – Roos – Amoroso – Kalecki – Keynes and many others) and my way of thinking: they simply move on planes different from mine and I feel perfectly free to use any of them for those peripheric problems for which they are intended.[18]

By a causal system, G. D. Birkhoff and D. C. Lewis, Jr., mathematicians at Princeton and Harvard Universities respectively, meant that if a system includes measurable endogenous variables and if their values are known in its initial condition, the subsequent development of the system is uniquely determined by a set of differential equations (Birkhoff and Lewis 1935, 304–5). Because innovation in Schumpeter's system is not a variable subject to differential equations, his system is uncertain and unpredictable; it is not a causal system in the above sense. Schumpeter's favorite statement that innovations are changes emerging from within an economic system is a sort of rhetoric, and they are better described as an exogenous variable in the system. This interpretation is justified by his quotation above. In his view, the system that includes, as its essential part, such a variable as innovation must be formulated by an evolutionary model, if any, that is neither of the two queries in Marschak's question.

At any rate, given Schumpeter's talent, the task for which he could enjoy comparative academic advantage was the integration of history and theory through work in economic sociology. This was the field in which he was trained in the tradition of German and Austrian academism and in which he hoped to display his fullest talent, although the tradition was out of vogue in face of the increasing precision and quantification of scientific methods. By conducting further socioeconomic investigations and gathering together the threads of sociological thought spun during his earlier academic life, he wrote *Capitalism, Socialism and Democracy*, which revealed amazingly original thought and scored a success.

Why, then, did Schumpeter make a challenge in the field for which he was unfit? His efforts were heroic, but there was no knowing what the results would be. In fact, he did not succeed in mathematical economics and econometrics, but it was his ambition that counts. He had a comprehensive idea about economics as a social science and could not help designing the whole system by himself. He tried to depict the total picture of what economics should be and to construct a logical connection with its major fields and the methodological foundation for them rather than to confine what he could do about technicalities to a single aspect of the whole research object. To depict the total picture of economics required a synthetic understanding of the economy and society. Schumpeter presented imposing and complex problems for a new paradigm that future generations should be concerned with. Despite his unsuccessful works such as *Business Cycles* and *Das Wesen des Geldes*, his goal was to contribute to a universal social science. Although Schumpeter must have known the thesis of the sociology of leadership – that a superior talent is limited to a small number of people and flourishes only in a limited field – he risked going beyond the bounds, dreaming of an *uomo universale* (an omnipotent genius in the age of the Italian Renaissance).

The economic picture of capitalism

Schumpeter explored economic development theory on the basis of his original idea. It was a coordinate with and a supplement to static theory, but he did not formulate it into a mathematical system comparable to the Walrasian system. Rather, he utilized his rhetorical skills to describe the nature of a dynamic economy. It can be argued that rhetoric is a method for describing vision. We owe a great deal to Schumpeter's talent for developing the dynamic image of capitalism. Before proceeding to his economic sociology and an overall picture of capitalism, we will now take a look at various aspects of the economic picture of capitalism within the scope of economics that he depicted by means of a superb rhetorical power.

The economics of rhetoric

First of all, Schumpeter emphasized the dynamic nature of capitalism. "Unlike other economic systems, the capitalist system is geared to incessant economic change ... Whereas a stationary feudal economy would still be a feudal economy, and a stationary socialist economy would still be a socialist economy, stationary capitalism is a contradiction in terms" (1943, 116–17). Later he wrote:

The essential point to grasp is that in dealing with capitalism we are dealing with an evolutionary process ... Capitalism, then, is by nature a form or method of economic change and not only never is but never can be stationary ... The fundamental impulse that sets and keeps the capitalist engine in motion comes from the new consumers' goods, the new methods of production or transportation, the new markets, the new forms of industrial organization that capitalist enterprise creates ... This process of Creative Destruction is the essential fact about capitalism. It is what capitalism consists in and what every capitalist concern has got to live in. (1950a, 82–83)

Second, economic development in the capitalist system is perceived to depend on spontaneous changes in the endogenous factors of the system. "By 'development,' therefore, we shall understand only such changes in economic life as are not forced upon it from without but arise by its own initiative, from within" (1934, 63). Another feature of economic development is discontinuous change. "What we are about to consider is that kind of change arising from within the system which so displaces its equilibrium point that the new one cannot be reached from the old one by infinitesimal steps. Add successively as many mail coaches as you please, you will never get a railway thereby" (1934, 64). As seen from the fact that Schumpeter called this sentence "another more exact definition" of the dynamic phenomenon, the rhetoric here seems to conceal difficulties with theoretical formulation.

Third, the leading part in capitalism is played by entrepreneurs, who develop innovations. "The entrepreneur is our man of action in the economic area. He is an economic leader, a real commander, not merely seeming to be commander like a static economic agent" (1912, 172).

In Schumpeter, the entrepreneur is typified by neither more nor less than his innovative role in the economy. The nature of civilization that the entrepreneur has brought about does not matter. It is not true that Schumpeter glorified the capitalistic entrepreneur. Thus he wrote that:

we do not observe, in this case, the emergence of all those affective values which are the glory of all other kinds of social leadership. Add to this the precariousness of the economic position both of the individual entrepreneur and of entrepreneurs as a group, and the fact that when his economic success raises him socially he has no cultural tradition or attitude to fall back upon, but moves about in society as an upstart, whose ways are readily laughed at, and we shall understand why this type has never been popular, and why even scientific critique often makes short work of it. (1934, 89–90)

Whereas Schumpeter sympathized with the external aspect of entrepreneurship in that "the entrepreneur never relies on tradition and connection; he is a real lever to break up all restraints and has nothing to do with a system of superindividual values in a stratum from which he has come as well as a stratum into which he has been raised" (1926a, 134), he did not conceal his contempt for its internal aspect in that "the entrepreneur is the pioneer of a jejune way of thinking, of a utilitarian philosophy – the brain that was first able and had reason to reduce beefsteak and the ideal to a common denominator" (1926a, 134).

Fourth, in Schumpeter's view, capitalist firms are in keen competition; they are exposed to "the perennial gale of creative destruction" (1950, 84). This conception of competiton is markedly different from the traditional one of neoclassical economics. Schumpeter explained the difference as follows:

Economists are at long last emerging from the stage in which price competition was all they saw. As soon as quality competition and sales effort are admitted into the sacred precincts of theory, the price variable is ousted from its dominant position. However, it is still competition within a rigid pattern of invariant conditions, methods of production and forms of industrial organization in particular, that practically monopolizes attention. But in capitalist reality as distinguished from its textbook picture, it is not that kind of competition which counts but the competition from the new commodity, the new technology, the new source of supply, the new type of organization (the largest-scale unit of control for instance) – competition which commands a decisive cost or quality advantage and which strikes not at the margins of the profits and the outputs of the existing firms but at their foundations and their very lives. This kind of competition is as much more effective than the other as a bombardment is in comparison with forcing a door ... Now a theoretical construction which neglects this essential element of the case neglects all that is most typically capitalist about it; even if correct in logic well as well as in fact, it is like *Hamlet* without the Danish prince. (1950a, 84, 86)

The reason is, "Capitalist reality is first and last a process of change. In appraising the performance of competitive enterprise, the question whether it would or would not tend to maximize production in a perfectly equilibrated stationary condition of the economic process is hence almost, though not quite, irrelevant" (1950a, 77).

As a corollary of Schumpeter's conception of competition, the market power of firms in the form of production restriction and price control in the process of creative destruction has acquired a new meaning:

In analyzing such business strategy *ex visu* of a given point of time, the investigating economist or government agent sees price policies that seem to him predatory and restrictions of output that seem to him synonymous with loss of opportunities to produce. He does not see that restrictions of this type are, in the conditions of the perennial gale, incidents, often unavoidable incidents, of a long-run process of expansion which they protect rather than impede. There is no more of [a] paradox in this than there is in saying that motorcars are traveling faster than they otherwise would because they are provided with brakes ...

What we have got to accept is that it has come to be the most powerful engine of that process and in particular of the long-run expansion of total output not only in spite of, but to a considerable extent through, this strategy which looks so restrictive when viewed in the individual case and from the individual point of time. In this respect, perfect competition is not only impossible but inferior, and has no title to being set up as a model of ideal efficiency. (1950a, 88, 106)

The question of whether technical progress is likely to occur more easily in oligopolistic and monopolistic situations, one of the Schumpeterian hypotheses, became a broad topic of empirical research after World War II.

Fifth, what was the economic performance of capitalism? Schumpeter wrote:

It is the cheap cloth, the cheap cotton and rayon fabric, boots, motorcars and so on that are the typical achievements of capitalist production, and not as a rule improvements that would mean much to the rich man. Queen Elizabeth owned silk stockings. The capitalist achievement does not typically consist in providing more silk stockings for queens but in bringing them within the reach of factory girls in return for steadily decreasing amounts of effort. (1950a, 67)

It is not an accident because the engine of capitalism is mass production, production for the masses. Thus capitalism has increased the standard of living of the masses through its very mechanism. Yet the initiative of this process is not in consumption but in production.

Sixth, Schumpeter related that the capitalist incentive system based on the criterion of money and wealth creates extraordinarily vigorous economic activity in capitalism and dominates not only economic but all aspects of a society:

Burgeois society has been cast in a purely economic mold: its foundations, beams and beacons are all made of economic material. The building faces toward the economic side of life. Prizes and penalties are measured in pecuniary terms. Going up and going down means making and losing money ... The game is not like roulette, it is more like poker ... Spectacular prizes much greater than would have been necessary to call forth the particular effort are thrown to a small minority of winners, thus propelling much more efficaciously than a more equal and more "just" distribution would, the activity of that large majority of businessmen. (1950a, 73–74)

Seventh, Schumpeter's view of depressions is unique: "Capitalism and its civilization may be decaying, shading off into something else, or tottering toward a violent death. The writer personally thinks they are. But the world crisis does not prove it and has, in fact, nothing to do with it. It was not a symptom of a weakening or a failure of the system. If anything, it was a proof of the vigor of capitalist evolution to which it was – substantially – the temporary reaction" (1939, 2, 908). His thesis on the fall of capitalism does not follow from an economic investigation of capitalism alone, but from a study of the capitalist society as a whole in the perspective of economic sociology.

Schumpeter's explanation of the world depression in the early 1930s was particularly aesthetic: the depression phases of the three waves – the Kondratieff cycle, the Juglar cycle, and the Kitchin cycle – that he employed as an analytic schema overlapped during this period: "the economic organism always does bleed from many wounds which it bears lightly in three out of the four cyclical phases, and which spell discomfort when one cycle, distress when two, catastrophe when all the cycles are in the depression phase" (1939, 2, 911). This is typically a rhetorical explanation. The four cyclical phases mean prosperity, recession, depression, and recovery.

The consequences of rationalization

Finally, Schumpeter distinguishes between competitive capitalism and trustified capitalism. His picture of the entrepreneur relates to competitive capitalism and must be modified under trustified capitalism, the large enterprise system. The innovative entrepreneur in nineteenth-century capitalism typically appeared in new small firms in defiance of old ones. Because innovation under these circumstances is a risky and difficult thing, one must possess the capacity to foresee the future and the courage to go beyond customary channels in order to enter the darkness of uncertainty. The scarcity of such capacity and energy is a prerequisite for the entrepreneur.

If anyone can easily calculate situations in an era of increasing rationalization, the importance of the entrepreneurial function will recede. In a large enterprise system, existing firms can control and plan the market; innovations become routine work based on the advice of experts in large firms. Entrepreneurs are not as necessary in daylight as they are in darkness. Innovations are different from inventions and discoveries; it was Schumpeter's hypothesis that there are abundant possibilities of innovations, which newly combine existing inventions and knowledge. Under a transparent condition, scarce capacity is not necessary to start things. "As soon as the success is before everyone's eyes, everything is made very much easier by this very fact" (1928, 384). As large enterprises accumulate their own surplus and become more dependent on direct financing in the money market, the role of bank credit will decrease. In *Entwicklung*, in which the concept of entrepreneur was advanced, Schumpeter was already discussing the process by which the importance of the entrepreneur type would decline.[19]

Schumpeter's picture of capitalism is not exhausted by its economic conditions. For him, limiting an observation to the economic aspects of a society overlooks the evolutionary nature of capitalism. To observe the society in the perspective of historical development requires one to see the total process in which various aspects of the society change through their inter-dependence and interaction. As shown in chapter 8 (see page 203), combining the viewpoints of development and the unity of social life was the fundamental idea he had acquired from the German Historical School of economics. Schumpeter, whose subject was capitalist economic development, had to proceed to an analysis of the development of capitalism as a whole through the interactions between economic and other aspects of society, that is, sociocultural development. This is the viewpoint of his economic sociology. His clearest indication of the shift from the economics of capitalism to the economic sociology of capitalism came in this statement: "Capitalism, whilst economically stable, and even gaining in stability, creates, by rationalising the human mind, a mentality and a style of life incompatible with its own fundamental conditions, motives and social institutions, and will be changed, although not by economic necessity and probably even at some sacrifice of economic welfare, into an order of things which it will be merely [a] matter of taste and terminology to call Socialism or not" (1928, 385–86).

CHAPTER 8

A methodology of economic sociology

Schumpeter may have drawn on Walras and Marx for the ideology on which he based his vision (see chapter 4), but he paid as much attention to Gustav von Schmoller, the leader of the younger German Historical School of economics. Whereas Schumpeter owed to Marx his vision of the development of society as a whole, he was more associated with Schmoller with regard to the practical method of research in historical perspective.

Thus Schumpeter appraised the research program of Schmoller as a prototype of economic sociology and characterized its goal as a "unified sociology or social science as the mentally ('theoretically') worked out universal history" (1926b, 382). He remarked that Schmoller was the only practitioner in the history of economics who not only proposed such a research program but also conscientiously carried it out (1926b, 354). Schmoller did this work not only individually but also by displaying leadership strong enough to form a school. Later, when Schumpeter surveyed the entire spectrum of the whole areas of economics in the *History of Economic Analysis*, he regarded economic sociology as one of the tools in economics, defining it as "a sort of generalized or typified or stylized economic history" (1954a, 20). As a simplified expression, he used "a reasoned (= conceptually clarified) history" (1939, 1, 220).[1] These words are the key expression for his conception of social science. Specifically, economic sociology is the study of institutional factors that are treated as noneconomic givens in economic theory, and thus it is a method for addressing the issue of sociocultural development as a whole (see pages 49–50). In my interpretation, economic sociology is the attempt to integrate history and theory through the analysis of institutions, because the specification in terms of institutions will make the method incorporating a generalization, typification, and stylization of history less ambiguous.

Beyond the *Methodenstreit*

The 1880s witnessed the bitter *Methodenstreit* between Schmoller and Menger over the relative importance of the theoretical and historical methods in economics. The antagonism between them became emotional and was typically shown by the following exchange of insults. According to Schmoller, Menger only confined himself to "a corner of the large house that represents our science" and took it for "the whole house" or "the best and fanciest salon in the house" (Schmoller [1883] 1888a, 293–94). In response, Menger asserted: "Schmoller's view is like that of a navvy who wants to be regarded as an architect because he carried some stones and sand to a construction site" (Menger 1884, 46). Solely because of emotional bias, the two economists could not achieve a reconciliation. The *Methodenstreit* continued for decades in the German-speaking world and produced much literature by theorists, historians, and philosophers.

Most current economists would agree with Schumpeter's appraisal of the *Methodenstreit*. In the *History of Economic Analysis*, he wrote: "In spite of some contributions toward clarification of logical backgrounds, the history of this literature is substantially a history of wasted energies, which could have been put to better use" (1954a, 814). This nihilistic assessment not only diverts one's attention from the perennial issue on theory versus history in economics but also makes one overlook important contributions, including that of Schumpeter himself, to the resolution of the conflict. The *Methodenstreit*, even if a waste of time and energy in itself, stimulated methodological inquiries about the foundations of social science and was rewarded with fruitful results. Although Schumpeter did not directly participate in the dispute, he was inspired by it and very much concerned with the methodological and methodical issue of the relationship between theory and history throughout his life. His apparent attitude toward the *Methodenstreit*, as shown in the extract from *History of Economic Analysis*, might reflect his habit of avoiding a discussion of his own work on the issue.

Separation and cooperation between theory and history

On two occasions Schumpeter gave different reasons why the debate over methods reflected a "history of wasted energies." First, in *Wesen* he insisted that because historical and theoretical methods are concerned with different problems, different interests, different categories of hypotheses, and different goals, it is useless to quarrel about the superiority of the different methods. To support his contention he developed instrumentalist methodology (see chapter 5) and strongly advocated the separation and differentiation of history and theory for peaceful coexistence. From this methodological standpoint, a specific method can only claim usefulness for the treatment of a specific problem. In *Wesen* Schumpeter stated:

With regard to their general argument, both sides [Schmoller and Menger] are mostly right. But one fails to appreciate the limits of argument and overlooks the fact that two parties often consider different problems. Each method has its distinct areas of application, and it is useless to struggle for its universal validity ... This standpoint can be briefly characterized by the observation that historical and abstract methods are not mutually inconsistent, that the sole difference between them lies in their interest in different problems. (1908, 6–7)

Although, in principle, instrumentalism demanded a truce between history and theory when it was applied to the *Methodenstreit*, in *Wesen* Schumpeter actually intended to clarify the methodological foundation of theoretical economics and defended theory against history at a time when the German Historical School suppressed theory and elevated history to a dominant position.

Second, when Schumpeter later launched a study not only of economic development but also of economic sociology, he focused on the cooperation of history and theory, instead of their separation and differentiation, in order to deal with complex dynamic problems. In this context, he regarded the controversy between history and theory as useless for a different reason. Both inductive and deductive methods or empirical and abstract methods were required for what might be called joint research of theory and history. In his essay "Gustav v. Schmoller und die Probleme von heute" (1926b), Schumpeter provided a methodological appraisal of Schmoller's historical and ethical economics and characterized his approach as economic sociology in which history and theory could be integrated.[2]

It does not make sense to argue merely in general terms that inductive and deductive methods or empirical and abstract methods do not contradict each other but should be mutually supportive, as has often been done in appraisals of the *Methodenstreit*. This argument did not resolve the *Methodenstreit*; as a matter of fact, cooperation could not be expected either in Schmoller's detailed historical studies or in Menger's abstract theoretical studies. It was rather essential to find a field where the interests of historians and theorists were in agreement and where cooperation between them was necessary and feasible. Schumpeter characterized economic sociology as "a specific discipline that, owing to the nature of its subject matter, is not only a detailed and fact-finding discipline but also a theoretical inquiry" (1926b, 369–70). He held that its subject matter consisted of institutions in general and social classes, business cycles, and public finance in particular. Interestingly, these themes indicated the areas of his own contributions to economic sociology. From Schumpeter's standpoint, if economic sociology is a theory at all, then its epistemological status must be construed as an instrument. Thus, for him, instrumentalism played the dual role of first separating and then integrating history and theory in the resolution of the *Methodenstreit*.

Schumpeter, Schmoller, and Weber

The methodology of Max Weber was also partly an attempt to resolve the *Methodenstreit* and was closely related to the epistemology of neo-Kantianism, especially that of Heinrich Rickert. Neo-Kantian philosophers asserted the possibility of the cultural or historical sciences as distinct from the natural sciences and provided a philosophical and epistemological foundation to the approach of the German Historical School. What, then, was the relationship between the methodology of Mach and Schumpeter, on the one hand, and that of Rickert and Weber, on the other, both of which addressed the resolution of the *Methodenstreit*? This question has not been considered either by Schumpeterian or by Weberian commentators.[3] It seems appropriate to compare Schumpeter's methodological position with that of Weber in order to identify the distinctive features of the former with respect to economic sociology because Weber's scientific methodology for this discipline has been much discussed.

The purpose of this chapter is to ask what sort of methodology Schumpeter employed when he launched his study of economic sociology. Because he did not work out such a topic himself, this question has never been raised. I shall show that Schumpeter applied his instrumentalist methodology, as forged first for static economic theory, *mutatis mutandis* to economic sociology by trying to establish economic sociology as a theoretical science. To sustain my argument I shall discuss how Schumpeter interpreted Schmoller's research program of historical economics, on the one hand, and how he evaluated Weber's methodology of historical science (which was a methodological reconstruction of the approach of the German Historical School), on the other. In both instances, it will be seen that Schumpeter recognized and practiced economic sociology as theory, not as history. The comparison of Schumpeter with Weber will suggest any differences between the positivist and idealist schools of thought in the research of historical knowledge. Although Schumpeter apparently opposed Weber's methodology with regard to a number of crucial points, I shall argue that Schumpeter's methodology was very close to that of Weber – despite their different origins – by demonstrating an interpretation of Weber's methodology as instrumentalist. Through this observation I hope to uncover a parallelism between the two ideas that were preeminent during the crisis of economics at the turn of the century in Germany, both of which aimed at not only providing an epistemological foundation to economics but also constructing a branch of economic sociology that went beyond economic theory.[4]

I also hope to establish the relevance of Schumpeter's methodology for economic sociology to the current debate on institutional economics. Schumpeter perceived economic sociology as a theoretical analysis of economic institutions and their changes in time. The current issues in institutional economics, including the methodological disparities between the old institutional economists (such as Veblen and Commons) and the new institutional economists (based on neoclassical economics), can be more effectively examined in light of the Schmoller-Schumpeter-Weber nexus. Because the difference between the old and the new institutionalism can be seen, in a sense, as a facsimile of the confrontation between Schmoller and Menger, Schumpeter's methodological position vis-à-vis the *Methodenstreit* and his practice of economic sociology will be of relevance to the current issues.

Economic sociology and the concept of institutions

How did Schumpeter arrive at his concept of economic sociology? There have been various attempts to integrate history and theory, so that the nature of his choice should be clarified in light of other possibilities. His 1926 essay on Schmoller is important in that it includes his own examination of the overall possibilities. Below his discussion is summarized by distinguishing between the use of theory in historical research and the use of history in theoretical research.

The scientific approach to history

In historical research, historical description was originally devoted to the portrayal of individual events such as epics, and the techniques of historiography were developed for that purpose. Then it was realized that historical description had to depend on some interests and viewpoints that reflected a cognitive purpose. As interests were made explicit, historical research was carried out from the individual viewpoints of politics, economy, law, religion, and so on, and methods of concept formation and analysis in individual disciplines were applied to history. Thus emerged specific disciplines of history such as political history, economic history, legal history, and religious history. Furthermore, as historical research began to examine not only individual events but also interrelated courses of events, it became necessary to explain the historical relationship by universally valid conceptual schema, so that the tendency developed to place historical materials, as it were, into the individual flasks of the social sciences. Undeniably in the process of the "scientization of historical description" history and theory achieved some degree of cooperation. But one of the difficulties is that the individual sciences clipped parts of history so arbitrarily that the unity of history was often destroyed. Rather, in the field of historical research the methods of individual sciences should be matched like the pieces of a jigsaw puzzle. For Schumpeter, only when the boundaries between the existing social sciences vanish in historical research, does a "prospect of a universal social science" emerge (1926b, 365).

Therefore, it is more important to consider how theory will be changed under the influence of historical research than how theory is applied unilaterally to history.[5] So let us consider, in turn, the use of history in theoretical research. According to Schumpeter, historical theory in a broad sense includes (1) the whole body of interrelationships between historical facts, (2) the conceptual apparatus and methods for historical description, (3) the philosophy of history as it concerns the power of motive underlying the historical process, and (4) the theory of handling historical materials. These four cases relate to the "theory of history," whereas cases (5) to (11) relate to "theory obtained from history": (5) theory illustrated by history (Wilhelm Roscher), (6) theory applied to historical conditions (Adam Smith's theory of Mercantilism), (7) theory concerning historical relativity (Friedrich List's system of commercial policy), (8) theory explaining something by reference to history (Friedrich Wieser's theory of money), (9) theory of the genesis of social types and institutions (Schmoller's theory of enterprise), (10) theory of the comparative economic process in historical terms, and (11) theory of generalizing history. Schumpeter attached the greatest importance to the last case; here, theory claims validity beyond the scope of the historical materials from which it is derived, and individual historical research can be linked to general social scientific knowledge; in other cases, theory remains realistic and not general in the sense that it is historical and concrete rather than theoretical and abstract, a view held by the German Historical School.

In *Wesen* Schumpeter confined the meaning of theory to "exact hypothesis" in contrast to "historical hypothesis"; similarly, in the *History of Economic Analysis* he limited it to "simplifying schemata or models" in contrast with "explanatory hypothesis" (see pages 45 and 112). Cases (5) to (10) relate to historical or explanatory hypothesis; case (11) is defined by Schumpeter as economic sociology. He regarded Schmoller as its founder and Arthur Spiethoff, Werner Sombart, and Max Weber as its subsequent representatives (1954a, 815–16).

Implications of the concept of institutions

Before examining Schmoller and Weber closely, it is useful to consider some important methodological features of Schumpeter's economic sociology and implications of the concept of institutions in this discipline.

First, while Schumpeter regarded social institutions as the determinants of actions, motives, and dispositions of agents, he supposed at the same time that these institutions themselves, in turn, change as a result of the interactions among agents in a historical process, as shown in the analysis of the evolution of the capitalist economic system in *Capitalism, Socialism and Democracy*. Thus economic sociology can be conceived of as dealing with the complicated interactions of social and economic forces, which he called sociocultural development. This relationship between the whole and its individual parts does not merely signify methodological holism, because the unintended results of individual actions as a whole contradict the holistic idea that the whole is more than the sum of its parts; that it has its own aims, interests, and motivations; and that it cannot be explained in terms of its parts. Nor is the relationship exhaustively explained on the basis of methodological individualism, which often assumes the rationality of abstract, autonomous individuals. Social institutions, in fact, constrain the behaviors of an individual, so that he might be seen as a product of culture and institutions. Thus any reductionist approach emphasizing either the whole or individual parts is inadequate for economic sociology. The nature of interactions between institutional conditions and individual behaviors is best described as evolutionary.[6] In order to develop an evolutionary approach based on the interpretation of the relationship between individual and society as evolutionary, it is necessary to have another perspective in which methodological individualism and holism are to be treated synthetically. On this point the view of Joseph Agassi is noteworthy.[7]

Second, as a practical strategy of research, economic sociology does not incorporate all factors excluded from the scope of economic theory; it confines itself to an analysis of institutions. This strategy of economic sociology has an important bearing on theory. Because institutions provide a set of rules in observance of which certain individual acts recur regularly, they have their own *modus operandi* and can be conceptualized in general terms. Herein lies the reason why a theoretical analysis of institutions abstracted from history is possible. Viewed in this way, institutions are social rules in a broad sense and include not only legal institutions but also social customs, morals, and values. The essence of Schmoller's approach to economics, often labeled as historical and ethical, was the recognition that institutions are not only physical and technical but also ethical and psychological, thus enabling individual agents to behave according to plural motivations.

Third, the concept of institutions also has a significant implication for the analysis of history. Analogically speaking, it resembles a system of mathematical equations involving a set of variables in the sense that institutions allow for different acts of individuals insofar as they conform to the rules set by the institutions. Whereas statistics for the variables in an equational system indicate the historical records under certain institutions, different institutions would represent different systems of equations with different structures and parameters. The concept of institutions is a means of generalizing historical events, but it is limited in generality because it is historically relative. Thus it can be conceived of as a compromise between the generality meant by theory and the individuality meant by history. If all economic behavior is characterized by perfect uniformity, whenever and wherever it may occur, there is no use talking about institutions for which certain economic behavior is typified; only one meaningful institution would exist. On the other hand, if all economic behaviors are *sui generis*, one could not categorize them according to a particular type or group; there would be such an infinite variety of behavioral patterns that it would be useless to consider types. Economic sociology, with its focus on the concept of institutions, is based on a typology in historical research,[8] and it thus allows the use of Weberian "ideal types" in the analysis of historical institutions.

Schumpeter's concept of institutions is thus congenial to the theoretical formulation of social phenomena, on the one hand, and is subject to historical constraints, on the other. In this sense it can mediate theory and history and form important connections with the works of Schmoller and Weber, both of which were much concerned with this perennial issue in the social sciences.

Schmoller's research program and the German Historical School

In his 1926 essay on Schmoller, Schumpeter interpreted Schmoller's approach as economic sociology, but he did not accept Schmoller's research program as it stood. He critically reconstructed it from the viewpoint of the relationship between history and theory. Schumpeter's idea of economic sociology demanded a reconstruction of the scope, method, and methodology of Schmoller's research program so as to develop its strengths and suppress its weaknesses; yet a radical change was required not so much in scope and method as in methodology. At this juncture it is useful to examine how Schumpeter viewed the formal aspect, the substantive aspect, and the methodology of Schmoller's research program in order to develop his own idea of social science.

The formal aspect of the research program

Schumpeter described the fundamental character of the German Historical School as follows: "the essence of the historical school lies ... in the fact that it put historical and altogether descriptive work on details into the forefront as the most important, or at any rate as the primary task, of social science" ([1914a] 1954c, 154). Admitting that the Historical School was oriented differently from classical and neoclassical economic theory, Schumpeter called its tradition economic sociology and regarded Schmoller as its real leader. Schmoller explained that the school's research procedures consisted of three steps: the observation and description of facts, the definition and classification of facts, and the causal explanation of facts and recognition of their interrelations (Schmoller 1911, 455). Although Schumpeter called this set of procedures "Schmoller's program,"[9] I shall interpret it as the formal aspect of Schmoller's research program. The two volumes of his *Grundriss der allgemeinen Volkswirtschaftslehre* (1900–1904) summarize the outcome of his program, covering the three kinds of research activities. Schumpeter called the book a "comprehensive mosaic."[10]

A kind of academic folklore surrounds the German Historical School – that it opposed theory on principle and proposed an apparently endless scenario of detailed historical studies. This is a misconception. The German Historical School only repudiated existing theory, and it did pursue a historical theory or a theoretical formulation of history. As Schmoller's tripartite scheme indicates, research was not restricted to the collection and description of historical data. He never excluded the methods of the natural sciences, general concepts, laws, and the like from economics: "I always stressed that all the progress of induction brings us deductively applicable propositions and that the completed science is generally deductive" (Schmoller 1911, 478). His emphasis on the importance of the collection and summarization of historical data through the accumulation of historical studies was rooted, first, in his basic recognition that because economics must deal with complicated phenomena, it had not advanced sufficiently to allow the use of deductive–abstract methods and the formulation of laws. Second, it was also based on his belief in scientific realism, which held that assumptions themselves should be realistic. According to Schmoller, economic theory should not be derived from a priori assumptions; it should be a generalization of facts gathered from diverse historical processes. The position of the German Historical School was not the denial of theory in general but the need for more empirical studies before the theoretical formulation of broad and complicated phenomena in the historical perspective could be undertaken productively.

Comparing empiricism with rationalism, Schmoller held that the development of human knowledge had taken place by alternating empirical and rational methods of science; he insisted that, in view of the present stage of the development of economics, one must engage in empirical research instead of making rash generalizations that lacked a solid empirical grounding (Schmoller 1888b, 147–50). He articulated the following principle: "We do not think that we must have laws at once at any price; we do not believe that we can pick them like blackberries, because we look first of all for true knowledge, i.e., necessarily and universally valid judgment. Where no law exists, we must be content with [1] the extensive observation of reality, [2] the classification of these materials, and [3] the inquiry of causes" (Schmoller [1883] 1888a, 283–84). As we have seen, these three research steps actually constitute his entire program, which excludes deductions from assumptions that cannot be judged as realistic. For Schmoller, what was meant by a causal explanation was not based on theories deduced from assumptions but on *ad hoc* conjecture.

Schumpeter expressed a deep appreciation for Schmoller's belief in the importance of the historical perspective, but he emphasized the need to construct a theory rather than to be content with the mere collection, classification, summarization, and *ad hoc* explanation of data. For Schumpeter, economic sociology was essentially characterized by the continual interaction between history and theory. The task of economic sociology was not merely to apply existing theories to historical experience in order to explain fact; nor was it simply to make a summary of historical materials. He expected that new theories would be formulated through the feedback between history and theory. As Schumpeter remarked: "Continuous interaction between the two [history and theory] pertains to, and constitutes, the essence of the matter. Schmoller's program will produce a new system of theory in a more important sense than is potentially implied by the mere provision of materials" (1926b, 375). Schumpeter wanted to put a brake on what might have appeared to be an endless process of data collection in Schmoller's research program, a bottomless pit into which historical economists were liable to fall. To do so, he had to resort to a methodological perspective.

The substantive aspect of the research program

It is the substantive aspect of Schmoller's research program that defines the content of his historical–ethical approach. This relates to the presuppositions of empirical research that give a set of specific visions and preconceptions on how to perceive the subject matter. In his early work on the history of economic doctrines and methods, Schumpeter summarized six basic viewpoints of the German Historical School ([1914a] 1954c, 175–80): (1) a belief in the unity of social life and the inseparable relationship among its components, (2) a concern for development, (3) an organic and holistic point of view, (4) a recognition of the plurality of human motives, (5) an interest in concrete, individual relationships rather than the general nature of events, and (6) historical relativity. We can hope for no better analysis of the methodological characteristics of the German Historical School than this.[11]

Considering that the German Historical School was a branch of German historicism, a major intellectual stream in nineteenth-century Germany, we cannot ignore the strong influence of its political and moral ideas on German historical economics. Of the three sets of ideas regarded as central to German historicism, namely the concept of the state, the philosophy of value, and the theory of knowledge (Iggers 1983, 7–10), Schumpeter was careful to isolate the first two and to concentrate on the third in discussing the scientific viewpoints of German historical economics.

For Schumpeter, the greatest significance of the historical method was the recognition that historical materials reflect the development phenomenon and indicate the relationship between economic and noneconomic facts, thus suggesting how the disciplines of the social sciences should interact. This recognition of the unity of social life and development, a combination of (1) and (2) above, was the essence of the German Historical School as Schumpeter understood it and constituted his central idea of a universal social science. Although in the short run or static perspective, a social scientist can isolate each area of social life and regard other areas as exogenously given, he must take into account all areas of social life that will change interdependently if he is to view the social life in a long-run dynamic perspective. Hence an outlook that goes beyond that of individual social sciences is required. According to Schumpeter, the need for an all-encompassing social science is met by historical studies. Historical research is important not so much in informing us of detailed knowledge about a certain time and place as in providing us with an understanding of the way in which a society as a whole actually changes. It is for this reason that he found in Schmoller's research program the "prospect of a universal social science" (1926b, 365), where the conventional lines of demarcation between separate disciplines disappeared in historical research. He later described why historical research should lead to a universal or all-encompassing social science: "the historical report cannot be purely economic but must inevitably reflect also 'institutional' facts that are not purely economic: therefore it affords the best method for understanding how economic and non-economic facts *are* related to one another and how the various social sciences *should* be related to one another" (1954a, 13).

Schumpeter had high praise for those scholars who had an all-encompassing program of research covering both historical development and intertwining social aspects. Marx was one of them; Schmoller was another. Schumpeter termed Marx's analysis of social evolution "unitary social science" (1954a, 441) in the same sense that he called Schmoller's program a "universal social science." But he noticed an important difference between the two economists. He was critical of Marx's economic interpretation of history; Marx, he asserted, reduced the whole historical process to the actions of one or two factors. He called this a simple hypothesis of the "Comte-Buckle-Marx kind" (1954a, 811) and contrasted it with Schmoller's pluralist approach, which was more compatible with his own thinking.

While viewpoints (1) and (2) of the German Historical School relate to the scope of its subject matter, (3), (4), (5), and (6) concern its methods. Schumpeter recognized a purely scientific value in the claims of (3) and (4), which are distinct from the assumptions of neoclassical economics, those of methodological individualism and utility maximization. As for (3), the organic and holistic view of society, he repudiated the School's contention that a national economy has its own distinct aims and interests and thus cannot be split up into a collection of independent economic agents, a position basically influenced by the philosophy of value in German historicism. Instead, he considered the belief that individuals do not live in a vacuum but are conditioned by the institutional and cultural factors of a society more acceptable; thus he interpreted Schmoller's view as follows: "the individual economic agents, which together comprise the national economy, stand in intimate mutual relations with each other. These relations are far more important than the ones which economic theory describes and which influence the individual member of the economy. They enforce in fact upon the individual a behaviour which is of a different kind and which must be explained in a way which is quite different from the one of which economic theory speaks" ([1914a] 1954c, 180). This viewpoint is closely related to viewpoint (4), the recognition of the plural motives of individuals, because in historical economics institutions play a central role in influencing the behaviors of individuals. Rejecting the assumption of the rational maximizing behavior of autonomous individuals, Schmoller held that customs, laws, and morals constitute the institutional framework of a society and that the plural values, especially ethical ones, are formed by institutions.

Referring to viewpoints (3) and (4), Schumpeter described the direction of research in the German Historical School that was labeled "historical–ethical": "the school professed to study *all* the facets of an economic phenomenon; hence *all* the facets of economic behavior and not merely the economic logic of it; hence the *whole* of human motivations as historically displayed, the specifically economic ones not more than the rest for which the term 'ethical' was made to serve, presumably because it seems to stress hyperindividual components" (1954a, 812). It is viewpoints (3) and (4) that the old institutional economics emphasized, whereas the new institutional economics based on neoclassical economics refuted them.

Schumpeter did not show much interest in viewpoints (5), the issue of individuality versus generality, and (6), the issue of relativity versus the universality of social knowledge. General knowledge is independent of individual situations; universal knowledge applies to all cases. Although the position of historicism used to be bound up with an interest in individuality and relativity, Schumpeter argued, this should not deny the possibility of general and universal knowledge. He found that (5) and (6) are not fruitful issues; thus, he was critical of neo-Kantian philosophy, which, he said, went too far into these issues. A different methodology for bridging the gap between theory and history was required to resolve these questions. Max Weber's methodological work, consisting of the concepts of "understanding"

(*Verstehen*) and "ideal types," was a solution to the problems concerning viewpoints (3), (4), (5), and (6).

Interestingly, Schumpeter found that Schmoller was basically pro-theory, sticking neither to the individuality nor to the relativity of historical phenomena:

[H]e recognized ... how essentially similar the causal nexus in social science and natural science is; he also described the explanation of social phenomena in the form of cause and effect and in the form of laws ... as the aim of scientific effort. Indeed we find even the far-reaching proposition that all perfect science is "deductive," that is, that the state of ideal perfection is only reached when it has become possible to explain concrete phenomena completely with the help of theoretical premises. This proposition implies the acknowledgment that such a state of the science is possible in principle – even if in actual fact it should remain unattainable for us. It also implies a complete rejection of the specifically historical belief in the "incalculable" and essentially "irrational" nature of social events. Schmoller goes further here than most of the theorists would have been prepared to do. ([1914a] 1954c, 170–71)

According to Schumpeter, Schmoller was interested in history not for the sake of its individuality or relativity but simply because it was the source of knowledge. Despite his appreciation of Schmoller's potentiality for theory, Schumpeter had to reject Schmoller's methodological standpoint because it, in fact, precluded Schmoller from undertaking substantive theoretical work.

In light of the difference between the so-called old and new institutional economics, Schumpeter's generous acceptance of the plurality of human motives can be contrasted with the assumptions of the rational maximizer in the new institutional economics. A crucial aspect of the new institutional economics is that it uses formal economic models and assumes the general validity of laws derived from the assumptions of methodological individualism and a rational utility maximizer in the explanation of institutions. But Schumpeter went far beyond the neoclassical approach in economics, a basis of the new institutional economics: he was able to incorporate the notion of institutions and social rules as the determinants of individual behavior, as well as the assumption of nonutility maximizers such as entrepreneurs. Schumpeter's economic sociology is characterized by the interdependence between economic and social forces, by the alternation of the individualistic and institutional viewpoints, and by the interaction between static and dynamic forces; hence it can be described as evolutionary.

A methodology of economic sociology

Schumpeter's view was that economic sociology is part of theory in that it is a sort of generalized economic history with a focus on the analysis of institutions, although its subject matter is different from that of economic theory. There-fore, it can be subject to instrumentalist methodology. This methodological standpoint served as a basic test for Schmoller's research program.

In later years, in recalling the *Methodenstreit*, Schmoller seemed to have reached the same conclusion as Schumpeter:

> Today this controversy [between history and theory] has retreated into the back-ground, owing to the recognition that each researcher may naturally use either more induction or more deduction or both methods, depending on the personal quality and nature of the inquiry, problems and questions to be dealt with, a narrower or broader scope of study, and whether the project is a study of unsettled questions or a description of settled ones; and owing to the recognition that in general it is not possible to speak of the superiority of one method over another. (Schmoller 1911, 479)

This is indeed a remarkable statement compared with his observations during the *Methodenstreit*, but there still remains an important difference between Schmoller and Schumpeter. Although Schmoller admitted that in a historical science there are universal phenomena to which the methods of the natural sciences, general concepts, and universal laws can be applied, he maintained that deductive theorizing for complex social phenomena is possible only after a sufficient amount of inductive work has been accumulated, because, according to him, a theory is no more than a summary or generalization of empirical facts. Thus if one confines the scope of economics to exchange and values as in neoclassical economics, he argued, deduction from simple psychological assumptions can legitimately explain the phenomena in ques-tion, but in a more complex field only historical experience can make a solution possible. In Schmoller's long-term view of economics, only the continuous efforts of detailed historical research, coupled with a perception of overall relationships in a society, will bring imperfect theories closer to an indisputable truth that is accepted by everyone (Schmoller 1897, 26). The question relates more to a methodology of economic sociology than to that of economic theory in the narrow sense.

Schumpeter's instrumentalism, in contrast, asserts that assumptions or hypotheses are arbitrary creations of the human mind and need not be justified by facts. Also, theories deduced from assumptions are not descriptive statements in themselves but instruments for understanding and explaining facts. Therefore, a theory is neither true nor false; it proves useful if it can cover a large number of facts. Instrumentalism facilitates deductive attempts even when empirical data are not sufficient according to the Schmollerian standard. A theory is useful not only as a device for collecting, classifying, and systematizing a given body of observable facts but also as a guide for exploring, predicting, and discovering facts undetected thus far. For this reason a theory is rather essential for achieving the priority agenda in

Schmoller's research program. One need not engage in the never-ending process of fact-finding in order to finally develop realistic assumptions. Rather, one should have a feedback process for theory construction and fact-finding in order to achieve a "unified sociology or social science as the mentally ('theoretically') worked out universal history" (1926b, 382), which was the scientific goal of Schmoller.

Although, in principle, Schmoller did not reject theory, he remained, in fact, a naive empiricist because he did not have a coherent methodological view. When he considered the nature of concept formation, he argued that concepts are an auxiliary means to organize thought, not a perfect copy of reality, admitting nominalism instead of realism (Schmoller 1911, 467–68). Because abstraction, to him, meant a deviation from reality, it was natural that he could not confer any real status to concepts. From this position it was only a step to instrumentalism. But he was so absorbed in the classification of particulars into universal categories, rather than in the role of concept formation, that he emphasized only the negative – that concepts cannot describe real individuality and consequently fundamental truth. As a result, he was only concerned with extensive data collection so as to endow concepts with as rich an empirical content as possible. His conception of a developed, ideal science seems to have been such that concepts and definitions already contained enough truth to deduce significant results. He could not proceed to instrumentalist methodology from the nominalist notion of concepts and allow an instrumental role of assumptions and hypotheses as deliberate mental constructs, because in spite of his nominalist position his ultimate goal was still scientific realism. There was a serious contradiction between nominalism and realism in Schmoller's methodological outlook.

Schumpeter's criticism of Weber

Schumpeter, Weber's junior by nineteen years, seems to have been not only impressed by his energetic and variegated academic activities but also spurred to compete with him.[12] In his obituary essay on Weber, Schumpeter described the distinctive feature of Weber's methodological work and in doing so revealed his own ideal:

They [Weber's works on methodology] were not speculative, they were focused on concrete problems, and they are inextricably connected with his great sociological works. They were primarily concerned with conquering the stronghold of epistemological difficulties, the scientific treatment of history ... In no other author do we find a comparable fusion of methodological theory and productive research. Each of his special studies mirrors the totality of his reflections on questions of principle. Every account of his reflections on questions of principle pulsates with the life of his individual investigations. In every line of both we find his entire personality. ([1920] 1991, 223)

Nevertheless, Schumpeter challenged and was ostensibly critical of Weber's methodological views. Before examining his critique of Weber, it will be helpful to review Weber's methodological orientation and his critical appraisal of the approach of the German Historical School.

Weber's understanding and ideal type

Weber had one foot in German historical economics and the other in neo-Kantian philosophy. Although the German Historical School emphasized the importance of historical research in economics, it lacked, as did Schmoller's view, a methodological foundation that could explain the existence and validity of historical science. The task of methodological inquiry was left to the neo-Kantian philosophers in Germany at the turn of the century, such as Wilhelm Dilthey, Wilhelm Windelband, Heinrich Rickert, and Max Weber. They sought to establish an epistemological basis for the historical, cultural, and social sciences through criticism of Immanuel Kant, who denied historical knowledge a scientific status because it did not fulfill the criterion of general validity. They contrasted the historical sciences with the natural sciences and showed how knowledge of historical individuality is possible as a science. The upshot of neo-Kantian philosophy was that the natural sciences were seen, to use Windelband's terminology, as "nomothetic" and the historical or cultural sciences as "idiographic" in accordance with the difference of a cognitive interest in the generality versus the individuality of reality between the two sciences (Windelband 1894). If the dispute between Menger and Schmoller is viewed in terms of the conflict between the natural scientific method and the historical scientific method as they apply to economics, the basic issues in the *Methodenstreit* were given philosophical reflection by the neo-Kantian philosophers. In fact, Menger distinguished between a historical science and a theoretical science in economic research and regarded each of them as based on a different cognitive interest, that is, the specific versus the general (Menger [1883] 1985, 38).

The starting point for Rickert and Weber was the recognition that in order to overcome the infinite variety of concrete reality, natural or social, some principles of selection and abstraction are indispensable for the establishment of knowledge. They asserted that there are two such principles – general-ization and individualization – each corresponding to a different scientific interest. The principle of generalization requires one to select those elements that are common to all concrete phenomena, whereas that of individualization requires one to choose those elements of individual phenomena that constitute their unique features. The former gives rise to general concepts for the natural sciences, and the latter results in individual concepts for the historical, cultural, or social sciences. In historical science, abstraction from reality must be carried out in such a way that the individuality and uniqueness of phenomena are not lost in the process of concept formation. In order to give this procedure a scientific status, Rickert tried to relate those phenomena concerned with science to generally valid cultural values; a phenomenon is selected because it embodies a particular cultural value and is therefore objectively significant. This is what is known as the principle of value-relevance (*Wertbeziehung*) (Rickert [1899] 1962).

Weber's own contribution to methodology was to put forward two conceptual devices to clarify the logical status of historical knowledge constructed by means of value-relevance: "understanding" (*Verstehen*) and "ideal type" (*Idealtypus*). I contend that these two devices are in fact a methodological reconstruction of viewpoints (3), (4), (5), and (6) attributed to the German Historical School by Schumpeter.

In his first methodological essay, "Roscher und Knies und die logischen Probleme der historischen Nationalökonomie," Weber took issue with the two major figures in the German Historical School concerning the logical problems of the relationship between concept and reality (Weber 1903–6). Weber criticized the curious combination between organicism and realism that was inherent in the traditional thought of the School and rejected its emanational conception, which would explain, on the basis of a biological analogy, the developmental sequence of historical and cultural phenomena in terms of their relationship to metaphysical factors such as *Volksgeist* (national spirit). Emanationism regarded a national economy as a coherent whole, like an organism, and vested it with the ideals and characters of a nation, which were considered as the emanational ground of cultural phenomena. On the other hand, in his essay, "Die 'Objektivität' sozialwissenschaftlicher und sozialpolitischer Erkenntnis" (1904), Weber found fault with historical economists who, as proponents of scientific realism who believed that the goal of science was a true copy of reality, were absorbed in the collection of empirical data. Weber asserted that history should be constructed by theory on the explicit assumption of evaluative values. Thus he fought on two fronts: he tried to replace organicism or holism with methodological individualism, on the one hand, and to replace scientific realism with instrumentalism, on the other. "Understanding" and "ideal type" were the result.

The method of "understanding" is to explain social action by referring to the motives, desires, and emotions of individuals, which are assumed to be the source of values attached to meaningful phenomena. It is an attempt to reconstruct methodologically the problems involved in viewpoints (3) and (4) – the organic and holistic view of society and the recognition of the plurality of human motives – because it assumes methodological individualism without denying the possible influences of social institutions on individual behavior and allows for the plurality of human motives, not only rational but also irrational. Weber used the term *Verstehen* to indicate the scientific procedure in which an observer understands the actions of individuals by reference to their subjective meaning. The same procedure can be expressed by the term *subjectivism* if a reference to the subjectivity of motives, desires, and so forth of observed individuals is to be emphasized.

Weber's other device, the "ideal type," clarifies the logical status of historical concepts. It is a universal concept that, unlike a generic notion in the natural sciences, emphasizes the individuality of historical phenomena, viewpoint (5) of the German Historical School, and the relativity of historical knowledge, its viewpoint (6). The ideal type does not describe the elements that a class of phenomena have in common in the empirical world, but rather the elements that they have in common in a theoretically constructed imaginary world or a model. Thus it makes viewpoints (5) and (6) of the Historical School valid in an imaginary world without denying the logic of the natural sciences. The world described by means of ideal type concepts is an imaginary world of utopia; a theory constructed by means of ideal type concepts is not a copy of reality but a heuristic instrument to deal with reality.

Schumpeter's critique of Weber can be divided into four areas: natural science versus cultural science, value-relevance, ideal type, and understanding of meaning.

Natural science versus cultural science

Schumpeter was critical of the distinction, put forward by the neo-Kantian philosophers, between natural science and cultural (or historical) science, which was based on the differences between the nomothetic and the idiographic, between the abstract and the concrete, and between the general and the individual. These differences were fundamentally attributed to the dissimilarity between cognitive interest in the natural and the cultural sciences, and when brought into economics, unnecessarily intensified the conflict between theory and history. Schumpeter remarked:

Generally, this sharp contrast between the concrete and the abstract in our field is only less infelicitous than – certainly logically false – the contrast between induction and deduction. If by the "concrete" we understand "unanalyzed," then there is nothing concrete in either historical description or economics. If we make a contrast of the concrete versus the abstract coincide with a contrast of the individual versus the general, then interest in the concretely significant and interest in the generally true, or more correctly, in the universally applicable, can indeed be distinguished in conception, but in practice they immediately join together again. ... The concrete and the abstract merely show – and this is the only meaning of the contrast in practical terms – degrees of difference in the asymptotic approach to the individuality of specific cases. (1926b, 362–63)

Schumpeter argued that there is no fixed demarcation between concrete and abstract aspects, or between individual and general aspects, of phenomena. The distinction is only relative and depends on the degree of abstraction from reality, which in turn reflects the cognitive interest of research.

According to Schumpeter, the neo-Kantians tried to distinguish between the two sciences on the basis of the unrealistic notions of difference. Referring to Windelband, Rickert, and Dilthey, he wrote:

> Their minds had been formed by the tasks and the training of the philosopher, historian, and philologist. So when they proceeded, with enviable confidence, to lay down the law for us, they drew an entirely unrealistic dividing line between the "laws of nature" and the "laws of cultural development" or the "formulation of laws" (nomothesis) and "historical description" (idiography), forgetting that great parts of the social sciences ride astride this dividing line, which fact seriously impairs its usefulness (though, for the truly philologico–historical disciplines it does retain validity). They were simply strangers to the problems and the epistemological nature of those parts of the social sciences, yet failed to add the proper qualifications to their arguments. That this was apt to mislead the many economists who listened to them – Max Weber, e.g., was strongly influenced by Rickert – was as inevitable as it was regrettable. But let us note the striking saying of Dilthey that reads like a motto of Max Weber's methodology: "We *explain* the phenomena of nature, we *understand* the phenomena of the mind (or of culture)." (1954a, 777)

Here Schumpeter ridiculed the distinction between explanation and understanding.

Schumpeter's criticism is valid for Rickert and Windelband, but not for Weber. From the early stage of his methodological inquiry, Weber was critical of the dichotomy between generality and individuality, between positivism and historicism, and between nomothesis and idiography, and his concepts of ideal type and cultural meaning were devices to overcome the difficulties surrounding the dichotomy and to lay the foundation of the cultural sciences.

The principle of value-relevance

At first sight Schumpeter seems to have accepted the principle of value-relevance in his actual social-scientific work. In his 1926 essay he referred to "universal human interests" (1926b, 362) as an indispensable analytic lever for empirical research. The opening page of *Entwicklung* also asserts the necessity of arbitrary abstraction in establishing objects of research: "The social process is really one indivisible whole. Out of its great stream the classifying hand of the investigator artificially extracts economic facts. The designation of a fact as economic already involves an abstraction, the first of the many forced upon us by the technical conditions of mentally copying reality" (1934, 3). This clearly indicates that Schumpeter accepted the neo-Kantian view that reality has such infinite elements and aspects that it is impossible to copy it.

But Schumpeter did not delve into the problem of value-relevance because, from the standpoint of instrumentalist methodology, the relevance to cultural value and interest emphasized by Rickert and Weber, however useful it may be in constructing knowledge, is still an arbitrary hypothesis and it is not necessary to justify it by any means in order to establish its truth. Schumpeter would definitely have denied the justificatory function of the principle of value-relevance. Here again, his criticism holds true for Rickert but not for Weber. Whereas Rickert tried to relate historical phenomena to what he called universally valid cultural values in order to justify the validity of historical knowledge, which amounted to metaphysical justification, Weber was committed to the pluralism of cultural values and emphasized the evaluative values of observers as the foundation of historical and cultural work, as is well known by his discussion of objectivity in the social sciences (Weber 1904).[13]

Indeed, there remains a difference of appearance between the methodologies of Weber and Schumpeter, but this is not a crucial point. As an illustration, consider the views of Weber and Schumpeter on the foundations of marginal utility theory. In his article "Die Grenznutzlehre und das 'psychophysische Grundgesetz,'" Weber criticized the assertion of Lujo Brentano, a German historical economist, that the marginal utility theory depends on the erroneous psychophysical law of E. H. Weber and G. T. Fechner (Weber 1908). In the marginal utility theory, according to Brentano, the valuation of economic agents, which produces externally observable acts of exchange, is explained by a sensation caused by an external impulse (that is, the amount of goods) in accordance with a certain psychophysical law. In contrast, Weber argued that the marginal utility theory represents an understanding of the meaning of human action in light of its specific cognitive objective. The cognitive objective of economic theory, according to Weber, is to clarify the significance of rationality embedded in the civilization of capitalism. Thus economic action is interpreted as based on a rational "calculation of merchants." Specifically, economic agents are assumed to act rationally to achieve the goal of want satisfaction, and this assumption has nothing to do with psychology. Weber's argument, which identified rationality with "the mind of merchants" and discovered the starting point of the marginal utility theory in "the method of commercial bookkeeping," clearly reflected his methodological principle of cultural value-relevance. But this does not mean that the cultural meaning of rationality is objectively valid.

On the other hand, in *Wesen*, which appeared in the same year as Weber's article on Brentano and the psychophysicists, Schumpeter too rejected the attempt to base marginal utility theory on psychology, but for a different reason (see pages 115–16). In his view, the assumption of the utility function is arbitrary and needs no justification; it is merely an assumption to explain an exchange equilibrium in the market. The assessment of an assumption rests on whether a theory deduced from it fits reality. Whereas Weber embellished the starting point of a theory with a meaning that is related to certain values, Schumpeter, as an instrumentalist, regarded the results of a theory as the criterion of validity. As a proponent of the "ideal type" methodology, Weber explicitly agreed that theory is a heuristic device as well as a constructive instrument for the analysis of empirical diversity. But as a successor of the neo-Kantian axiological theory of knowledge, he still adhered to the cultural significance of phenomena involved in concept formation and emphasized incessant changes in values.

The concept of ideal type

The concept of ideal type is an important idea that defines the methodological nature of theoretical concepts in the social sciences. But the use of ideal types involves questions. Can we say that Schumpeter fully agreed with Weber's methodology of ideal type? The answer is no, as illustrated in these remarks:

This method of (logically) Ideal Types has, of course, its uses, though it inevitably involves distortion of the facts. But if, forgetting the methodological nature of these constructions, we put the "ideal" Feudal Man face to face with the "ideal" Capitalist Man, transition from the one to the other will present a problem that has, however, no counterpart in the sphere of historical fact. Unfortunately, Max Weber lent the weight of his great authority to a way of thinking that has no other basis than a misuse of the method of Ideal Types. Accordingly, he set out to find an explanation for a process which sufficient attention to historical detail renders self-explanatory. He found it in the New Spirit – i.e. a different attitude to life and its values – engendered by the Reformation ... The historical objections to this construction are too obvious to detain us. Much more important is it to see the fundamental methodological error involved. (1954a, 80–81)

Elsewhere Schumpeter draws the same conclusions.[14]

What exactly is "the fundamental methodological error"? Was this accusation of Weber justified? Weber's notion of the ideal type was essentially intended to reveal the structure of linkage between theory and history, not to exaggerate the distinction or dichotomy between the two. Specifically, it was a solution to the question of how historical concepts can be general and yet not lose their individuality. With regard to this question, Schumpeter had dismissed the importance of the neo-Kantian distinction between the abstract and the concrete, between the general and the individual, because the one requires the other in a continual process of concept formation. In earlier methodological studies of Weber's ideal type, it had been asserted that one should not put into one category diverse kinds of ideal types that vary in their levels of abstraction and thus include the concepts of abstract economic theory (such as utility, competition, and economic man) as well as those of historical elements (such as early Christianity, the medieval city economy, and Protestant economic ethics). The most famous criticism to this effect was Alexander von Schelting's (1922), but it was offered for the first time by Schmoller (1911, 467–68). For Schumpeter, however, the issue of diversity did not matter because, in his view, historical concepts contain various levels of the abstract and the concrete, and it is natural that ideal types include diverse concepts derived from different degrees of abstraction. The critics of diversity, such as Schmoller and Schelting, ignored Weber's intention of constructing historical individuality based on universal concepts and adhered to Rickert's naive dichotomy of nature and culture.

The difficulty concerns the way in which ideal types are used, rather than the way in which they are constructed. What Schumpeter meant by "the fundamental methodological error" of Weber lies in his assertion that Weber confused ideal types with historical concepts and used them directly for historical description. Since in the conception of ideal types even specific historical concepts are granted a certain degree of generality as far as their typical elements are concerned, they are still thought constructs and instruments. It will be recalled how in *Wesen* Schumpeter distinguished between historical and theoretical description (see page 112): whereas historical description provides a catalogue of specific facts through selection and classification, theoretical description gives a general scheme by way of the abstraction and transformation of individual facts (1908, 42). In other words, Schumpeter distinguished between an *ad hoc* explanatory hypothesis about historical facts and an instrumental hypothesis or a general simplifying scheme or model (1954a, 14–15). It was the latter that he was concerned with as the object of economic methodology and that he regarded as an instrument. Ideal type concepts are not *ad hoc* explanatory hypotheses but instrumental hypotheses, even if they include diverse categories based on different degrees of abstraction and are part of economic sociology as well as economic theory. From this standpoint, Weber could be accused of confusing theory and history, of using the ideal types as if they were historical explanatory hypotheses.

Weber, however, was careful to guard against misunderstanding in this regard, as his following critique of the German Historical School indicates. The German Historical School strongly held that the goal of science is to order its empirical data into a system of concepts whose aim is assumed to be the reproduction of objective reality. The school's recurrent attacks on theoretical work in economics rested on the unreality of concepts. Weber explicitly rejected this realist contention:

If one perceives the implications of the fundamental ideas of modern epistemology which ultimately derives from Kant; namely, that concepts are primarily analytical instruments for the intellectual mastery of empirical data and can be only that, the fact that precise genetic concepts are necessarily ideal types will not cause him to desist from constructing them. The relationship between concept and historical research is reversed for those who appreciate this; the goal of the Historical School then appears as logically impossible, the concepts are not ends but are means to the end of understanding phenomena which are significant from concrete individual viewpoints. Indeed, it is just *because* the content of historical concepts is necessarily subject to change that they must be formulated precisely and clearly on all occasions. In their application, their character as ideal analytical constructs should be carefully kept in mind, and the ideal-type and historical reality should not be confused with each other. (Weber [1904] 1949, 106–7)

Regardless of whether Weber actually succeeded in capturing the relationship between the Protestant ethic and capitalism without overloading abstract concepts with substantive historical contents, Schumpeter's critical view seems to confirm their basic agreement on the instrumentality of the ideal type.

The understanding of meaning

Schumpeter also found fault with another of Weber's methodological contributions: his thesis regarding the understanding of meaning. According to Weber, the cultural sciences are comprised of meaningful human actions. Knowledge of culture amounts to understanding actors' motives, desires, and intentions in contradistinction to knowledge of nature, which consists of meaningless facts – physical things and processes. Thus Weber distinguished between "understanding" (*Verstehen*) or knowledge of culture and "grasping" (*Begreifen*) or knowledge of nature. He arrived at this thesis by developing Rickert's view that value-relevance relates to values entertained by historical actors, not by historians. Those phenomena to which humans attach values become meaningful.

Schumpeter responded ironically to the distinction between understanding and grasping by observing that "it makes precious little difference to the practical work of a theorist whether Mr. Methodologist tells him that in investigating the conditions of a profit maximum he is investigating 'meant meanings' of an 'ideal type' or that he is hunting for 'laws' or 'theorems'" (1954a, 819). The distinction between understanding and grasping meant nothing to Schumpeter, who did not need to relate to any cultural values in posing problems.

In his 1940 essay on rationality ([1940] 1991), Schumpeter did consider the problem of understanding in terms of the distinction between the values of an observer and those of observed actors, specifically with regard to the concept of rationality, the major theme of Weber's economic sociology. Schumpeter distinguished between hypothetical rationality attributed to agents by an observer (*objective rationality*) and conscious rationality in agents (*subjective rationality*) and regarded the former as more important in the social sciences. This thesis seems to oppose Rickert and Weber's thesis of understanding. Whereas in Rickert and Weber the observer draws out the values from the objects of study, in Schumpeter the observer sets up his own values to observe the objects of study. This position was also a direct consequence of Schumpeter's instrumentalist methodology, which enabled him to discuss phenomena without reference to prevailing cultural values.

On close examination, however, Schumpeter's criticism does not apply to Weber. It might be important to distinguish between two different senses of meaning in Weber (see Oakes 1988, 26–32). One is the *subjective meaning* that actors ascribe to their actions; the other is the *cultural meaning* that observers ascribe to a phenomenon. Neo-Kantian value-relevance, in terms of which a phenomenon becomes the object of the cultural sciences and an ideal type is correspondingly constituted, relates to the cultural meaning. The subjective meaning of actions is determined by the valuation of actors and gives a criterion of demarcation between natural phenomena as the domain of the meaningless and human actions as the domain of the meaningful. Wilhelm Dilthey contrasted humanities with natural science because he wanted to find the stamp of human spirit in social reality. Therefore, the subjective meaning of a phenomenon is a necessary condition for its cultural meaning, but the latter is not reduced to the former. Schumpeter's argument concerning objective rationality and subjective rationality is simply another version of Weber's cultural meaning and subjective meaning.

An interpretation of Weber's methodology

In spite of Schumpeter's harsh criticism and partial misunderstanding of Weber's methodology, the substance of their methodologies appear to be the same. If this is true, it is rather remarkable that at the critical juncture of the *Methodenstreit* Schumpeter and Weber worked out similar solutions although they were influenced by different schools, Schumpeter by the early positivists and Weber by the neo-Kantians. By *similar solutions* I mean that they similarly developed instrumentalist methodology and similarly addressed economic sociology.[15]

Both *Verstehende* sociology and the ideal type concept are widely recognized as Weber's characteristic tools, and in the above discussion I have shown them to be a reconstruction of the methodological views of the German Historical School. *Verstehen*, however, is simply a particular assumption of methodological individualism; it does not present Weber's general methodological position.

Similarly, ideal type is merely a kind of concept formation, not a general methodological perspective. What has been lacking in the literature on Weber is an effort to define his central methodological propositions in sociology, which I suggest, can be interpreted as instrumentalism. By instrumentalism I do not mean the narrow version currently attributed to Milton Friedman, but rather the broader version that I expounded with respect to Schumpeter's methodological view in chapter 5. Through this procedure, Schumpeter's instrumentalist methodology, which was first developed in the context of economic statics, will assuredly be valid in the broader field of economic sociology.

Interpretation as instrumentalism

The structure of Weber's instrumentalist methodology can be seen in some passages from his writings:

For the purposes of a typological scientific analysis it is convenient to treat all irrational, affectually determined elements of behavior as factors of deviation from a conceptually pure type of rational action ... The construction of a purely rational course of action in such cases serves the sociologists as a type (ideal type) which has the merit of clear understandability and lack of ambiguity ... Only in this respect and for these reasons of methodical convenience is the method of sociology "rationalistic." It is naturally not legitimate to interpret this procedure as involving a rationalistic bias of sociology, but only as a *methodical device*. It certainly does not involve a belief in the actual predominance of rational elements in human life, for on the question of how this predominance does or does not exist, nothing whatever has been said. (Weber [1922b] 1978, 1, 6–7, emphasis mine)[16]

It is important to recognize Weber's general view that *Verstehen* is only a methodical (not methodological) or instrumental assumption, not a description of real fact, although in this context he is specifically concerned with the hypotheses of an instrumental rationality (*zweckrational*) as an extreme case of methodical individualism. The instrumentalist view on the cognitive status of theories is that theories are neither true nor false because they are mere instruments.

Weber conceived the nature of law as follows: "It is customary to designate various sociological generalizations, as for example 'Gresham's Law,' as 'laws.' These are in fact typical probabilities confirmed by *observation* to the effect that under certain given conditions an expected course of social action will occur, which is understandable in terms of the typical motives and typical subjective *meaning* of the actors" (Weber [1922b] 1978, 1, 18, emphasis mine).[17] Observation (*Beobachtung*) and meaning (*Sinn*) are the key words. In order to understand what Weber actually meant here, it is useful to refer to the distinction between three basic concepts, introduced in chapter 5 (see page 106):

"hypotheses" (axioms, postulates, or assumptions), "theories" (laws, principles, or theorems), and "facts" (observations, data, or phenomena). To paraphrase Weber, "theories" in *Verstehende* sociology must be based on "hypotheses" about the subjective meaning of individual action, on the one hand, and must be justified by objective "facts" of social phenomena, on the other.

Weber added further explanations to emphasize the importance of the roles he attributed to "hypotheses" and "facts," or meaning and observation:

A correct causal interpretation of a typical action (an understandable type of action) means that the process that is claimed to be typical is conceived to be *meaningfully adequate* to some degree and at the same time is confirmed as *causally adequate* to some degree ... Only statistical uniformities that correspond to the understandable subjective meaning of social action constitute the understandable type of action in the sense of words used here and thus "sociological generalizations." (Weber [1922b] 1978, 1, 12, emphasis mine)[18]

Here Weber presented two requirements for right theories in the sense of a right causal explanation of social phenomena: "meaningfully adequate" (*sinn adäquat*) and "causally adequate" (*kausal adäquat*). The former relates to the dependence of "theories" on subjectively meaningful "hypotheses" and the latter to the correspondence of "theories" with empirically observed "facts."

What then is the correspondence between "theories" and "facts"? In this regard, it is worth recalling that Weber refuted the view of the German Historical School that "the knowledge of historical reality can or should be a 'presuppositionless' copy of 'objective' facts" (Weber [1904] 1949, 92). He was not of the opinion that facts as such exist independently of theories and that observation can support theories even in a probabilistic form. In order to answer this question, we have to examine Weber's ideal type concept because for him theories were conceived as ideal types. To illustrate his view by reference to abstract economic theory, he stated:

Substantively, this construct [economic theory] in itself is like a *utopia* which has been arrived at by the analytical accentuation of certain elements of reality. Its relationship to the empirical data consists solely in the fact that where market-conditioned relationships of the type referred to by the abstract construct are discovered or suspected to exist in reality to some extent, we can make the *characteristic* features of this relationship pragmatically *clear* and *understandable* by reference to an *ideal-type*. This procedure can be indispensable for heuristic as well as expository purposes. The ideal typical concept will help to develop our skill in imputation in *research*: it is no "hypothesis" but it offers guidance to the construction of hypotheses. It is not a *description* of reality but it aims to give unambiguous means of expression to such a description. (Weber [1904] 1949, 90)

In instrumentalist methodology, the roles of a theory include organization, classification, reconstruction, and – through all these efforts – the understanding of facts, and they amount to what Weber called *heuristic*.

A well-known claim of instrumentalism is that the realism of assumptions does not matter. Although Weber was not a theoretical economist, he did not deny the value of economic theory. In his evaluation of theoretical economics, his instrumentalist perspective is clearly revealed:

We have in abstract economic theory an illustration of those synthetic constructs which have been designated as "ideas" of historical phenomena. It offers us an ideal picture of events on the commodity-market under conditions of a society organized on the principles of an exchange economy, free competition and rigorous rational conduct. This conceptual pattern brings together certain relationships and events of historical life into a complex, which is conceived as an internally consistent system. (Weber [1904] 1949, 89–90)

The ideal types of social action which for instance are used in economic theory are thus unrealistic or abstract in that they always ask what course of action would take place if it were purely rational and oriented to economic ends alone ... The more sharply and precisely the ideal type has been constructed, thus the more abstract and unrealistic in this sense it is, the better it is able to perform its functions in formulating terminology, classifications, and hypotheses. (Weber [1922b] 1978, 1, 21)

Finally, how is the practical success of theories evaluated? Weber wrote: "Here, too, there is only one criterion, namely, that of success in revealing concrete cultural phenomena in their interdependence, their causal conditions and their *significance*. The construction of abstract ideal-types recommends itself not as an end but as a *means*" (Weber [1904] 1949, 92). This criterion of success corresponds to a moderate, weak version of instrumentalism, not to that of an extreme, strong version of instrumentalism that restricts the instrumental role of theory to prediction.

Sociology, in Weber's view, belongs to the category of theory in that it tries to formulate type concepts and provide uniform generalizations of social phenomena. Therefore it is subject to instrumentalist methodology; in fact, Weber explained the essence of instrumentalism using his own ideal type concept.

The concept of ideal types and institutions

Adopting the German Historical School's viewpoint of historical development as a global process, Schumpeter proposed a conceptual framework for the theoretical research of history, namely, economic sociology, focusing on the concept of institutions that would make it possible to apply generalizations to the objects of historical individuality. On this basis Schumpeter could apply his instrumentalist methodology to economic sociology, and his methodological view is quite similar to that of Weber.

Based on this finding, I can say that if Weber's concept of the ideal type was the methodological exploration of concept formation in economic sociology, Schumpeter's concept of institutions was a substantive specification of the ideal type concept. The equivalence of the ideal type concept and the institution concept is a conclusion that we have reached through an investigation of the ways in which Weber and Schumpeter sought the mutual cooperation of theory and history. In this sense the methodologies of Weber and Schumpeter paralleled one another and were essentially rooted in instrumentalism, except for the significant difference in their backgrounds and appearances – Rickert's idealism versus Mach's positivism. Schumpeter's methodological position differed from Weber's insofar as it eschewed idealistic elements. Schumpeter's final word on Weber – "His work and teaching had much to do with the emergence of Economic Sociology in the sense of an analysis of economic institutions, the recognition of which as a distinct field clarifies so many 'methodological' issues" (1954a, 819) – can be understood to imply that an analysis of institutions will help clarify all the methodological issues concerning the relationship between history and theory.

As this chapter is concerned with Schumpeter's methodology of economic sociology, it does not cover his substantive analyses in that field. But here two points are appropriate. First, although the methodologies of Schumpeter and Weber reveal many similarities, there was a big difference in the substance of their economic sociologies. Weber's sociology was much more concerned with comparative static social systems than the dynamic process of evolution. This may explain why evolution-minded Schumpeter felt closer to Marx and Schmoller. And second, the above methodological discussion may throw light on Schumpeter's famous thesis on the decline of capitalism in *Capitalism, Socialism and Democracy* (1942), his major work of economic sociology. His thesis that capitalism will decline because its economic success will lay the groundwork for social circumstances unfavorable to it should not be interpreted as historical determinism. It has nothing to do with a historical hypothesis or prediction; rather, it is a theoretical hypothesis derived from certain assumptions about the interaction between economic and social factors, and its validity rests on the instrumental roles in understanding reality. Schumpeter would certainly have objected to the explication of his thesis as a historical hypothesis, in the same way that he disagreed with Weber's use of ideal type concepts to explain the historical rise of capitalism by the Protestant ethic.

Between positivism and idealism

Right or wrong, Schumpeter participated in the stream of positivist thought of the twentieth century, but inherited the outlook of the nineteenth-century German Historical School. Whereas in the seventeenth and eighteenth centuries the Enlightenment in Britain and France brought about the rise of social sciences based on rationalism, positivism, and universalism, historicism was formed in Germany under the influence of idealism as a critique of the Enlightenment.

Positivism, historicism, and idealism

In his early speculation on the history of thought, Schumpeter made an interesting observation about the German Historical School. He regarded Thomas Carlyle, Auguste Comte, and the German Historical School as a reaction to positivism and the Enlightenment in the social sciences that occurred in the eighteenth century, and he located the Historical School at the midpoint between Carlyle and Comte. Schumpeter wrote:

> On the one hand, this school, like the Romanticists, reproached the barrenness and banality of theoretical analysis, praised the national spirit and the unity of personality, and demanded the revival of philosophical observations. On the other hand, however, this school proclaimed "exact factual research" as its principle, as opposed to "nebulous speculation." Both directions cannot coexist ... Yet, when did a scientific program ever have logical unity? ... This school floated at the same time both in the stream of reaction of philosophical volition against analysis and in the stream of reaction of positivism against philosophy. (1915, 75–76)

Although the philosophical and idealist elements were particularly distinct in the old Historical School, they receded in the younger Schmollerian Historical School. But insofar as Schmoller had a teleological viewpoint, he was not completely free from metaphysical elements.

Did Schumpeter, like the Historical School, maintain an ambivalence toward positivism and idealism? Although Schumpeter affirmed the value of the achievements of economics on the positivistic line that had been attained through a specialization narrow in scope, he could not help identifying with historicism in grasping the overall picture of a society. For him, the relationship between positivism and historicism was not like the conflict between natural science and historical science, or between generalization and individuation, as was conceived in the neo-Kantian philosophy, but rather the relationship between pure economics and an all-encompassing social science. It was for this reason that he relied on economic sociology in addition to economic theory. On the other hand, idealism was almost foreign to Schumpeter. After the third generation of the German Historical School consisting of Weber, Spiethoff, and Sombart, German economics became the political economy of the totalitarian ideology during the interwar period. Schumpeter, standing on positivistic ground, drew a dividing line between totalitarian economists and himself. He appreciated the philosophy of science but opposed idealism.

Three levels of historicism

It is useful to summarize the conceptions of historicism in order to confirm the place of Schumpeter in the intellectual field of social science. Herbert Schnädelbach distinguishes between three meanings of historicism (Schnädelbach 1974, 19–23). The first relates to scientific practice that emphasizes detailed empirical research and that sometimes prevents the systematization and theoretical formulation of knowledge by absorption in never-ending data collection. The second is a style of thought that maintains a historical relativity of knowledge and denies a universal system. The third is a characteristic *Weltanschauung* that views things as emerging historically and resists naturalism, a view that is nothing more than the position of Romanticism as opposed to the Enlightenment. Although Schnädelbach calls these positions the three meanings of historicism, they are conceptions defined on three different levels that may be properly labeled the method, methodology, and vision of historicism, respectively.

When the first conception (method) and the second conception (methodology) of historicism are combined, the theoretical formulation of history, or *histoire raisonée*, to use Schumpeter's favorite expression, is likely to be denied. A historicism that indulges in relativism is in danger. Schumpeter objected to anti-theory and advocated feedback between theory and history on the basis of instrumentalist methodology. Although he admitted that data collection and theory formulation are different types of work, he characterized economic sociology as collecting data as well as formulating theory. Practically speaking, the concept of institutions in economic sociology was a device that facilitated compromise between the general and the individual. Weber's ideal type was also a conceptual device to support the theoretical formulation of history.

Viewed in this way, the third conception (vision) of historicism is its essence. Thus different visions make different systems of thought possible. Weber focused on *Verstehen* sociology, which was different from the naturalistic and mechanistic view of society. Schumpeter similarly emphasized social science, which included human beings. Yet Weber's various sociologies produced a comparative typology of social systems, whereas Schumpeter's economic sociology addressed the historical evolution of social systems.

CHAPTER 9

Economic sociology as an evolutionary science

After the publication of *Theorie der wirtschaftlichen Entwicklung* in 1912, Schumpeter diverted his research interest from economics to economic sociology. His first topic in economic sociology was social classes, an idea he had developed in his lectures on "State and Society" at the University of Czernowitz (1910–11), "The Theory of Social Classes" at Columbia University (1913–14), and "The Problem of Social Classes" at the University of Graz (1915–16). His first article on the subject, "Die sozialen Klassen in ethnisch homogenen Milieu" (1927a), was published on the occasion of his 1926 lecture on "Leadership and Class Formation" at the University of Heidelberg.

During the same period Schumpeter also brought out several sociological works: *Die Krise des Steuerstaates* (1918), "Zur Soziologie der Imperialismen" (1918/19), and "Sozialistische Möglichkeiten von heute" (1920–21). All of these studies were based on the vision of changing capitalism, and, together with his theory of social classes, would be finalized as *Capitalism, Socialism and Democracy* (1942).[1]

This chapter aims to interpret and reconstruct Schumpeter's sociological work and discusses, for that purpose, the development of his thought on *Capitalism, Socialism and Democracy* in terms of a series of component theories of leadership, social classes, tax state, imperialism, and socialism. Some might consider sociological themes such as the tax state and imperialism to be digressions from Schumpeter's major research areas. But in my view this is not true. Schumpeter's entire body of sociological work was an investigation of what he called a sociology of the *Zeitgeist* (the spirit of the time) from the perspective of social classes, paying special attention to Marx's conceptual framework for the economic interpretation of history. A sociology of the *Zeitgeist* is an analysis of the culture, ways of thinking, and value schemes of the time; for Schumpeter, it was an essential ground for developing his thesis on the transformation of capitalism into socialism. Although he had completed a series of studies on economic sociology earlier in his career, he attempted to expand and consolidate them in later life (in *Capitalism, Socialism and Democracy*), just as he had done with his theory of economic development and his history of economic thought.

Although Schumpeter did not present an explicit system of economic sociology as a conceptual paradigm, his framework can be reconstructed from the materials he left. He did not complete his analysis of fluid reality, but his work is sufficient to show a paradigmatic scheme of social science.

From leaders to social classes

An essential link between Schumpeter's theory of social classes and his previous economic research was his thesis of leadership. He regarded entrepreneurs, that is, innovators in the economic area, as a special group of leaders who comprised a small number of people. Generally speaking, there are a limited number of people in various areas of social life, who, after overcoming all resistance, are able to destroy existing orders through the introduction of innovations and thereby succeed in creating the current of the time, in contrast to the majority of people who stick to adaptive and customary types of behavior. Such leaders in various areas, each in his own way, ascend the upper rank of society and form a set of social classes. For Schumpeter, a theory of social classes sums up the performance of various social areas, including the economy, and thus serves as a conceptual pivot for his idea of a universal social science.

Schumpeter's theory of social classes, combined with his theory of leadership, mediated between economics and economic sociology when he explored historical changes in a capitalist system. Thus an analysis of a changing capitalist system became a unified task of his universal science. He did not deal with each of the social areas equally, but distinguished strategically between the economic area, on the one hand, and noneconomic areas, on the other, to focus on the actions and reactions between economy and noneconomy. Noneconomy was conceptualized, as Mach's thought economy so to speak, to indicate in the simplest way the institutional framework or the *Zeitgeist* that circumscribes the economy. This setup basically constituted Schumpeter's economic sociology, which was the first approximation of a universal social science.

In chapter 3 I paid attention to the perspective of a universal social science, which Schumpeter presented – beyond the domain of a theory of economic development – in chapter 7 of the first edition of *Theorie der wirtschaftlichen Entwicklung*. This perspective broadened his vista from the phenomena of economic development that were caused by entrepreneurs to the phenomena of sociocultural development as a whole that were abundantly colored by the activities of leaders in various areas. It is noteworthy that before Schumpeter painted a picture of the overall development of a society (section 13 of chapter 7) in the first edition of *Theorie*, he discussed social classes (section 11) and the social atmosphere of a capitalist economy (section 12). His argument in the two sections, prior to his sociological articles, was submitted as a "theoretical scaffold" (1912, 525) for his move from economics to economic sociology. It is particularly meaningful because the major issues of social classes that he later addressed in his economic sociology were already described here.

Schumpeter's major points were as follows: Entrepreneurs can stand on the top of not only the economic but also the social pyramid and exert influence on the spirit, culture, and politics of the time. However, there are leaders other than entrepreneurs; the social pyramid is not solely composed of economic material. The social pyramid is not single-peaked but consists of old and new strata involving a historical time lag. The categories of classes in economics are meaningless when they are employed as the concepts of social classes in sociology. The moral and spiritual atmosphere of a capitalist society cannot be explained by economic phenomena alone.

The upshot of Schumpeter's argument is that a theory of economic development, including his own, has only limited power in understanding social structure. Hence, just as he had tried to develop a dynamic theory by defining the limits of static theory, so too did he aim at developing economic sociology by asserting the limits of dynamic theory. In this undertaking he sought a breakthrough in developing a theory of social classes, stating its reason as follows: "Social class is a complicated, certainly not purely economic, perhaps generally not unified phenomenon. Therefore, when we speak about the social structure of a capitalist economy, we do not believe that the economic mechanism easily explains the social mechanism at its core" (1912, 529).

Leaders and social classes

The relationship between leaders or elites and social classes had already been addressed by writers like Vilfredo Pareto and Gaetano Mosca who offered non-Marxian theories of social classes. According to Pareto, elites are a class of people who possess the greatest ability in their area of activity (Pareto [1916] 1935, 3, 1423). More specifically Mosca observed:

If a new source of wealth develops in a society, if the practical importance of knowledge grows, if an old religion declines or a new one is born, if a new current of ideas spreads, then, simultaneously, far-reaching dislocations occur in the ruling-class. One might say, indeed, that the whole history of civilised mankind comes down to a conflict between the tendency of dominant elements to monopolise political power and transmit possession of it by inheritance and the tendency toward a dislocation of old forces and an insurgence of new forces; and this conflict produces an unending ferment of endosmosis and exosmosis between the upper classes and certain portions of the lower. (Mosca [1896] 1939, 65)

Schumpeter combined this thesis of leadership and social classes with his sociology of the *Zeitgeist*.

At the outset of his 1927 article on social classes, Schumpeter noted that the concept of classes he was going to use related to historical and social entities, not to a conceptual artifact like landowners and workers constructed in economic theory. A class is more than a mere aggregate of its members and has its own peculiar life and characteristic spirit. This specification clearly means that a theory of social classes is a sociology dealing with institutional and environmental conditions that circumscribe the behavior and thought of individuals and that methodological individualism does not hold in this discipline. Among a variety of sociological questions about classes, Schumpeter considered the question of why a society is not homogeneous but always forms a social ladder or pyramid. His answer was a thesis of leadership.

That Schumpeter's sociological approach was based on a theoretical formulation of history or *histoire raisonée* is manifested in the following idea: every social situation is the heritage of preceding situations, and therefore the social pyramid is not a single entity but takes over the preceding social structure and concentration of power. In other words, the social pyramid is not single-peaked but multiple-peaked. Thus he maintained:

first, that any theory of class structure, in dealing with a given historical period, must include prior class structures among its data; and then that any general theory of classes and class formation must explain the fact that classes coexisting at any given time bear the marks of different centuries on their brow, so to speak – that they stem from varying conditions. This is in the essential nature of the matter, an aspect of the nature of the class phenomenon. ([1927a] 1951b, 145)

Specifically, in considering the aristocratic class of European feudalism and the industrial bourgeoisie of capitalism, Schumpeter attached great importance to the fact that the feudal lords survive in the modern era and maintain a symbiotic relationship with the industrial bourgeoisie. "It was feudalism run on a capitalist basis; an aristocratic and military society that fed on capitalism; an amphibial case very far removed from bourgeois control" (1954a, 144). Such a social structure has a paramount influence on the future of capitalism.[2]

Schumpeter dealt with the relationship between social classes and the superstructure as Marx did but, based on his view of social structure, developed a theory quite different from Marx's economic interpretation of history or historical materialism, saying that:

The social pyramid is never made of a single substance, is never seamless. There is no single *Zeitgeist*, except in the sense of a construct. This means that in explaining any historical course or situation, account must be taken of the fact that much in it can be explained only by the survival of elements that are actually alien to its own trends ... Another implication is that the coexistence of essentially different mentalities and objective sets of facts must form part of any general theory. ([1927a] 1951b, 144–45)

Schumpeter did not deny the importance of studying the superstructure and the *Zeitgeist*, but he tried to explain them in terms of historically complex elements of social classes. In interpreting his framework, in which social classes are conceptualized by reference to leaders in various social areas and the superstructure is to be accounted for by reference to social classes, it is useful to focus on two fundamental concepts: *social values* (or social leadership) and the *Zeitgeist*. These concepts are essential for an economic sociology that is constituted on the basis of theories of leadership and social classes.

Social values and the Zeitgeist

Each social area has a social function to undertake the specific tasks of a society imposed by the environment, and to contribute to the formation of social classes. Those who succeed in fulfilling the social functions can ascend the ladder of each social class. Schumpeter's metaphor was that "each class resembles a hotel or an omnibus, always full, but always of different people" ([1927a] 1951b, 165). When he discussed social science as well as social classes, he was not explicit about which areas of social life were to be distinguished, though the economy was always mentioned. According to Michael Mann, human beings pursue a diversity of objectives and in various ways create the intersecting networks of social interaction as institutional devices for these purposes. The most important networks are the economic, ideological, military, and political (Mann 1986, 1, 22–28). If the ability to achieve objectives is called power, the four major areas are conceived to be the sources of social power; a relatively influential power structure will emerge, depending on the particular period in history.

In Schumpeter's view, the social functions attributed to individual social classes do not have equal rank. A hierarchy of classes constitutes the social order. Schumpeter's answer to the question, why do the social functions have higher or lower ranks, was that one function might signify more important social leadership than other functions at a given time. The point here is not leadership within each area of social life but leadership across all the areas. The feudal nobility had the military function to wage wars; the modern industrial bourgeoisie has the economic function to implement technological innovations. These classes represent instances of social leadership in different historical periods. Whereas the ultimate foundation of class phenomena is, as the thesis of leadership holds, the differences of the capacity of individuals to undertake specific social functions and a leadership role, the factor that differentiates the relative importance of social classes is social leadership in meeting the demands of the time. Thus, the rank of a class is determined, first, by the social importance of the functions attached to the class and, second, by the success of its members in performing the functions. For these reasons, the relative rank of social classes rises and falls. Although Schumpeter did not use the word "power," his term "social leadership" can be understood to mean social power.

In each area of politics, economy, religion, science, and so forth, we see leaders who challenge the customary ways of life and lead people in new directions. However, all the areas do not always fulfill the most crucial functions for the social order. The relative rank of social classes depends on the relative importance of social functions in the historical circumstances. Thus Schumpeter used the concept "social values" to mean the aptitude for fulfilling socially necessary functions in a certain historical situation. Class structure is a hierarchy in which individual families are arranged according to their social value. The superstructure of a society is established as consciousness, culture, and institutional framework, which are peculiarly related to the class endowed with social leadership in view of its contribution to social values. Schumpeter's concept of the *Zeitgeist* can be used to symbolically denote the superstructure. Thus, *social values*, which integrate social classes into a hierarchical system, and the *Zeitgeist*, which is the ideological expression of this hierarchy, characterize the nature of a society as a whole. For example, the manorial system of feudalism and the private enterprise system of capitalism are different institutional systems with different social values and a different *Zeitgeist*. It is possible that social values and the *Zeitgeist* will conflict; in that case Schumpeter's famous thesis on the fall of capitalism is, in a nutshell, reduced to the argument that the social values demanded by capitalism and the *Zeitgeist* produced by capitalism may collide.

As the power of the state rose in Europe, the status of the nobility declined; although the patrimonialization of public office, land ownership, and human relationships continued for the previous nobility, military force was no longer a lifestyle and the major function of the nobility lost ground. Patrimonialization means that a class, once established, keeps its routine work and stabilizes its status so that even after its core institutions are lost, its form remains. Although conducting public business within a state machinery, managing one's own farmland, and so on became new functions of the former feudal lords, these functions could not defend the class status that had been associated with their proper social functions. The function of warriors had already become obsolete, and they were expected to apply their skills in new spheres of activity.

In capitalism the social leadership is comprised of entrepreneurs, and they form the bourgeois class. If the entrepreneurial function becomes obsolete, the bourgeois class must decline, as was argued in Schumpeter's thesis on the demise of capitalism. His 1927 article, which was structured according to a set of concepts, social leadership, social values, the *Zeitgeist*, class symbiosis, and patrimonialization, developed a general theory of the rise and fall of social classes, using the examples of the nobility and the bourgeoisie. Schumpeter's argument on the decline of capitalism, the germ of which dated from the 1910s, was not incorporated into the 1927 article, but before long was integrated with the framework of his theory of social classes.

The place of the theory of social classes

Paul Sweezy once presented an interpretation on the place of Schumpeter's theory of social classes in the grand design of his thought. According to Sweezy, a complete theory of capitalism requires, à la Marx, the theory of origins, the theory of functioning and growth, and the theory of decline; most of Schumpeter's work (*Theorie der wirtschaftlichen Entwicklung* and *Business Cycles*, in particular) concerns the theory of functioning and growth, his article on "Die sozialen Klassen" is his central work on the theory of origins, and *Capitalism, Socialism and Democracy* is his theory of decline (Sweezy 1951, xiii–xiv). Sweezy is right in attempting to locate Schumpeter's theory of social classes within his grand system, instead of neglecting it or regarding it as a fragmentary piece, but his interpretation is questionable because it assumes that all four works named above use the same scientific approach and are distinguished only by different subjects of study.[3]

I disagree. Whereas *Entwicklung* is an economic analysis of given institutions (*Business Cycles* goes over the frame a bit), "Die sozialen Klassen" and *Capitalism, Socialism and Democracy* are works of economic sociology that deal with the institutional framework of an economy. I also contend that Schumpeter's theory of social classes is meant to be a link between the economic and noneconomic areas, as one of the basic concepts of economic sociology, rather than an analysis of the origins of capitalism.

This issue can be understood more fully by clarifying the differences and similarities between Schumpeter's theory of social classes and Marx's economic interpretation of history. The main thrust of Marx's original argument was to view production structure as the determinant of class structure and class structure, in turn, as the determinant of superstructure. Thus class structure and production structure were regarded as an integral whole; the class struggle between capitalists and workers represented the mechanism of change in the economic and social structures; the economic working of a society, thus shaped by production and class relationships, determined the cultural and ideological superstructure of a society. Schumpeter praised

Marx's view, saying that "the so-called Economic Interpretation of History is doubtless one of the greatest individual achievements of sociology to this day" (1950a, 10).[4] But he presented a modification and reconstruction of Marx's view in a shape that he could accept (see page 81). In this context, Schumpeter's critical objection to Marx's class theory was stated as follows: first, Schumpeter refused to approach class phenomena from economic interest alone but explained them from the standpoint of social leadership in the complex of social areas; and second, he declined to explain class structure in terms of a dominant class of the time, but defined it as a multiple-peaked pyramid involving the class structure of a preceding age.

Alan Dyer, in his interesting essay on the relationship between "Die sozialen Klassen," *Theorie*, and *Capitalism, Socialism and Democracy*, asserts that "Die sozialen Klassen" presented general theories of social order and social change, whereas *Theorie* applied the general theory of social order to a capitalist economy and *Capitalism, Socialism and Democracy* involved the application of the general theory of social change (Dyer 1988). In my view, "Die sozialen Klassen" did not offer a large-scale general theory from which Schumpeter's two books could be derived; it only defined the concept of classes as a basic category of economic sociology and did not include an economic and sociological analysis of the mechanism of a capitalist society. Although Dyer, in fact, regarded this as a serious flaw in Schumpeter's theory of social classes, his negative evaluation is merely the outcome of his own excessive characterization of Schumpeter's class theory.

Nevertheless, it is certain that Schumpeter's theory of social classes occupies an important place in his idea of a universal social science. To sum up the structure of his theory of social classes: it starts from the general theory of leadership, it defines various social areas as the fields in which *social functions* are fulfilled, it arranges the complex of social areas in terms of *social values* or *social leadership* (the aptitude of fulfilling the social functions) to derive a social hierarchy (social classes), and it summarizes in the word *Zeitgeist* the spiritual and cultural expressions that correspond to the hierarchical social classes thus derived. Because in the age of capitalism, the economic area has the greatest social function and determines the principle ideas of the society, it seems natural from the standpoint of scientific strategy that Schumpeter's idea of a universal social science focuses on economic sociology that is concerned with the interactions between the economy and institutions. In this picture of the society, the concept of social classes is pivotal, mediating the interactions between economic machinery endowed with social leadership, on the one hand, and the institutional superstructure, on the other.

Schumpeter called his article, "Zur Soziologie der Imperialismen," an inquiry into the sociology of the *Zeitgeist* that was concerned with the relationship between the social classes and their consciousness, spirit, and culture

([1918–19] 1951b, 8). In the same place he labeled his work, *Die Krise des Steuerstaates* (1918), a study of the *Zeitgeist* from another angle. Furthermore, he mentioned that because "Zur Soziologie der Imperialismen" treated economic problems only cursorily, it would be supplemented by a forthcoming study of neomercantilism and related ideas would be dealt with in another work, "Die Ideenseele des Sozialismus."[5] Neomercantilism, in *Business Cycles*, was the label on the third Kondratieff wave, which started in the 1890s, in order to identify the era in which the metamorphosis of capitalism through change in the social atmosphere was occurring in the face of private monopolization and government control (1939, 1, 398).

In this way, Schumpeter intended to analyze the relationship between the development of economic machinery and the institutional superstructure based on his theory of social classes in the latter half of the 1910s and the early 1920s. But during this period he left the academic world and missed the chance to complete this research plan in its original form. He resumed the investigation twenty years later, and his findings appeared as *Capitalism, Socialism and Democracy*. His 1941 Lowell lecture, "An Economic Interpretation of Our Time," though not published, was literally an attempt to provide an economic interpretation of the *Zeitgeist*. In the later years Schumpeter thought that in order to reach scientific conclusions about the future of the entrepreneurial function, the following fundamental sociological problems must be explored: "the nature of the class structure of capitalist society; the sort of class civilization which it develops and which differs so characteristically from the class civilization of feudal society; its schema of values; its politics, especially its attitudes to state and church and war; its performance and failures; its degree of durability" (1947, 158). Although these questions were addressed in *Capitalism, Socialism and Democracy*, he still urged further study of these issues in order to produce valid generalizations – as opposed to impressions – on the working of a capitalist system.

From the theory of social classes to imperialism

Theories of imperialism were developed primarily by Marxists during the first twenty years of the twentieth century. John A. Hobson, a British non-Marxist economist and the author of *Imperialism* (1902), pioneered the work in this field; the core of the doctrine consisted of *Das Finanzkapital* (1910) of the Austro-Marxist Rudolf Hilferding and *Imperialism* (1917) of the Russian Bolshevik leader Vladimir Lenin, among others.[6] Schumpeter's essay "Zur Soziologie der Imperialismen" (1918–19), triggered by this trend, attacked the Marxist theory that imperialism was the inevitable external expansion of capitalism based on the interest of the capitalist class, especially of finance capital. Schumpeter is remembered in this field of research as a proponent of the atavistic theory of imperialism, which regards imperialism as a legacy from the medieval lords. But he did not simply digress into this area. His theory of imperialism was worked out within his framework of economic sociology in that, first, it applied the idea of the multiple-peaked social pyramid as a critique of the Marxian economic interpretation of history; second, it placed socialism, not imperialism, at the highest level of capitalist economic development; and third, it concluded that the value scheme of capitalist civilization was essentially anti-imperialistic and pacifist according to the sociology of the *Zeitgeist*. In view of the fact that Lenin's *Imperialism* was a serious assault on revisionist Marxists like Karl Kautsky and Edward Bernstein, the resemblance of Schumpeter's theory of imperialism to their views, which has been pointed out by some writers, is not necessarily wide of the mark.[7]

The atavistic theory of imperialism

Schumpeter defined imperialism as "the objectless disposition on the part of a state to unlimited forcible expansion." This disposition is derived from the behavior of nations and classes "that seek expansion for the sake of expanding, war for the sake of fighting, victory for the sake of winning, dominion for the sake of ruling" ([1918–19] 1951b, 7, 6). This is not an a priori definition. Schumpeter surveyed world history on the causes of wars and external expansion, beginning with ancient Egypt, Assyria, Persia, Arabia, and Rome, and including the medieval and modern ages. This is an example of a *histoire raisoneé* that derived a theoretical hypothesis from brilliant historical description. His mode of historical writing is quite different from his theoretical writing in *Wesen*. His analysis of historical facts made clear, first, that external military expansion, which is an end in itself, plays a large role in human history; second, that once the warrior class is established and its psychological habits and social structure are shaped, its disposition and structure survive even after its purpose and function no longer have meaning; and third, that, as a secondary factor that helps promote the survival of the warrior class, the interest of a new ruling class and the influence of people benefiting from the war policy contribute to the belligerence of nations.

Schumpeter discusses the meaning of imperialism in capitalism from the standpoint of social leadership. After the Industrial Revolution, the ruling bourgeois class was shaped by economic concerns; then as its political and social status increased, its lifestyle and value scheme became dominant in the society. The ideologies of the bourgeoisie were democracy, individualism, and rationalism. These ideologies prevailed not only in the bourgeois class but also in the labor class, intellectual class, rentier class, and all classes shaped by capitalism. Over time, traditional and instinctive customs became obsolete and the society devoted its energies to economic activities. There was little vigor left to find an outlet in war and conquest. Hence in the capitalist climate the imperialistic impulse is stifled. It was Schumpeter's theoretical conclusion that capitalism is inherently pacifist.

In order to test this conclusion, Schumpeter not only described the various ways in which pacifism penetrates all quarters of society under the rationalistic ideology of capitalism, but also demonstrated that the imperialistic tendency, which is apparent in the reality of capitalism, did not arise from capitalism itself but was taken over from outside capitalism from the previous absolute monarchy. Arms merchants, who naturally have an interest in expansionist policies are likely to encourage this tendency, but the capitalist class as a whole has little incentive to fight wars, and the labor class has never advocated war. Thus Schumpeter concluded that imperialism is atavistic. Contrary to the Marxist belief, he said, imperialism does not arise from existing production relationships but is a legacy from the past social structure and psychological habits. Because the social leadership in a capitalist society does not demand war and conquest, the more capitalism develops, the more it turns away from imperialism and toward peace.

Schumpeter's argument, however, seems to be modified for capitalism at the stage of monopoly instead of free competition. Protectionist policies, monopoly pricing, and export dumping lead to international conflicts of interest. It is now the concern of influential social classes to appeal to arms in order to monopolize foreign markets especially in areas with a political vacuum. Thus Marxist ideology regarded imperialism as a consequence of trustified capitalism. Schumpeter, however, still maintained that the growth of large-scale firms does not create export monopolies and a demand for protectionist tariffs, and that the orientation in favor of control is a remnant of the influence of the guild and monopoly in precapitalist times. Again, Schumpeter rejected the view that capitalism itself causes imperialistic external expansion at its fully developed stage.

The basis of Schumpeter's argument was the thesis of the multiple-peaked social pyramid delivered in "Die sozialen Klassen." He developed the concept in the context of the sociology of imperialism as follows: if the ruling class of the Middle Ages, the war-oriented nobility, had changed its function and become the single ruling class of a capitalist society, or, on the contrary, if the bourgeoisie had swept away the nobility from the capitalist world to occupy the single ruling post, then much would have been different in the life of the capitalist world. Actually, neither case of the single-peaked social pyramid occurred; instead, a double-peaked social pyramid with the two groups in symbiosis has been formed. As a result, while bourgeois industrialism is pacifist, the battle instincts of the medieval knights have survived via the autocratic state to the modern state. Schumpeter concluded that "it is a basic fallacy to describe imperialism as a necessary phase of capitalism, or even to speak of the development of capitalism into imperialism" ([1918–19] 1951b, 118).

Appraisal of Schumpeter's theory of imperialism

Schumpeter's concept of imperialism is unique to him and might be taken as sophistry. Among several appraisals, that of Murray Greene is rather severe. According to him, Schumpeter's argument consists of the following syllogism: what is not the expression of a warrior-class social structure is not imperialism; capitalist society is not a warrior-class social structure; therefore capitalist society is not imperialistic (Greene 1952, 456). Another observer calls it a dice-loading technique (Davis 1960, 18). These commentaries point out Schumpeter's characteristic style of thought in full relief. In working on specific topics in economic sociology, he made a theoretical hypothesis from historical materials, not an *ad hoc* explanatory hypothesis. In his discussion of the relationship between theory and history, the distinction between an *ad hoc* explanatory hypothesis and a general theoretical hypothesis was of funda- mental importance. Therefore, even if Schumpeter's definition of imperialism appears one-sided in that it seems to ignore the case of purposeful external economic expansion, its usefulness in understanding reality is not to be judged by the apparent plausibility of his definition. He did not neglect the imperialistic elements of modern capitalism at all but tried to analyze them by taking account of the atavistic phenomena associated with older classes. This is an approach to history by means of a theoretical hypothesis. Part of the reality that remains unexplained after the application of the atavistic hypoth- esis is meant to be explained by a capitalist model.

Schumpeter constructed an ideal type of capitalism that was pacifist. With regard to nationalism and militarism, both of which are closely related to imperialism *per se*, he wrote: "the mode of life that flows logically from the nature of capitalism necessarily implies an antinationalist orientation in politics and culture ... According to the 'pure' capitalist mode of life, the bourgeois is unwarlike. The alignment of capitalist interests should make him utterly reject military methods, put him in opposition to the professional soldier" ([1918–19] 1951b, 126). Here capitalism is obviously conceptualized as a logically pure type. When he said, "It [modern imperialism] would never have been evolved by the 'inner' logic of capitalism itself" ([1918–19] 1951b, 128), capitalism is nothing but a logical construct. But it seems that Schumpeter was inconsistent regarding this position, because the fit to reality must be considered.

It is interesting to see what Schumpeter thought of the same topic twenty years later. He made two observations. First, in discussing the period called neomercantilist Kondratieff in *Business Cycles*, he remarked: "A glimpse of a view that now seems to the writer to be nearer the truth than either the Marxist or his own theory is embodied in Karl Renner's concept of Social Imperialism (Sozialimperialismus)" (1939, 2, 696). Although Schumpeter thought that under capitalism the labor class did not support imperialism, this was not the case in Germany during the interwar period. Second, in the Lowell lecture, with regard to the Marxist theory of imperialism and his own atavistic theory, he stated that: "In the light of later events we may well suspect that both were wrong" ([1941] 1991, 345). In his writings in the 1940s, including *Capitalism, Socialism and Democracy*, whereas the Marxist theory of imperialism is still rejected and the thesis of pacifist capitalism is still maintained, there is no insistence of the atavistic theory.

What must have constituted a serious problem in Schumpeter's mind was, I suspect, the issue of monopoly. In his 1920–21 essay, "Sozialistische Möglich-keiten von heute," he argued that the growth of large enterprises, concentra-tion, and monopolization tended to promote the development of socialism, but he maintained his previous view that the propensity to monopolize was not derived from a free competitive economy but from the customs of the preceding ages and led to imperialism. He wrote:

If mammoth enterprises and trusts that controlled the industries of whole countries and even more were established, and if a free competitive economy receded increasingly as a result of the struggle with large monopolistic firms, the cause would be more than merely economic. Among other things, the influence of nationalistic, militaristic, and imperialistic fighting instincts cannot be explained solely by the economic situation of our time. (1920–21, 313)

In *Capitalism, Socialism and Democracy*, in contrast, he asserted that industrial organization including the formation of large enterprises is the outcome of capitalist economic development, and that restrictive measures by monopo-listic firms have a positive impact on the process of creative destruction. He continued to maintain that the propensity to monopolize promotes a leaning toward socialism, but he no longer claimed that this propensity is the atavism of precapitalistic elements while the essential nature of capitalism consists of competition and peace. Instead, Schumpeter attacks the textbook concept of competition and affirms, as the essence of capitalism, the dynamic concept of competition leading to monopolistic positions. Thus he considered "a theory of a phenomenon that is not necessarily imperialist in itself, modern protec-tionism" (1950a, 51). In this way, he filled in the gap between the theory of imperialism and the theory of socialism at the sacrifice of dropping the atavistic concept from the theory of imperialism. Even at this cost, the contention of the dynamic concept of competition might be sufficiently rewarding to him in view of its profound impact on the basic thinking in economics.

Schumpeter's study of economic sociology, which began around 1912, came to fruition in *Capitalism, Socialism and Democracy*, and established a thesis that capitalism would decline because of its success. Among a series of studies Schumpeter conducted in economic sociology, a glimpse of the seminal thesis in its earliest form is given in "Zur Soziologie der Imperialismen" and *Die Krise des Steuerstaates*. The following observation in the former article is relevant here: "Capitalism is its own undoing but in a sense different from that implied by Marx. Society is bound to grow beyond capitalism, but this will be because the achievements of capitalism are likely to make it superfluous, not because its internal contradictions are likely to make its continuance impossible" ([1918–19] 1951b, 108). In this essay Schumpeter repudiated the Marxist theory of imperialism, which argued that capitalism developed into imperialism, but in order to avoid the misunderstanding that he believed in the continuance of capitalism, he provided, in a footnote, a glimpse of his vision of changing capitalism, though the context of the article is different.

From fiscal sociology to the theory of socialism

Schumpeter's small book *Die Krise des Steuerstaates*, presented as a lecture at the Vienna Sociological Society and published as *Zeitfragen aus dem Gebiet der Soziologie*, vol. 4, was intended to contribute to fiscal sociology. Fiscal sociology originated in the advocacy of Rudolf Goldscheid (1917) during the World War I. His thought was influenced by his ideology on state and economy; he claimed that the state should eliminate economic and social evils and be released from the hands of private capitalists. For this purpose, he advocated "state capitalism" in which the state had property and the economy was socialized. A tax state or debt state was a state that did not own property and had to depend on taxes. In spite of his ideological bias, Goldscheid demanded a reorientation of social science in view of two shortcomings of traditional theories. First, he declared, the traditional theory of public finance was replete with institutional description and party politics without sufficient social scientific cognition and, second, traditional sociology and political science developed fictional ideal pictures of the state without sociological analysis of the state. In his advocacy of a fiscal sociology, Goldscheid proposed to build a bridge between public finance and sociology through the historical study of state finance.[8]

Die Krise des Steuerstaates

When Goldscheid talked about social scientific cognition, abstract economic theory was out of the question. What he called fiscal sociology rejected fiscal theory based on Austrian economics and was close to the German Historical School as well as Austro-Marxism. Because state finance undoubtedly provides an institutional framework for a national economic system, a fiscal sociology that depended on financial history would constitute an important part of economic sociology as far as Schumpeter was concerned.

In *Die Krise des Steuerstaates*, Schumpeter, quoting from Goldscheid that "the budget is the skeleton of the state stripped of all misleading ideologies," said that "the fiscal history of a people is above all an essential part of its general history" and paid attention to the important influence of fiscal policy on the development of an economy, all forms of life, and all aspects of a nation's culture. In this book, he tried to develop fiscal sociology through a historical approach in order to grasp "the view of the state, of its nature, its forms, its fate, as seen from the fiscal side" ([1918] 1991, 100, 101).

Based on this general view, Schumpeter asked specific questions about whether a capitalist economic system would break down under the excessive tax burden imposed by World War I and whether it would be reorganized by the state and transformed into a new system. He concluded that such a system would not collapse under the shock of the war, but a collapse would be inevitable over the long term.

Schumpeter's description of the fall of the manorial economy and the rise of the modern state in *Die Krise des Steuerstaates* represents the most historical research that he conducted. However, at the same time this research is characterized by a sharp theoretical touch. The crisis of the manorial economy was due to a shortage of the warfare expenses under the falling feudal organization. Out of the common exigency, Schumpeter argued, the public and private spheres that had been united in the feudal system were divided, and it was agreed that the state would collect taxes. The interpretation that fiscal demand for the purpose of solving the common exigency and realizing common aims had established the tax state represents the benefit approach to taxes. In contrast to the private subordination among princes, lords, and farmers under feudalism, the tax state in the public sphere coexists with the private economy in the private sphere. A mixed economy in this sense is the essence of capitalism. On the other hand, under socialism, where all social life is socialized, the state as a separate entity from private ones does not exist. Therefore the tax state exists only in capitalism. The crisis of the tax state means the collapse of big government under the capitalist system as well as the breakdown or transformation of the private economy, which is the counterpart of the government. A mixed economy collapses because there is a limit to the expansion of the tax state and to the collection of taxes from the private sector.

A lifetime theme of socialism

At the outset of *Capitalism, Socialism and Democracy*, published in 1942, Schumpeter wrote: "This volume is the result of an effort to weld into a readable form the bulk of almost forty years' thought, observation and research on the subject of socialism" (1942, xiii). His forty years' interest in socialism dates from his introduction to socialist thought through his friendship with Austro-Marxists in his student days beginning in 1901, when he entered the University of Vienna. After World War I, he had a chance to participate in the politics of socialism in Austria and Germany. His last piece of writing, composed on the evening before his death, was an article entitled "The March into Socialism" (1950b). In view of this history, it is fair to say that socialism was Schumpeter's lifetime theme. This subject was naturally incorporated into his system of thought which addressed the grand problem of the evolution of capitalism, because, for him, socialism was both the future of capitalism and the product of capitalism.

The gist of his supposition on the future of capitalism was as follows: "The thesis I shall endeavor to establish is that the actual and prospective performance of the capitalist system is such as to negative the idea of its breaking down under the weight of economic failure, but that its very success undermines the social institutions which protect it, and 'inevitably' creates conditions in which it will not be able to live and which strongly point to socialism as the heir apparent" (1950a, 61). This seemingly paradoxical presumption was stated explicitly in "Sozialistische Möglichkeiten von heute" (1920–21), but the idea first appeared in *Die Krise des Steuerstaates*, where the thesis, though primitive, was all the more strongly contended:

If the will of the people demands higher and higher public expenditures, if more and more means are used for purposes for which private individuals have not produced them, if more and more power stands behind this will, and if finally all parts of the people are gripped by entirely new ideas about private property and the form of life – then the tax state will have run its course and society will have to depend on other motive forces for its economy than self-interest. This limit, and with it the crisis which the tax state could not survive, can certainly be reached. Without doubt, the tax state can collapse. ([1918] 1991, 116)

The last sentence of the book reads:

And yet it is the first precondition for the socialized community that capitalism has done its work and an economy exists which is satiated with capital and thoroughly rationalized by entrepreneurial brains. Only then it is possible to look forward calmly to that inevitable slowing down of merely economic development which is the concomitant of socialism, for socialism means liberation of life from the economy and alienation from the economy. This hour has not yet struck. The war has postponed it.

The hour that is belongs to private enterprise, to economic effort to the very limit of its strength. And with private enterprise the hour also belongs to the tax state ... Nevertheless the hour will come. By and by private enterprise will lose its social meaning through the development of the economy and the consequent expansion of the sphere of social sympathy ... Society is growing beyond private enterprise and [the] tax state, not because but in spite of the war. That too is certain. ([1918] 1991, 130–31)

This small book, of course, does not contain all the points developed in the thesis; as the two quotations above indicate, Schumpeter argued that when the public sector has grown sufficiently to realize the common social aims and when the private sector has exerted fully the vitality of capitalism, then a society will be relieved of the burden of economic need. I call this socialism at the highest stage of capitalism. The enumeration of those factors that contribute to the arrival of the highest stage within this framework was left to Schumpeter in his later years.

The possibilities of socialism

The year of the publication of *Die Krise des Steuerstaates* saw the end of world war. After the Russian revolution in 1917, the storm of socialism raged in Europe. At the end of 1918, when the German socialist cabinet set up the German Socialization Commission, Schumpeter became a member. In 1919 he joined the Austrian coalition cabinet of the Social Democratic Party and the Christian Social Party as minister of finance. On the basis of his experience and observations during this period, he wrote the fifty-six page article, "Sozialistische Möglichkeiten von heute" (1920–21).

The aim of this essay was to determine whether or not it is possible to recognize an objective tendency toward socialism in economic and social phenomena, apart from ideological wishes and political activities in favor of socialism. His answer was yes, but he argued that when the objective conditions are not fulfilled, political actions of socialization are untimely and will encounter great resistance, and that even when all conditions are met, deliberate actions are needed for socialization, as Marx had argued. This is an important point in understanding Schumpeter's thesis of socialism. He wrote: "Even in the 'fullness of time,' when everything is ready, direction for achieving socialism, i.e., socialization, would be still necessary; without it a competitive economy does not vanish by itself" (1920–21, 323). Schumpeter here defined socialism as control over the means of production and the planning of production, as distinct from capitalism based on private ownership, private initiative, and credit creation; he claimed that in order to move to socialism, significant institutional reforms must be undertaken. Premature action in terms of objective conditions will inevitably result in economic and political failure. From this standpoint, Schumpeter wrote two scenarios –

socialization in a state of maturity and socialization in a state of immaturity –
in chapter 19 of *Capitalism, Socialism and Democracy*, where he discussed the
transition from capitalism to socialism.

It should be noted that whereas the definition of capitalism includes private
ownership, that of socialism does not need public ownership. According to
Schumpeter, as the idea of private ownership and inheritance has declined,
only social control, not social ownership, of the means of production matters.[9]

Schumpeter used the words "evolution" and "revolution" to denote the
objective tendency toward socialism and the political choice of socialism,
respectively. When evolution and revolution are in agreement, he said,
"Socialism has naturally to provide a new life form of mankind, new habits of
thought and feeling, and new culture. It will slow down economic development, but its meaning to some extent just lies in that it releases the best of
human energy from economic concern" (1920–21, 344).

He comprehensively enumerated complex factors that lead to socialism:
economic development brings about large-scale enterprises and their concentration, so that a national economy becomes easily controllable; a competitive
economy rationalizes an economy and economic activity, and the process of
rationalization produces the idea of organizing an economy from the social
point of view; under the big enterprise system, technological innovation
becomes automatic and dehumanized and does not need entrepreneurial
activity; with the forfeiture of the entrepreneurial function, the entrepreneurial
class declines; through the separation of ownership and control, the necessity
of private ownership diminishes; the liberation from economic need weakens
family ties and eliminates the incentive to achieve family fame; and the
human spirit proceeds from self-interest to altruism, and human concerns
expand from the private sphere to the public sphere.

Schumpeter qualified the saturation of capital and the constancy of
population as the prerequisites of socialization, because the most difficult task
of the socialist system, which gives less priority to the economy, is to
accommodate an increase in capital and population. Under the above
tendencies, he emphasized, although socialism gradually becomes feasible and
the resistance against it weakens, these tendencies do not indicate the
automatic realization of socialism. "Therefore," he concluded, "in economic
and social things as well as in the spirit, there are insurmountable forces
working toward socialism that are independent from the will directed to it,
and ultimately from any will, as well as from the will against it. To be more
precise, these forces tend to make socialism more 'feasible' physically as well
as psychologically and to eliminate the resistance against it more completely.
Of course, this does not mean that these forces must realize it automatically at
any time" (1920–21, 322).

It is now clear that Schumpeter's thesis of socialism was shaped after World

War I, and that his inquiries were directed to the likelihood of socialism in Germany and Austria. He concluded that socialization in Germany would be possible but difficult and would exact a high cost, and that it would be even more problematic in Austria where the economic foundation was not mature. Premature socialization would meet with strong resistance from the bourgeoisie. Above all, both countries had to depend on a capitalist economy in order to recover from the confusion and poverty caused by the war.

Finally, two questions may be raised. First, how did Schumpeter, in the early 1920s, regard the case of Soviet Russia, where evolution and revolution did not coincide? He thought that whereas even developed countries were not socialized, socialization in economically backward Russia would end in failure or poverty or oppression. "Russian Bolshevism is, after all, completely understandable when one considers it as the successor of czarism" (1920–21, 332). In a different place in the same period, he wrote:

Russian and Hungarian Bolshevism is and was an interesting phenomenon with principles of little significance – not to be taken seriously from the standpoint of sociological analysis. Above all, it is not to be taken seriously by robust Marxian socialists, because if it were possible to implant ideas by means of the bayonet – though this is the most favorable interpretation – the socialist lifestyle in a land that lacks its economic and social prerequisites, the Marxist vision of the social development process must be false. (1924, 295)

Second, in view of his emphasis on leadership as the central thesis of social phenomena, how did Schumpeter view leadership regarding the tendency toward socialism? He anticipated the position offered in *Capitalism, Socialism and Democracy*:

Of course, today we still stand at the beginning of this development [of socialism]. But finally – though in the distant, nebulous future – we shall arrive at the situation where a national economy itself becomes a single huge machine operating automatically. In allocating men to this machine, there will still be a distinction between guiding labor and guided labor, between upper and lower ranks; creative labor will also be indispensable. But it will no longer be crystallized in the personality of leaders, but in a specifically qualified form of systematized bureaucratic labor. (1920–21, 317–18)

This means that the working of an economy under socialism will be mechanized and bureaucratized, so that social leadership will not be a factor in the economy.

Methodological notes to *Capitalism, Socialism and Democracy*

After emigrating to America, Schumpeter resumed a thread of thought on socialism in 1936, when he gave a lecture entitled "Can Capitalism Survive?"

([1936b] 1991) at the United States Department of Agriculture Graduate School. This lecture contains nothing new, compared with his thought in the 1920s, but the title was used for Part II of *Capitalism, Socialism and Democracy* and became a catchphrase for embracing all the factors tending toward socialism.

Capitalism, Socialism and Democracy (1942) has been Schumpeter's most widely read work. The second edition was published in 1947 and the third edition in 1950, each with new chapters, new essays, and new prefaces. According to his wife Elizabeth, "After herculean labor, J. A. S. had finished his monumental *Business Cycles* in 1938 and sought relaxation in *Capitalism, Socialism and Democracy*, which he regarded as distinctly a 'popular' offering that he expected to finish in a few months. He completed it some time in 1941" (1954a, v). According to Gottfried Haberler, "It was written within a year or two and the author regarded it as nothing more than a *parergon*" (Haberler 1951a, 39). John K. Galbraith made a similar observation: "Joseph Schumpeter ... once told me that among his books this one inspired his special loathing. It lacked, he said, scientific depth and precision, although a more important reason was his vanity. This required that he disavow any work that had won a popular audience. He wrote for the elect. The book remains, nonetheless, the only volume by which he is now remembered" (Galbraith 1977, 74).[10]

Although the book was written in a relatively short period, it represented a synthesis of forty years of thought, observation, and research on the dynamics of capitalism in historical perspective. It developed for the first time in one book the idea of a universal social science, and it analyzed the process of change in capitalism as civilization through the investigation of long-term interactions between economic and noneconomic areas. As indicated in its title, the book examines the tendency to move from capitalism to socialism, on the one hand, and the consistency between socialism and democracy, on the other; various psychological, cultural, and social factors were incorporated into these system concepts, economic and political. The foremost concept of economic sociology that Schumpeter found in the research program of the German Historical School was the integration of the viewpoint of the unity of social life with that of development, the idea of the endogenous evolution of society as a whole through interactions among various areas. *Capitalism, Socialism and Democracy* is interpreted as an attempt to introduce economic sociology as an evolutionary science.

The book begins with a fifty-page examination of Marxist doctrine. Schumpeter was not a socialist, but he emphasized the similarities between his and Marx's visions regarding the development of a capitalist system. What is common to both is the explanation that the process of economic development and transition is endogenous, that is, it is created from within the economic system. After examining the theories of Marx, Schumpeter remarked that in spite of all his errors and dogmas, Marx produced one truly great achievement, the vision of the endogenous evolution of the economic process. "Thus, the author of so many misconceptions was also the first to visualize what even at the present time is still the economic theory of the future for which we are slowly and laboriously accumulating stone and mortar, statistical facts and functional equations" (1950a, 43).

Before we proceed to the substantive arguments in *Capitalism, Socialism and Democracy*, let us examine methodologically the formal characteristics of the endogenous theory of evolution of capitalism. It is necessary to make methodological notes regarding Schumpeter's paradoxical thesis – that capitalism will destroy its own foundation not by its failure but by its success and inevitably produce socialism – in order to avoid any misunderstanding of his concept.

The subject matter of Schumpeter's thesis

By socialism Schumpeter did not mean the development-oriented system actually adopted by less developed nations. He believed that as capitalism grows and matures, it must change itself in the historical process; in its development phase it is called the capitalist system and in its mature form socialism. Socialism in this sense is, to borrow the subtitle of Lenin's *Imperialism*, "the highest stage of capitalism." It is, of course, possible to consider socialism in the conventional sense, but that was not Schumpeter's concern, for the prerequisites of his conception of socialism, that is, the mature conditions of capitalism, which were his major focus, were absent in the socialist countries of that time. Therefore, the readers of Schumpeter should not confuse the two understandings of socialism. It is erroneous to suppose that the existing socialist countries had matured beyond the capitalist system.

Schumpeter's thesis also does not contend that capitalism will automatically bring about a socialist system; rather, if the tendency toward socialism inherent in capitalism should fully work itself out, socialism would be feasible. As can be seen from his arguments of the 1920s, socialism as an institutional system can be realized only by political choice, not spontaneously. Moreover, in order for socialism to be a feasible political choice, certain objective conditions are necessary. Schumpeter's thesis on the fall of capitalism claimed only that these conditions are spontaneously created in the process of capitalist economic development.

Most reviewers of Schumpeter's thesis have criticized the prediction that capitalism would be replaced by socialism in view of the fact that present-day capitalism is far from dying and moving to socialism; on the contrary, socialism has collapsed and is moving to capitalism. This argument misunderstands Schumpeter in confusing not only his conception of socialism with the conventional one, but also his description of tendencies with deterministic predictions. Moreover, insomuch as he consistently asserted that the premature socialization of countries before "the fullness of time" would result in economic failure and political oppression, the breakdown of the socialist countries in the contemporary world rather demonstrates the truth of his thesis.

In *Capitalism, Socialism and Democracy* Schumpeter reiterated his former position on evolution and revolution:

The capitalist process shapes things and souls for socialism. In the limiting case it might do this so completely that the final step would not be more than a formality. But even then the capitalist order would not of itself turn into the socialist order; such a final step, the official adoption of socialism as the community's law of life, would still have to be taken, say, in the form of a constitutional amendment. (1950a, 220)

The evolution of capitalism inevitably develops the conditions for socialism, but without revolution socialism is not realized. This was also Marx's problem. As Schumpeter remarked: "Evolution was for him the parent of socialism. He was much too strongly imbued with a sense of the inherent logic of things social to believe that revolution can replace any part of the work of evolution. The revolution comes in nevertheless ... It [the Marxian revolution] is essentially revolution in the fullness of time" (1950a, 58)

Thus viewed, Schumpeter's thesis does not mean that capitalism is deterministically destined to adopt socialism. It is possible that the subjective choice of a society should be against socialism, even if the objective conditions for socialism were established, and that it should revert or weaken the tendency toward socialism. In the third edition of *Capitalism, Socialism and Democracy*, Schumpeter replied to the charge that his argument was defeatist:

The report that a given ship is sinking is not defeatist. Only the spirit in which this report is received can be defeatist: The crew can sit down and drink. But it can also rush to the pumps. If the men merely deny the report though it be carefully substantiated, then they are escapists. Moreover, even if my statements of tendencies amounted more definitely to prediction than they were intended to do, they would still not carry defeatist suggestions. What normal man will refuse to defend his life merely because he is quite convinced that sooner or later he will have to die anyhow? (1950a, xi)

This passage clearly shows that his thesis is not a prediction but a description of tendencies.

Although his concept is often interpreted as deterministic, Schumpeter did not regard the tendency toward socialism as a law of nature in which there is no room for human action. Knowing the tendencies in a certain direction is one thing, acting on them, quite another. The actual steps of a system, therefore, will follow a zigzag course of advance and retreat around the tendencies. Keeping this course in mind, Schumpeter said that "a century is a 'short run' " (1950a, 163).

In addition to replying to the defeatist charge, he answered the criticism of determinism: "Thus, prediction of whether or not the capitalist order will survive is, in part, a matter of terminology. If it is to be more than that, it depends upon the likelihood of a reversal not only of existing tendencies, but also of an established state of things, and therefore upon the answer to the question where the political forces are to come from that will be able and willing to effect such a reversal" ([1946a] 1951c, 204). It might appear that political factors are artificially raised here as a *deus ex machina* to deny determinism, but this is not so. As we see later, this problem has an important bearing on his implicit thesis that the crucial determinant of a system is not an economy itself but political action. Most importantly, Schumpeter advocated the way to corporatism in order to obstruct the tendency toward socialism (see pages 300–1).

The structure of the paradox

Schumpeter's thesis on the demise of capitalism resulting from its success appears at first glance paradoxical. But is it really so? There are elements of rhetoric in the thesis. This thesis is constructed by combining the arguments in economics and economic sociology that the economic success of capitalism, through its effect on noneconomic factors and reactions from them, negatively affects economic performance and leads to the decay of capitalism. If one considers the economic world in the abstract, capitalism would develop by the driving force of innovation and stabilize itself through business cycles; it would not breed its own bad performance. But since capitalism is actually a comprehensive system of civilization, it does not continue to work indefinitely within the economic world alone. As a result of economic success and prosperity, the social, political, and cultural circumstances surrounding the capitalist economic machinery will have to change so that they gradually restrict vigorous economic development. In other words, the economic success of capitalism brings about noneconomic circumstances inimical to its own working and favorable to socialism. The economic machinery of capitalism works very well and continues to work if noneconomic conditions remain equal, but as a result of its success, surrounding conditions will change as if sand were thrown into the machine from outside. Each of the following two statements is quite understandable in itself: that as economic prosperity and rationalization proceed, the value system of human beings will be changed, and that if surrounding conditions are inimical to economic development, the economy does not work smoothly. When they are combined, however, the cognitive gap between the abstract economic picture and the broad picture of society may create the impression of a paradox on the part of the readers, who are not necessarily used to thinking in terms of a universal social science.

In "The Instability of Capitalism" (1928), Schumpeter attempted to account for this paradox by distinguishing the stability or instability of the capitalist *system* from that of the capitalist *order*. The problem of system relates to the question of whether capitalism works smoothly with respect to economic performance, and the problem of order relates to the question of whether capitalism can survive as an economic system (1928, 363). These terms also appear in *Capitalism, Socialism and Democracy* (1950a, 42). What his paradoxical thesis actually means is that whereas the capitalist system is stable, the capitalist order is unstable. Furthermore, in order to appreciate the consistency of Schumpeter's overall structure of thought, one must understand that his apparently conflicting visions of "Walras as ideology" and "Marx as ideology" are united into the ideas underlying the apparently paradoxical thesis now in question, which combines economic and socioeconomic observations (chapter 4).

Thus Schumpeter's inference in his thesis depends on the dramatic effects of comparing the picture of the economic world with that of society as a whole, or, in other words, of comparing the stability of the capitalist system with that of the capitalist order. If we follow the process of inference closely, the fall of capitalism is caused by the unworkability of the capitalist economic functions owing to changes in the surrounding conditions. In Schumpeter's characteristic view, this is not the result of a functional disorder or the violent destruction of capitalism, as Marx argued, but of maturity and exhaustion of vigor in developed capitalism. However, if we call the lasting unworkability of economic functions economic failure, Schumpeter's thesis is a simple statement about the decay of capitalism owing to the failure of capitalism.

In the series of inferences in the thesis, (A) the success of capitalism $\Rightarrow$ (B) the emergence of unfavorable circumstances $\Rightarrow$ (C) the failure of capitalism $\Rightarrow$ (D) the decay of capitalism, if we focus on relation (C) $\Rightarrow$ (D), the thesis seems to accord with common sense; but if we focus on the relationship (A) $\Rightarrow$ (D), the thesis seems paradoxical. For example, the following passage is typical of Schumpeter's rhetoric: "The true pacemakers of socialism were not the intellectuals or agitators who preached it but the Vanderbilts, Carnegies and Rockefellers" (1950a, 134). Of course, Schumpeter did not intend simply to mystify his readers through rhetoric, but perhaps he wanted to attach importance to the relationship (A) $\Rightarrow$ (B) rather than the relationship (C) $\Rightarrow$ (D) because the former relationship was undoubtedly the cause of the latter. In fact, after he constructed and examined the thesis from several angles, he added: "In the end there is not so much difference as one might think between saying that the decay of capitalism is due to its success and saying that it is due to its failure" (1950a, 162).

The integration of economics and economic sociology

It is more important to deal with methodological questions concerning the link between economics and economic sociology in Schumpeter's thesis than with superficial questions about determinism and a paradox concerning it. He introduced an important idea relating to this problem: "Things economic and social move by their own momentum and the ensuing situations compel individuals and groups to behave in certain ways whatever they may wish to do – not indeed by destroying their freedom of choice but by shaping the choosing mentalities and by narrowing the list of possibilities from which to choose" (1950a, 129–30). When discussing Schumpeter's methodological individualism in *Wesen*, I paid attention to his remark that methodological individualism applies to economics but not to sociology (see page 140). The economic picture based on methodological individualism must be modified when a broader perspective of the world, including the influence of economic activities on noneconomic areas and the reactions of noneconomic conditions to economic activities, is taken into account.[11] These interactions constitute the evolutionary process of a society, the subject matter of economic sociology, and Schumpeter's thesis on the transformation of capitalism is just an example.

Specifically, economic agents in economic theory are consumers and producers, both with adaptive behavior, and entrepreneurs with innovative behavior. These concepts are functional and do not constitute classes in actual society. Adaptive consumers and producers are traditionally called economic men. On the contrary, the economic agents dealt with in Schumpeter's economic sociology are classes such as the bourgeoisie and feudal lords. For him:

Class is something more than an aggregation of class members. It is something else, and this something cannot be recognized in the behavior of the individual class member. A class is aware of its identity as a whole, sublimates itself as such, has its own peculiar life and characteristic "spirit." Yet one essential peculiarity – possibly a consequence, possibly an intermediate cause – of the class phenomenon lies in the fact that class members behave toward one another in a fashion characteristically different from their conduct toward members of other classes. ([1927a] 1951b, 140)

Based on this conception, Schumpeter spoke of the culture and spirit of capitalism emanating from the bourgeois class and of economic behavior conditioned by these cultural data.

Pareto versus Schumpeter

Besides Marx and Weber, one may regard Vilfredo Pareto as one of the thinkers who attempted to develop a universal social science through the integration of economics and sociology, and compare him to Schumpeter in order to elucidate the profound originality of Schumpeter's thought.

Pareto was a member of the Lausanne School, and his work was animated by the idea of social equilibrium in a global sense, which was an extension of the general equilibrium concept in economics. His sociology addressed the interdependence of the various elements in society as a whole, embracing economics in a modified form of the science of interests. He distinguished between logical and nonlogical actions of human beings and argued that whereas the basic, invariable elements (the "residues") in nonlogical actions are identified by inductive methods, the reasoning and justification of nonlogical actions (the "derivations") are clarified by logical deduction. Thus he called his method logico–experimental. A logical action is defined in terms of subjective and objective coherence between ends and means. In Pareto's view, although interests (the central notion of economics) are not limited to the economic sphere but typically govern the logical actions in various social areas, the dominant type of actions in a society is nonlogical (but not necessarily illogical). It was the core of Pareto's sociology to dissect nonlogical actions and complex social networks using the concepts of the residues, the derivations, or, in other words, underlying sentiments and justificatory ideologies. He also developed a theory of social classes focusing on the circulation of the elites who would manipulate ideological tactics. The changing composition of the social classes represents the cycles of a social equilibrium that is based on social heterogeneity. Thus in Pareto's sociological investigations the major elements that determine a social equilibrium are the "residues," the "derivations," interests, and the social classes.

How can Pareto be compared with Schumpeter regarding the grand visions of a universal social science, especially the relationship between economics and sociology? The two scholars share several basic conceptions: social equilibrium based on general interdependence, the distinction between logical and nonlogical behaviors, social heterogeneity of the elites (or leaders) and the masses, and the circulation of the elites. But the textures of their universal social sciences are different. First, in Pareto's comprehensive body of sociology, economics or the science of interests is located beside the general scheme of the analysis of nonlogical actions in terms of the residues and the derivations. Schumpeter's universal social science, by contrast, is practically composed of sciences for the economic sphere and the noneconomic sphere, both of which are primarily concerned with statics and dynamics rather than logical and nonlogical behaviors. Schumpeter based the interdependence of a social system on the Marxian dichotomy between the superstructure and the substructure rather than on the Walrasian general equilibrium scheme.

Second, Pareto did not enter into the substantive relationship between the economic sphere and the noneconomic sphere; he thus did not clarify the place of the social class theory in the overall scheme of social theory although he did address the circulation within a class in a general way. In Schumpeter, the two spheres were closely linked in the sociological dimension, and the social classes played a role in integrating the various spheres of society and possessed the historical content that allowed him to depict the scenario of falling capitalism.

Third, whereas Pareto consistently applied methodological individualism to each sphere of social research in order to derive a social equilibrium, Schumpeter explicitly held that dualism consisted of methodological individualism in economic research and methodological holism in sociological investigations, which primarily included economic sociology and the sociology of knowledge.

In his appraisal of Pareto's sociology, Schumpeter found two different analytic schemata: a morphology of society and social psychology (1951a, 136–42). The morphological schema focuses on the dynamics of the social classes and the socio-psychological schema is concerned with the functions and structure of the derivations. Schumpeter argued that if the derivations were defined in terms of group interests, and if group interests were defined in terms of the social location of groups within a society's productive organization, there would be an affinity between Pareto and Marx. Actually, however, Pareto tried to explain the derivations merely in terms of the residues, the psychology of instincts; as a result, the analysis of ideologies was diverted from an evaluation of the social dynamics that would be linked with the morphological schema. In light of his own "two-structure approach to mind and society," Schumpeter's comment virtually pointed out the absence of a connection between the morphological schema and the socio-psychological schema in Pareto's system and led to his conclusion that Pareto's sociology was not a technical achievement of the first order.

Instrumental theory construction

It was clear to Schumpeter, who had a definite view of methodology, that to discuss the future of capitalism was neither prophecy nor prediction. When we have a set of facts linked together by certain relations, "in cases where these relations are very invariant over very long periods of time, of course this kind of statement [about the future] comes practically to the same as a forecast – in astronomy, for instance. But where these relations vary, there is no sense in forecasting, no sense in extrapolating in functions, and so on, if one wants to be logical and neat and correct" ([1936b] 1991, 299). Moreover, when we observe the capitalist process from the perspective of the interactions between economic and noneconomic areas, even the variables and functions involved are not clear. The method of observation must be limited to the extent that, assuming certain conditions and tendencies based on a grand vision, certain results will be derived.

Before launching into observations in *Capitalism, Socialism and Democracy*, Schumpeter described the methodological nature of his statement about the future:

What counts in any attempt at social prognosis is not the Yes or No that sums up the facts and arguments which lead up to it but those facts and arguments themselves. They contain all that is scientific in the final result. Everything else is not science but prophecy. Analysis, whether economic or other, never yields more than a statement about the tendencies present in an observable pattern. And these never tell us what *will* happen to the pattern but only what *would* happen if they continued to act as they have been acting in the time interval covered by our observation and if no other factors intruded. (1950a, 61)[12]

Schumpeter's characteristic style of thought will be made clear if we look closely at the way in which he analyzed the relationship between economic and noneconomic areas. His argument that the success of capitalism brings about its fall was exemplified through the roles played by noneconomic factors. This is based on the supposition that the economic mechanism of capitalism in itself produces excellent performance. If the economic performance of capitalism is actually bad, it must be attributed to unfavorable circumstances produced by social, political, and cultural factors. This argument appears to depend on a one-sided supposition, for it excludes other notional possibilities: first, the possibility of the inherent instability of a capitalist economy; second, the possibility of the positive influence of capitalist economic success on noneconomic factors; and third, the possibility of the successful intervention of political factors to make up for the economic failure of capitalism. But this peculiar method of dissecting the social process again reflects Schumpeter's instrumental theory construction, which was revealed in his analysis of the relationship between capitalism and imperialism, and should not be blamed for the alleged lack of realism in individual hypotheses.

Whether or not the capitalist economic mechanism should be conceived of as inherently stable and full of vigor is a problem of definition and hypothesis as well as that of fitness to facts. As the reality is composed of a variety of economic and noneconomic factors and their interrelationships, the abstraction of an economic aspect of capitalism in such a way that it is viewed as essentially stable and vigorous, though depending on belief and vision in the ultimate sense, is permitted in science only in the instrumental sense. Schumpeter's technique of constructing a picture of a stable and vigorous capitalist economic system by resorting to such rhetorical definitions as "capitalism is essentially a process of (endogenous) change ... The atmosphere of industrial revolution – of 'progress' – is the only one in which capitalism can survive" (1939, 2, 1033) and "stationary capitalism is a contradiction in terms" (1943, 117) and of then attributing the overall success or failure of the capitalist order to noneconomic circumstances resembles his approach to a thesis on imperialism, where he determined that "capitalism is by nature anti-imperialist" ([1918–19] 1951b, 96) and attributed the imperialistic tendencies actually found in capitalism to the pre-capitalistic structure and psychology. It was his consistent view that as definitions and hypotheses are instruments for dissecting complex reality, their values depend on how efficiently they explain the reality.

Schumpeter's hypothesis that while the capitalist system is stable, the capitalist order is unstable in the sense defined above, involves the attribution of the destiny of capitalism to noneconomic factors. In his exposition of the Great Depression of the 1930s, which is often regarded as a failure of the capitalist system, he explained it as an accident of overlapping troughs of three business cycles with different lengths and by external factors such as the failure of the banking system and New Deal policy, which in his view was anti-capitalist.

Even if one accepts the position that the economic engine of capitalism is essentially sound, there are still second and third possibilities with regard to theorizing the behavior of noneconomic factors. In those capitalist countries that maintain economic growth and avoid heavy inflation and unemployment, it is possible to imagine a stable government and a rich middle class so that conservative, yet a touch liberal political power contributes to the survival of capitalism. On the other hand, it is also possible to imagine that the economic failure, not success, of capitalism brings about a series of government interventions so that the government regulation of markets becomes an obstacle to the vigor of capitalism. Among the diverse reactions of non-economic factors (including politics), Schumpeter chose to stress the consequences of economic rationality upon the dimension of an institutional system as a bold main line of argument. The problem of rationality was basic to Max Weber's social science. Although Schumpeter compared his thesis with the scope of Marx's economic interpretation of history, its content is comparable with Weber's theory of rationality.

The economic sociology of systemic evolution

Having dealt with the methodological points in *Capitalism, Socialism and Democracy*, the question now arises, what is the logical structure of economic sociology in this book? From this standpoint, it is much more important to understand the universal social science that Schumpeter adopted to analyze the grand problem of systemic evolution than to determine whether his thesis on the transformation of capitalism to socialism was correct.[13] His method was to explore the consistencies or inconsistencies between an economy and a civilization of capitalism. Most commentaries on *Capitalism, Socialism and Democracy* have agreed with the evaluation that his argument was wrong but his writing was fascinating and have been unconcerned with his framework of economic sociology, which basically constituted the essence of the book.[14]

The basic ideas

Schumpeter found that inherent in the successful development of capitalism is its tendency to change. What he meant by capitalism was not only the economic system consisting of the market mechanism, private ownership, and credit creation, but also civilization including politics, science, culture, ways of thinking, value systems, ways of life, and so on. In other words, capitalism refers to a social system that comprises the economic mechanism and the superstructure as a whole. For him, a science that could handle this all-encompassing subject was economic sociology. His theory of economic development had the task of examining the dynamics of a market economy with its focus on innovations by entrepreneurs; it could be jointed with a system of economic sociology and bear the weight of a major pillar of economic sociology, because his concept of entrepreneurs was designed as a special case of social leadership. The success of innovating entrepreneurs reorients the class structure of a society, and the rationalistic ideology of the bourgeois class affects the cultural, social, and psychological character of capitalism. Thus the endogenous evolution of a capitalist system as civilization is explained by the interactions between economy and noneconomy through the mediation of the concept of social leadership.

Indeed, Schumpeter's splendid writing may conceal the underlying logical structure of his economic sociology. The reader may not notice that there is a solid framework behind his sparkling sentences. But the essence of his argument lies ultimately, in my view, in the conflicting relationships between entrepreneurs and the bourgeois class, between anti-rationalistic entrepreneurship and rationalistic bourgeois mentality. Let me clarify this reasoning.

Schumpeter assumed that a capitalist society consisted of the following classes: farmers, businessmen, rentiers (or capitalists), intellectuals, white-collar workers, skilled workers, and unskilled workers ([1946a] 1951c, 196). The bourgeois class is the sum of the business class and the capitalist class. Entrepreneurs do not constitute a class, but successful entrepreneurs, irrespective of their origins, enter the bourgeois class together with their family. "Economically and sociologically, directly and indirectly, the bourgeoisie therefore depends on the entrepreneur and, as a class, lives and will die with him" (1950a, 134). According to Schumpeter's multiple-peaked social pyramid concept, in the capitalist age the bourgeois class and the class of the feudal nobility and knight were in an ideal symbiosis. The bourgeoisie supported the nobility economically, and the nobility supported the bourgeoisie politically. The ideology of the bourgeois class is rationalism, as is the civilization of capitalism. Schumpeter emphasized that rationalism was born in the economic world: "I have no hesitation in saying that all logic is derived from the pattern of the economic decision or, to use a pet phrase of mine, that the economic pattern is the matrix of logic" (1950a, 122–23). This is the logic of economic statics, which he had placed at the bottom of the economic system in *Wesen* but was now located at the center of the capitalist civilization in his framework of economic sociology.

Yet the rationalistic ideology emanating from the bourgeois class adversely affects itself and its protective strata, the noble class, by breaking many of the surrounding fetters and barriers, as a boomerang rebounds to where it started. The bourgeois class does not have the political power to protect itself; the industrialist and merchant by nature have no trace of the charisma that is required to rule people.

The stock exchange is a poor substitute for the Holy Grail. We have seen that the industrialist and merchant, as far as they are entrepreneurs, also fill a function of leadership. But economic leadership of this type does not readily expand, like the medieval lord's military leadership, into the leadership of nations. On the contrary, the ledger and the cost calculation absorb and confine ... The bourgeois fortress thus becomes politically defenseless. Defenseless fortresses invite aggression especially if there is rich booty in them. (1950a, 137, 143)

Social and economic policy that Schumpeter regarded as anti-capitalistic was introduced into a political vacuum, and the intellectual class, fundamentally fostered in the scientific and rationalistic atmosphere of capitalism, developed a moral disapproval of the capitalist order. "The most glamorous of these bourgeois aims, the foundation of an industrial dynasty, has in most countries become unattainable already" (1950a, 156).

In this manner, the economic world loses the only source of romance and heroism that survived in the form of entrepreneurship even in the unromantic and unheroic civilization of capitalism. Schumpeter provided an excellent summary, focusing on the consequences of rationalism on the extra-capitalist *structural* and *ideological* bases of capitalism: "the capitalist order not only rests on props made of extra-capitalist material but also derives its energy from extra-capitalist patterns of behavior which at the same time it is bound to destroy" (1950a, 162). The inconsistency between heroic entrepreneurship and rationalistic bourgeois ideology is the basic idea underlying Schumpeter's thesis, a thesis concerned with the conflict between social values required by capitalism and the *Zeitgeist* produced by capitalism (see pages 227–28). This conflict exactly corresponds to what I mean here by the inconsistency between heroism and rationalism. *Capitalism, Socialism and Democracy*, in my view, should be read with reference to the sociological framework of social values versus the *Zeitgeist* and in the ideological context of heroism versus rationalism. A series of discussions in that book are multifarious developments of this basic idea.

Can capitalism survive?

Schumpeter asked, "Can capitalism survive?" and replied, "No." As noted above, he did not mean that capitalism automatically leads to socialism, but that it establishes the conditions that make socialism feasible. According to the summary in his posthumous manuscript, "The March into Socialism," the reasons for this are as follows: (1) as innovations are organized, automatized, and routinized, economic development becomes the task of experts in governmental bureaucracy, so that the function of entrepreneurs tends to become obsolete and their social status is lost; (2) owing to the development of rational habits of mind, the pre-capitalistic elements that supported the working of capitalism with regard to moral, disciplinary, habitual, and institutional aspects are destroyed; (3) the development of capitalism has created a political system of democracy that is interventionist in the interest of workers and an intellectual class that is hostile to capitalism; (4) the value scheme of capitalist society, with wealth as the standard of success, loses its hold, and there is an increased preference for equality, social security, government regulation, and leisure time (1950a, 417–18).

Based on the fact that during the half century since the publication of *Capitalism, Socialism and Democracy*, capitalist countries have not been moving toward the establishment of socialism as an institution, Schumpeter has been frequently criticized. But most of the criticism suffers from methodological failures. What is crucially important for systemic evolution is political decision and action toward socialism after the necessary conditions have been met. Socialist countries in the former Soviet Union, Eastern Europe, and other areas that belong to the development-oriented type of economy do not have the kind of socialism that develops from mature capitalism. These countries actually failed because of their economic inefficiencies and political oppression, and this proves that Schumpeter was correct in concluding that premature socialization cannot succeed. Moreover, the experience of socialist countries has brought disillusionment with, and a decisive rejection of, socialism. Schumpeter located a moment of political choice at the last crossroad in the process of systemic evolution, but it is possible that capitalist countries, even in their "march into socialism," declined to adopt socialism at that moment.

What then, can we deduce from Schumpeter's observation about the maturity of capitalism resulting in a tendency toward socialism? His diagnosis was correct in that the concerns of the public sector carry more weight in the economic decisions of a society, and capitalist countries have more or less adopted a system called the welfare state or a mixed economy. The major reasons for the shift in this direction have been changes in the value scheme of capitalist societies and the emergence of a big government, as discussed under factors (2) and (4) above. These changes occurred because capitalist economic development led to affluence but tended to work against private incentives and to lessen the vigor of capitalism. This is nothing but a disease of advanced countries – for instance, a British disease – and it is fair to say that its prototype was first analyzed by Schumpeter. He called capitalism at this stage "capitalism in fetters" (1950a, 201) or "capitalism in the oxygen tent" (1943, 123). With regard to this, too, political action by the conservatives in advanced countries worked to remove the fetters and to have smaller government.

Schumpeter had a tendency to stress the negative effects of factor (3) – the intellectual class is not always critical of capitalism; it also desires a small government and the vitalization of a capitalist economy. The conservative intellectual class sometimes coexists with the ruling strata of conservative government, bureaucracy, and the business class. But, as the political machinery of democracy must more or less compromise, the politicization of the economy and the expansion of the public sphere is an inevitable trend. Therefore, the relevance of factors (2), (3), and (4) are high.

On the other hand, with regard to factor (1), it is also true that capitalism after World War II still had a remarkable capacity for development and adaptation. Indeed, under trustified capitalism, innovations tended to come not from individuals but from large organizations, but as long as there remained plenty of room for an unregulated market economy, the increasing generation of innovations in large corporations did not necessarily weaken the pace of technological progress in dynamically competitive situations. After the war innovations became large-scale and the competition for innovations intensified both domestically and internationally. If the decline of innovative activity was observed, it must have been due to a decrease in entrepreneurial incentives and in the scope of the market economy through government regulation and protection. Schumpeter's image of capitalist economic development was that of the sporadic emergence of small new enterprises, probably privately owned, and emphasized the dreams, desires, and performance of romantic adventurers. So far as there has been room for so-called venture business alongside big corporations, the industrial organization of an economy has not been as bureaucratic and rigid as he predicted, and it is likely to produce risky projects of innovative destruction more intensively than the nineteenth-century competitive economy.

The crucial question in this context is whether the present method of recruiting human energy into the economic sphere (in other words, that of seeking social leadership for economic activities) will come to an end. Schumpeter conceived of socialism at the stage where capitalism becomes mature, and wants and technology are saturated; unless these conditions are met, there is no reason to choose socialism. Socialism, therefore, is a system whose essence does not exist in economic change. If people want economic change, and if circumstances promoting capitalism are provided, then it is quite natural that the age of socialism will not arrive.

Schumpeter thought that after capitalism had accomplished the task of increasing the standard of living through economic development, another system would take its place, one based on a highly rationalized economy that would allocate resources from a social point of view and relieve people from the burden of economic life. Because economic development would no longer be necessary in the new system, the natural result would be the slowing down of development. "There would be nothing left for entrepreneurs to do. They would find themselves in much the same situation as generals would in a society perfectly sure of permanent peace ... Human energy would turn away from business. Other than economic pursuits would attract the brains and adventure" (1950a, 131).

In addition to the mode of capitalist civilization, in which entrepreneurs gain the surplus of a society in the form of profits and plow them back into investments, there are other ways of recruiting leaders and utilizing the social surplus. The nature of a social system in the history of civilization is determined by where the social leadership is allocated and what the social surplus is used for. Today, all countries with a mature capitalist system are facing this question and are asked to allocate much more innovation and social leadership to broader areas of a society rather than to the narrow economic area. For Schumpeter, a social scientist, this approach would not be pessimistic.

Can socialism work?

Schumpeter defined socialism as "that organization of society in which the means of production are controlled, and the decision on how and what to produce and on who is to get what, are made by public authority instead of by privately-owned and privately-managed firms" (1950a, 415).

To the question, "Can socialism work?" he answered, "Of course it can." Because he spoke of socialism as constituting the highest stage of capitalism, so to speak, he could logically assume the economic superiority of socialism over capitalism in that it not only has a feasible mechanism of resource allocation, but also can avoid unemployment, frictions, and wasted resources – all of which are inevitable in the dynamic operation of capitalism. He believed in the feasibility of economic calculations in socialism based on the theory of competitive socialism or market socialism, tracing back to Enrico Barone and developed by Oscar Lange and others. In short, he thought that socialism could work according to the economic logic dwelled on in *Wesen*. Thus he could say "that socialization means a stride beyond big business on the way that has been chalked out by it or, what amounts to the same thing, that socialist management may conceivably prove as superior to big-business capitalism as big-business capitalism has proved to be to the kind of competitive capitalism of which the English industry of a hundred years ago was the prototype" (1950a, 195–96).

It is important to recognize that Schumpeter's thesis on the feasibility of socialism was limited to the economic dimension. To use his terminology for diagnosing capitalism, it is a thesis concerning the workability of the socialist *system*; in order to determine the workability of the socialist *order*, one must examine the noneconomic circumstances – in particular, civilization and the value scheme – shaped by the management of socialism. Although he argued that the tendency toward rationalization, individuation, and democratization had emerged from capitalism, and that it would make socialism eventually feasible, he did not make clear what would occur in a socialist society. He admitted, of course, that socialism represented a new cultural world but thought that socialism could permit diversity in the political, social, religious, and spiritual aspects of a society. Referring to this as "the Cultural Indeterminateness of Socialism," he did not attempt to specify the unique cultural and spiritual traits of socialism (1950a, 170). This proposition is very important in order to understand his argument on socialism.

Whereas the capitalist economic *system* is conceived of as dynamic as well as stable in the framework of economic dynamics, Schumpeter argued in the wider context of economic sociology that the comprehensive capitalist *order* cannot survive the unfavorable reactions of the noneconomic areas. In contrast, with regard to socialism he merely said that the socialist economic *system* is workable in itself and did not comment on the workability of the socialist *order* on account of "the Cultural Indeterminateness of Socialism," except regarding the future of the premature case of Bolshevism. In order to be consistent, Schumpeter should have answered, "Nobody knows yet," to the question, "Can socialism work?"

"The Cultural Indeterminateness of Socialism" means that various forms of civilization are possible in a post-capitalist society. Innovative entrepreneurs working in the economic area of capitalism are a special type of leadership. Those who carry out excellent innovative projects in other areas of a society, especially those who are concerned with the creation of systems of knowledge and information, may take the place of entrepreneurs in light of their growing importance in promoting the dynamics of a society as a whole. This has nothing to do with socialism; rather, to use Schumpeter's sociological concept, it involves the shift of social leadership from economic to other areas.

How does democracy work?

Viewed from this perspective, Schumpeter's treatment of democracy in *Capitalism, Socialism and Democracy* is interesting. In the preface he wrote: "The problem of democracy forced its way into the place it now occupies in this volume because it proved impossible to state my views on the relation between the socialist order of society and the democratic method of government without a rather extensive analysis of the latter" (1950a, viii). In discussing socialism, he criticized the traditional theory of democracy and proposed an alternative theory. His position was to maintain the indeterminateness thesis just described, on the one hand, and to regard democracy not as a normative value but as an institutional arrangement, on the other. Hence, it was incumbent on him to ask how it works.

According to Schumpeter, the classical theory of democracy is summarized by the proposition: "that 'the people' hold a definite and rational opinion about every individual question and that they give effect to this opinion – in democracy – by choosing 'representatives' who will see to it that that opinion is carried out" (1950a, 269). On the contrary, Schumpeter's theory is based on the following definition: "the democratic method is that institutional arrangement for arriving at political decisions in which individuals acquire the power to decide by means of a competitive struggle for the people's vote" (1950a, 269). He asserted, there is no uniquely defined common good or public interest to be realized in the political process. The will of the people is manufactured by politicians or exponents of economic interest, and democratic politics is nothing more than the activities of politicians, motivated by self-interest, to get votes in order to become members of parliament and ministers. Democracy in the political system and markets in the economic system are functional parallels in that both are competitive systems for selecting leadership.

Schumpeter's theory of democracy, in the systemic context, intended to separate the traditional ties between socialism and democracy; he argued that they may be combined or stand alone. Although he did not deny the possibility of democratic socialism, he also admitted the possibility of autocratic socialism. From the economic point of view, he gave socialism a favorable evaluation because it would be a sequel to the economic performance of capitalism at the highest stage; however, with regard to its noneconomic functions, he not only asserted the indeterminacy of socialist culture but also pulled down the idol of socialism from the pedestal of democracy.

What does his theory of democracy mean in relation to capitalism?

Democracy was the product of the bourgeoisie, but its disciplined operation was not necessarily realized in capitalism because the self-control required by a democracy was lost and the politicization of economic problems increased through the activities of pressure groups. This has something to do with factor (4) described earlier, and democracy can be interpreted as an institutional route to eroding the capitalist economy.

Schumpeter's hypothesis about capitalism was that although the economy works well, political, social, and cultural circumstances will ultimately disband the system. Similarly, I infer, his hypothesis about socialism might be that although the economy functions effectively, political autocracy will destroy the system. In both cases, the economy does not determine the eventual destiny of a system; this was Schumpeter's message to the world.

CHAPTER 10

The historical world of economics

Schumpeter, who maintained a great interest in the history of economics throughout his academic career, produced an extensive body of work in this field, covering the literature from the Greek period to contemporary times. His books on the subject include *Epochen der Dogmen- und Methodengeschichte* (1914a), *Vergangenheit und Zukunft der Sozialwissenschaften* (1915), *Ten Great Economists* (1951a), *History of Economic Analysis* (1954a), and *Dogmenhistorische und biographische Aufsätze* (1954b). *Ten Great Economists* and *Aufsätze* are collections of his separate articles edited and published after his death. The *History of Economic Analysis,* a revision and expansion of his 1914 study, was left unfinished at his death; it was edited and finally published through the efforts of his wife.

A two-structure approach to mind and society

The *History of Economic Analysis,* a magnum opus exceeding 1,200 pages, is a distinguished achievement among the studies of the history of economics. Outstanding features include its broad scope, the astonishing polymathy and unique judgment of its author, and his penetrating insight in constructing a scenario of scientific history. Although there exist fine historical studies in specific fields of economics and on individual economists, there is no precedent for attempting a doctrinal history that covers such a wide range of economic disciplines, includes not only the top-ranking authors but also many minor figures, and describes the history of economics against an intellectual and social background tracing back to the sources of the Western thought. Nothing has taken its place; nothing has equaled it. Many will agree with Jacob Viner, who said:

There is, as we shall see, much in this book which is redundant, irrelevant, cryptic, strongly biased, paradoxical, or otherwise unhelpful or even harmful to understanding. When all this is set aside, there still remains enough to constitute, by a wide margin, the most constructive, the most original, the most learned, and the most brilliant contribution to the history of the analytical phases of our discipline which has ever been made. (Viner 1954, 894–95)

The history of science as science: its tasks

However, to consider Schumpeter's work as unsurpassable would mean the end of history, so to speak, and arrest the growth of study. *History* should be interpreted not as an artistic work but as a scientific work. Because Schumpeter advocated the theoretical formulation of history or the *histoire raisonnée*, it was incumbent on him to develop a theoretical framework in the study of history – be it the history of an economy or the history of economics. History, of course, is subjective; no objective schema or scenario for historical description is acceptable to everyone. However, the rules of procedure by which to analyze the sometimes implicit framework of historians yielding subjective scenarios should be made explicit. What is the basic idea that characterizes Schumpeter's approach to the history of economics?

In *History* a set of metatheories (the philosophy of science, the history of science, and the sociology of science), a set of substantive theories (economic statics, economic dynamics, and economic sociology), and a set of analytic tools (theory, history, statistics, and institution) are discussed simultaneously to describe the history of economics and represent the components of a theoretical framework for Schumpeter's historical study.

The following five major issues, which overlap to some extent, are the focus of this chapter. First, what are the method and framework of periodization in history? Second, how and when was economics established as an autonomous science? Third, what was the relationship between external history and internal history, or between the philosophy of science and the sociology of science in the context of economics? Fourth, how was the genealogy traced for each theoretical system of economics (economic statics, economic dynamics, and economic sociology)? And fifth, if individual scholars are practical test cases of the sociology of science, what meaning does a biographical study have in the history of science?

An evolutionary science of mind and society

In the first sentence of chapter 1 of *History*, Schumpeter wrote: "By History of Economic Analysis I mean the history of the intellectual efforts that men have made in order to understand economic phenomena or, which comes to the same thing, the history of the analytic or scientific aspects of economic thought" (1954a, 3). Most people who have read the book, including Jacob Viner, have been puzzled by the gap between Schumpeter's statement that the book is literally the history of economic analysis and what *History* is *actually* about. They have complained that this work, which also delves into other history, policy, culture, and related disciplines, includes redundant and inconsistent material in disarray.[1] But this is a faulty understanding of Schumpeter's method for constructing a history of science, for the following reasons.

First, in undertaking a history of the developments in one area of social life Schumpeter did not mean to deny the importance of other areas. Rather, he believed that in order to write an accurate account of the changes in a particular field, one must consider the interrelationship between that field and other fields. The German Historical School believed in integrating the perspectives of development and unity in social life. According to this viewpoint, it was necessary for historians of economics to examine all other factors and to discern what was relevant.

Second and more specifically, Schumpeter intended to distinguish between economic thought and economic analysis. When human beings acquired some ideas about an economy, they did not separate economic analysis from economic thought. The further one goes back in time, the more often it will be found that the two were intermingled, and thus it is necessary to extract the analytic elements from the primitive ideas of an economy. Schumpeter wrote that

the frontiers of the individual sciences or of most of them are incessantly shifting and … there is no point in trying to define them either by subject or by method. This particularly applies to economics, which is not a science in the sense in which acoustics is one, but is rather an agglomeration of ill-coordinated and overlapping fields of research in the same sense as is "medicine." (1954a, 10)

The mixing of economic thought and economic analysis cannot be avoided even today, because the economy is the ordinary business of ordinary people, and they are not barred from forming an understanding of it. Moreover, this remark of Schumpeter's cannot be disregarded: "Let us recall our distinction between Economic Thought – the opinions on economic matters that prevail at any given time in any given society and belong to the province of economic history rather than to the province of the history of economics – and Economic Analysis – which is the result of scientific endeavor in our sense" (1954a, 52). Because, in his view, the tools of economic analysis consist of history, theory, statistics, and economic sociology, economic thought that provides information about the history and institutions of an economy is indispensable to a history of economic analysis.

Third, in a more fundamental sense, the diversity of the material in *History of Economic Analysis* is due to what I call the "two-structure approach" that Schumpeter properly developed for his volume. Schumpeter's total work includes the "system of theory" about economy and the "system of metatheory" about economics. His system of theory consists of three layers: economic statics, economic dynamics, and economic sociology. Analogically, his system of metatheory also has three layers: the philosophy of science, the history of science, and the sociology of science; the three metatheories are concerned with scientific activity from the perspective of statics, dynamics, and sociology, respectively. In economics, these metatheories relate to the inquiry of its static structure and rules of procedure (economic methodology), the inquiry of its dynamic developments (history of economics), and the inquiry of its activity in a social context (sociology of economics), respectively. The history of economics provides not only the context in which the three layers in the system of theory are historically examined, but also reveals the structure of the three layers in the system of metatheory in which economics is conditioned by economic methodology and the sociology of economics, so that the history of economics is explained internally and externally.

It is possible to interpret the two systems from a different viewpoint: as the system of theory for the two different social areas, that is, economy and thought, rather than as the system of theory for the economic area and the system of its metatheory. Thought and science are elements of culture, mind, and consciousness in a wider sense and represent the superstructure of society as defined by Karl Marx. Therefore, an inquiry into the relationships between the two systems has a perspective that is similar to the economic interpretation of history in Marx. Schumpeter's two-structure approach was fully developed in the *History of Economic Analysis*.

Referring to Giambattista Vico, the eighteenth-century Italian thinker, Schumpeter discussed the two-structure approach as follows:

His New Science (*scienza nuova*) is best described by the phrase "an evolutionary science of mind and society." But this must not be interpreted to mean that the evolution of the human mind shapes the evolution of human society; nor, though this would be nearer the truth, that the historical evolution of societies shapes the evolution of the human mind; but that mind and society are two aspects of the same evolutionary process. (1954a, 137)

Nothing expresses the nature of Schumpeter's view of social science better than this passage. He identified the social sciences in the form of eighteenth-century moral philosophy with "the sciences of 'mind and society' " (1954a, 141). Thus it can be argued that the history of "an evolutionary science of mind and society" was the task of *History*.

Regarding John Stuart Mill's *A System of Logic* (1843) as one of the great books of the nineteenth century, representing one of the leading components of its *Zeitgeist*, Schumpeter pointed out the family likeness that existed between Mill's *Logic* and his *Principles of Political Economy* (1848). According to Schumpeter, Mill was so modest that he did not claim to give the world a new theory of intellectual operations and of economic processes, but in fact he applied similar approaches to mind and society in order to coordinate existing knowledge, to develop it, and to solve unsettled problems.

Figure 6 summarizes Schumpeter's two-structure approach to social science, where theory and metatheory are concerned with society and mind, especially with economy and economics, respectively. Each structure consists of static analysis, dynamic analysis, and sociological analysis. Society and mind are in the process of evolution with bilateral relationships between them.

The two-structure approach represents a critique of other approaches that tended to interpret the evolution of mind and society unilaterally. On the one hand, Marx's economic interpretation of history explained human history by the modes of material production, and on the other hand, Hegel's idealistic philosophy of history and the "intellectualist evolutionism" of Jean Antoine Condorcet, Auguste Comte, and Henry Thomas Buckle emphasized the mind as the determinant of a society (1954a, 438–43). Schumpeter lumped the two approaches together, calling it a "single hypothesis of the Comte-Buckle-Marx kind" (1954a, 811), and claimed that mind and society were interdependent and interactional.

The classical situation and the filiation of scientific ideas

On what methodology does the two-structure approach depend? Let us begin with a formal framework. Schumpeter introduced the concept of the "classical situation" as a device of periodization in history; he defined it as "the achievement of substantial agreement after a long period of struggle and controversy – the consolidation of the fresh and original work which went before" (1954a, 51). This quotation is from the editor of *History;* although Schumpeter planned to discuss the concept generally, he did not do so. However, the intent of the concept is clear enough in his description of the three classical situations.

Interpretation of the three classical situations

Schumpeter defined the first classical situation as the establishment of economics as "tooled knowledge" (1954a, 7) in the latter half of the eighteenth century, when two sources of economics, that is, philosophy and politics, were joined in Adam Smith's *Wealth of Nations* (1776). This scenario will be examined more closely below; here the establishment of economics with Adam Smith is assumed. To be precise, the years around 1790 are regarded as the period of the first classical situation, allowing twenty years for acceptance of Smith's work. The second classical situation refers to the years after Adam Smith when classical economics matured and was formulated by

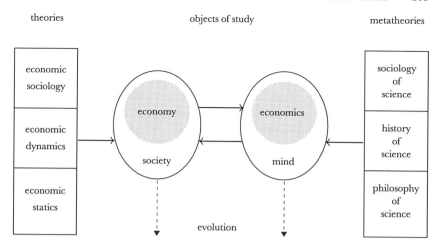

Figure 6   *Schumpeter's two-structure approach*

John Stuart Mill in his *Principles of Political Economy* (1848). The third classical situation was the identification of neoclassical economics in the *Principles of Economics* (1890) by Alfred Marshall and *Über Wert, Kapital, und Rente* (1893) by Knut Wicksell after the Marginal Revolution around 1870, allowing twenty years for their absorption.

Schumpeter's concept of the classical situation looks very much like Thomas Kuhn's concept of the establishment of normal science, which was made possible by the development of a paradigm. The formulation of a paradigm is achieved, first, when the conflict and competition among schools are over and a certain theory is supported by the dominant group of scholars, and second, when such a theory has been equipped with clearly articulated problems and methods and indicates the direction of the entire research activity. After the fall of logical positivism and logical empiricism, however, various positions on the philosophy of science were proposed by Kuhn, Karl Popper, Imre Lakatos, and others. In view of the differences they perceived among those positions, it would be misleading to emphasize only the similarity between Schumpeter and Kuhn. In fact, it is possible to regard Schumpeter as similar to Lakatos on the problem of verification and falsification and on the relationship between statics and dynamics. Rather than comparing aspects of Schumpeter's approach fragmentally with others', it is more useful to define his own theory of scientific history from his description of a scenario in the history of economics. In this context of the history of science, it is important to recognize that he had views on the methodology of science and the sociology of science – specifically, on instrumentalism, schools, and vision – because these views must be applied to, and tested by, the actual process of scientific activity.

Werner Stark, a student of the history of economics and the sociology of knowledge, asked why the great syntheses of economics that Schumpeter expressed by the concept of the classical situation occurred in certain periods of time, a question, in Stark's opinion, that Schumpeter failed to answer. Stark argued that the classical situation in economics reflected an analogous crystallization and equilibrium in social and economic situations, and that the intervals between two classical situations were characterized not only by a disintegration of the theoretical reflection of reality but also by a disintegration of the reality itself. His argument was based on the idea that "these two concomitant developments are really only aspects of one total stream of happening" (Stark 1959, 58). This idea does not differ from Schumpeter's belief that "mind and society are two aspects of the same evolutionary process" quoted above, or from my notion of the two-structure approach. Yet Stark's further claim that a consolidation, crystallization, and equilibrium of thought reflect the parallel developments in reality seems far-fetched and unacceptable. Schumpeter denied the unilateral causation from society to mind.

My general interpretation of Schumpeter's two-structure approach to mind and society is that because society is the object of thought and the field in which thought is created, society naturally influences thought, but thought has its own logic so that the relationships between mind and society are flexible. The exact nature of the relationships depends on specific cases and cannot be described in advance. Although the philosophy of science and the sociology of science are often developed in abstract terms, it is the task of the history of science to examine them in a specific context. My pragmatic interpretation is to relate the periodization of the three classical situations to that of the Kondratieff long cycles developed in Schumpeter's *Business Cycles* (1939).

In *Business Cycles* Schumpeter used the Kondratieff long cycles with a wave length of fifty to sixty years as the framework for the analysis of capitalist economic development, for two purposes: first, to analyze the Juglar cycles of nine to ten years and the Kitchin cycles of about forty months and to describe economic and industrial history within a period of the Kondratieff cycle, and second, to characterize the nature of a Kondratieff wave length in terms of not only epochal technological innovation but also sociological features, including civilization and the *Zeitgeist*. Thus, the first wave was called Industrial Revolution Kondratieff (characterized by cotton textile, iron, and steam power), the second wave Bourgeois Kondratieff (railroads), and the third wave Neomercantilist Kondratieff (electricity, chemicals, and the automobile).

In Schumpeter's view, Kondratieff long-waves start from the neighborhood of economic equilibrium; according to the chronology by Kuznets, which

Schumpeter eventually approved, the first wave began in 1787, the second in 1843, and the third in 1898 (Kuznets 1940). These three dates almost coincide with the dates of the classical situations in *History*. With these double heuristic frameworks Schumpeter tried to deal with developments in the economy and in economics. In this sense, the descriptions of economic history in *Business Cycles* and the history of economics in the *History of Economic Analysis* are parallel. The composition of *History*, however, does not follow the dating of the classical situations: Part II covers the period from Plato to the acceptance of Adam Smith's *Wealth of Nations* (around 1790); Part III, classical economics (1790–1870); Part IV, neoclassical economics (1870–1914 and after); and Part V, the present (to the 1940s). The division depends on the mechanism of scientific development.

Mechanism of scientific developments: revolution and synthesis

Schumpeter planned to write a methodological introduction as Part I after completing the substantive portion of *History*. Chapters 1 to 3 of Part I were finished; for chapter 4, entitled "The Sociology of Economics," section 1 ("Is the History of Economics a History of Ideologies?") was written; for two more sections ("The Motive Forces of Scientific Endeavor and the Mechanisms of Scientific Development" and "The Personnel of Science in General and of Economics in Particular"), Schumpeter left only fragmentary paragraphs. As I discussed in chapter 4, however, his sociology of science, which was more fully developed elsewhere, focused on vision (or ideology) and schools (or groups of scientists). Here I will examine how he applied his sociology of science and methodology of science to the study of the history of science in *History* to explain his idea of the mechanism of scientific development. His concept of the "classical situation" is part of that mechanism; another part is provided by his concept of the "filiation of scientific ideas." By combining the two, I will set forth an interpretation of Schumpeter's leading idea in *History*, which until now has remained rather ambiguous, as compared with his evaluation of individual figures, in which scholars have shown a keen interest.

A classical situation is a period that represents the establishment of uniform ideas about the method and problems of economics, a time during which advances that have been made over a number of decades are consolidated and coordinated. Doctrines are formulated and standardized by influential textbooks, and a comprehensive school, such as the classical or neoclassical schools, in economics is established for the discipline as a whole. The appearance of a classical situation is a remarkable phenomenon of the sociology of science. After this the scientific development enters a phase of gradual growth, an age of normal science, as Thomas Kuhn put it, during which one can speak of the progress of science according to the standard of scientific methodology.

Prior to consolidation and coordination, new ideas must be presented, leading to struggles and controversies among competing schools as they pursue legitimacy. Also, in the process after consolidation, new ideas will soon appear. To command the stream of ideas in this new age of disturbance, scientists need a conscious and an unconscious strategy. Even if one were prominent, he might diverge from the right course of scientific development in the long run; or conversely, even if one hit on a good idea, it might not be accepted at the time. Therefore, the history of science must engage not only in the follow-up of the mainstream but also in the critical evaluation of why other potentialities failed in light of the sociology of science as well as the methodology of science.

Concerning the success of a revolution, the rise in fame, or the neglect of valuable contributions, Schumpeter observed:

Owing to the resistance that an existing scientific structure offers, major changes in outlook and methods, at first retarded, then come about by way of revolution rather than of transformation and elements of the old structure that might be permanently valuable or at least have not yet had time to yield their full harvest of result are likely to be lost in the process. (1954a, 46)

Historical performances are rarely like erratic blocks in a plain. They are more like peaks that rise from clusters of smaller eminences. In other words, a science develops by small accretions that create a common fund of ideas from which, by chance as well as by merit, emerge the works that enter the hall of fame. Therefore we must add at least a few of those writers who, though they failed to achieve historic fame, yet did important work and exerted an influence upon developments in analysis that are anonymous but not negligible. (1954a, 480)

To explain the emergence of new ideas, Schumpeter's thesis of vision is applicable. Because scientific acts consist of the formation of vision and its theoretical formulation, a revolution can take place on either side. According to Schumpeter, "it is much more difficult for the human mind to forge the most elementary conceptual schemes than it is to elaborate the most complicated superstructures when those elements are well in hand" (1954a, 602). But unless vision is provided, economics has no object of recognition and elaboration. The history of economics is partly a history of the attempts to formulate a vision by means of theoretical structures: "To a great part, advance in theoretical analysis precisely consists in elaborating implications of older thought that had not been seen or not clearly seen before" (1954a, 674). The combination of vision and theory over time produces continuity in thought, and this is what Schumpeter called the filiation of scientific thought. In many places in the history of economics he actually found the lines of filiation, such as that of equilibrium theory from Richard Cantillon to Jacque Turgot and Jean-Baptiste Say to Léon Walras. As this example indicates, the Marginal Revolution had some predecessors and from the stream of ideas progress in analytic techniques can be perceived; the filiation of scientific ideas, along with development within a paradigm established during a classical situation, shapes another concept of progress in science.

It is clear from the following sentence that Schumpeter regarded revolution and synthesis as the two moments in scientific development:

> so far as pure theory is concerned, Walras is in my opinion the greatest of all economists. His system of equilibrium, uniting, as it does, the quality of "revolutionary" creativeness with the quality of classical synthesis, is the only work by an economist that will stand comparison with the achievements of theoretical physics. (1954a, 827)

If by the emergence of a classical situation, as its definition signifies, synthesis establishes a universal basis of a science, revolution makes scientific thought continuous in human history through the discovery of the filiation of cognate ideas. The thesis that revolution implies continuity with the past appears to be a paradox that would please Schumpeter. The ordinary concept of revolution is one-sided in emphasizing the critical aspects of revolutionary versus mainstream thought; a science could make significant (rather than piecemeal) progress if a novel idea could look back to past thought that had been neglected.

Joseph Spengler, in discussing the endogenous and exogenous influences on the development of economics, presented the noteworthy view that the relative importance of influences depends on how the scope of economics is defined (Spengler 1968). If economics is perceived as a kit of tools, exogenous influences exert little influence on its development. If, however, economics is conceived of more broadly to also include ideological, philosophical, and preanalytic elements, it becomes sensitive to exogenous influences. This view accords with Schumpeter's; as I have noted (see pages 70–71), he thought that the role of preanalytic vision is important for the analysis of long-term changes in an economy and that exogenous influences including ideology have a larger role to play in this type of research. Moreover, an association with past neglected thought through the visionmaking of later authors sometimes produces revolutionary leaps, whereas the progress of analytic techniques and the elaboration of theoretical structures depends on the internal development of science.

Vision as well as theoretical tools, however, cannot permit foreseeable development. Schumpeter observed that "science as a whole has never attained a logically consistent architecture; it is a tropical forest, not a building erected according to blueprint" (1954a, 10). Nevertheless, his philosophical idea that a science would take a reasonable course *ex post* might partly presume the idea of natural law in history and partly reflect the biologism of Ernst Mach and Henri Poincaré.[2] Although, like evolution in an economy, evolution in thought cannot be explained *ex ante*, it is argued that, in the analogy with biological evolution, thought changes so as to adapt to facts; otherwise a theory cannot survive. Intellectual history is a history of the survival of the fittest, and theories must compete with each other in a competition for the fit to facts.

Survivors, however, are not necessarily superior. Schumpeter rejected the view that important concepts, methods, and conclusions were all embodied in the current theories and argued that only a recollection and conversation with the past would ensure the filiation of scientific ideas. In *The Science of Mechanics* (1883), Mach warned that the prevailing theories were not inevitable and might not have taken over important past ideas.[3]

A scenario of the establishment of economics

Two sources of economics

In *Epochen der Dogmen- und Methodengeschichte*, Schumpeter developed a scenario that economics, as it was established as a science at the end of the eighteenth century, had two different sources in Europe: the speculation of philosophical *Weltanschauung* and the debate of current topics ([1914a] 1954c, 9–10). The first source was the thought of philosophers on society, beginning with Aristotle, progressing through medieval theology, and crystallizing in eighteenth-century "moral philosophy." The second source was the "vulgar economics" discussed by merchants and officers who were engaged in ordinary economic practice; it was called mercantilism and cameralism. The *History of Economic Analysis* adopted the same scenario. Investigating the sources of a science includes answering the question of how a science was established thereafter as an autonomous science, the first question that the history of a science always encounters. Schumpeter acknowledged the separation of these two sources as an expository device, implying that his history of economics was based on the instrumentalist formulation of history.

For the sake of convenience, the two sources can be called philosophy and policy. According to Schumpeter, "Social problems interest the scholarly mind primarily from a philosophical and political standpoint; scientifically they do not at first appear very interesting or even to be 'problems' at all" (1954a, 53), because economic life is merely an ordinary experience in which everyone participates.

The first stream of thought, he argued, began in Greece and the Roman Empire, then skipped five hundred years from the sixth to the tenth century (Schumpeter called this period "the great gap"), and finally ran into medieval scholasticism, the natural law, and moral philosophy. Schumpeter admitted that this stream of thought was dominated by the moral, legal, and normative perspective, but paid scrupulous attention to the analytic viewpoint, which might be involved and stimulated. "There is no point in throwing out the analytic baby with the philosophic bath-water" (1954a, 111). The analytic elements he wanted to uncover in history were always those of economics and sociology.[4]

Let us examine a few examples of resolving a mixture of analytic and philosophical elements. Schumpeter called Aristotle's *Nicomachean Ethics* and *Politics* the first known systematic presentation of a unitary social science. Aristotle's economic sociology consisted of a discussion of institutions such as private property, slavery, communism, and the family. Schumpeter took notice of Aristotle's embryonic pure economics that was based on wants and their satisfaction and regarded his analyses of values, exchange, and money as the starting point of later economics. Although it had been held that Aristotle was so preoccupied with the philosophical and ethical problems of justice in exchange that he was diverted from the analytic issues of actual pricing, Schumpeter interpreted the normal competitive prices in Aristotle as standards of commutative justice. Similarly, he regarded the concept of just price in the work of St. Thomas Aquinas as belonging to pure economics and identified his sociology with a study of the social function of private property focusing on the concept of public good.

In this stream, Schumpeter observed, the most important element was the thought of natural law, which had a fundamental significance as the origin of all of the social sciences. According to him, a science originated where a body of interdependent phenomena was recognized; this recognition was a prerequisite to analyzing apparently commonplace phenomena. Social science discovered itself in the concept of natural law. *Natural* meant the nature of things or naturally right things. The quote, "just as we may look upon the physical universe ... as a logically consistent whole that is modeled upon an orderly plan – so we may look upon society as a cosmos that is possessed of inherent logical consistency" (1954a, 114) was based on this concept.

On the other hand, philosophers of the seventeenth and eighteenth centuries tried to find natural law through a psychological inquiry into universal human nature. In this way, the scholastic concept of public good was formulated into the utilitarian doctrine of the greatest happiness of the greatest number. Schumpeter saw utilitarianism as the last system of the natural law. Utilitarianism had widely influenced the social sciences, among them economics, based on the formulation of human motives in terms of egoism and the pursuit of pleasure. Moral philosophy, including utilitarianism, had emerged as a comprehensive theory of society that covered broad areas of the social sciences.

Two points that Schumpeter discussed in *History* with regard to natural law (the postulate of individual rationality and the discovery of the order in social phenomena) had been more sharply emphasized as the formative ideas of science in his previous book, *Epochen der Dogmen- und Methodengeschichte*: "We shall, therefore, understand that on the one side thinkers arrived at an individualist point of view, which saw in the world of motives within the individual the key to an understanding of social problems, while on the other side they maintained that there was an immutable and universally valid order which alone corresponded to Reason" ([1914a] 1954c, 18). Schumpeter interpreted this earlier recognition as strictly scientific in the modern sense.

The second stream leading to economics encompassed the debates of contemporary economic policy. With the fall of the feudal society and the rise of monarchy after the fourteenth and fifteenth centuries, the authority of the Roman Catholic Church and thus the international cultural world of the Middle Ages gradually declined. In contrast, the nation-states appeared on the stage, and they were concerned about economic policy. Their goals were to raise government revenue internally and to increase trade surplus externally. Schumpeter labeled the authors of economic literature during sixteenth- and seventeenth-century mercantilism and cameralism in Europe, before Adam Smith, "Consultant Administrators" and "Pamphleteers."

One of the major policy debates was about the program for the development of industry and commerce, and the main results were discourses on trade and money. Although they aimed directly at solving practical issues, the logic inherent in the economic process was gradually uncovered. Another major debate was on public finance.

The discovery of economic circulation and the integration of economics

Schumpeter, having discussed the history of economic thought by referring to philosophical thought and practical policy issues as the sources of economics, faced the task of judging whether economics was established as a science somewhere in the latter half of the eighteenth century. His two studies on the history of economics provided different conclusions. This might mean a change of mind, but more important, it gave rise to a theoretical problem about periodization in history. In *Epochen der Dogmen- und Methodengeschichte* Schumpeter had emphasized the "discovery of economic circulation" by the Physiocrats. They not only belonged to the stream of thought of natural law, but also supported a policy favoring agriculture; therefore, they represented the confluence of the two mainstreams: "Before the Physiocrats appeared on the scene only local symptoms on the economic body, as it were, had been perceived, while they enabled us to conceive this body physiologically and anatomically as an organism with a uniform life process and uniform conditions of life, and it was they who presented to us the first analysis of this life process" ([1914a] 1954c, 44). Primitive and elementary as the *Tableau Economique* was, Schumpeter attributed the establishment of economics to François Quesnay, who acquired through this framework a recognition of the interdependence of economic phenomena.[5]

In the *History of Economic Analysis*, in contrast, the two streams were joined at Smith's *Wealth of Nations*. Although Schumpeter here, too, emphasized the importance of the work of the Physiocrats, he did not treat them as epoch-makers; the two streams from the Greek period, still not confluent at the Physiocrats, ran further to Adam Smith.[6]

In both books Schumpeter thought that after Quesnay a synthesis of existing elements of economics was still needed. The Physiocrats, a true school, had appeared and disappeared like a shooting star. In *Epochen* Schumpeter regarded Turgot and Smith as qualified to undertake the synthesis. Smith actually performed the task, but Schumpeter's evaluation was that "he [Smith] was a man of systematic work and balanced presentation, not of great new ideas, but a man who above all carefully investigates the given data, criticizes them coolly and sensibly, and co-ordinates the judgment arrived at with others which have already been established" ([1914a] 1954c, 65). In *History* the two streams were united at the *Wealth of Nations*, but Schumpeter, unlike most scholars, did not regard Smith as the founder of economics:

No matter what he actually learned or failed to learn from predecessors, the fact is that the *Wealth of Nations* does not contain a single analytic idea, principle, or method that was entirely new in 1776. (1954a, 184)

But though the *Wealth of Nations* contained no really novel ideas and though it cannot rank with Newton's *Principia* or Darwin's *Origin* as an intellectual achievement, it is a great performance all the same and fully deserved its success. The nature of the one and the causes of the other are not hard to see. The time had come for precisely that kind of coordination. And this task A. Smith performed extremely well. He was fitted for it by nature: no one but a methodical professor could have accomplished it. (1954a, 185)

Schumpeter marked the epoch by Smith's synthesis of economics and called it the first classical situation.

These contrasting views about the birth of economics as a science do not mean that either one is the right version by itself. The question is which one more appropriately explains the historical reality. Without a doubt Quesnay was epochal to Schumpeter, who attached the highest importance to the recognition of general equilibrium in an economy. This view, however, makes it difficult to interpret the process from Quesnay to Smith as a synthetic development because Smith did not follow Quesnay's whole system. As Schumpeter admitted, the analytic work of Quesnay was not comprehended by his contemporary and later economists; because it included a curious thing like the *tableau*, the scrupulous Smith did not link Quesnay's ideas with his system.[7] "Karl Marx was the only first-rank economist to give Quesnay his due" (1954a, 232). As long as Marx was influential enough to form a paradigm and a school, Quesnay was for the first time brought into the process of the filiation of scientific ideas.

It can be argued that although the discovery of economic circulation by the Physiocrats was epochmaking in terms of the criterion of the philosophy of science, it did not have a great influence in actually shaping a paradigm in economics.[8] In contrast, Smith's framework of economics was far from ideal from the standpoint of the philosophy of science. Owing to its external success, however, it engendered considerable power in professional circles from the outlook of the sociology of science. What is important from the latter perspective was that, in view of Schumpeter's third definition of science – that science is carried out by groups of professional scientists – Adam Smith was not a bureaucrat, a politician, a merchant, or even a doctor, but a typical university professor. "From about 1790 on, Smith became the teacher not of the beginner or the public but of the professionals, especially the professors" (1954a, 193–94). Schumpeter found Smith's larger success to be his influence on professionals rather than in the number of books he sold. In other words, Quesnay was epochal in terms of internal history but Smith was in terms of external history. In the internal history describing the filiation of scientific ideas, Quesnay was later linked with Walras, who was to establish the Magna Carta of economic theory, in addition to Marx. Unlike the *Epochen*, a small book that did not encompass the sociology of science, *History*, with its broader scope, introduced the sociology of science as another coordinate axis for describing the history of economics.[9]

Theoretical exercises in the sociology of science

History reveals very interesting thought in the sociology of science. In this volume Schumpeter attempted to compare the ability of three contemporaries Jacques Turgot, Adam Smith, and Cesare Beccaria to perform the integration of economics, which was the demand of the age. According to him, Turgot was undoubtedly the most brilliant of the three. Turgot's *Réflexions sur la formation et la distribution des richesses*, though no more than an elaborate analytic table of contents for the book that he planned to write, was distinctly superior to the skeleton of Smith's *Wealth of Nations* ; if their outlines were compared, nobody would have admired Smith's (1954a, 248). In comparing Smith and Beccaria, too, Schumpeter remarked, Beccaria's *Elementi di economia pubblica,* though only lecture notes, was superior to Smith's lectures at the University of Glasgow. Schumpeter reflected that if Beccaria had spent his time expanding the notes for as many years as Smith did instead of working for the Milanese administration, the outcome would have been comparable with the *Wealth of Nations*. Smith's success was attributed to the fact that, as a university professor, he could invest enough time in writing (1954a, 180–81).

This conjecture might sound unreasonable to Smith's adherents. But what Schumpeter did in *History* was to present a theoretical analysis of the factors responsible for the success of the *Wealth of Nations* by making counterfactual assumptions. He found that Smith's work was "the product of patience, of meticulous care, of self-discipline," and that its success was due to "its mature wisdom, its luxuriant illustrations, its effective advocacy of policies" and, in addition to intellectual performance, to "elaboration, application, and illustration" (1954a, 248). Schumpeter's evaluation, based as it was on the imagination and analytic inference, is rare in the study of the history of economics.

Schumpeter made similar comparisons for Heinrich von Thünen (and Antoine Cournot) versus David Ricardo in the period of the classical school and for Léon Walras versus Alfred Marshall in the period of the neoclassical school. In every comparison his judgment was against the British.

The genealogy of statics, dynamics, and economic sociology

After Adam Smith, economists reached a consensus about the fundamentals of economics such as the subject matter, method, and goals of economics. This permitted the integration of analytic efforts. The classical situation, in terms of the synthesis of the economic system, was established by Smith and the development of classical economics (1790–1870) began. What did the economics of this period mean to Schumpeter, who thought that economics as an autonomous science was first realized by Walras?

Relative immaturity

Responding to this question, Schumpeter characterized this period as one of "relative immaturity" (1954a, 463). Indeed, the solidification of a certain framework of economics by Adam Smith meant that "relative maturity" was achieved. By relative immaturity Schumpeter meant that important advances were recognized not immediately but only later, so that the progress of economics was obstructed. The Smithian synthesis overlooked and sterilized some development possibilities contained in the work of his predecessors. Moreover, the prevalence of Ricardian economics made economic research stray from the pursuit of a general equilibrium theory. Thus the discoverers of the marginal utility theory, such as Antoine Cournot, Jules Dupuit, Hermann Gossen, and William Lloyd, did not attract much attention; instead, the labor theory of value gained currency. The forerunners of the demand-and-supply theory of exchange values, such as James Lauderdale, Jean-Baptiste Say, and Robert Malthus, were ignored. Heinrich von Thünen, the great neglected economist who conceived of the marginal productivity theory and applied differential calculus to maximization (economizing), the central problem of economics, was the second scholar (next to Cournot) to express the general interdependence of economic magnitudes by an equation system. John Rae, who anticipated the Austrian capital theory, was also overlooked.

Following the comparative evaluation of Turgot (and Beccaria) versus Smith, Schumpeter compared Thünen with Ricardo. He said that if judged exclusively by his purely theoretical abilities, Thünen was superior to Ricardo and to all economists of the time except Cournot (1954a, 465). According to him, Ricardo's major influence stemmed from his findings on the current policy issues. Rejecting Schumpeter's emphasis of Cournot, Lionel Robbins asked, whether the withdrawal of Cournot or Ricardo would have caused the greater impoverishment of economics if their contribution had been withdrawn (Robbins 1955, 5). This is a mediocre rebuttal, because Schumpeter did not try to compare the actual achievements and influences of the two economists, but to separate the causes of their performances into factors by counterfactual assumptions.

In fact, Ricardo formed a school, whereas, in Schumpeter's view, the Ricardian system was distorted by a policy-oriented viewpoint and digressed from the development of economics. Schumpeter regarded the work of John Stuart Mill as the core of classical political economy and that of Smith-Mill-Marshall as the mainstream representing the British line of economic statics. In France, the line of Cantillon-Quesnay-Turgot-Say-Cournot-Walras grasped the economic equilibrium (1954a, 492).

In the age of classical economics, the apparent dynamic elements found in Smith, Ricardo, and Mill were not concerned with changes emerging from the economic process but with responses to changes in exogenous data; their vision of a future economy was no more than the discussion of the stationary state that the economy would achieve. Schumpeter complained about the poverty of vision in the British Classical School: "The most interesting thing to observe is the complete lack of imagination which that vision reveals. Those writers lived at the threshold of the most spectacular economic developments ever witnessed. Vast possibilities matured into realities under their very eyes. Nevertheless, they saw nothing but cramped economies, struggling with ever-decreasing success for their daily bread" (1954a, 571). He compared it with the grand vision of Karl Marx.

The only development in dynamic economics during this period was that of Marx; Schumpeter called it "the only genuinely evolutionary economic theory that the period produced" (1954a, 441). The idea, forged by economic sociology, that the capitalist order is a phenomenon in a historical phase and will be transformed into another by virtue of its own inherent logic belonged to Marx alone (1954a, 544). In the second German edition of *Theorie der wirtschaftlichen Entwicklung*, the description of stationary flow in chapter 1 is followed by an appendix that provides a summary of the history of economics in order to demonstrate the static nature of the previous theories. This appendix is not translated in the English version. Here, too, Schumpeter wrote that "the only great attempt to tackle development problems is that of Marx" (1926a, 84), because apart from the historical vision in the economic interpretation of history, Marx set forth the economics of the inherent evolution of the economic process.

After the Marginal Revolution

The Marginal Revolution by William Stanley Jevons, Carl Menger, and Léon Walras achieved the establishment of the general equilibrium system and was linked with the latent line beginning with Richard Cantillon. Schumpeter wrote:

It was only in the period under discussion that the conception of an economic cosmos that consists of a system of interdependent quantities was fully worked out with all its problems, if not quite satisfactorily solved, at least clearly arrayed and with the idea of a general equilibrium between these quantities clearly established in the center of pure theory. (1954a, 918)

According to Schumpeter, the most important among the three was Walras; the revolutionariness of the Marginal Revolution was not marginal utility or marginal analysis but the recognition of general equilibrium.

After neoclassical economics had been developed as static theory, Schumpeter must have been confident that his theory of economic development was a real contribution to dynamic theory. His theory was the filiation of scientific ideas that linked only with Marx in the entire history of economics. But he did not claim it explicitly in his study of the history of economics. In the *History of Economic Analysis* Schumpeter tried to discover dynamic theory in the development of economics after World War I and II, but he did not find a theory of endogenous economic evolution that was related to Marx's vision. Despite the influence of Keynesian economics, Schumpeter referred to it as aberrations leading to what he called the "Ricardian vice."

Economic sociology and a universal social science

I have paid attention to the fact that Schumpeter traced the descent of economic sociology as well as economics in the *History of Economic Analysis*. Until economics gained scientific autonomy, economic thinking had been inseparable from the overall view of society and was often combined with sociological thinking. Schumpeter called this overall view a "unitary Social Science" and applied the concept to Aristotle (1954a, 58), utilitarianism (1954a, 429), and Marx (1954a, 441); similarly, he called the thought of the scholastic writers and of the philosophers of natural law a "universal social science" (1954a, 141). Although he was fascinated by a grand approach, he was critical of a monolithic view that explained social phenomena by a single factor. Thus he rejected a "single hypothesis of the Comte-Buckle-Marx kind" that attempted to attribute historical evolution to simple factors (1954a, 811).

Schumpeter was particularly interested in the structure of the unitary social science of Marx and examined it closely to find out whether Marx's synthesis rested on the same concept of social classes in both economics and sociology. He admitted that such a synthesis without a doubt enhanced the analytic vitality:

The ghostly concepts of economic theory begin to breathe. The bloodless theorem descends into *agmen, pulverem et clamorem*; without losing its logical quality, it is no longer a mere proposition about the logical properties of a system of abstractions; it is the stroke of a brush that is painting the wild jumble of social life. Such analysis conveys not only richer meaning of what all economic analysis describes but it embraces a much broader field – it draws every kind of class action into its picture, whether or not this class action conforms to the ordinary rules of business procedure. (1950a, 45–46)

Schumpeter, nevertheless, pointed out that the unity of the social sciences in Marx also suffered from defects. Viewing the economic category "labor" and the social class "proletariat" as identical might conceal the diversity of wage earners. In such a monolithic synthesis a theory would be directed to a single purpose and liable to lose its usefulness: "A valuable economic theorem may by its sociological metamorphosis pick up error instead of richer meaning and vice versa. Thus synthesis in general and synthesis on Marxian lines in particular might easily issue in both worse economics and worse sociology" (1950a, 46). Therefore, Schumpeter proposed to break down Marx's system into economics and economic sociology. The model of economic sociology, in Schumpeter's view, was that of the German Historical School, and he determined that his work in economic sociology would belong to this line of thought.

Another relative immaturity

In the trend of the specialization of sciences in the first half of the twentieth century, the synthetic and comprehensive orientation of economic sociology lost its appeal. As time went on, the work of economic sociology was on the decline. As for economic dynamics, some aspects of the analytic technique gradually began to make progress in the field of macroeconomics, but no theory was related to Marx's vision. From Schumpeter's evaluation of the immaturity of dynamic economics and economic sociology, even the false interpretation that the *History of Economic Analysis* was an absolutist history headed for the static general equilibrium theory might follow. But, in fact, his investigation included not only static theory but also dynamic theory and economic sociology. His principle of eliminating his own work from the history of economics might obscure the fact that he traced the lines of dynamic economics and economic sociology from the Greek period to the present. He would have viewed the post-World War I period as another era of relative immaturity.

Portrait gallery of masters

Joseph Alois Schumpeter and John Maynard Keynes were the two greatest biographers in the field of economics in the first half of the twentieth century. As early as the 1910s Schumpeter, whose talent for constructing portraits of economists was already recognized, prepared a series of obituary essays for acquaintances. He was fond of writing biographical essays and continued this work throughout his life. The economists he wrote about were Walras, Böhm-Bawerk, and Marx in the 1910s, Weber, Menger, Böhm-Bawerk, Knapp, and Wieser in the 1920s, Bortkiewicz in the 1930s, and Marshall, Taussig, Marx, Keynes, Fisher, Pareto, and Mitchell in the 1940s. They were all his contemporaries and, except for Marx, he knew them all personally. In addition, he presented numerous sketches of past scholars in *History*.

Biography as art

In his review of Keynes's *Essays in Biography* (1933b), Schumpeter wrote: "Biography is the art of focussing an epoch and an environment in the story of an individual" (1933b, 652). He enumerated the combination of abilities required to write a good biography: first, vision of the age and environment; second, acquaintance with the disciplines of prominent figures; and third, a gift for art. Keynes, he believed, had rare abilities in this respect, especially for artistic writing: "There are pages in this book every sentence of which is a master-stroke directed by the highest 'Kunstverstand,' a term which I have never been able to translate" (1933b, 652). Schumpeter himself showed incomparable talent in his biographical work and wrote in an elevated style.

Schumpeter had high praise for Keynes's essay on Marshall, which, he said, was "the gem of its genus, the most brilliant and profound biography of any scientist the present writer ever read, the great monument to the great leader" (1933b, 653).

Nevertheless, he did not hesitate to raise doubts about Keynes's interpretation of economists in history. Whereas we have seen Schumpeter's criticism of Keynes's theoretical work, it is interesting to examine his appraisal of Keynes's biographical contribution:

(a) Regarding Marshall's belief in perfectionism and his methodicalness in academic activities, Keynes wrote the following celebrated passage: "Economists must leave to Adam Smith alone the glory of the quarto, must pluck the day, fling pamphlets into the wind, write always *sub specie temporis*, and achieve immortality by accident, if at all" (Keynes [1924] 1972, 199). Schumpeter remarked that making Marshall a pamphleteer would not have made him more famous, and that Marshall was the type of man who resolutely refused to give up to the hour what was meant for the centuries. He found a similarity, from the viewpoint of the sociology of science, between Smith's *Wealth* and Marshall's *Principles*: "they are the result of the work of decades and fully matured, the products of minds that took infinite care, were patient of labor, and indifferent to the lapse of years" (1954a, 835).

(b) Schumpeter placed a higher value on Walras than on Marshall. He sarcastically grumbled at Keynes's extreme praise of Marshall at the expense of Jevons and Walras. Referring to the Greek myth that a tragedy began because Anchises boasted of his son Aeneas, Schumpeter suggested that although Marshall had as a pupil Keynes, Jevons and Walras did not have pupils to be proud of. Keynes, in his essay on Marshall, characterized the relationship between Marshall and Jevons as follows: "Jevons saw the kettle boil and cried out with the delighted voice of a child; Marshall too had seen the kettle boil and sat down silently to build an engine" (Keynes [1924] 1972, 185). Schumpeter said that if there were Jevonians, they would protest against it, yet he had to admit, "what a beautiful passage all the same!" (1933b, 654). Keynes's parable renders unnecessary the argument that either Jevons or Marshall was superior.

(c) In his essay on Malthus, Keynes wrote: "If only Malthus, instead of Ricardo, had been the parent stem from which nineteenth-century economics proceeded, what a much wiser and richer place the world would be to-day!" (Keynes [1933] 1972, 100–101). Although this was written before *General Theory*, Schumpeter condemned it as a self-seeking argument.

Biography as a sociology of science

A biography is an idiographic work in the sense that it is concerned with a specific person; it is a world in which the tool of rhetoric and the composition of scenario can be dominant. Thus it is a work of art. A biographical work, however, does not deal with a fictitious character but is restricted by various historical facts relating to an actual person. A biography describes the circumstances and the motives, character, and talent the figure under study possessed to develop his intellectual life. It is his work in the history of thought that should be explained. Viewed in this way, a biography has the task of describing and interpreting the "story of an individual," according to Schumpeter, as it relates to intellectual activity, through his characteristic talent and personality with reference to "an epoch and an environment" in order to help others better understand his work and thought.

Generally speaking, the sociology of science is concerned with the relationship between thought and society, without denying the procedural rules that are prescribed by the philosophy of science. But thought and society do not relate to each other uniquely unless the two are mediated by individual thinkers. Individuals are conditioned from two sides. On the one hand, they are not a mechanical catalyst that produces certain scientific work under certain circumstances but rather enjoy a unique existence endowed with individual peculiarities. On the other hand, their activities are subject to the objectively given intellectual field and to the procedural rules of science. The task of a biography as a sociological work of science is to resolve the conflict between objectivism and subjectivism in the explanation of the nature of thought. In other words, a biography is an attempt by the sociology of science to explore the relationship between an "epoch" and "thought," focusing on an "individual." Alternatively, it sheds light on the process in which "thought" is produced from the interaction between an "individual" and an "epoch." If a biography is to clarify such a relationship and process, a concept that often remains implicit in the ordinary discourse of the sociology of science should be made explicit. That is the *habitus*, in Pierre Bourdieu's terminology, that intermediates between an "epoch" and an "individual." When the *habitus* or the intellectual habit is conceived through abstraction not merely as personal but as social and transposable, one can produce a biography not as a work of art but as a sociological work of science.

In Schumpeter's instrumentalism, a theory is an arbitrary creation of the mind for the purposes of understanding a reality. Because the reality does not necessarily exist in an exact and objective form independently of a theory, the fitting of a theory to the reality should be interpreted with flexibility. Basically the same thing applies to biography as sociology of science. Although a biography is regarded as such an artistic piece that the subjectivity of the writer sometimes dominates, the biography still must fit objective facts. In other words, the facts must test and justify a biography. Insofar as a biography passes the test, it can contribute, from the viewpoint of the sociology of science, to the understanding and evaluation of the intellectual performance of the individual in question, and eventually to the grasp of the *Zeitgeist*.

Schumpeter's critique of Keynes's biographical works illustrates the ways in which interpretative assertions in a biographical work are confirmed or falsified. In case (a) above, Schumpeter meant that whereas there are economists who contribute to economics through pamphlets on current issues or academic articles, Marshall was not one of them, and asked for an explanation of the full personality. In case (b), concerning the place of prominent figures in history, Schumpeter pointed out that an unbalanced evaluation is likely to result in rejection of the biography. Schumpeter's appraisal of Walras has been well received, but his low rating of Adam Smith, Ricardo, and Marshall has not. There is a wide margin of interpretation in this respect, so that iconoclasm in the case of great thinkers and the discovery of neglected thinkers are both possible. Case (c) is concerned with reading one's own viewpoint into an individual's work; Schumpeter's valuation of Walras and Marx is an example. This method is inevitably self-seeking, on the one hand, but represents a modern interpretation of the past and achieves Schumpeter's filiation of scientific ideas, on the other.

Cases (a), (b), and (c) may not exhaust all the criteria of evaluating a biographical work, but these cases demonstrate that each of the three elements constituting biographical studies (vision, science, and art) has a part to play with a high degree of freedom. In this area Schumpeter could work in a lively fashion without constraints.

Types of habitus

If Keynes's essay on Marshall (Keynes 1924) is an obituary for a teacher on whom the pupil's "love and labour have been lavished" (1933b, 653), then Schumpeter's article on Böhm-Bawerk (1914b) is the most elaborate of his biographical essays in its praise of a teacher's immortal achievements. The former is a monumental work of sixty-two pages in the *Economic Journal*, and the latter is one of seventy-five pages in *Zeitschrift für Volkswirtschaft, Sozialpolitik und Verwaltung*. The two differ in their style of description. Whereas Keynes developed the thought of Marshall through biographical description, Schumpeter discussed the theory of Böhm-Bawerk exclusively and drew his portrait in abstract terms. Schumpeter's other essays have this same level of abstraction. In this sense, he based his biographical studies on the conceptualization and standardization of the subject's *habitus*.

With regard to the attributes required for the study of economics, Keynes's essay on Marshall includes this well-known passage:

He [the economist] must reach a high standard in several different directions and must combine talents not often found together. He must be mathematician, historian, statesman, philosopher – in some degree. He must understand symbols and speak in words. He must contemplate the particular in terms of the general, and touch abstract and concrete in the same flight of thought. He must study the present in the light of the past for the purposes of the future. No part of man's nature or his institutions must lie entirely outside his regard. He must be purposeful and disinterested in a simultaneous mood; as aloof and incorruptible as an artist, yet sometimes as near the earth as a politician. (Keynes [1924] 1972, 173–74)

Among the diverse talents in this list, Schumpeter thought most highly of historical awareness (1954a, 12–13). He remarked that Ricardo had no sense of history; he was only fit for theoretical study. By a historical sense Schumpeter meant von Thünen's fact-minded approach to work from the unformed clay of objective materials. According to Schumpeter, Ricardo was not a genuine theorist; his fame was due to the ingenious combination of theory with the brilliant advocacy of policies. Schumpeter regarded politician-like talent and propensities harmful to economics if they entailed a policy-oriented approach. He despised this approach and in this respect found a similarity between Ricardo and Keynes. He rated Ricardo highly for using the concept of a theoretical model or an analytic engine as a tool, but criticized him for lacking the comprehensive vision of the universal interdependence of all elements of the economic system and for producing a defective analytic engine, distorted by virtue of policy orientation, and concluded that Ricardian analysis was a detour (1954a, 474).

On the contrary, it was leadership, Schumpeter admitted, that was Ricardo's most important contribution. Leadership is not only the result of a blend of various talents; it is also based on a set of the *habitus* that can be shared in a scientific field. This fact demonstrates the importance of strategy in attaining a position of leadership in a scientific field. A strategy is the art of directing others through appeal. Schumpeter would compare primitive economic models with toys; in this case, he said: "Very quickly his [Ricardo's] circle developed the attitude – so amusing but also, alas!, so melancholy to behold – of children who have been presented with a new toy" (1954a, 473–74). In the case of Ricardo, too, Schumpeter maintained, there was a gap between leadership and scientific progress, between performance seen from the perspective of the sociology of science and performance from the standpoint of analytic technique.

It is illuminating to compare the *habitus* of Smith, Mill, and Marshall, who served to define Schumpeter's classical situations by the overwhelming success of their books. "He [Smith] was conscientious, painstaking to a degree, methodical, well-poised, honorable" (1954a, 182). The cause of Adam Smith's success, Schumpeter argued, was that despite, or, rather because of, his lack of originality, Smith was endowed with the innate ability to coordinate and synthesize various lines of thought and thus devoted twenty-five years to producing the *Wealth of Nations*. "He [Smith] was effective not only by virtue of what he gave but also by virtue of what he failed to give" (1954a, 185). Brilliance, difficult and ingenious methods, recondite truth, and prodigy – these Smith could not give.

John Stuart Mill aimed at a modern version of the *Wealth of Nations*, but invested too little time (a few years) to the writing of his *Principles*, because he was confident that most of the necessary thinking had already been done. Schumpeter believed that this attitude led to sterility and superficiality. Moreover, the severe intellectual training by Mill's father from early childhood made Mill immature and devoid of vitality: "Jevons reads fresh and stimulating even where he utters a platitude; Mill never reads fresh and stimulating even where he speaks valuable wisdom. That was the fault of his early training" (1954a, 452). And, "To a greater part it is due to Mill's judicial habit of mind that forced him to consider all aspects of each question" (1954a, 531). Although Mill did not have Smith's diligence, by virtue of an exceptionally wide range of interests he could synthesize a variety of thought and write on both economics and methodology. But Mill's investigations were never in depth.

Schumpeter found a similarity in the achievements and historical place of Smith and Marshall: "Both the *Wealth* and the *Principles* are what they are, partly at least, because they are the result of the work of decades and fully matured, the products of minds that took infinite care, were patient of labor, and indifferent to the lapse of years" (1954a, 835). But "Marshall's powerful engine of analysis – though it may look antiquated by now – was the result of a creative effort and not of a synthetic one" (1954a, 837). What was the source of Marshall's creativity? "Reader will discover a quality that comes near to constituting Marshall's chief claim to immortality: in Marshall he beholds not only a high-powered technician, a profoundly learned historian, a sure-footed framer of explanatory hypotheses, but above all a great economist" (1954a, 835–36). Schumpeter meant to say that Marshall understood the nature of business and the inner workings of capitalism; in short, he had a historical sense. Marshall, therefore, is in striking contrast to Mill, who "never knew what life really is" (1954a, 528).

It is more difficult to explain original talent than synthetic talent. Schumpeter called the achievement of Walras, his greatest admirer, the unity of revolutionary creativeness and classic synthesis. William Jaffé, through his studies of Walras's correspondence, later found the source of the general equilibrium theory in Louis Poinsot's *Eléments de Statique*, Achille Isnard's *Traité de richesse*, and personal consultation with Paul Piccard, a professor of mechanics at Lausanne, and Hermann Amstein, a professor of mathematics at Lausanne (Jaffé 1983). Although Schumpeter had regarded Isnard as a precursor of Walras (1954a, 217), he did not know of these other connections, writing that: "He [Walras] did it without help and without collaborators, until he himself had created them – without any encouragement other than that which he found within himself" (1951a, 79). But, even if Schumpeter had been aware of these sources of Walras's theory, his view would still have been that it is the work of originality to apply existing thought in unforeseen directions.

Portraits in miniature

Throughout the *History of Economic Analysis* Schumpeter gives unique descriptions of many authors and their work in the footnotes. No note exceeds thirty lines of fine print. Although the editor of the *History* refers to the notes as "biographical sketches," it would seem more appropriate to call them "vignettes." These are wonderful pieces that combine concision, artistry, and judgment – qualities that are usually not allowed in a biographical dictionary. Schumpeter took advantage of them to give full play to his ingenuity. He condensed much of the biographical information into these vignettes, which give portraits not by mere abstract expression but by concrete stories. They still serve as guides for bibliographies. For example:

Victor Riquetti, Marquis de Mirabeau (1715–89), called the elder to distinguish him from his son, the Mirabeau of the Revolution, was an eccentric aristocrat of exuberant vitality and irrepressible impulses. It is difficult to understand – except on the hypothesis that force of temperament and glowing phrases will always carry everything before them – how it was that this man, whose unquestioned ability was completely spoiled by lack of judgment, could have enjoyed, though only for a few years, an international and national fame much greater than that of any other economist before or after, not excluding A. Smith or K. Marx. This happened in the first part of his career, that is, before he had joined the physiocrats, and on the strength of a performance that cannot be called impressive in anything except passionate phraseology. This performance, anonymously published in three parts under the title *L'Ami des hommes, ou traité de la population* (1756), will have to be mentioned again in our chapter on population. Of all the other works of Mirabeau – he left dozens of volumes besides a quantity of unpublished material – only the subsequent parts (4–6) of *L'Ami* (1758 and 1760), the *Philosophie rurale* (1763), and the *Théorie de l'impôt* (1760) call for notice in this book. The last two are, however, physiocratic, at least in principle, and therefore need not detain us here. (1954a, 175)

In a footnote concerning the Age of French Enlightenment, whose intellectual orientation and social background had been widely described in the literature, Schumpeter, referring to a brief essay by Lytton Strachey, a Bloomsbury writer, on Abbé André Morellet, wrote: "half an hour invested in reading it plus another half-hour of pondering over it will do more for the reader than would many hours spent on heavier works" (1954a, 123). Strachey's piece is contained in his *Portraits in Miniature and Other Essays* (Strachey 1931).

The so-called Victorianism that had dominated nineteenth-century biographical writing in Britain, demanded biographies that praised heroes and provided spiritual nourishment for the morality of people. Strachey was renowned as an iconoclast in the area of biography, and it is instructive to read his requirements for that genre. In the preface to his *Eminent Victorians*, Strachey stated:

To preserve, for instance, a becoming brevity – a brevity which excludes everything that is redundant and nothing that is significant – that, surely, is the first duty of the biographer. The second, no less surely, is to maintain his own freedom of spirit. It is not his business to be complimentary; it is his business to lay bare the facts of the case, as he understands them. (Strachey [1918] 1948, 10)

Strachey's volume of *Portraits* is really a collection of fine vignettes that satisfy the requirement of concision to an extreme degree; no essay exceeds five pages. I do not mean to imply that Schumpeter had learned the style of vignette writing from Strachey, but that because he particularly admired Strachey's short essays on biography, he must have been fully aware of their merits.[10]

The footnotes in *History* achieved an ideal type of biography in the sense of economy of thought. They reveal Schumpeter's particularly clear judgment and unique expertise for evaluation in a very short passage. The important figures in *History* are dealt with in the text, not in footnotes. According to my accounting, *History* contains about three hundred portraits in miniature. They are not necessarily inferior because they are footnoted. Schumpeter depicted a much wider stage than economics; the briefly described persons were outstanding in their own fields but here do no more than support more prominent figures. Thus *History* provides the grand drama of a comprehensive intellectual history from the perspective of economics.

CHAPTER 11

Value judgments and political economy

The economics of Gustav von Schmoller, the leader of the German Historical School, utilized a historical and ethical approach (Schumpeter 1954a, 812). In the essay "Gustav v. Schmoller und die Probleme von heute" (1926b), Schumpeter interpreted Schmoller's historical approach as the prototype of economic sociology which attempted to integrate theory and history (see page 200). In fact, Schumpeter discovered, at the same time, another important point in Schmoller's ethical approach to economics. Little attention has been given to this aspect of Schumpeter's essay, which seems to shed new light on his ideas, especially his thinking on norms.

This chapter, starting from Schumpeter's thought on value judgments expressed in his Schmoller essay, presents a profile of his *Weltanschauung*, social philosophy, and political economy. The conventional view of Schumpeter seems to be too focused on his scientism to pay attention to his general outlook on life and the world, following faithfully his apparent emphasis on science rather than policy, on facts rather than values, and on functions rather than ideals. However, he grappled with such broad problems of mind and society that he naturally did not dispense with ideas on the *Weltanschauung*, policy, values, and ideals.

The essential trend of history

Schmoller's ethical approach

Before we consider Schumpeter's argument, let us consider the characteristics of Schmoller's ethical approach. After history, the next leading idea in Schmoller's economics was ethics. He believed that the historical evolution of institutions should be the theme of economics and he focused on ethical norms, including customs, laws, and morals, as the social determinants of institutions. Ethics gave meaning and direction to historical research in Schmoller's economics. It is a mistake to reject his ethical approach because of the stereotyped notion of a value-free science. His approach had three significant features (Shionoya 1995).

First, by morals Schmoller did not mean his own subjective moral judgments but objective moral convictions in the sense of historical facts. It is true that ethical and political ideals simply based on metaphysical and nonempirical grounds cannot be supported scientifically. In contrast, for Schmoller ethical values were empirical materials in the historical research of institutional change because these values are more or less embodied in institutions. His ethical approach, it should be stressed, was not an attempt to mix values with facts, as some claimed, but to deal with factual values. He argued: "As ethics becomes more and more empirical so that it describes ethical duty, virtue, and good in the form of historical development rather than teaching norms, the elements of beliefs and their function in ethics naturally decline. Thus ethics resembles social science or state science or what we call today sociology" (Schmoller 1911, 438).

Second, in dealing with factual value judgments, Schmoller opposed the partial values advocated by political parties and social classes; he wanted to discuss universally valid values that were concerned with the total interests of society and shared by all of its members. He believed in the trend toward the empirical unification of ethical systems: "One might dispute many individual points, the derivation of ethical truth, and the scientific construction of an ethical system, but on the most important, practical value judgments, good and cultivated people of the same nation in the same cultural age tend to agree more and more. When one seeks ethical value judgments that have meaning for an economy, a society, and the state order, these are the real questions above all" (Schmoller 1911, 494–95).

Third, Schmoller asserted that the ethical approach not only aims at the recognition of moral facts but is also framed in a teleological form. Teleology is contrasted with causality. In explaining a phenomenon, teleology focuses on the relationship between end and means, not between cause and effects. Teleology appeals to goals that account for human actions and social systems. If a society, a group of individuals, can be regarded as a unified entity with its own objectives – in other words, if holism can be assumed – teleological inquiry is possible. Because moral values are to govern a society as a whole, teleology is effective in the study of institutional organizations that embody ethics. For Schmoller, the major component of teleology was the principle of justice. He argued: "The economic organization of a nation is not a natural product as was thought for a long time, but mainly a product of current ethical views about what is right and just in relation to different social classes. So far all progress in economic organization has been a triumph of ethical ideas and will continue to be so in the future" (Schmoller [1874] 1890, 55–56).

That ethics plays a system-constructing role in Schmoller's research program can be best understood in terms of the methodological importance of teleology in his thought. He regarded teleology as a heuristic device that supplements an empirical science when empirical knowledge is insufficient; it assumes that individuals behave as if they would purposefully serve the ends of the whole. Thus, "Teleological investigation is the most important method because it grasps the totality of phenomena, whose inner causal relations are not yet known, as if the whole has a meaning. It is similar to a systematic investigation insofar as the latter approach systematizes and grasps the total of phenomena or truth consistently" (Schmoller 1911, 437). This clearly indicates the methodological purpose of Schmoller's teleology, which has nothing to do with the justification of a specific ideology. That purpose is to provide a preliminary vision or *Weltanschauung* in order to draw a systematic picture of the world. Schmoller's teleology is an example of methodological holism. When one deals with the outcomes of individual behavior within a given social framework, as is the case with neoclassical economics, it is appropriate to assume methodological individualism. But there is much room for the use of methodological holism to explain individual behavior and its consequences under a changing institutional framework.

Schmoller's values as the guiding ideas in historical research relate not to subjective but objective values, not to partisan but universal values. These objective and universal values, viewed statically, are more or less embodied in institutions and form the basis of agreement among people; viewed dynamically, the interactions, conflicting or accommodating, between these values and social institutions bring about the evolutionary process of a society. In a teleological view, the telos of systems and institutions is generally considered to be self-survival and accounts for the mechanism of their establishment and transformation in terms of the goal-directed behavior of the systems. The teleological explanation of an evolutionary process is based on a future goal as an always desired but not yet attained objective; it cannot predict a future course. Teleology only understands a process as we track it down.

Science and policy objectives

Schumpeter's essay on Schmoller is divided into three parts – "value-freedom and the setting of objectives," "history and social science," and "detailed study and theory" – and discusses problems of values prior to those of history. Schumpeter asked what value judgments and the setting of objectives meant in Schmoller's ethical economics and how Schmoller could make value judgments and choose objectives.

Of course, Schumpeter admitted that science is concerned with *Sein* and not *Sollen*, but he contended that the difficulties of value judgments do not involve the impossibility of the scientific justification of values. Rather, the real difficulties lie in two areas:

First, in our field, the actions of and reactions to all behaviors of a nation, a group, or an individual differ, depending on the time span and the outlook of the observers, and are so complicated after all, that unequivocal answers to practical questions become impossible. Second, value judgments and objectives are in fact so sharply divided, particularly in view of class interests, that there is in sight no common ground of a total society or for the general welfare; this is so even when each individual and group only want to behave for the general good, because each views the general welfare and social ideal differently. (1926b, 340–41)

This means that if the reality could be seen from the same viewpoint, and if the objectives could be set according to the same viewpoint, then value judgments could avoid division.

Schumpeter illustrated the case of medicine. Nobody can prove the desirability of health, and it is difficult to define precisely what health is. But everyone is equally eager for health.[1] In economics, by contrast, the two points above are crucial. The first concerns the plurality of the viewpoint from which to see the reality; this in itself is not a value judgment, but involves differences between short-term and long-term viewpoints, between economic and social viewpoints, and so forth. This is likely to be entangled with the second point, the differences in valuation, so that agreement in objectives is much more difficult to reach. Nevertheless, Schmoller's viewpoint was distinct in that he put forward policy without advocating a particular partisan position, without defending the existing social order, and without indicating his own preference. Schumpeter noted that "Schmoller spoke from the standpoint of the nation, or what was the same thing for him, from the standpoint of the whole, the social totality" (1926b, 343). How was that possible? This was Schumpeter's question.

Schumpeter paid attention to the fact that when different political parties, with different ideals and programs, take office, they tend not to frame extremist policies. In the world of practical politics, real situations force governments to adopt more or less similar measures that do not necessarily correspond with the subjective intentions of political parties. What should be done in particular circumstances is inevitably fixed and cannot be changed. Ultimate ideals are not essential to current policy issues. If this point is forgotten, there is a danger of failure. Disasters are generally to be avoided, desirable things are to be done, and what was started is to be continued. He also took notice of the coexistence of interests made possible by practical policies, while the conflict between classes was often emphasized. In other words, the conflict is not qualitative but quantitative, and the conflict in principle usually occurs when man and society are too primitive to foresee the future.

Schumpeter understood the diminishing conflicts of interest in the context of the trend of rationalization in capitalism: "Rationalization, equalization, mechanization, and democratization, all of which constitute an aspect of the nature of capitalist civilization, facilitate the unity of aspirations all the more. In the rationalized world of capitalism, political parties lose their sacred banners" (1926b, 350). By the development of science and realistic politics, conflicts based on ideological illusion will be reduced. Just as rationalism expels ideology from science, it excludes ideology from society. "The time will soon come, when social preferences are unified so that in every given situation the choice of goals is made possible by means of science" (1926b, 351). I would call this the "essential trend of history." According to Schumpeter, Schmoller thought that, based on the essential trend of history, the unity of policy objectives will be realized.

Schumpeter's argument on the diminishing conflicts of interest and the unity of objective setting may seem rather optimistic. If so, he may appear to defend Schmoller's ethical approach. But this argument must be carefully interpreted methodologically.

Schumpeter observed that Schmoller's historical research on institutions and policy emphasized historical relativity, on the one hand, and the inevitability of social situations, on the other; in other words, there was a mixture of determinism and nondeterminism of history in Schmoller's writing. This was a result of Schmoller's unique approach. Schumpeter was right in methodologically evaluating Schmoller's view of the state as the subject of unified aspirations. Although Schumpeter emphasized the underlying trend toward the unification of policy objectives, he regarded, as an interpretation of Schmoller, the state as a hypothetical instrument to set and realize policy objectives; the aspirations of the state or general aspirations were used only in this sense. This is exactly what I mean by a teleological framework. Unified preferences of the state should be regarded as an instrument to explain the evolution of institutions by methodological holism.

For Schumpeter, the essential trend of history pointed toward the socialization of capitalism. But he did not believe it was a desirable ideal. His thesis on the tendency toward socialism should be viewed in light of the above first difficulty in value judgments, that is, plural viewpoints in the perception of reality. The thesis indicates what the trend of capitalism would be when one considers the longest time span and the broadest perspective. "One can take the view, for example, that the present society will sooner or later adopt the socialist form of life, but he does not necessarily desire it just as a doctor who foresees the early death of a patient does not necessarily desire it" (1926b, 346). Based on the perception of the essential trend of history, it is the task of the political economy to evaluate the trend and advocate what is to be done. Because Schumpeter did not want to influence people regarding the political economy, he did not discuss it in detail. But he was of the opinion that the private enterprise system should be maintained.

Capitalism as civilization

Within the framework of what I call the two-structure approach to a universal social science, Schumpeter was most interested in the human mind as well as the economy. That area covers thought, science, art, and civilization, which are basically shaped by invisible elements inherent in a society such as mental attitudes, value schemes, and ways of thinking. This section examines his view of capitalist civilization in order to reveal his values and *Weltanschauung*. In his essay on Schmoller, he said: "Everyone keeps the ultimate yardstick of his wishes to himself. Science cannot tell him what he should wish, what he should value highly, what he should hate" (1926b, 340). Schumpeter never explicitly disclosed his ideals for society. He once said of Marx: "Also, he never taught any ideals as set by himself. Such vanity was quite foreign to him. As every true prophet styles himself the humble mouth-piece of his deity, so Marx pretended no more than to speak the logic of the dialectic process of history. There is dignity in all this which compensates for many pettinesses and vulgarities with which, in his work and in his life, this dignity formed so strange an alliance" (1950a, 7). Unlike Marx, the trend of history Schumpeter grasped was not his ideal. Can one discover his ideals under his veil of dignity?

Rationalism and heroism in capitalism

Schumpeter characterized civilization and the spirit of capitalism (which is the cultural complement of its economy) basically as rationalism. The rational attitude stemmed from the economic necessity of human beings and was not peculiar to capitalism but it was promoted by capitalism and spread to all areas of the society. The definiteness and quantitativeness of money was the driving force behind the rationalization of the human mind. Capitalism not only shaped the rational mental attitude, but also provided a social field for rational men and their activities. In addition to politics, the military, and ideological areas (religion and science), the economy attracted many people with avarice and ambition. Schumpeter observed: "Not only the modern mechanized plant and the volume of the output that pours forth from it, not only modern technology and economic organization, but all the features and achievements of modern civilization are, directly or indirectly, the products of the capitalist process" (1950a, 125). The most comprehensive view of a society ever produced by the rationalism of capitalism was utilitarianism, which he described as the grand principle of action, in both the private and public spheres, integrating rationalism, hedonism, and individualism (1950a, 248).

It can be argued that the value of capitalism is expressed by what is produced from the system, but also by what is discarded and expelled by it. According to Schumpeter:

> The capitalist process rationalizes behavior and ideas and by so doing chases from our minds, along with metaphysical belief, mystic and romantic ideas of all sorts ... Also, capitalist civilization is rationalistic "and anti-heroic." The two go together of course. Success in industry and commerce requires a lot of stamina, yet industrial and commercial activity is essentially unheroic in the knight's sense – no flourishing of swords about it, not much physical prowess, no chance to gallop the armored horse into the enemy, preferably a heretic or heathen – and the ideology that glorifies the idea of fighting for fighting's sake and of victory for victory's sake understandably withers in the office among all the columns of figures. (1950a, 127–28)

What is sacrificed by capitalist rationality is heroism. But heroism was nothing more than the social value that capitalism demanded of innovations. The gap between the social value demanded by capitalism and the *Zeitgeist* produced by capitalism was the central theme of *Capitalism, Socialism and Democracy* (see pages 227–28); in substantive terms, the gap is now represented as a divide between heroism and rationalism.

Schumpeter's image of entrepreneurs overlapped with the image of the romantic, heroic knights of the medieval times. The dream and the will to found a private kingdom and a dynasty, the will to conquer for conquering's sake, and the joy of creation, which he enumerated as the entrepreneurial motives, were characterized as anti-hedonistic and heroic. However, the bourgeois class, which successful entrepreneurs joined, has lost the qualities of adventure, romance, and mystery in the midst of rationalist civilization. In Schumpeter's view of the multi-peaked social pyramid, these qualities were possessed in the capitalist age by the descendants of the medieval princes, lords, and knights, who ruled the area of politics as the protecting strata of the bourgeois class. Schumpeter's comparison between the medieval princes and the modern industrialists sharply indicates his own preference. The lords and knights have become rulers by means of their mystic glamour and prestige; the upstart industrialists do not have such character but they have money. By the symbiosis of both classes the order of the capitalist system was maintained. It can be argued that Schumpeter's autocratic tastes and hatred of utilitarianism were connected with his understanding of the core of capitalist civilization.

Schumpeter's conception of entrepreneurship was based on the function of family fortunes in business life. For him, the decay of family relations and the evaporation of substance in the idea of property under rationalist civilization meant the deterioration of the image of entrepreneurs. Instead, a different kind of *homo oeconomicus* had emerged in the rationalist world, and "he loses the only sort of romance and heroism that is left in the unromantic and unheroic civilization of capitalism – the heroism of *navigare necesse est, vivere no necesse est* (seafaring is necessary, living is not necessary)" (1950a, 160).

Schumpeter said that value judgments about capitalist performance are of little interest because man is not free to choose under the essential trend of history (1950a, 129). But his preference was undoubtedly for the aristocratic and knightly elements rather than the bourgeois elements in capitalism. Capitalism with a vigorous civilization was, for him, not simply the world of technological innovation; it also must be the world of entrepreneurship. It was not simply the world of entrepreneurship; it also must be the world of heroism. When capitalism ceases to be so, he declared, the essence of capitalism has been lost.

Anti-utilitarianism

Schumpeter's extreme hatred and contempt of utilitarianism represented the crucial point of his thought and the reverse side of his view emphasizing the role of leadership in a society. In the *History of Economic Analysis,* he called utilitarianism a comprehensive system of social science with broad fields of application and analyzed its threefold functions (1954a, 132–34). First, he said, it is a philosophy of life exhibiting a scheme of ultimate values; second, it is a normative system regulating laws and morals; third, it is a comprehensive system of social science embodying a uniform method of analysis.

Based on the instrumentalist methodology, Schumpeter could separate utilitarianism as an analytic tool from utilitarianism as a philosophy of life and a normative theory and admit that it is logical and possible to accept utilitarianism as an analytic tool. He distinguished four areas in economics and examined the applicability of the utilitarian hypothesis in each area. (1) Positive economics may apply the assumption of utility maximization in the accounting of economic equilibrium; the assumption was not harmful, Schumpeter thought, but unnecessary (see pages 117 and 135). (2) In welfare economics, he argued, the notion of a common good or general welfare as the sum of individual utility does not hold universally. One aspect of Schumpeter's criticism of the classical theory of democracy was to reject the view that the general welfare can be conceived unequivocally on the basis of utilitarianism. (3) In economic history, he asserted strongly, it is completely useless to view social phenomena as evolving historically by the utilitarian motive of human beings. (4) In the psychological analysis of motivations, the utilitarian view is worse than valueless. Though all of these points relate to the usefulness of the utilitarian hypothesis as an analytic tool, Schumpeter's appraisal of areas (2), (3), and (4) suggests that the use of the utilitarian hypothesis in any substantive sense is not desirable.

How then could Schumpeter criticize utilitarianism as a philosophy of life and a normative theory, represented in the principle of "a calculus of pleasure and pain" or "the greatest happiness of the greatest number"? He called utilitarianism the shallowest of all conceivable philosophies of life. His primary objection was that "the utilitarians reduced the whole world of human values to the same schema, ruling out, as contrary to reason, all that really matters to man" (1954a, 133). What he had in mind here was the distinction between static man and dynamic man, which occupied the center of his observation of a society (see pages 38 and 169):

From the viewpoint of observers, the fundamental meaning of economic activity, i.e., the meaning that explains why economic activity exists at all, manifests itself in a circular flow. In this sense, the acquisition of goods as the essence of the economic motive is naturally the acquisition of goods for the satisfaction of wants ... But, the motive of our type [the entrepreneur] is essentially different ... His economic motive, the effort to acquire goods, is not anchored in a feeling of pleasure, which is caused by the consumption of acquired goods. If the satisfaction of wants in this sense is the criterion for economic activity, then the behavior of our type is generally irrational or of a different kind of rationalism. (1926a, 133–34)

According to Schumpeter, entrepreneurs and leaders in general are dynamic men characterized as energetic and nonhedonistic, whereas the average man only adapts his behavior according to given social habits and conventions. The criterion of want satisfaction can be applied to the average man, but the behavior of leaders changes the framework of social life and cannot be evaluated by the existing criteria. The value of their behavior lies in their superhuman and creative actions as such and does not depend on the consequences. Of course, the consequences will always appear, and if creative destruction succeeds, they transcend evaluation by the existing standards. As the history of a society includes major changes in the framework of thought and institutions, Schumpeter believed, it is erroneous to apply the utilitarian principle to a design of institutions and an interpretation of history. His image of leaders was that of a hero or superman; the summation of wants of common men would neither explain the history that included the emergence of leaders and heroes nor provide the norm for a desirable form of society and institutions. His idea of innovation, in whatever areas of social life, described a deviation from the traditional situation or state of equilibrium that is explained in terms of utility; it is properly viewed as an anti-utilitarian social philosophy and probably belongs to the kind of approach that emphasizes excellence and virtues.

Although Schumpeter admitted that utilitarianism had grown up in the capitalist world, he suggested, interestingly, that it was not a philosophy of the capitalists and bourgeoisie by origin or social tendency but showed an unmistakable kinship to socialism in its way of thinking ([1918–19] 1951b, 92). What he meant was that the normative utilitarian principle defined the sum total of the wants of the masses as the criterion of social values; this is exactly what Friedrich von Hayek meant when he identified utilitarianism as constructivist rationalism (Hayek 1976, 17–23). Whereas Hayek rejected utilitarianism because of its constructivism, Schumpeter despised it because of its vulgarism.

Socialism as a practice

The unusual relationship, if any, between Schumpeter and socialism is characterized less by any positive or negative ideological commitment to socialist thought than by his practical engagement in socialist politics. He did not accept Marxism in theory but had high praise for Marx's vision of capitalist development. For Schumpeter, however, socialism was not only notional but, though temporarily, a problem of political practice in his role as "consultant administrator." When asked why he, an anti-socialist, accepted a post in the German and Austrian socialist governments after World War I, he replied, "If somebody wants to commit suicide, it is a good thing if a doctor is present" (Haberler 1951a, 31).

Austro-Marxism

Schumpeter's membership of the German Socialization Commission in 1918, established by the coalition government of the Social Democratic Party and the Independent Social Democratic Party, and his position as finance minister in the Austrian coalition government in 1919, established by the Social Democratic Party and the Christian Social Party, were both a result of his friendship with Austro-Marxists at the University of Vienna.

At the end of the nineteenth century, Austria – along with Germany – was a center of the European socialist movement. Under the influence of Professor Carl Grünberg, who has been called the father of Austro-Marxism, the Free Union of Socialist Students and Academicians was formed in 1895; almost all of the prominent members were his students: Max Adler, Friedrich Adler, Otto Bauer, Gustav Eckstein, Rudolf Hilferding, and Karl Renner. The union was more like a scientific seminar than a social club and became the underpinning of Austro-Marxism. These Austro-Marxists actually formed a school and exerted a noticeable influence both politically and scientifically in the first twenty years of the twentieth century. They belonged to the Social

Democratic Party and occupied the middle point between Bernstein's revisionism and Bolshevism.

These people were senior to Schumpeter, but when Böhm-Bawerk returned to the University of Vienna in 1904 and later held a seminar, Schumpeter, as a student, could join this seminar along with Bauer, Hilferding, and others. He thus studied Marxist theory under the Austro-Marxists.

After World War I, socialist governments were established in Germany and Austria under a republican regime. Both countries experienced violent struggle, including bloodshed, among socialists over the choice between a democratic republic and a proletarian republic. Also in both countries the Social Democratic Party, unlike the extreme leftists, contemplated a moderate type of socialism. Because there was little knowledge about the operation of socialism, the activities of the Austro-Marxists had important meaning, exhibiting the relationship between the theory and practice of socialism. Among others, Bauer published many books and took an active part as the leader of the party, a member of parliament, foreign minister, and chairman of the Socialization Commission. In a miniature portrait in the *History of Economic Analysis*, Schumpeter wrote: "Otto Bauer (1881–1938), a man of quite exceptional ability and not less exceptionally high character, was to some extent in the same predicament even before he rose to the position of leadership" (1954a, 881). These words are worthy of attention in light of the conflict that occurred between them.

Schumpeter and Bauer

In March 1919 Schumpeter became finance minister of Austria. His political life *per se* is not my concern here.[2] Rather, it is his position regarding the relationship between the theory and practice of socialism, as seen in the differing views of Schumpeter and Bauer on the program of socialization.

Bauer supported socialization at a slow pace, that is, he advocated a piecemeal approach to socialism, starting with concentrated industries such as mining and steel and gradually reaching the whole economy. Socialized firms, he asserted, should be managed not by government but by tripartite organizations of producers, consumers, and government. As for the political regime, a parliamentary democracy, not a Bolshevik dictatorship, should be established.[3]

As a member of the cabinet Schumpeter had to agree in principle with Bauer's program but did not think that the postwar era was an appropriate time to begin socialization in Germany and Austria. He noted in his 1920–21 essay that the development and maturity of capitalism would make the transition to socialism possible (see pages 239–40). Then the problem was the political aspect of his argument. As finance minister he faced two major challenges: recovery of the impoverished Austrian economy and redemption of war bonds. Economic recovery required the use of capitalist vigor, and for that purpose, the acquisition of foreign currency, especially the introduction of foreign capital, which was necessary to import foreign materials, including foods. Under this circumstance, socialization of the economy should not be attempted except on a limited basis. For the redemption of the war bonds, he thought, the government should impose a capital levy instead of reducing the real value of bonds through inflation or declaring a termination of the redemption. The capital levy would suppress inflation and bring about sound government finance. Schumpeter believed that the annexation of Austria to Germany would be unfavorable to the recovery and development of the Austrian economy.

Bauer had a different view on these matters. He claimed that in order to promote socialization, the revenue from a capital levy should be used to compensate socialized firms, because socialization was the way to economic recovery. The idea of redeeming war bonds through a capital levy was not Schumpeter's; according to März, it was proposed from both the right and the left wings during the war years (März 1983, 135–36). From the right, two finance ministers before Schumpeter had advocated the imposition of a tax on property, and from the left, Goldscheid had urged it as the means to socialization. Thus, although both Schumpeter and Bauer seriously considered the previous policy proposals, they differed on the purpose of the policy.

Bauer was in favor of the annexation; on the occasion of the fall of the Austria-Hungary currency bloc, he approached Germany with the unified currency proposal. Schumpeter opposed it, claiming that Vienna should be the financial center of Central Europe. And finally, the Alpine Montan Company affair made the fissure between the two decisive. This company was the largest steel maker and the owner of the most important source of iron ore in Austria. With the proposal for socialization, the share price of the company declined sharply. The Vienna banking house of Richard Kola, who had been assigned to deal with foreign currency as an agent of the ministry of finance, bought a large number of the Kola shares at the request of Italians. The share price rose to high levels. Since it was impossible for the Austrians to buy back the shares from the victorious country, the planned socialization of the Alpine Company became deadlocked. The Social Democratic Party's newspaper claimed that Minister Schumpeter, although he had known about the deal, did nothing to stop it. The cabinet established an investigating committee to look into the affair. The fact that the findings of the investigation had totally exonerated Schumpeter was brought to light by the recent publication of the Cabinet Protokol (1992, 195–99). By this unfounded accusation he was politically assassinated; at a cabinet reshuffle in October 1919, he resigned.

Schumpeter served for only seven months as finance minister. While he was in office, the country was in disarray after the war, and until it concluded a peace treaty with the Allies, Austria was deprived of the freedom of a domestic policy. It was not until September 1919 that the treaty was signed. Schumpeter made the finance plan public barely one day before his resignation.

Science and politics

As his political activity shows, Schumpeter was not an ideological socialist. He strongly maintained that it was premature for objective conditions for socialism in Germany and Austria to exist. There the economic conditions and the spirit of the people were not in harmony, although the political circumstances supported the spiritual conditions of socialism. While he believed in the essential trend of history toward socialism, he was against a premature revolution from the standpoint of science. In this period he was attacked by socialists for being conservative and reactionary, but his opposition to socialism was not ideological. This perspective was unique to Schumpeter, and his attitude seems to make an important statement about policy. It represents a criticism of the view that politics is a value judgment after all.

Indeed, as far as ideology was concerned Schumpeter had a negative attitude toward socialism. But he did not assume that practical policies should be determined by ideology and tastes alone. Under given circumstances, he believed, the logic of a situation should derive a single understanding of the process that must be shared by everyone no matter who the policymaker was. This position on policy would require that scientific knowledge be explored from short-term as well as long-term perspectives, covering economic as well as noneconomic areas, so that the ideological aspects of politics would be minimized. For Schumpeter, a science of society should be universal and evolutionary in order to avoid differences in viewpoints and scope produced by different understandings and to construct and broaden the scientific base of remedies.

The possibility of a scientific remedy, in fact, could not be accepted so easily even in academic circles, but Schumpeter boldly adopted this view in the world of politics. As a result, he experienced failure and disillusionment in politics. At that, he seems to have devoted himself to scientific work and remained independent of policy and politics. But he still believed in the possibility of scientific solutions. He thought that the control of ideology is attained not simply by excluding ideology from science for the purpose of keeping a value-free science, but mainly by expanding the field of science itself for the purpose of acquiring an understanding of a social process that can be accepted by anyone regardless of his ideology. Thus, in 1939 he wrote: "What our time needs most and lacks most is the understanding of the process which people are passionately resolved to control. To supply this understanding is to implement that resolve and to rationalize it. This is the only service the scientific worker is, as such, qualified to render. As soon as it is rendered everyone can draw for himself the practical conclusions appropriate to his individual interests or ideals" (1939, 1, vi).

In the *History of Economic Analysis* Schumpeter analyzed the attitude of John Stuart Mill toward socialism in order to understand his *Weltanschauung* by means of a specific conceptual framework (1954a, 532–33). That framework can also be applied to Schumpeter. He divided the development of Mill's thought into three stages. First, from the beginning, Mill was emotionally drawn to socialism; socialism at that time was a so-called utopian socialism, and he accepted it as a beautiful dream. Second, though Mill regarded socialism as "an ultimate result of human progress" and recognized it explicitly as the ultimate goal, he opposed untimely socialism because of "the unprepared state of mankind in general, and of the labouring classes in particular."[4] Third, whereas he believed that capitalism was approaching the completion of its work and that socialism was coming soon, he was against the idea of transition by revolution. Schumpeter called it evolutionary socialism. What, then, was Schumpeter's thinking? First, unlike Mill, Schumpeter hated socialism. Second, like Mill, he recognized socialism as the ultimate goal but opposed the socialization policy because it was untimely. Third, also like Mill, Schumpeter leaned toward evolutionary socialism, which recognizes the coming of socialism as realistic.

The difference between Mill and Schumpeter was that Schumpeter was not sympathetic to socialism and in this sense was not a socialist. Nevertheless, both scholars regarded socialism as "an ultimate result of human progress" and agreed on "evolutionary socialism." In spite of their ideological differences, they demonstrated an insight into the essential trend of history and delivered a truth that was unpalatable to both socialists and anti-socialists.

An alternative of political economy

Schumpeter called the sum total of views about practical questions and the underlying scheme of values, political economy (1954a, 1141), as distinct from analytic or scientific economics. Because he regarded political economy as nonscientific and always emphasized the harmful influences caused by an interest in practical solutions, people paid little attention to political economy when it was proposed by Schumpeter himself.[5] His political economy was a large-scale attempt to prescribe an alternative to socialism (assuming a transition from capitalism to socialism). In *Capitalism, Socialism and Democracy*, he said that there was an alternative to sitting down and waiting for socialism to take over, room for political action. To avoid misunderstanding Schumpeter's thesis on the future of capitalism, we must pay attention to his political economy. He proposed corporatism.

The Montreal lecture

In a lecture at Montreal in November 1945, entitled "L'avenir de l'entreprise privée devant les tendances socialistes modernes," Schumpeter addressed the question of how the private enterprise system should be preserved in light of the tendency toward socialism. He argued:

Will the solution to this grave problem spring from authoritarian statism, which may doubtless assume more than one form but of which the perfect example is bolshevism? Not at all. Does it come from democratic socialism? Again, no. But where then is it necessary to look? It will be necessary to turn to corporate organization in the sense advocated by *Quadragesimo Anno*. It is not the economist's role to praise a moral message of the Pope. But he can draw out an economic doctrine from it. This doctrine does not call upon false theories. It does not rest on so-called tendencies that do not exist. It recognizes all the facts of the modern economy. And, while bringing a remedy to the present disorganization, it shows us the functions of private initiative in a new framework. The corporate principle organizes but it does not regiment. It is opposed to all social systems with a centralizing tendency and to all bureaucratic regimentation; it is, in fact, the only means of rendering the latter impossible. ([1946b] 1975, 297)

Quadragesimo Anno was the encyclical of Pope Pius XI "On Reconstructing the Social Order" (Pius XI 1931). Referring to the political advocacy of the Catholic Church in the early twentieth century in the *History of Economic Analysis*, Schumpeter wrote:

something that was new developed toward the end of the [nineteenth] century, namely, a definite scheme of social organization that, making use of the existing elements of groupwise co-operation, visualized a society – and a state – operating by means of self-governing vocational associations within a framework of ethical precepts. This is the "corporative" state adumbrated in the encyclical *Quadragesimo Anno* (1931). Since it is a normative program and not a piece of analysis, no more will be said about it in this book. (1954a, 765)

Also, in his address, "The March into Socialism," given before the American Economic Association in December 1949 nine days before his death, he stated that a reorganization of society on the lines of the encyclical *Quadragesimo Anno* was an alternative to socialism that would avoid the omnipotent state (1950a, 416).

Corporatism means economic management through cooperation among firms in each industry, or cooperation among industries, or cooperation between groups of workers and groups of capitalists. It aims at a middle position between capitalism and socialism, before the existing tendencies to destroy the atomistic market mechanism in capitalism work themselves out and finally arrive at centralized socialism. In corporatism, while individual freedom is maintained, cooperation among individuals is necessary from the point of view of a society as a whole. In a competitive market system, atomistic individuals are allowed to pursue their own interests, but in order to move to a system of cooperation among groups with some market power, Schumpeter thought, acceptance of the notion of social responsibility is required. Social responsibility, in turn, requires moral reform, because the formation of groups is not to be imposed by a state but by a social contract among those concerned. In this sense, corporatism in the Schumpeterian sense was different from the state-led system in a totalitarian Fascist society.

After World War II the incomes policy introduced in advanced countries was a sort of corporatism based on a social contract among industry, labor, and government. It was a program aimed at achieving price stability through consultation among groups with sizable market power in the determination of wages, profits, and prices. A triangular relationship involving politics, government, and industry in Japan is sometimes called corporatism without labor. Generally, to distinguish between the corporatism before and after World War II, the word "neocorporatism" is used for the postwar period.[6]

Schumpeter's call for moral reform meant that in order to maintain the corporatist social system, a spiritual superstructure consistent with it was indispensable. The thesis of the decline of capitalism and the argument in favor of corporatism were combined in Schumpeter as follows. One of the reasons for the decay of the capitalist system was the change in the inner value scheme of individuals and the loss of the values of family life under the trend of growing individualism and rationalism. Because the innovative activity of entrepreneurs is not motivated by short-term self-interest, but by the incentive to raise the family's social status, the fall of the bourgeois value scheme is crucial to a capitalist system itself:

it is very easy to indicate the two general causes which tend to produce social decomposition: it is the lack of faith among the governing class and the lack of what one calls "leadership." Families, workshops, societies do not function if nobody accepts his duties, if no one knows how to make himself accepted as leader and if each applies himself to constantly drawing up a balance-sheet of his personal and immediate benefits and costs at any given time. ([1946b] 1975, 296)

Against these tendencies, Schumpeter asserted the need for change in the value scheme.

The doctrine of the papal encyclical

In 1891 Pope Leo XIII distributed the encyclical letter *Rerum Novarum* on "Capital and Labor" and made public the normative view of the Catholic

Church on the social problems of his day. This initiated a social lecture by the church. Forty years later, in 1931, Pope Pius XI published the encyclical letter *Quadragesimo Anno*. Whereas the former was concerned with the problems of workers, the latter addressed all the problems of the social order. When Schumpeter talked about corporatism as his own political economy, he always had in mind *Quadragesimo Anno,* but his reference was too brief to indicate what he actually meant. Therefore it is important to examine the content of the encyclical to establish his idea. Its tenets can be summarized as follows.

First, the abolition of private ownership does not result in the advantage of the working class, as is claimed by socialists. The right of property must be defended by all means on the clear understanding of the twofold character of ownership: individual and social. Unless the harmony of the individual and the social character of ownership is attained, there is an inevitable danger of collectivism and individualism. Second, capital and labor must cooperate with each other, because neither capital can do without labor nor labor without capital. The huge disparity between the few exceedingly rich and the countless propertyless poor is the source of the gravest evils today, and a fair distribution must be made. Third, the work contract must be modified by a partnership contract, taking into account the conditions of the overall economy. Entrepreneur (mind), capitalist (capital), and worker (work) all must combine and form, as it were, a single whole. Fourth, for the reconstruction of the social order two things are particularly necessary: the reform of institutions and the correction of morals. Specifically, "the principle of subsidiary function" and "corporatism" were proposed, and these were most relevant to Schumpeter's view.

The principle of subsidiary function prescribes how the state should aid individuals and associations in drawing a proper distinction between the public and the private spheres. The appropriate role of government is to help individuals help themselves so they can develop according to their own ideas and abilities. The state should not take from individuals and small organizations what they can accomplish by their own initiative and industry.

Corporatism advocates the establishment of industrial and professional associations that would facilitate cooperation between individuals and the state, in place of the warring labor and capitalist classes. Most important, the purpose of these organizations would be to promote cooperation in the pursuit of the common good of the country, not particular interests. This would require moral reform.

If the two leading ideas on institutional reform – the principle of subsidiary function and corporatism – are combined, there is no doubt that the papal doctrine rejected statist control and implied criticism of the Fascist corporatist state of Mussolini, but it caused misunderstanding.[7]

The encyclical made a heroic critique of the tendencies toward socialism. It proclaimed that although socialism appeared to side with the weak in a society, it fundamentally contradicted Catholicism with regard to social theory. The pope explained the difference as follows:

according to Christian teaching, man, endowed with a social nature, is placed on this earth so that by leading a life in society and under an authority ordained of God he may fully cultivate and develop all his faculties unto the praise and glory of his Creator; and that by faithfully fulfilling the duties of his craft or other calling he may obtain for himself temporal and at the same time eternal happiness. Socialism, on the other hand, wholly ignoring and indifferent to this sublime end of both man and society, affirms that human association has been instituted for the sake of material advantage alone. (Pius XI [1931] 1942, par. 118)

Schumpeter did not mention the Catholic doctrine, but he seemed to agree with its criticism of the utilitarian ideas in socialism.

A century is a short run

Schumpeter's view may appear conservative and revivalistic; his reference to the concept of professional association with a flavor of the medieval guild especially could give this impression. It was perhaps natural for him to think that, as far as capitalist development is concerned, "a century is a 'short run' " (1950a, 163), which assumes many twists and turns in the long process leading from the fall of an atomistic market system to centralized socialism. How to live during that process would determine the destination of a society. If we take into account the underlying trend of history and changes in actual conditions, his political economy was not backward looking. The conception of individuals within a group rather than atomistic individuals would mean a forward-looking attitude in groping for new possibilities of capitalism.[8]

During the Montreal lecture, Schumpeter made this immortal statement: "Except in time of war, those who live in poverty are the people who have not known the system of private enterprise" ([1946b] 1975, 294). Parallel with economic affluence, the capitalist countries have adopted democratic regimes replete with trials and errors. It is true that under democracy a free society tends to become a system of representatives who are working on behalf of their own interests, and though this tendency is still within the range of the trend described by Schumpeter, this does not immediately mean socialization. It is also true that the economic structure of capitalism tends to become a large corporate system, but this does not immediately mean socialization if the boundaries between the public and private spheres are preserved and the brakes are put on the growing bureaucracy. In order to maintain the market economic system and the democratic political system, Schumpeter urged moral reform rather than economic and social reform. The substance of the moral reform was to emphasize the independence and responsibility of individuals without easy request of social services, and to give full play to individuality without easy conformity to ordinary rationalism. Independence and individuality were a prerequisite of leadership.

Through his social scientific observation in *Capitalism, Socialism and Democracy*, Schumpeter argued the basic tendency to move from capitalism to socialism, on the one hand, and concluded the cultural indeterminateness of socialism in the sense of the political, social, religious, and spiritual neutrality in a socialist system, on the other. In contrast, through his argument for a political economy, he chose capitalism and democracy as desirable and rejected socialism emotionally. But if capitalism and democracy is to be consistent, moral reform is required to implement corporatism. When capitalism has accomplished its economic tasks and reached a mature stage where the choice of socialism is feasible, gifted leadership would be more and more demanded in the field of politics. Chapter 9 concludes that, according to Schumpeter's scientific inference, politics would be crucial to the possibilities of capitalism as well as socialism. Here, also, according to his argument for political economy, politics would be crucial to realize the possibilities of the survival of capitalism. However, is it not the greatest irony for Schumpeter, who regarded democracy not as the ideal system but as the institution of gathering votes, to advocate moral reform under democracy?

CHAPTER 12

Conclusion: Schumpeterian synthesis

Schumpeter was once depicted by George Stigler as: "immensely learned and immensely clever, and as a minor foible, a *poseur* in abstract economic theory" (Stigler 1988, 100). Even if Stigler is partly right, it is far more important to recognize the great possibilities of Schumpeter's alleged "minor foible." By acting as if he were an abstract economic theorist, Schumpeter left large-scale heterodox concepts that would never have been formulated by ordinary theoretical economists.

Vision and theory construction

One of Schumpeter's greatest torments in the academic world was probably the gap between his vision and his construction of theory. His original ideas, such as technological innovation, long swings, monopolistic firms, dynamic competition, and evolutionary economics, which were offered from a dynamic point of view, were not fully developed by him, but they were recognized by later economists as highly relevant themes and led to prolific results in the fields of theoretical and empirical analysis. These themes helped broaden the frontier of economics.

In later years Schumpeter wrote: "The highest ambition an economist can entertain who believes in the scientific character of economics would be fulfilled as soon as he succeeded in constructing a simple model displaying all the essential features of the economic process by means of a reasonably small number of equations connecting a reasonably small number of variables" (1946c, 3). Related in Stigler's style, this passage, where he talked as if he were a competent abstract economic theorist, has often been understood to be Schumpeter's dream. But this interpretation is not correct, because he explicitly denied the values of such simple models, except as a possibility of future economics. In the same essay, he continued: "I must confess to a feeling that at present the premature and irresponsible application to diagnosis, prognosis, or recommendation, of what of necessity are as yet provisional and flimsy constructions can produce nothing but error and can only result in discrediting this pioneer work" (1946c, 3). Simply elegant models that do not embody "all the essential features of the economic process" did not mean anything to him. He thought the elaboration and sophistication of theory without vision should be rejected.

Synthesis and evolution

Schumpeter's vision extended beyond economics to recognizing both the unity of social phenomena and the evolution of society. This recognition is what he meant by his basic idea of the synthesis of theory and history, or the *histoire raisonée*, and what he understood to be the surviving elements of the German Historical School. The perspective of the unity of social phenomena provides, as it were, a horizontal axis from which to observe a society that consists of various areas of social life; it must be combined with a vertical axis, which represents the viewpoint of the evolution of society. For Schumpeter, the object of social science is the process by which various areas of social life are interrelated horizontally (simultaneously), on the one hand, and by which a society evolves vertically (intertemporarily), on the other. To view a society comprehensively does not necessarily mean to view a society evolutionarily. The general equilibrium view of society characterizes the static method of observing a society. Rather, the dynamic, intertemporal vantage point of observation makes the comprehensive outlook of a society indispensable, and not vice versa. As far as we are going to focus on the long-term development of a society, we cannot concentrate on changes in a single area of that society, because in a dynamic process all the areas of a society are interrelated and change simultaneously.

Economic sociology is concerned with the interdependence of various aspects of a society, with economy being the center of the observation. Evolutionary science, on the other hand, is concerned with the spontaneous development of a society, with changes in various areas being involved in the process of economic change. Economic sociology can acquire a dynamic nature only if it becomes evolutionary science. Schumpeter's final goal was an evolutionary science, and consequently, a universal social science. In his view, the source of evolution was leadership and innovation in various social areas, and his idea of social science located the core principle of leadership in the perspective of Marx's scheme of the super- and substructure of society.

Specialization and synthesis

In his early work *Vergangenheit und Zukunft der Sozialwissenshaften* (1915), Schumpeter predicted the future direction of the social sciences: improvement of theoretical formulation, closer cooperation of basic theory and special studies, advancement of empirical and quantitative research, and so on. At the same time, he asked whether this direction was ever desirable. He replied: "The more a science goes this way, the more certainly it loses something very beautiful: the charm of literary play" (1915, 127). This brings to mind his argument in *Capitalism, Socialism and Democracy* that the rationalization of economic society makes its civilization mechanized and dull. This was certainly his serious observation on the effect of rationalization on a variety of social areas including science. Characteristically enough, he did not forget the opposite truth that professional training was essential to science; following the conventions makes possible supreme and original achievements.[1]

The same thing applied to vision: "What is even more common in this regard is that the researcher has a vague feeling about the important feature of phenomena until they become evident in a more precise form only in detail and through detail. This feeling is everything" (1915, 131). Vision about essence springs not from abstract notions but rather from the pursuit of particulars and individuals in reality. This was Schumpeter's conception of vision and similar to his methodological approach in which a methodological principle could not be separated from particular methods.

In this way, Schumpeter foresaw the possibility of synthesizing through specialization in the new fruitful epoch. He called it "Soziologisierung" of the social sciences: "The substance of the new epoch is revealed by the tendency to understand as many things around us as possible – i.e., law, religion, moral, art, politics, economy, even logic and psychology – from sociology. The analysis of cultural phenomena is the lighthouse that the total fleet of different ships on different courses is headed for. And an epoch similar to the eighteenth century in many respects is approaching" (1915, 132–33). This expresses the leitmotiv running throughout Schumpeter's life.

In an interview with the *Harvard Crimson* in 1944, Schumpeter called his long-standing research program "a comprehensive sociology" and observed: "All my failures are due to observance of this program and my successes to neglect of it: concentration is necessary for success in any field."[2] For him, there was a dilemma between socially determined academic success and his own conception of an academic ideal. Indeed, his efforts based on the research program had not been rewarded with wide acceptance by the academe; even *Capitalism, Socialism and Democracy*, an attempt at synthesis, had proved successful only as a popular book and had not been considered as a serious work of economic sociology or comprehensive sociology. But he never gave up his pursuit of the program. Perhaps because the *habitus* for a universal social science was second nature to Schumpeter, he could not find an easy solution to this dilemma.

Schumpeter's habitus

Schumpeter accepted many different streams of thought and constructed a comprehensive approach to the mind and society. In Bourdieu's terminology, the former was the intellectual field Schumpeter was concerned with, and the latter was his total work as practice. It is now time to ask, what ultimately made these possible? In other words, what was his organizing principle or *habitus*? I suggest that his synthesizing methods were (1) the substantive tool of sociology, (2) the methodological tool of instrumentalism, and (3) the literary tool of rhetoric.

First, Schumpeter habitually relied on the simultaneous use of economics and sociology to analyze the overall nature of the problems in question. This is shown in the titles of his essays, "Economics and Sociology of Distribution" (a section of his 1916–17 article on "The Fundamental Principles of Distribution"), "Economics and Psychology of the Entrepreneur" (1929a), "Economics and Sociology of the Income Tax" (1929b), "Economics and Sociology of Capitalism" (a section of his 1946 article on "Capitalism"), and "The Communist Manifesto in Sociology and Economics" (1949b), to name a few.

Marx, too, used economics and sociology to explain the evolution of the capitalist process, but Schumpeter rejected Marx's monolithic structure of a universal social science integrating economics and sociology (1950a, 45). He proposed that a distinction be made between economics and sociology in the evaluation of Marx's system: "No question of principle is involved in this distinction. It is simply an expository device that, in itself, is incapable of being 'right' or 'wrong' and is to be judged merely from the standpoint of the categories 'convenient' or 'inconvenient'" (1949b, 204). This expresses his instrumentalist methodology. Indeed, he worried that this distinction would destroy the unity of Marx's system but regarded it as useful to preserve the truth in Marx rather than to abandon the whole system (1950a, 9). If it is possible to cut the whole into pieces, it is much easier to combine the separate pieces. The simultaneous use of economics and economic sociology did not raise serious methodological questions according to Schumpeter. His idea of a universal social science did not mean a seamless texture. What mattered to him was the usefulness of tools for the analysis of specific problems.

Second, the methodological principle underlying the Schumpeterian synthesis was instrumentalism, explored in his first book, *Wesen*. In fact, his instrumentalism was presented as a solution to the *Methodenstreit* between theory and history. According to this methodological principle, no contradiction exists between theory and history; the difference between theoretical and historical methods is explained in terms of the different concerns of theorists and historians with regard to the problems they are interested in. Multifaceted analyses of reality are attempted for their pragmatic usefulness and made compatible with each other on the basis of instrumentalism. As in *Capitalism, Socialism and Democracy,* the simultaneous application of economics and economic sociology will produce a fresh, though seemingly paradoxical, thesis and provide a new perspective to the reality. These results explain the success of theory construction as an instrument.

The same applies to the relationship between Schumpeter's statics and dynamics. Most of the objections to his dichotomy are concerned with a formal argument of methodology for the sake of methodology. For instance, there is the often repeated criticism that his simultaneous acceptance of Walras's idea and Marx's idea is a contradiction. It is quite natural that a theoretical structure differs according to the objectives and problems of researchers. It is unnecessary from a methodological standpoint to demand that all theories be monolithic even if they are entertained by one person. To use Schumpeterian rhetoric, does it cause any inconvenience or contradiction that one has a key for a room and another a key for a car? Because only the usefulness of instruments is important, no one thinks that one must have one master key.

Of course, the systems of thought in a universal social science must be coherent. In Schumpeter's system, statics, dynamics, and economic sociology are coherent, though they are concerned with different problems and methods. The recognition that each area of social life is interrelated through actions and reactions presupposes that there is a consistent relationship among the knowledge of each area. In the view of science based on instrumentalism, theory is not a description of the real world but a convenient tool to understand reality. While the criterion for a successful instrument is usefulness, coherence theory must hold for the network of knowledge. According to coherentism, various statements are justified by their coherent interdependence. It can be argued that Schumpeter's synthesis presented a network of useful knowledge organized by the criterion of coherence.[3]

For Schumpeter, just as Walras (who discovered the essence of the economic system) was the greatest theoretical economist and just as the general equilibrium theory was the Magna Carta of economics, *Das Wesen und der Hauptinhalt der theoretischen Nationalökonomie* was the core of his total work about society and mind. The static economic mechanism, which explains the adaptive adjustment forces of an economy, constitutes the logic of an economy as such. Even in the dynamic sphere, the static mechanism absorbs the impact of destructive innovations on the economy and leads to a reorganization of the economy; furthermore, in the perspective of economic sociology, it represents the concept of rationality, the essential characteristic of capitalist civilization. The success of capitalism means vigorous economic development by innovation; though rationality is the basis of economic development and innovation, paradoxically, it eventually destroys capitalism.

Third, in order to break into unexplored fields Schumpeter depended on the literary tools of rhetoric, metaphor, and analogy. These are not to be disdained; rather, they are indispensable to the conveyance of empirical and inductive knowledge in the form of vision. Insofar as a prescientific idea is located only in the mind of one scholar and remains there as tacit knowledge, it is not socially shared. Science is socially shared knowledge, but vision is not necessarily so unless it is presented through the tool of rhetoric. Schumpeter admitted that the role of vision is significant in the study of a long-term process of change because theoretical formulation and its justification in this field are so difficult that vision must remain as vision. We owe him our understanding of the dynamism of capitalism, expressed in his admirable form of rhetoric.

Schumpeter's argument concerning vision indicates not only that vision must precede the construction of a theory, but also that it must be the object of social understanding and communication, insofar as scientific activity is carried out in a society, not in the mind of a scientist alone. Hence, vision must be subject to certain procedural rules. In the case of vision, such a rule is rhetoric. Even before science, the process of human thought has a rule. Schumpeter was distinctive because of his use of rhetoric; without it, he could not have presented even the vision of his wide-ranging system of a universal social science. His "charm of literary play" was to the utmost extent exhibited in *Capitalism, Socialism and Democracy;* therefore it is the treasure of vision.

The idea of a universal social science

I refer to sociology, instrumentalism, and rhetoric as the tools of Schumpeterian synthesis in order to show that his achievement was due not solely to his talent, but to durable, transposable dispositions that were essentially helped by these tools. The capacity and the propensity to accept and utilize these tools were Schumpeter's *habitus*. His idea of a universal social science, the substance of which was evolution based on leadership and innovation in various social spheres, was made possible by his *habitus* thus defined. To the Anglo-Saxon positivists his methods appeared awkward; his inclinations and education were too outdated for him to succeed in that forum. Beyond the age of specialization, however, he predicted the coming of an age, like the eighteenth century, when knowledge would be globally synthesized. By bringing this less appealing system of thought into economics, Schumpeter tried to introduce a unique mix of historicism and positivism. His universal social science came too early. I do not mean that harmony and equilibrium always prevailed in his research; rather, his internal tension and conflict produced his Herculean effort to achieve harmony, equilibrium, and coherence. In this effort his inner *habitus* found the supplementary tools to implement itself, and thereby his social scientific work was expressed in an objective form. The harmony between tools and propensity is important to scholars because science is a social as well as a subjective activity.

Two thousand five hundred years ago, Confucius advocated the virtue of the mean: "When there is a preponderance of native substance over acquired refinement, the result will be churlishness. When there is a preponderance of acquired refinement over native substance, the result will be pedantry. Only a well-balanced admixture of these two will result in gentlemanliness" (*The Analects*, Book VI, par. 18). As the minute of Harvard University revealed, based on the Western standards of civilization and morality, "he [Schumpeter] remained to the end the cultivated Austrian gentleman of the old school" (Haberler, Harris, Leontief, and Mason 1951, ix).

Notes

1 Introduction

1 Schumpeter also adhered to this principle in his lecture. Haberler observed: "The content of all these courses would be varied from year to year, but they all suffered from one defect: by listening to Schumpeter's lectures and studying his reading assignments and suggestions, students could have never found out that he himself had ever written anything on those subjects" (Haberler 1951a, 39).

2 Schumpeter used the term "universal social science" for Gustav von Schmoller (Schumpeter 1926b, 176) and the term "unitary social science" for Karl Marx (Schumpeter 1954a, 441), both in an affirmative sense.

3 Schumpeter's views on vision and ideology are examined in chapter 4. This discussion is traditionally called the sociology of science, and its central question is to explain the social conditioning of science. But the same social factors do not necessarily yield the same vision and knowledge; there is much room for personal factors. Thus "this [vision] should be extended even to peculiarities of his [man's] outlook that are related to his personal tastes and conditions and have no group connotation – there is even an ideology of the mathematical mind as well as an ideology of the mind that is allergic to mathematics" (1949a, 351).

4 These essays are collected in Schumpeter (1951a, 1954b).

5 I have been working on Schumpeter's methodology (Shionoya 1986, 1990a, 1990b, 1991, 1992a). Although Augello regarded methodology as a separate area of study in his comprehensive survey of the Schumpeteriana, works classified in that area were actually not concerned with methodology but with method (Augello 1990). Machlup (1951) is rather an exception; recently, Bottomore's research emphasized methodology (1992). In appropriate places in the book, I shall discuss these works mainly from a critical point of view.

6 Schumpeter's meaning of the word "metatheory" is different from mine. According to him, it addresses social phenomena as ordinary theories do, but it denotes investigations of all the facts that lie beyond or behind the research objects of ordinary theories. For instance, he said, metasociology or philosophical anthropology denotes inquiries into the formation of habits or into the properties of physical environments; he used the word in connection with the seventeenth-century natural philosophers (1954a, 120).

7 Because Schumpeter's methodology of science and his explication of static theory were developed simultaneously in *Das Wesen und der Hauptinhalt der theoretischen Nationalökonomie*, the neglect of his methodology and of his contribution to statics was a combined affair.

8 Since this book differs wholly from most studies on Schumpeter in the setting of problems, it seldom refers to the existing literature. The authors of books on Schumpeter published after World War II are Clemence and Doody (1950), Harris (1951), Khan (1957), Lehnis (1960), Perroux (1965), Schneider (1970), Predöhl (1972), Heertje (1981), Frisch (1982), März (1983), Winterberger (1983), Bös and Stolper (1984), Seidl (1984), Coe and Wilber (1985), Helburn and Bramhall (1986), Wagener and Drukker (1986), Timmermann (1987), Oakeley (1990), Müller (1990), Naderer (1990), Allen (1991), Brouwer (1991), Swedberg (1991a), Wood (1991), Bottomore (1992), Shionoya and Perlman (1994), Stolper (1994), Vecchi

(1995), and Moss (1996). For a bibliography of works on Schumpeter, see Stevenson (1985) and Augello (1990).

2 Schumpeter and his surroundings: an overview

1 For a general survey of Viennese cultural activities at the turn of the century, see Johnston (1972), Janik and Toulmin (1973), Schorske (1980), and Berner, Brix, and Mantl (1986).

2 For biographies of Schumpeter, see Haberler (1951a), Schneider (1970), März (1983), Allen (1991), and Swedberg (1991a). The following description of Schumpeter's life draws on these materials.

3 For the Schumpeter family tree, see Shionoya (1989a).

4 A picture of Schumpeter's house in Třešt' appears in Shionoya (1989b) and Swedberg (1991a).

5 Arthur Smithies mentioned two factors that were decisive in the formation of Schumpeter's character: first, "he spent most of his first ten years as the only son of a young widowed mother," and second, "while he was of middle-class origin and undistinguished lineage, he was brought up in a highly aristocratic environment" (Smithies 1951, 16).

6 According to *Jahres-Bericht des Gymnasiums der K. K. Theresianischen Akademie in Wien* (1901), the annual report of the Theresianum, eight out of the twenty-eight graduates had excellent records; Schumpeter was one of them.

7 For Schumpeter's curriculum vitae, records at the Habilitation, and lecture plan at the University of Vienna, see Yagi (1993).

8 For Austro-Marxism, see Bottomore and Goode (1978).

9 Schumpeter's own handwritten record in *Stammbuch (II) der Philosophischen Fakultät der Universität Bonn*. I thank Professor Richard Swedberg for kindly providing me with a copy of this material.

10 This essay seems to be Schumpeter's first description of his famous thesis on the sacred decade of fertility, but the abridged English translation in *Ten Great Economists* (Schumpeter 1951a) omitted this paragraph.

11 One of his biographers described Schumpeter's peculiarities and faults in these terms: pretentious arrogance, a sense of self-importance and superiority, elaborate manners, omniscient attitude, elitist, a snob's snob, conspicuity, ambition; spats, an unusual vest or cravat, a bracelet, colored or two-toned shoes, a silver-headed cane; flamboyant yet impeccable manners (Allen 1991, 1, 55).

12 This expression was quoted from the obituary in the *Harvard Crimson*, January 10, 1950. There are variations of this sentence: "but I failed to become the greatest horseman in Austria" (Morgan 1983, 4); "but, unfortunately, the seat I inherited was never of the topmost caliber" (Samuelson 1981, 7). See also Allen (1991, 2, 171).

13 It has been variously reported that Seaver was twelve years older than Schumpeter (Smithies 1951, 119), twenty-four years older (Schneider 1970, 13), twelve years older (Date 1983, 31), and two years younger (Seidl 1984, 190). Smithies and Schneider did not give the source of their information. Date's account was based on the marriage register in London and Seidl's from the police register at Graz.

14 For the Socialization Commission, see Stolper (1994).

15 For Schumpeter's public activities during this period, see Schumpeter (1985, 1992a) and Stolper (1994).

16 For Schumpeter's writings on current issues while and after he was bank president, see Schumpeter (1985, 1993).

17 The biographical essays by Smithies (1951) and Haberler (1951a) both state that Schumpeter had Anna educated in France and Switzerland to equip her to be his wife. Although this must be what he told people, the story is not true and illustrates the way in which Schumpeter kept up appearances. See Allen (1991, 1, 193).

18 This story was first made public by Allen (1991, 1, 225–27). The key to this puzzling practice was provided in the 190-page report of Erica Gerschenkron, who deciphered the Gabelsberger shorthand. See "The Diaries of Anna Reisinger-Schumpeter: A Report by Erica Gerschenkron," Harvard University Archives, HUG (FP) 66.90, Box 4.

19 *Epochen* was translated into English in 1954, after Schumpeter's death, with the permission of Elizabeth B. Schumpeter. Before the publication of the English version, *Epochen* was translated into Greek (1939), Japanese (1950), and Italian (1953). See Augello (1990, 119–20).

20 Haberler related the following incident: "In 1944, when Roosevelt was running for his fourth term as president, a lady who was unaware of Schumpeter's intense aversion asked him at a cocktail party whether he would vote for Roosevelt. He answered: 'My dear lady, if Hitler runs for President and Stalin for Vice President, I shall be happy to vote for that ticket against Roosevelt'" (Haberler 1981, 74).

21 About Schumpeter Paul Sweezy wrote: "He made no attempt whatever to form a group of disciples around him, and yet I have never known a teacher who took a more personal and painstaking interest in his students ... he saw it as his function, one might even say duty, to help those who were living through that period to bring every bit of talent in them to fruitful expression. For this, what they needed was encouragement, sometimes advice, but above all an atmosphere of intellectual clash and excitement which would sharpen their interest and challenge their ambition. And throughout the thirties, when his physical vigor still matched his mental vigor, Schumpeter spared no pains to see that just such an atmosphere existed for the best graduate students in economics at Harvard" (Sweezy 1951, xxii–xxiii).

22 Harvard University Archives, HUG (FP) 4.6, Box 3.

23 See also Bourdieu (1975, 1985, 1990a, 1993).

3 The scope and methods of Schumpeter's research program

1 In quoting from *Theorie der wirtschaftlichen Entwicklung*, I distinguish between three versions: *Entwicklung* (1st edition, 1912), *Entwicklung* (2nd edition, 1926), and *The Theory of Economic Development* (1934). There are significant differences between the first and the second German editions. The English version is an abridged translation of the second German edition, so that it cannot fully replace the latter.

2 Chapter 7 is divided into thirteen sections: 1. Preliminary Remarks, 2. Two Problems of Economic Theory, 3. Historical and Theoretical Problems of Development, 4. Discussion of the "Environment Theory" of Development, 5. Discussion of the "Growth Theory" of Development, 6. Three General Propositions of Economic Development, 7. The Influence of Development on Individual Economic Agents, 8. The Most Important Special Case, 9. A Model of a Total Socio-Economic Process, 10. An Overview of Our Analysis of the Production Process and Some Applications, 11. On the Economic Structure of Society and the Problems of Social Class Structure, 12. The Social Atmosphere of the Capitalist Economy, 13. The Analogy of Economic Development in Other Areas of Social Life: A Social Phenomenon. Broadly speaking, while sections 1–10 were summaries of the theory of economic development and later absorbed into chapter 2 of the second edition, sections 11–13 presented investigations of sociocultural development and were omitted in the second edition. I pay attention to Schumpeter's idea in these three sections.

3 In the study of the history of economics, Schumpeter found the first recognition of order by social scientists in the concept of the natural law, which was discovered through their inquiries into human nature (see page 271).

4 Schumpeter used the term *methodological individualism* as distinct from *political individualism* in *Wesen* (1908, part 1, chapter 6). He is considered to be the first to use this term – see Machlup (1951, 100). But the label is misleading, because it actually means the assumption of a certain mode of behavior of individuals and not the epistemological justification of the assumption. Therefore, it should be labeled *methodical individualism* or *assumptive individualism*.

5 This involves a problem of functional versus causal relationships. As indicated in chapter 5 of this volume, Schumpeter argued in *Wesen* that economic theory is not concerned with the causal relationship but the functional relationship. As we have just seen, however, in *Entwicklung* he discussed the causal relationship. Machlup, therefore, maintains that Schumpeter changed his mind (1951, 97), but this is completely wrong. What Schumpeter meant in *Wesen* is that only a functional relationship (general interdependence) exists among endogenous elements in an economic system, but in the sense that the configuration of these elements is uniquely conditioned by a set of exogenous factors outside the system to which the causal

explanation applies. What Schumpeter referred to in *Entwicklung* was just the causal relation-ship between economic and noneconomic factors; he did not change his mind. Machlup quotes from Schumpeter's *Business Cycles* to support the point; contrary to Machlup's interpretation, however, that quotation means that "until we have assembled in one model causes, mechanisms, and effects, and can show how it works" (Schumpeter 1939, 1, 34), we can raise the question of causation between exogenous and endogenous variables. Nor is there a change of mind here.

6 See Meiners and Nardinelli (1986, 521).

7 Mannheim's speech at the Congress of German University Teachers of Sociology. Quoted from Meja, Misgeld, and Stehr (1987, 43).

4 The sociology of science and Schumpeter's ideology

1 The account in this paragraph is based on Kordig (1978).

2 A survey of the logical positivist view of science and its criticism is given in Suppe (1977).

3 For a survey of the recent sociology of science, see Knorr-Cetina and Mulkay (1983), Coats (1984), and Mäki (1992).

4 The common English translation "knowledge is existentially determined" is not appropriate, for it conveys the one-sided causal determination from society to knowledge. It is strange to encounter this translation at the place where Mannheim warns that the word *Seinsverbundenheit* does not indicate the exact nature of the correlation between society and knowledge (Mannheim [1931] 1936, 239). See also Wolff (1993, 42).

5 The following remarks might be misleading: "the original vision *is* ideology by nature" (1949a, 351); "vision is ideological almost by definition" (1954a, 42). What Schumpeter meant here was that there is nothing for vision but to embody ideology.

6 This article was published in Japan after Schumpeter's revision of the lecture notes. Recently, his Kobe lecture notes were printed in slightly different forms by Allen (Schumpeter [1931c] 1982) and Swedberg (Schumpeter [1931d] 1991).

7 According to Schumpeter's plan, section 1 of chapter 4 of *History*, which discusses the relationship between science and ideology, was to be followed by sections on "The Motive Forces of Scientific Endeavor and the Mechanisms of Scientific Development" and "The Personnel of Science in General and of Economics in Particular." See the editor's note (1954a, 44–45).

8 A little later, at his farewell speech at Bonn, Schumpeter expounded the same view: "I have never tried to bring about a Schumpeter School. There is none and it ought not to exist ... Economics is neither a philosophy of economy nor a world view ... Hence there can be no 'schools' in our field" (Schumpeter [1932], 1952, 600–3).

9 See Tsuru (1983, 8) and Allen (1991, 1, xx).

10 Bottomore criticizes Schumpeter for neglecting the progress of science through confrontation between rival theories (Bottomore 1992, 21–22, 25–27). But, as can be seen from the above, this is far from the truth. Furthermore, in the same place he attributes the idea of the progress of science as "slow accretion" to Schumpeter by quoting Schumpeter (1954a, 9) and criticizes him for not providing more recent conceptions of scientific revolution. Again, this is not true. Schumpeter spoke about "slow accretion" only for the origins of "a science as distinguished from the origins of a particular methods or the foundation of a 'school'"; for the latter, there was obviously a dramatic breakthrough (1954a, 9). Bottomore does not understand that Schumpeter did have a framework for his statics–dynamics dichotomy, i.e., a conception of scientific growth within a paradigm and that of a paradigmatic change.

11 For the contrast between phenomenology and historicism, see Mannheim ([1925] 1952, 154–79).

12 In the second edition of *Entwicklung* Schumpeter abandoned the double dichotomy of statics–dynamics with respect to the phenomena as well as to the theoretical tools (1934, 64). The customary use of the word *dynamics* increasingly had been to indicate analysis that links quantities pertaining to different points of time, following the idea of Ragnar Frisch. In his own system Schumpeter now used stationary state versus evolutionary state (or development) for phenomena, and statics versus the theory of development for analysis. See also Schumpeter

(1954a, 963–67). But we do not think it necessary to follow such a strict usage; we apply the word dynamics for his system.

13 The first three pairs of the static–dynamic dichotomy were given in the second edition of *Entwicklung* (1934, 82–83). The fourth pair was mentioned in the first edition in place of the first pair (1912, 512–13).

14 Weintraub specifies the hard core of the neo-Walrasian research program by the following propositions: (1) economic agents exist, (2) agents have preferences over outcomes, (3) agents independently optimize subject to constraints, (4) choices are made in interrelated markets, (5) agents have full relevant knowledge, and (6) observable economic outcomes are coordinated, so they must be discussed with reference to equilibrium states (Weintraub 1985, 109).

15 A similar interpretation is given by Mark Blaug. According to him, "Lakatos's 'hard core' expresses an idea similar to that conveyed by Schumpeter's notion of 'Vision' – 'the preanalytic cognitive act that supplies the raw material for the analytic effort' or Gouldner's 'world hypotheses,' which figure heavily in his explanation of why sociologists adopt certain theories and reject others" (Blaug 1976, 157). If it is assumed that one of Schumpeter's visions was Walras, then Blaug's general view of hard core vis-à-vis vision might coincide with my interpretation of statics vis-à-vis dynamics.

16 Karl Marx and Friedrich Engels, *The German Ideology* ([1845–46] 1939).

17 Quoted in chapter 28 ("The Consequences of the Second World War") of *Capitalism*, which was added to its second edition (1947). This saying is also attributed to Count Axel Oxenstierna of Sweden (1583–1654). A. Partington (ed.), *The Oxford Dictionary of Quotations*, 4th ed., 1992, 503.

18 This view is best expressed by Haberler (1951a, 45–47). See also Allen, who supports Haberler's view (1991, 2, 255–56).

19 The word was suggested by Martin Bronfenbrenner.

20 According to Augello's work on the Schumpeter bibliography, there were about 200 entries on Schumpeter – including books, articles, and other materials – during his lifetime, 360 in the fifties, 200 in the sixties, 250 in the seventies, and 900 in the eighties. Although the last figure reflects the influence of his centenary in 1983, it is true that there has been a growing interest in appraising his work and in formulating his vision.

5 The economic methodology of instrumentalism

1 For the methodological study of neoclassical economics before Schumpeter, see Carl Menger (1883), John Neville Keynes (1890), and Vilfredo Pareto (1896–97).

2 In Vienna early in the twentieth century Friedrich von Hayek observed: "It [positivism] was almost entirely the influence of Ernst Mach, the physicist, and his disciples. He was the most influential figure philosophically. At that time, apart from what I had been reading before I joined the army, I think my introduction to what I now almost hesitate to call philosophy – scientific method, I think, is a better description – was through Machian philosophy. It was very good on the history of science generally, and it dominated discussion in Vienna. Joseph Schumpeter had fully fallen for Mach" (Hayek 1994, 49).

3 *Wesen* was reprinted by Augustus M. Kelley (New York) in 1970 and by Verlag Wirtschaft und Finanzen (Düsseldorf) in 1990. *Wesen* was translated into Japanese in 1936 and into Italian in 1982.

4 According to Robbins, "Economics is the science which studies human behaviour as a relationship between ends and scarce means which have alternative uses" (Robbins 1935, 16). His definition is based on the Austrian tradition of economics.

5 For a survey of the history of economic methodology, see Blaug (1980), Caldwell (1982), Pheby (1988), and Redman (1991). See also the anthologies of Caldwell (1984, 1993) and Hausman (1984).

6 The English title of *Wesen* is not uniquely fixed among economists because the book has not been translated into English. The literal translation is *The Essence and Main Contents of Theoretical Economics*, but the metaphysical implication of "essence," I think, should be avoided in view of Schumpeter's opposition to metaphysics.

7 Carl Menger (1883) distinguished in the field of economy between (1) historical science

(inquiry into individuality) and (2) theoretical science (inquiry into generality) and differentiated within the latter (2a) between empirical research and (2b) exact research. Schumpeter's theoretical or pure economics corresponded to Menger's exact theoretical research. Menger asserted that although theoretical economics consisted of exact theoretical research, empirical research advocated by the German Historical School could not take the place of an exact theoretical approach. This criticism initiated the *Methodenstreit*.

8 Schumpeter later wrote about the situation in Germany in *History of Economic Analysis*: "As we know, in Germany *Sozialpolitik* and the work of the historical school asserted their influence upon general economics more than in any other country. These interests did not entirely destroy tradition nor did they entirely crush out the 'theoretical' component in general economics. But in places they came near doing so: although a reaction had set in by 1900 and was running strong by 1914, the men who were then in their twenties were practically untrained in the art of handling analytic tools and some of them actually conceived of 'theory' as consisting of philosophies about socialism or individualism and the like and of quarrels about 'methods' – they had no conception of theory as a 'box of tools' " (1954a, 843).

9 In this paragraph, the titles *Principles of Economics* and *The Scope and Method of Political Economy* refer to Alfred Marshall (1890) and John Neville Keynes (1890), respectively. The composition of Schumpeter's *Wesen* is quite different from that of those two books, as can be seen from its contents: Part 1 Basic Theory; Part 2 Problems of Static Equilibrium; Part 3 Theory of Distribution; Part 4 Variation Method; Part 5 The Summary of Conclusions with regard to the Nature, Cognitive Values, and Development Possibilities of Theoretical Economics.

The areas covered by parts 2 and 3 corresponds with almost all of Marshall's description of economic theory in *Principles*, but Schumpeter's description is directed not so much to substantive theory as to its epistemological clarification. (More specifically, part 2 is divided into two sections: the first is a purely methodological discussion of statics; the second is a survey of each branch of statics.) Part 4 is an extension of statics, developed in parts 2 and 3, and corresponds with what is currently called comparative statics. Substantive theory in parts 2–4 is located between part 1 and part 5, which are introductory and concluding descriptions of economic methodology, respectively, and resemble Keynes's book.

10 The term *methodological tolerance* is Machlup's (1951, 95). It is ironic that Machlup, who was sensitive to the distinction between method and methodology, attached such a label, since Schumpeter claimed to tolerate the diversity of methods by quoting the adage "To understand all means to approve all." Methodical tolerance is an appropriate labeling.

11 Duhem writes: "A physical theory is an abstract system whose aim is to *summarize* and *classify logically* a group of experimental laws without claiming to explain these laws ... To explain is to strip reality of the appearances covering it like a veil, in order to see the bare reality itself" (Duhem 1962, 7); "A physical theory is not an explanation. It is a system of mathematical propositions, deduced from a small number of principles, which aim to represent as simply, as completely, as exactly as possible a set of experimental laws" (19).

12 Leplin's volume offers an overview of the current debate between realism and antirealism.

13 Nagel's definition of instrumentalism, quoted above, is followed by the remark: "However, those who adopt this [instrumentalist] position do not always agree in their answers to the question whether physical reality is to be assigned to such theoretical entities as atoms" (Nagel 1961, 118).

14 For a summary of Mach's philosophy of science, see Oldroyd (1986, 176–82). For recent discussions of his works, see "A Symposium on Ernst Mach" in *Synthèse* (April 1968), Cohen and Seeger (1970), Bradley (1971), and Blackmore (1972).

15 According to Hayek, the view that science should aim not at a personified "explanation" of nature but at a complete "description" of nature was first formulated explicitly in Kirchhoff's *Vorlesungen über mathematische Physik* and later spread by Mach's philosophy of science (Hayek, 1952, 30).

16 In his explanation of economic equilibrium in *Wesen*, Schumpeter refers to Mach's equation representing the maximization problem (1908, 204).

17 For the methodology of Pareto, see Tarascio (1966).

18 For this interpretation, see Laudan (1981, 202–25).

19 Quoted from Laudan (1981, 224).

20 For recent studies of Poincaré's philosophy of science, see Giedymin (1982, 1991) and Stump (1989).

21 For a recent discussion of the relationships between instrumentalism, conventionalism, and pragmatism, see Boland (1982, 141–52).

22 This can be compared with Mach's remark that "our concepts, it is true, are formed consciously and purposely by us, but they are nevertheless not formed altogether arbitrarily, but are the outcome of an endeavor on our part to adapt our ideas to our sensuous environment" (Mach [1883] 1960, 318).

23 See Giedymin (1976, 200).

24 See Friedman (1953), Wong (1973), and Boland (1979).

25 Caldwell later admitted that he made a mistake in characterizing Friedman as an instrumentalist in the standard sense (1992). He now tries to give Friedman the label "predictionist instrumentalist" based on cognitivism.

26 See pages 43–49 for a discussion of the relationship between theoretical and historical methods from the standpoint of technical method. Here I am concerned with the two methods from the standpoint of methodology.

27 Schumpeter, however, uses the term *historism* in *History* (1954a, 807–8).

28 See Kauder (1965) and Jaffé (1976).

29 Since Wieser seldom discussed methodology, this review article is very rare. Hayek wisely adopted it as one of Wieser's typical works on methodology in his compilation of Wieser's essays. See Hayek (1929, xiii).

30 Chapters 6 and 7 of Caldwell (1982) discuss the conflicts between Robbins and Hutchison, and between Hutchison and Machlup, respectively. The aim of my argument here is to introduce Schumpeter into this context and to relate him to the economic methodology after Robbins.

31 The English translation of *Entwicklung* does not include any preface from the first, second, or fourth German editions. The preface to the fourth edition, consisting of nine pages, is important because it explains the development of instrumentalist methodology.

32 The conversation between Schneider and Schumpeter is supposed to have taken place between 1929 and 1932 when they were together in Bonn.

33 I am grateful to Richard Swedberg for showing me Lachmann's memoir.

34 After receiving the Japanese translation, Schumpeter wrote to Takeyasu Kimura and Takuma Yasui. His letter, dated August 12, 1936, read in part as follows: "I looked upon it with mixed feelings. On the one hand, of course, I am delighted to see a contact established between myself and Japanese students. On the other hand, I have myself almost lost contact with that youthful performance of mine. I have never allowed a second German edition to appear, although the book has been out of print for more than twenty years. I hope to be able in another year or two to publish the results of my later thought in the field of economic theory, and much of it will sound rather differently from what I said in 1907" (Harvard University Archives, HUG(FP) 4.8, Box 2).

6 Static economics as an exact science

1 While today's economists rarely discuss *Wesen*, Wassily Leontief aptly characterizes its nature as follows: "Never translated or even republished, this remarkable book remains practically unknown in the English-speaking world and yet it contains the statement of his fundamental views which constitute the basis of Schumpeter's whole scientific *[W]eltanschauung*. Some of these were never restated again as explicitly or with so much *elan*. It is indicative of his turn of mind that the nearest approximation to exposition of the general principles of economics was undertaken by Schumpeter at the very beginning of his career. In a sense it is an inventory, but certainly not a stock-taking of finished products counted at the end of a working day. It is rather a survey of tools and material, a preliminary pilot study of the working processes" (Leontief 1950, 105).

2 This is not an example of Schumpeter's prejudice against Wieser. Erich Streissler writes: "Wieser was an opinionated and in many ways hopelessly confused man who must have infuriated many ... He also was a domineering figure, 'a priest in the service of truth,' as his successor, Mayer, said" (Streissler 1986, 85).

3 The following major articles (translated titles) were published in the 1906 issue of *Zeitschrift für Volkswirtschaft, Sozialpolitik und Verwaltung* (vol. 15), in which Schumpeter's essay appeared: "The Development of Commodity Transactions in Austria"; "On the Mathematical Method of Theoretical Economics" (by Schumpeter); "The Burden on Industry Posed by the Old Age Pension Scheme"; "The Current Outlook of World Economic Development"; "The Pensions of Private Employers"; "Practical Reform of the Austrian Administration"; "Reform of the Housing Tax"; "International Economic Situations"; "A Contribution to the Critique of the Marxian System"; "Professor Clark's Distribution Theory" (by Schumpeter); "The Recent Literature on Capital and Capital Interest"; "Schmoller's Economics"; "Income by Occupation and Status in Austria"; "The Origin of Capitalism in Western Jews in the Early Middle Ages"; "The Improvement of Alpine Stock Raising in Austria."

4 For the development of the general equilibrium theory, see Weintraub (1985, 1991).

5 See Negishi (1962) and Weintraub (1983). Cassel's study of a simplified version of Walras's theory was an overture to this tradition. Cassel's *Theoretische Sozialökonomie* (1918) was translated into English in 1923 and 1932.

6 There has been a growing literature on Austrian economics. See, for example, Littlechild (1990).

7 To be exact, Schumpeter calls utility function total value function (1908, 130) and limits value function to the marginal valuation. But he is not consistent: in one place (142–43) he defines value function as the relationship between the quantity of a good and the demand price (namely, demand function), and in another place (106) he defines it as the relationship between the quantity of a good and its marginal utility (namely, marginal utility function). I interpret his usage to mean that the most basic function is utility function, which he called value function.

8 Schumpeter (1954a, 917) records the name of the author of the term *opportunity cost* as D. I. Green (1894), coined during the discussion of the imputation problem. In today's economics the term *imputation* is completely forgotten, but *opportunity cost* survives.

9 In *History,* Schumpeter clearly talks about "marginal value (or utility) productivity": "Fundamentally, the Austrian marginal productivity was indeed a value productivity but one that did not presuppose the price of the product: it was not physical marginal productivity multiplied by any price but physical marginal productivity multiplied by some consumers' marginal utility" (1954a, 915).

10 For the controversy between Böhm-Bawerk and Schumpeter, see Böhm-Bawerk (1913a, 1913b) and Schumpeter (1913).

11 Samuelson, in a different place, examines the criticism that Lionel Robbins (1930) and Frank Knight (1935) leveled at Schumpeter (Samuelson 1943). According to him, Robbins was mistaken in claiming a positive rate of interest for a stationary state without a time preference. Knight asserted that even in a stationary state the marginal productivity of capital is not zero, but according to Samuelson nobody knows about the questions of technology.

12 See Schneider (1970, 19).

13 For the personality of Spann and Mayer, see Craver (1986).

7 The theory of economic development as a midpoint

1 Except for the part concerning the first and second propositions, the rest of the article became chapter 6 ("Das Wesen der Wirtschaftskrisen") of the first edition of *Entwicklung*. In the second edition, chapter 6 was rewritten and the title changed to "Der Zyklus der Konjunktur."

2 In a stationary economic process the values of prices and quantities remain constant given constant data, and in this case "*stationary flow* and *equilibrium* are analytically equivalent" (1939, 1, 42).

3 Elsewhere Schumpeter observed: "As a matter of history, it is to physiology and zoology – and not to mechanics – that our science is indebted for an analogous distinction which is at the threshold of all clear thinking about economic matters" (1939, 1, 37). In the *History of Economic Analysis* he pointed out that the distinction between statics and dynamics in economics was taken not from mechanics but from zoology, and he criticized John Stuart Mill for speaking of "a happy generalization of a mathematical phrase" (1954a, 417). Moreover, Schumpeter went

into the causes of the misunderstanding that the conceptual devices of statics and dynamics in economics were borrowed from mechanics: first, these devices plainly came from the more advanced physical sciences, and second, the mechanical analogy was very convenient for the diffusion of the devices (1954a, 965). Alfred Marshall's contrast between mechanical and biological analogy is well known: he claimed that the Mecca of the economist is economic biology rather than economic dynamics (Marshall 1898). In *Wesen*, Schumpeter rejected this idea because in statics the biological analogy was not relevant (1908, 537–38). Was it possible, then, for Schumpeter to accept Marshall's claim as far as dynamics was concerned? No, because Marshall's biological analogy visualized an economy as organic growth using trees as an example; this is not dynamics in the Schumpeterian sense.

4 Schumpeter distinguished between two types of hypotheses: theoretical hypotheses and historical hypotheses. See page 112.

5 The English translation of this sentence by Redvers Opie drops Schumpeter's famous rhetoric in German: "wie z. B. die Veränderung zwischen Postkutsche und Eisenbahn (for example, such changes as from a mail coach to a railway)" (1926a, 93–94).

6 Although Redvers Opie translated the general term "Neuerungen in der Wirtschaft" (1926a, 100) as "innovations in the economic system" (1934, 65), Schumpeter in *Entwicklung* used the term "new combinations" not "innovations" to denote the introduction of new goods, new methods of production, new markets, new sources of supply, and new organizations of industry. Indeed, regarding the production of new things, or of the same things by a different method, he explained that they meant to combine materials and forces differently (1934, 65). But, more generally, he defined production in the broadest sense as combination, referring to utilizing existing objects and processes (1934, 14). Fundamentally, he defined the activities of dynamic men as "creating new combinations of existing economic possibilities" (1912, 158). As Michio Morishima has pointed out (Morishima 1994,XX), while the English translators of Pareto's *Trattato di Sociologia Generale* (1916) adopted the term "combination" for the Italian *combinazione*, they noted that the Italian meaning is much more comprehensive than the English one; thus the instinct for combinations involves inventive faculties, ingeniousness, originality, imagination, and so on, representing the progressive element in human society (Pareto [1916] 1935, 2, 519). In *Business Cycles* Schumpeter introduced the term "innovation" (1939, 1, 84).

7 In *General Theory* Keynes treated the three fundamental psychological factors (the propensity to consume, the liquidity preference, and the marginal efficiency of capital), the rate of money wages, and the quantity of money as the ultimate independent variables determining national income and employment. His idea was that "our final task might be to select those variables which can be deliberately controlled or managed by central authority in the kind of system in which we actually live" (Keynes 1936, 247).

8 In the thirteenth letter (to Adam Smith) appended to Bentham's *Defence of Usury*, there is a description of projectors who have an adventurous spirit. Schumpeter probably meant this when he referred to Bentham's recognition of entrepreneurs. Bentham argued that projectors intending new things needed to borrow money, but the high interest rate would be a blow to them. Keynes once called the following quotation from Bentham "his finest passage" (Keynes 1936, 353): "The career of art, the great road which receives the footsteps of projectors, may be considered as a vast, and perhaps unbounded, plain, bestrewed with gulphs, such as Curtius was swallowed up in. Each requires a human victim to fall into it ere it can close, but when it once closes, it closes to open no more, and so much of the path is safe to those who follow" (Bentham [1787] 1952, 180). Whereas Schumpeter only compared successful entrepreneurs with imitators who followed, Bentham remarked that the sacrifice of numerous unsuccessful entrepreneurs made the work of imitators possible.

9 Reference can be made to Taymans (1949) on Tarde, Redlich (1955) on Bergson, Carlin (1956) and Macdonald (1971) on Weber, Santarelli and Pesciarelli (1990) on Nietzsche, and Morishima (1994) on Pareto.

10 For a comparison between Schumpeter and Keynes on money, see Vercelli (1985).

11 Later Schumpeter seemed to regret that he had not published the money book. Immediately after moving to the United States, he returned to his theory of money. At that time there was an advertisement of his forthcoming book on money by the Harvard University Press. In

Business Cycles, he indicated that he would bring out his book on money (1939, 1, 109). But because he could not complete the work to his satisfaction, he never published it. See Mann (1970) and Swedberg (1991a). See also Kulla (1989) and Stolper (1989) for a different view.

12 This was Mann's title. In Schumpeter's Bonn period, this book was announced as *Geld und Währung*.

13 For surveys of major achievements in this field, see Mensch (1979), Kamien and Schwartz (1982), Freeman (1983), Kleinknecht (1987), Dosi, Pavitt, and Soete (1990), Berry (1991), and Scherer (1992).

14 Schumpeter also referred to the Kuznets cycles (25 years) and the Wardwell cycles (15 years) but did not utilize them (1939, 1, 165).

15 *Business Cycles* does not give the dates of the Kondratieff cycles. Kuznets determined the chronology of the Kondratieffs, with Schumpeter's consent, as follows:

	Prosperity	Recession	Depression	Recovery
1st Kondratieff	1787–1800	1801–13	1814–27	1828–42
2nd Kondratieff	1843–57	1858–69	1870–84/85	1886–97
3rd Kondratieff	1898–1911	1912–24/25	1925/26–39	

16 Schumpeter wrote: "It should be emphasized once more that our model and its working is, of course, strongly institutional in character. It presupposes the presence, not only of the general features of capitalist society, but also of several others which we, no doubt, hold to be actually verified but which are not logically implied in the concepts either of economic action or of capitalism. Our argument rests on (abstractions from) historical facts which may turn out to belong to an epoch that is rapidly passing" (1939, 1, 144). Abstractions from history in terms of institutional change constitute Schumpeter's economic sociology.

17 The four propositions were the rise of a labor's political voice, the growth of white collar hostility to the bourgeoisie, the fall of precapitalistic strata that protected capitalist interests, the weakening of family ties, and the decay of the capitalist value scheme, and the formation of the anti-saving ideology.

18 Marschak had sent a draft of his book review of *Business Cycles* to Schumpeter beforehand asking for comments. The quotation is from Stolper (1994, 375–76), but "the logic of business cycles" in Stolper's quotation should read "the logic of the business organism."

19 In *Entwicklung* Schumpeter stated: "The more accurately we learn to know the natural and social world, the more perfect our control of facts becomes; and the greater the extent, with time and progressive rationalisation, within which things can be simply calculated, and indeed quickly and reliably calculated, the more the significance of this function decreases. Therefore the importance of the entrepreneur type must diminish just as the importance of the military commander has already diminished" (1934, 85–86). As we shall see in chapter 9, this argument traces back to his earlier description: "Long before we approach socialism, the entrepreneurs and the capitalist class as well as their major functions must recede in the same way that the significance of the nobility began to fade with the abolishment of the cavalry" (1920–21, 318).

8 A methodology of economic sociology

1 Referring to Tooke and Newmarch's *History of Prices* (1838–48) in the *History of Economic Analysis*, Schumpeter used the words *histoire raisonnée* to convey the meaning of "reasoned history" (1954a, 690). Viner pointed out that since the French words mean "conjectural history" (Viner 1954, 90), Schumpeter erred in his use of the term. But when Schumpeter discussed Werner Sombart's *Der Moderne Kapitalismus* (1902) elsewhere in *History*, he called it *histoire raisonnée* or systematized history with the accent on reasoning (1954a, 818). In view of Schumpeter's conviction that theory is nothing but conjecture or artifact, by "reasoned history" he actually meant "conjectural history." An economist at the highest level to whom Schumpeter attributed the term *histoire raisonnée* was Karl Marx: "He [Marx] was the first economist of top rank to see and to teach systematically how economic theory may be turned into historical analysis and how the historical narrative may be turned into *histoire raisonnée*" (1950a, 44). Schumpeter, with Schmoller in mind, added that the claim that Marx established the goal of the German Historical School could not be dismissed lightly.

2 Schumpeter's 1926 essay addressed the modern significance of Schmoller's work that was called "historical and ethical"; the first half of the essay dealt with ethics and the second with history. Whereas this chapter discusses the essay in connection with the problems of history and economic sociology, chapter 11 again takes it up to examine Schumpeter's beliefs regarding ethics and value judgments.

3 For an exception, see Osterhammel (1987). He regards both Schumpeter and Weber as nominalists and compares the former, who was influenced by Poincaré, with the latter, who was neo-Kantian.

4 Richard Swedberg argues that Schumpeter's 1926 essay provided an interpretation of Schmoller's work by the use of the term "*Sozialökonomik*," which he had borrowed from Weber (Swedberg 1991a, 66, 84–89). However, Schumpeter's intention there was to identify Schmoller's work as "economic sociology" and to present his own interpretation and definition. Contrary to Swedberg's claim, Schumpeter gave no substantial argument for *Sozialökonomik*. See also note 15 below.

5 In *Vergangenheit und Zukunft der Sozialwissenschaften*, Schumpeter wrote about the scientific approach to historical description in the eighteenth century as follows: "Historical materials step into the kingdom of scientific thinking when, on the one hand, they become the objects of applying scientific results, so that historical phenomena are analytically explained ... and when, on the other hand, historical raw materials become the basis of abstraction, so that regularities, which are more or less generally formulated, result directly from them and are based on them" (1915, 51–52).

6 R. A. Gordon summarizes the notion of institutional economics as follows: "Economic behavior is strongly conditioned by the institutional environment (in all its manifestations) within which economic activity takes place, and economic behavior in turn affects the institutional environment. This process of mutual interaction is an evolutionary one. The environment changes, and, as it does, so do the determinants of economic behavior. Hence the need for an 'evolutionary approach' to economics" (Gordon 1964, 124–25).

7 Agassi (1975) set forth the axis of psychologism versus institutionalism in addition to the traditional one of individualism versus holism in order to avoid extreme reductionism; from the combining the two axes he derives individualistic psychologism (traditional individualism), institutionalistic holism (traditional holism), holistic psychologism, and institutionalistic individualism. He argues that position (4) can deal with the interaction between individual actions and the influence of institutions on individuals.

8 For this typology, see Gerschenkron (1968, 77–78).

9 Schumpeter described Schmoller's approach, corresponding to the tripartite task of Schmoller, as follows: "If one wants to understand concrete situations of concrete nations and say something relevant about their concrete problems, all of what theoretical economics assumes as 'given' and thus is no longer concerned with *ex professo* (openly) ... becomes the main issues, the proper subject matter. The collection of facts becomes the [first] fundamental task, and their treatment becomes the prerequisite for all the rest. Classification and summarization of these facts is the second task. If one accomplishes this, even though only partially – it cannot be solved more definitely than the first task, and the work of collecting and arranging materials must continue indefinitely *pari passu* with the utilization of existing materials and the development of methods for their provision and handling – one can already answer many important questions directly. But, then [as the third task], there is a need for the analysis of technical relations, of the actual behavior of social groups and individuals, and of the nature and functions of social institutions such as state, property, and commercial law and so forth. From the totality of these analyses emerges the sociological and economic knowledge of an age, which one can try to weld together into a provisional synthesis" (1926b, 353–54).

10 Schmoller's major methodological writings appeared in Schmoller (1883, 1897, 1900 [Introduction], and 1911). For a critical evaluation of his methodology, see Shionoya (1989a, 1995).

11 The order of the six items here is not the same as Schumpeter's. Furthermore, he described viewpoint (4) as the "anti-rationalist point of view," which is not reasonable.

12 Two controversial dialogues between Weber and Schumpeter have been reported. One was

about socialism after the Russian revolution, the other about ideal type. See Tritsch (1953, 1955), Somary (1955), and Jaspers (1968).

13 In his 1904 essay on objectivity in the social sciences, Weber asserted, with Rickert, that there are infinitely many facts, and that it is, therefore, impossible to copy them all. Reality can only be constructed on the subjectively chosen value premises which highlight the specific aspects of reality that deserve scientific consideration. Value premises or value-relevance of the objects to be studied should be distinguished from value judgments. Whereas Rickert tried to justify the value-relevance by recourse to those general cultural values that are held by people in the society in which scientists live, Weber contended that value premises should be explicitly revealed on the basis of value freedom of scientists. A requirement of the objectivity of science should be found in the subjective efforts of scientists to realize the limitation of knowledge and reveal explicitly his own value premises.

14 In his article on "Capitalism" in the *Encyclopaedia Britannica*, Schumpeter wrote: "Some economists, among whom it must suffice to mention Max Weber, have felt the need of explaining the rise of capitalism by means of a special theory. But the problem such theories have been framed to solve is wholly imaginary and owes its existence to the habit of painting unrealistic pictures of a purely feudal and a purely capitalist society, which then raises the question what it was that turned the tradition-bound individual of the one into the alert profit hunter of the other. According to Weber, it was the religious revolution that, changing humanity's attitude toward life, produced a new spirit congenial to capitalist activity. We cannot go into the historical objections that may be raised against this theory. It is more important that the reader should realize that there is no problem" (1946a, 186). See also Schumpeter (1939, 1, 228).

15 Richard Swedberg asserts that Weber proposed to include economic theory, economic history, and economic sociology within the concept of *Sozialökonomik* as the solution to the *Methodenstreit* (however, Weber's attempt failed), and that Schumpeter, under the influence of Weber, worked within Weber's paradigm (Swedberg 1991a, 2; 1991b, 31–33). Schumpeter once used the term *Sozialökonomik* to mean economics, typically in his book *Epochen der Dogmen- und Methodengeschichte* (1914a), which was included in the series *Grundriss der Sozialökonomik* initiated by Max Weber as its editor. Chapter 1 of the book was entitled "Die Entwicklung der Sozialökonomik zur Wissenschaft" and section 1 "Die zwei Quelle der Sozialökonomik." Indeed, as his *History of Economic Analysis* indicates, Schumpeter's concept of economics and economic analysis is broad enough to include four areas (theory, history, statistics, and economic sociology) and may be interpreted as *Sozialökonomik*. In my view, however, Schumpeter specifically emphasized economic sociology rather than *Sozialökonomik*, economics in the broadest sense.

16 In this quotation I changed the English translation (edited by G. Roth and C. Wittich) of "methodischer Zweckmässigkeitsgrunde" from "methodological convenience" to "methodical convenience" and of "methodisches Mitte" from "methodological device" to "methodical device."

17 In this quotation I changed the English translation of "typisch gemeinter Sinn" from "typical subjective intentions" to "typical subjective meaning."

18 I changed the English translation of this quotation substantially. For Weber, "meaningfully adequate" and "causally adequate" are two requirements of correct theories. But the English translation of these sentences is not exact.

9 Economic sociology as an evolutionary science

1 According to Paul Sweezy (1951), Schumpeter in his later years counted as his major scientific writings four books, *Das Wesen und der Hauptinhalt der theoretischen Nationalökonomie, Theorie der wirtschaftlichen Entwicklung, Business Cycles,* and *Capitalism, Socialism and Democracy,* and two articles on imperialism and social classes. Needless to say, the posthumous *History of Economic Analysis* should be added to this list. Schumpeter attached importance to his two sociological pieces and moreover regarded them as distinct from his work on the transformation of capitalism into socialism represented by *Capitalism, Socialism and Democracy.* The two sociological articles are collected in *Aufsätze zur Soziologie* (1953); they are translated into English and edited in *Imperialism and Social Classes* (1951b).

2 Schumpeter also claimed the existence of a multiple-peaked social pyramid in feudal society: "The society of feudal times cannot be described in terms of knights and peasants any more than the society of capitalist times can be described in terms of capitalists and proletarians" (1954a, 74). Feudal society possessed classes of a bourgeois character whose origins were rooted in Roman industry, commerce, and finance; these classes had outgrown the framework of the feudal organization and established a commodity economy and towns. The church was another center of power.

3 O. H. Taylor criticized Sweezy for treating Schumpeter's system, though it consists of a two-part structure of economics and sociology, as a fully integrated, homogeneous, monolithic system. In the same place, Taylor mentioned that Schumpeter never explained how economics and sociology are related (Taylor 1951, 528–29), but, as we know, Schumpeter's view on this question appears in the exposition of four tools of economic analysis in his *History of Economic Analysis*.

4 Schumpeter thought that among Marx's theories the least valuable was the theory of social classes relating to class struggle (1954a, 439–40). But Schumpeter appreciated the fact that Marx's theory of social classes was linked with his economic interpretation of history. In 1924 he wrote: "Marx's theory of history is the first scientific theory of historical phenomena and is much more valuable even today, heuristically and systematically, than many adherents believe; it is not more materialistic than any other scientific thought … It maintains neither that economic self-interest is or must be the dominant motive of human behavior nor that the meaning of life and events is exhausted in the economy, but only that human mentality and social development find their sufficient explanation in economic relations and are shaped by them" (1924, 327). This interpretation did not change in his later writings: "The economic interpretation of history does not mean that men are, consciously or unconsciously, wholly or primarily, actuated by economic motives. On the contrary, the explanation of the role and mechanism of non-economic motives and the analysis of the way in which social reality mirrors itself in the individual psyches is an essential element of the theory and one of its most significant contributions" (1950a, 10–11).

5 Sweezy (1951, xxi) guessed that although the work Schumpeter called "Die Ideenseele des Sozialismus" did not appear under that title, part or all of its contents were published in his "Sozialistische Möglichkeiten von heute" (1920–21). But this is not known for certain.

6 Lenin's *Imperialism* was published in Russian in 1917 and in German and French in 1920. Therefore Schumpeter, who did not read Russian, did not have a chance to read Lenin before he published his own article on imperialism in 1918–19.

7 See Kautsky (1961) and Fletcher (1983). For a survey of Kautsky, Bernstein, and Schumpeter, see Semmel (1993).

8 For recent literature on fiscal sociology, see Musgrave (1980, 1992) and Backhaus (1994).

9 See Schumpeter (1920–21, 308; 1950a, 167, 415).

10 This is more than Schumpeter's vanity. With regard to the great success of Mrs. Jane Marcet's book in mid-nineteenth-century Britain, which he called economics for high-school girls, Schumpeter criticized the idea that the truth discovered in economics was so simple that it could be taught to schoolgirls. He added that a similar idea was also common among modern Keynesians (1954a, 477).

11 To use Joseph Agassi's words, this situation may be understood by institutional individualism. See chapter 8, note 7.

12 In Schumpeter's posthumously published manuscript "The March into Socialism," there is more comprehensive discussion about the fact that the observation in *Capitalism, Socialism and Democracy* was neither prophecy nor prediction (1950a, 416). He explained that his thesis was concerned with the consequences derived, on the basis of certain causal relations, from observable tendencies. These consequences are not a prediction of what will actually happen, because three conditions may change: first, factors other than those chosen for observation may appear; second, unlike astronomy, causal relations in a society may change; and third, existing tendencies may cease to work as a result of the balance between conflicting forces.

13 Richard Swedberg (1992) is one of a very small number of writers who claim that it is not fruitful to ask whether Schumpeter was right or wrong in his diagnosis of capitalism in

Capitalism, Socialism and Democracy, and that one should spotlight the concepts and methods that he introduced into his analysis of the evolution of institutional phenomena.

14 See Heertje (1981) and Coe and Wilber (1985).

10 The historical world of economics

1 Lionel Robbins remarked that there were two defects in the *History of Economic Analysis* (although they were not so serious as to detract importantly from its total achievement): undue length or discursiveness and overemphasis on certain scholars (Robbins 1955, 4–5).

2 Poincaré wrote: "The advance of science is not comparable to the changes of a city, where old edifices are pitilessly torn down to give place to new, but to the continuous evolution of zoologic types which develop ceaselessly and end by becoming unrecognizable to the common sight, but where an expert eye finds always traces of the prior work of the centuries past. One must not think then that the old-fashioned theories have been sterile and vain" (Poincaré [1905] 1929, 208).

3 Mach wrote: "We shall recognize also that not only a knowledge of the ideas that have been accepted and cultivated by subsequent teachers is necessary for the historical understanding of a science, but also that the rejected and transient thoughts of the inquirers, nay even apparently erroneous notions, may be very important and very instructive. The historical investigation of the development of a science is most needful, lest the principles treasured up in it become a system of half-understood prescripts, or worse, a system of prejudices. Historical investigation not only promotes the understanding of that which now is, but also brings new possibility before us, by showing that which exists to be in great measure conventional and accidental" (Mach [1883] 1960, 316).

4 For example, the following remarks are found in many places in the *History of Economic Analysis*: "Later on, especially in the sixteenth century, sociological and economic topics were treated within the system of scholastic jurisprudence" (1954a, 83). "Let us return to the classic period [of scholasticism], the thirteenth century, in order to search for elements of sociological and economic analysis" (1954a, 90). "All the facts presented above about eighteenth-century thought go to show that the natural-law approach to sociology and economics held its own to a considerable extent" (1954a, 141). "We simply recognize him [Marx] as a sociological and economic analyst whose propositions (theories) have the same methodological meaning and standing and have to be interpreted according to the same criteria as have the propositions of every other sociological and economic analyst" (1954a, 385). Clearly off the mark is the interpretation that in *History* Schumpeter pursued the genealogy of economic theory exclusively culminating in the formulation of general equilibrium by Walras.

5 The great figures among the Physiocrats were Quesnay, Cantillon, and Turgot. Schumpeter formulated a theory on the sociology of their scientific discovery and success. According to him, "Cantillon was the first to make this circular flow concrete and explicit, to give us a bird's-eye view of economic life. In other words, he was the first to draw a *tableau economique*" (1954a, 222). Thus he attributed the discovery of economic circulation not only to Quesnay but also to Cantillon. Regarding the *tableau,* Schumpeter emphasized that "most important, the Cantillon-Quesnay *tableau* was the first method ever devised in order to convey an explicit conception of the nature of economic equilibrium" (1954a, 242). In this connection he mentioned three criteria for attributing inventions to individuals: the scientific need for some tool; the idea of how to construct one; and the actual construction of the tool. Based on the view that the original perception of another man's work belongs to discovery, Schumpeter admitted that an essential part of the *tableau* was perceived through an analogy with the circulation of the blood in the human body discovered by William Harvey and credited to Quesnay's independence from Cantillon (1954a, 240).

6 Despite this scenario, Smith's place in *History* seems strange. In Part II, which deals with the development of economic analysis from the beginning to around 1790 when *Wealth of Nations* was accepted, Smith is located in chapter 3, section 4(e), before the description of the Physiocrats and mercantilism. As the editor of *History* noted (1954a, 181), Schumpeter removed the long account of Smith, including the Reader's Guide to the *Wealth of Nations,* from the manuscript. In restoring it, the editor did not insert it in the appropriate place. I

think it should have been located at the end of Part II, which would then conclude with the establishment of the first classical situation by Smith.

7 Although Schumpeter stated so in *History* (1954a, 232), he wrote in *Epochen* as follows: "In 1764 he [Smith] went with a fairly complete system to France where he established contact with the Physiocrats. In the serene years in Kirkcaldy he added those points in their system which we have described as essential to his own so that he burst its frame with the result that symmetry suffered seriously" ([1914a] 1954c, 66). In *Epochen*, since he marked an epoch by Quesnay, he might have had to regard Smith as succeeding Quesnay, although here Schumpeter meant that Smith was concerned with Quesnay's idea of productive and nonproductive labor, not with Quesnay's notion of the *tableau*.

8 By the criterion of the philosophy of science I mean that the general equilibrium theory was considered by Schumpeter as the complete economic model in the sense that it satisfied the requirements of the economy of thought, phenomenalism, and instrumentalism, as seen in chapter 5.

9 Robbins said that to discuss the whole history of economics from Plato and Aristotle to Adam Smith as one unit has two disadvantages: it tends to underestimate the achievements of Smith and Quesnay, and it tends to create a break between Smith and the Classical School (Robbins 1955, 6). According to Robbins, the arrangement of *Epochen*, which dealt with the discovery of Quesnay and Smith's economic system as a distinct period (excluding the earlier philosophers, consultant administrators, and pamphleteers) was superior. I disagree. In my view, as a result of that arrangement, *Epochen* failed to show the synthesis of developments from Quesnay to Smith.

10 If Schumpeter had read Strachey's essay on Nightingale in *Eminent Victorians*, he might have been delighted to find the following sentence: "The force that created was the force that destroyed" (Strachey [1918] 1948, 149).

11 Value judgments and political economy

1 In *Das Wesen des Geldes*, Schumpeter wrote: "A physician can make his prescriptions without having to add, each time, 'if you wish to become well,' because the criteria for the condition which we characterize as one of health apply to the great majority of people, and this majority has the desire to be 'well,' as defined by these criteria. In the same way, the economist could speak of right and wrong measures, and of good and bad currency conditions, without further explanation, if the goals set by people were in fact sufficiently similar to one another: the gulf of principle between the realm of analysis and that of volition would not disappear as a result of this, but its significance for the work of science and of practice would disappear if everybody wanted the same thing" ([1970] 1991, 511–12).

2 For Schumpeter's political life, see März (1983), Schumpeter (1985, 1992), Allen (1991), and Stolper (1994).

3 Bauer's *Der Weg zum Sozialismus* (1919) became the fundamental text on the socialization program.

4 Both quotations are from Mill's preface to the third edition (1852) of *Principles* (Mill [1848] 1965, 1, xciii).

5 There are, however, a few exceptions. See Solterer (1951), Cramer and Leathers (1981) and Stolper (1994).

6 For neocorporatism, see Schmitter and Lehmbruch (1979) and Lehmbruck and Schmitter (1982).

7 See Nell-Breuning (1977).

8 It is interesting to recall that John Maynard Keynes, in *The End of Laissez-Faire* (1926), proposed "a return towards medieval conceptions of separate autonomies," similarly groping for a middle position between individualism and socialism. Keynes wrote: "I believe that in many cases the ideal size for the unit of control and organisation lies somewhere between the individual and the modern State. I suggest, therefore, that progress lies in the growth and the recognition of semi-autonomous bodies within the State – bodies whose criterion of action within their own field is solely the public good as they understand it, and from whose deliberations motives of private advantage are excluded, though some place it may still be

necessary to leave, until the ambit of men's altruism grows wider, to the separate advantage of particular groups, classes, or faculties – bodies which in the ordinary course of affairs are mainly autonomous within their prescribed limitations, but are subject in the last resort to the sovereignty of the democracy expressed through Parliament" (Keynes [1926] 1972, 288–89). However, since Keynes found, after all, the remedy for capitalism in a macroeconomic demand management policy, this idea did not bear fruit in his political economy.

12 Conclusion: Schumpeterian synthesis

1   Regarding this point, Schumpeter quoted an episode from Goethe's *Gespräch mit Eckermann*: "During a meal, the ladies praised a portrait by a young artist. 'Wonderful!' they said, then added, 'He learned everything by himself.' This was quite obvious from a hand wrongly drawn breaking the rules. Goethe said, 'Yes, this young man has a talent. But we should not praise him because he has learned everything by himself; instead, we should blame him for that. A talent is born not to be left by himself, but to turn to techniques and good masters who will make him somebody'" (December 13, 1826). Should Schumpeter have turned to "good masters" to learn analytic techniques?

2   *Harvard Crimson*, April 11, 1944.

3   For the coherence theory, see Rescher (1973) and Lehrer (1974).

References

Agassi, Joseph. 1975. Institutional Individualism. *British Journal of Sociology* 26.2: 144–55.

Allen, Robert Loring. 1991. *Opening Doors: the Life and Work of Joseph Schumpeter*, 2 vols. New Brunswick: Transaction Publishers.

Augello, Massimo M. 1990. *Joseph Alois Schumpeter: a Reference Guide*. Berlin-Heidelberg: Springer-Verlag.

Backhaus, Jürgen G. 1994. The Concept of the Tax State in Modern Public Finance Analysis. In Yuichi Shionoya and Mark Perlman, eds., 1994, 65–94.

Barnes, Barry. 1974. *Scientific Knowledge and Sociological Theory*. London: Routledge & Kegan Paul.

Bauer, Otto. 1919. *Der Weg zum Sozialismus*. Vienna: Wiener Volksbuchhandlung.

Bentham, Jeremy. 1787. *Defence of Usury*. In W. Stark, ed., *Jeremy Bentham's Economic Writings*, vol. I, 121–207. London: George Allen & Unwin, 1952.

Berner, P., Brix, E., and Mantl, W., eds. 1986. *Wien um 1900: Aufbruch in der Moderne*. Vienna: Verlag für Geschichte und Politik.

Berry, Brian J. L. 1991. *Long-Wave Rhythms in Economic Development and Political Behavior*. Baltimore: Johns Hopkins University Press.

Birkhoff, G. D., and Lewis, D. C. Jr. 1935. Stability in Causal Systems. *Philosophy of Science* 2.3: 304–33.

Blackmore, J. T. 1972. *Ernst Mach: his Life, Work and Influence*. Berkeley: University of California Press.

Blaug, Mark. 1976. Kuhn versus Lakatos or Paradigm versus Research Programmes in the History of Economics. In S. J. Latsis, ed., *Method and Appraisal in Economics*, 149–80. Cambridge, UK: Cambridge University Press.

1980. *The Methodology of Economics: or How Economists Explain*. Cambridge, UK: Cambridge University Press.

Bloor, David. 1976. *Science and Social Imagery*. London: Routledge & Kegan Paul.

Böhm-Bawerk, Eugen von. 1913a. Eine "dynamische" Theorie des Kapitalzinses. *Zeitschrift für Volkswirtschaft, Sozialpolitik und Verwaltung* 22: 1–62. Reprinted in his *Kleinere Abhandlungen über Kapital und Zins*, Franz X. Weiss, ed. 520–85. Vienna: Hölder-Pichler-Tempsky, 1926.

1913b. Eine "dynamische" Theorie des Kapitalzinses: Schlussbemerkungen. *Zeitschrift für Volkswirtschaft, Sozialpolitik und Verwaltung* 22: 640–56.

Boland, Lawrence A. 1979. A Critique of Friedman's Critics. *Journal of Economic Literature* 17.2: 503–22.

1982. *The Foundations of Economic Method*. London: George Allen & Unwin.

Bös, Dieter, and Stolper, Hans-Dieter, eds. 1984. *Schumpeter oder Keynes? Zur Wirtschafts-politik der neunziger Jahre*. Berlin: Springer-Verlag.

Bottomore, Tom. 1992. *Between Marginalism and Marxism: The Economic Sociology of J. A. Schumpeter*. New York: Harvester Wheatsheaf.

Bottomore, Tom, and Goode, Patrick, eds. 1978. *Austro-Marxism*. Oxford: Clarendon Press.

Bourdieu, Pierre. 1975. The Specificity of the Scientific Field and the Social Conditions of the Progress of Reason. *Social Scientific Information* 14.6: 19–47.

1977. *Outline of a Theory of Practice*. Richard Nice, trans. Cambridge, UK: Cambridge University Press.

1984. *Distinction: a Social Critique of the Judgement of Taste*. Richard Nice, trans. Cambridge, Mass.: Harvard University Press.

1985. The Genesis of the Concepts of *Habitus* and of Field. *Sociocriticism* 2: 11–24.

1990a. *The Logic of Practice*. Richard Nice, trans. Stanford, Calif.: Stanford University Press.

1990b. *In Other Words: Essays towards a Reflective Sociology*. Mathew Adamson, trans. Stanford, Calif.: Stanford University Press.

1993. *The Field of Cultural Production: Essays on Art and Literature*. Randal Johnson, ed. New York: Columbia University Press.

Bradley, J. 1971. *Mach's Philosophy of Science*. London: Athlone Press.

Brouwer, Maria. 1991. *Schumpeterian Puzzles: Technological Competition and Economic Evolution*. New York: Harvester Wheatsheaf.

Caldwell, Bruce J. 1982. *Beyond Positivism: Economic Methodology in the Twentieth Century*. London: George Allen & Unwin.

1984, ed. *Appraisal and Criticism in Economics: A Book of Readings*. Boston: Allen & Unwin.

1992. Friedman's Predictivist Instrumentalism: A Modification. *Research in the History of Economic Thought and Methodology* 10: 119–28.

1993, ed. *The Philosophy and Methodology of Economics*, 3 vols. Aldershot: Edward Elgar.

Carlin, Edward A. 1956. Schumpeter's Constructed Type: The Entrepreneur. *Kyklos* 9.1: 27–43.

Cassel, Gustav. 1918. *Theoretische Sozialökonomie*. Leipzig: C. F. Winter. (*The Theory of Social Economy*. S. L. Barron, trans. London: T. F. Unwin, 1923; new revised ed. London : E. Benn, 1932.)

Clark, John Bates. 1907. *The Essentials of Economic Theory*. New York: Macmillan.

1909. Book Review of J. A. Schumpeter, *Das Wesen und der Hauptinhalt der theoretischen Nationalökonomie*. *Political Science Quarterly* 24.4: 721–24.

Coats, A. W. 1976. Economics and Psychology: The Death and Resurrection of a Resarch Programme. In S. J. Latsis, ed., *Method and Appraisal in Economics*, 43–64. Cambridge, UK: Cambridge University Press.

1984. The Sociology of Knowledge and the History of Economics. *Research in History of Economic Thought and Methodology* 2: 211–34.

Coe, Richard D., and Wilber, Charles K., eds. 1985. *Capitalism and Democracy: Schumpeter Revisited.* Notre Dame, Ind.: University of Notre Dame Press.

Cohen, Robert S., and Seeger, Raymond J. eds. 1970. *Ernst Mach: Physicist and Philosopher.* Dordrecht: D. Reidel Publishing Co.

Cramer, D. L. and C. G. Leathers. 1981. Schumpeter's Corporatist Views: Links among his Social Theory, *Quadragesimo Anno,* and Moral Reform. *History of Political Economy* 13.4: 745–71.

Craver, Earlene. 1986. The Emigration of the Austrian Economists. *History of Political Economy* 18.1: 1–32.

Date, Kuniharu. 1983. Schumpeter's First Wife (in Japanese). *Economic Seminar,* Supplement: 31.

Davis, H. B. 1960. Schumpeter as Sociologist. *Science and Society* 24.1: 13–35.

Dosi, G., Pavitt, K. and Soete, L., eds. 1990. *The Economics of Technical Change and International Trade.* Hemel Hempstead: Harvester Wheatsheaf.

Duhem, Pierre. 1906. *La théorie physique: son objet et sa structure,* 2nd edn. Paris: Chevalier et Rivière, 1914. (*The Aim and Structure of Physical Theory.* Philip P. Wiener, trans. New York: Atheneum, 1962.)

Dyer, Alan W. 1988. Schumpeter as an Economic Radical: an Economic Sociology Assessed. *History of Political Economy* 20.1: 27–41.

Edgeworth, Francis Y. 1881. *Mathematical Psychics.* London: C. Kegan Paul & Co.

Elliott, John E. 1983. Introduction to the Transaction Edition. In J. A. Schumpeter, *The Theory of Economic Development,* vii–lix. New Brunswick, N.J.: Transaction Books.

Feyerabend, Paul K. 1975. *Against Method: Outline of an Anarchistic Theory of Knowledge.* London: Verso.

  1981. *Realism, Rationalism and Scientific Method: Philosophical Papers.* Vol. I. Cambridge, UK: Cambridge University Press.

Fletcher, R. A. 1983. Cobden as Educator: The Free Trade Internationalism of Eduard Bernstein, 1899–1914. *American Historical Review* 88.3: 561–78.

Freeman, Christopher, ed. 1983. *Long Waves in the World Economy.* London: Butterworth & Co.

Friedman, Milton. 1953. The Methodology of Positive Economics. In his *Essays in Positive Economics,* 3–43. Chicago: University of Chicago Press.

  1969. *The Optimum Quantity of Money and Other Essays.* Chicago: Aldine Publishing Co.

Frisch, Helmut, ed. 1982. *Schumpeterian Economics.* New York: Praeger.

Galbraith, John K. 1977. Near or Far Right. *New Society* 40.758: 74–75.

Gerschenkron, Alexander. 1968. The Typology of Industrial Development as a Tool of Analysis. In his *Continuity in History and Other Essays,* 77–97. Cambridge, Mass.: Harvard University Press.

Giedymin, Jerzy. 1976. Instrumentalism and its Critique: a Reappraisal. In R. S. Cohen, P. K. Feyerabend, and M. W. Wartofsky, eds., *Essays in Memory of Imre Lakatos,* Boston Studies in the Philosophy of Science, vol. 39, 179–208. Dordrecht: Reidel.

  1982. *Science and Convention: Essays on Henri Poincaré's Philosophy of Science and the Conventionalist Tradition.* Oxford: Pergamon Press.

  1991. Geometrical and Physical Conventionalism of Henri Poincaré in Epistemological Formulation. *Studies in History and Philosophy of Science* 22.1: 1–22.

Giersch, Herbert. 1984. The Age of Schumpeter. *American Economic Review* 74.2: 103–8.

Goldscheid, Rudolf. 1917. *Staatssozialismus oder Staatskapitalismus: ein finanzsoziologischer Beitrag zur Lösung des Staatsschuldenproblem.* Vienna: Anzengruber.

Goodwin, Richard M. 1983. Schumpeter: The Man I Knew. *Ricerche Economiche* 37.4: 606–13.

Gordon, R. A. 1964. Institutional Elements in Contemporary Economics. In Joseph Dorfman *et al., Institutional Economics: Veblen, Commons, and Mitchell Reconsidered,* 123–47. Berkeley: University of California Press.

Greene, M. 1952. Schumpeter's Imperialism: a Critical Note. *Social Research* 19.4: 453–63.

Haberler, Gottfried. 1951a. Joseph Alois Schumpeter, 1883–1950. In S. E. Harris, ed., 1951, 24–47.

    1951b. Schumpeter's Theory of Interest. In S. E. Harris, ed., 1951, 72–78.

    1981. Schumpeter's *Capitalism, Socialism and Democracy* after Forty Years. In Arnold Heertje, ed., 1981, 69–94.

Haberler, G., Harris, S. E., Leontief, W. W., and Mason, E. S. 1951. Professor Joseph A. Schumpeter: Minute, Faculty of Arts and Sciences, Harvard University. In S. E. Harris, ed., 1951, ix–x.

Hanson, Norwood Russel. 1958. *Patterns of Discovery.* Cambridge, UK: Cambridge University Press.

Harris, S. E., ed. 1951. *Schumpeter: Social Scientist.* Cambridge, Mass.: Harvard University Press.

Hausman, Daniel M., ed. 1984. *The Philosophy of Economics: An Anthology.* Cambridge, UK: Cambridge University Press.

Hayek, Friedrich A. von. 1929. Friedrich Freiherr von Wieser. In Friedrich Wieser, 1929, v–xxiii.

    1937. Economics and Knowledge. *Economica* 4.13: 33–54. Reprinted in his *Individualism and Economic Order,* 33–56. London: Routledge & Kegan Paul, 1949.

    1952. *The Counter-Revolution of Science: Studies on the Abuse of Reason.* Indianapolis: Liberty Press.

    1976. *Law, Legislation and Liberty,* vol. 2, *The Mirage of Social Justice.* London: Routlege & Kegan Paul.

    1994. *Hayek on Hayek: An Autobiographical Dialogue.* Stephen Kresge and Leif Wenar, eds. Chicago: University of Chicago Press.

Heertje, Arnold, ed. 1981. *Schumpeter's Vision: Capitalism, Socialism and Democracy after 40 Years.* New York: Praeger.

Helburn, S. W., and Bramhall, D. F., eds. 1986. *Marx, Schumpeter, and Keynes: A Centenary Celebration of Dissent.* Armonk, N.Y.: M. E. Sharpe.

Hicks, John R. 1959. A "Value and Capital" Growth Model. *Review of Economic Studies* 26.3: 159–73.

    1974. *The Crisis of Keynesian Economics.* Oxford: Basil Blackwell.

    1976. 'Revolution' in Economics. In S. J. Latsis, ed., *Method and Appraisal in Economics,* 207–18. Cambridge, UK: Cambridge University Press.

Hilferding, Rudolf. 1910. *Das Finanzkapital: eine Studie über die jüngste Entwicklung des*

Kapitalismus. Vienna: Wiener Volksbuchhandlung. (*Finance Capital: a Study of the Latest Phase of Capitalist Development*. Morris Walnick and Sam Gordon, trans. London: Routledge & Kegan Paul, 1981.)

Hobson, John Atkinson. 1902. *Imperialism: A Study*. London: Nisbet.

Hutchison, T. W. 1938. *The Significance and Basic Postulates of Economic Theory*. London: Macmillan.

1981. *The Politics and Philosophy of Economics: Marxians, Keynesians and Austrians*. Oxford: Basil Blackwell.

Iggers, George G. 1983. *The German Conception of History*. Rev. edn. Middletown, Conn.: Wesleyan University Press.

Jaffé, William. 1976. Menger, Jevons and Walras De-homogenized. *Economic Inquiry* 14.4: 511–24.

1983. *William Jaffé's Essays on Walras*. Donald A. Walker, ed. Cambridge, UK: Cambridge University Press.

Janik, Allan, and Toulmin, Stephen. 1973. *Wittgenstein's Vienna*. New York: Simon & Schuster.

Jaspers, Karl. 1962. *Bemerkungen zu Max Webers politischen Denken*. Reprinted in his *Aneignung und Polemik: Gesammelten Reden und Aufsätze zur Geschichte der Philosophie*, Hans Saner, ed. Munich: R. Piper & Co. 1968. (*Karl Jaspers on Max Weber*, Robert J. Whelan, trans. 163–82. New York: Paragon House, 1989.)

Johnston, William M. 1972. *The Austrian Mind: An Intellectual and Social History, 1848–1938*. Berkeley: University of California Press.

Kamien, Morton I., and Schwartz, Nancy L. 1982. *Market Structure and Innovation*. Cambridge, UK: Cambridge University Press.

Kauder, Emil. 1957. Intellectual and Political Roots of the Older Austrian School. *Zeitschrift für Nationalökonomie* 17: 411–25.

1965. *A History of Marginal Utility Theory*. Princeton: Princeton University Press.

Kautsky, John H. 1961. Schumpeter and Karl Kautsky: Parallel Theories of Imperialism. *Midwest Journal of Political Science* 5.2: 101–28.

Keynes, John Maynard. 1923. *A Tract on Monetary Reform*. London: Macmillan. *The Collected Writings of John Maynard Keynes*, vol. 4, 1972.

1924. Alfred Marshall, 1842–1924. *Economic Journal* 34.135: 311–72. Reprinted in *The Collected Writings of John Maynard Keynes*, vol. 10, 1972.

1926. *The End of Laissez-Faire*. London: Hogarth Press. *The Collected Writings of John Maynard Keynes*, vol. 9, 1972.

1930. *A Treatise on Money*, 2 vols. London: Macmillan. *The Collected Writings of John Maynard Keynes*, vols. 5 & 6, 1971.

1933. *Essays in Biography*. London: Macmillan. *The Collected Writings of John Maynard Keynes*, vol. 10, 1972.

1936. *The General Theory of Employment, Interest and Money*. London: Macmillan. *The Collected Writings of John Maynard Keynes*, vol. 7, 1973.

Keynes, John Neville. 1890. *The Scope and Method of Political Economy*, 4th ed. London: Macmillan, 1917.

Khan, M. S. 1957. *Schumpeter's Theory of Capitalist Development*. Aligarh, India: Mustin University Press.

Kirchhoff, Gustav Robert. 1876. *Vorlesungen über mathematische Physik*, vol. 1, *Mechanik*. Leipzig: B. G. Teubner.

Kleinknecht, Alfred. 1987. *Innovation Patterns in Crisis and Prosperity: Schumpeter's Long Cycle Reconsidered*. New York: St. Martin's Press.

Knight, Frank H. 1935. Statics and Dynamics. In his *The Ethics of Competition and Other Essays*, 161–85. New York: Augustus M. Kelley.

Knorr-Cetina, Karin D., and Mulkay, Michael. 1983. Introduction: Emerging Principles in Social Studies of Science. In K. D. Knorr-Cetina and M. Mulkay, eds., *Science Observed: Perspectives on the Social Study of Science*, 1–18, London: Sage Publications.

Kordig, Carl R. 1978. Discovery and Justification. *Philosophy of Science* 45: 110–17.

Koyré, Alexandre. 1956. Concept and Experience in Newton's Scientific Thought. Reprinted in his *Newtonian Studies*, 25–52. Chicago: University of Chicago Press, 1965.

Kuhn, Thomas S. 1962. *The Structure of Scientific Revolutions*, 2nd edn. Chicago: University of Chicago Press, 1970.

Kulla, Bernd. 1989. Spiethoff, Schumpeter und »*Das Wesen des Geldes*«. *Kyklos* 42.3: 431–34.

Kuznets, Simon. 1940. Schumpeter's Business Cycles. *American Economic Review* 30.2: 257–71. Reprinted in his *Economic Change: Selected Essays in Business Cycles, National Income, and Economic Growth*, 105–24. New York: Norton, 1953.

Lachmann, Ludwig M. 1986. *The Market as an Economic Process*. Oxford: Basil Blackwell.

Lakatos, Imre. 1970. Falsification and the Methodology of Scientific Research Programmes. In I. Lakatos and A. Musgrave, eds., *Criticism and the Growth of Knowledge*, 91–196. London: Cambridge University Press. Reprinted in Lakatos, *The Methodology of Scientific Research Programmes*, Philosophical Papers, vol. 1, 8–101. Cambridge, UK: Cambridge University Press, 1978.

   1971. History of Science and its Rational Reconstructions. In R. C. Buck and R. S. Cohen, eds., *PSA 1970: In Memory of Rudolf Carnap*, Boston Studies in the Philosophy of Science, vol. 8, 91–135. Dordrecht: Reidel. Reprinted in Lakatos, *The Methodology of Scientific Research Programmes*, Philosophical Papers, vol. 1, 102–38. Cambridge, UK: Cambridge University Press, 1978.

Lange, Oscar. 1941. Book Review of J. A. Schumpeter, *Business Cycles*. *Review of Economic Statistics* 23.4: 190–93.

Laudan, Larry. 1981. Ernst Mach's Opposition to Anatomism. In his *Science and Hypothesis: Historical Essays on Scientific Methodology*, 202–25. Dordrecht: Reidel.

Lehmbruch, Gerhard, and Schmitter, Philippe C., eds. 1982. *Patterns of Corporatist Policy Making*. London: Sage Publications.

Lehnis, Felix. 1960. *Der Beitrag des späten Schumpeter zur Konjunkturforschung*. Stuttgart: Gustav Fischer Verlag.

Lehrer, K. 1974. *Knowledge*. Oxford: Clarendon Press.

Lenin, V. I. 1917. *Imperialism: The Highest Stage of Capitalism*. New York: International Publishers, 1939.

Leontief, Wassily. Joseph A. Schumpeter (1883–1950). *Econometrica* 18.2: 103–10.

Leplin, Jarrett, ed. 1984. *Scientific Realism*. Berkeley: University of California Press.

Levin, Michael. 1984. What kind of Explanation is Truth? In J. Leplin, ed., *Scientific Realism*, 124–39. Berkeley: University of California Press.

Littlechild, Stephen, ed. 1990. *Austrian Economics*, 3 vols. Aldershot: Edward Elgar.

Macdonald, Ronan. 1971. Schumpeter and Max Weber: Central Visions and Social Theories. In Peter Kilby, ed., *Entrepreneurship and Economic Development*, 71–94. New York: Free Press.

Mach, Ernst. [1882]. Die ökonomischen Natur der physikalischen Forschung. In his *Populär-wissenschaftliche Vorlesungen*, 203–30. Leipzig: Johann Ambrosius Barth, 1896a. (The Economic Nature of Physical Inquiry. In his *Popular Scientific Lectures*, 186–213. T. J. McCormack, trans. Chicago: Open Court Publishing Co., 1898.)

    1883. *Die Mechanik in ihrer Entwicklung: historisch-kritisch dargestellt*, 9th edn. Wiesbaden: Verlag F. A. Brockhaus, 1933. (*The Science of Mechanics: A Critical and Historical Account of Its Development by Ernst Mach*. T. J. McCormack, trans. La Salle, Ill.: Open Court Publishing Co., 1960.)

    1896b. *Die Principien der Wärmelehre: historich-kritisch entwickelt*, 3rd edn. Leipzig: J. A. Barth, 1919.

Machlup, Fritz. 1951. Schumpeter's Economic Methodology. In S. E. Harris, ed., 1951, 95–101.

    1955. The Problem of Verification in Economics. *Southern Economic Journal* 22: 1–21.

    1963. Problems of Methodology: Introductory Remarks. *American Economic Review* 53.2: 204.

    1978. *Methodology of Economics and Other Social Sciences*. New York: Academic Press.

Mäki, Uskali. 1992. Social Conditioning of Economics. In Neil de Marchi, ed., *Post-Popperian Methodology of Economics: Recovering Practice*, 65–104. Boston: Kluwer Academic Publishers.

Mann, Michael. 1986. *The Sources of Social Power*, vol. I. *A History of Power from the Beginning to AD 1760*. Cambridge, UK: Cambridge University Press.

Mannheim, Karl. 1925. Das Problem einer Soziologie des Wissens. *Archiv für Sozialwissenschaft und Sozialpolitik* 53. Reprinted in his *Wissenssoziologie*. Berlin: Luchterhand, 1964. (The Problem of a Sociology of Knowledge. In his *Essays on the Sociology of Knowledge*, P. Kecskemeti, trans. 134–90. London: Routledge & Kegan Paul, 1952.)

    1931. Wissenssoziologie. In A. Vierkandt, ed., *Handwörterbuch der Soziologie*, 659–80. Stuttgart: Ferdinand Enke. (The Sociology of Knowledge. In his *Ideology and Utopia*, L. Wirth and E. Shils, trans. 237–80. London: Routlege & Kegan Paul, 1936.)

Marget, Arthur W. 1951. The Monetary Aspects of Schumpeterian System. In S. E. Harris, ed., 1951, 62–71.

Marschak, Jacob. 1940. Book Review of J. A. Schumpeter, *Business Cycles*. *Journal of Political Economy* 48.6: 889–94.

Marshall, Alfred. 1890. *Principles of Ecnomics: an Introductory Volume*, 9th edn. London: Macmillan, 1961.

    1898. Mechanical and Biological Analogies in Economics. In A. C. Pigou, ed., *Memorials of Alfred Marshall*, 312–18. London: Macmillan.

Marx, Karl, and Engels, Friedrich. 1845–46. *Die Deutsche Ideologie*. (*The German Ideology*, R. Pascal, ed. New York: International Publishers, 1939.)

März, Eduard. 1983. *Joseph Alois Schumpeter: Forscher, Lehrer und Politiker.* Munich: R. Oldenbourg Verlag. (*Joseph Schumpeter: Scholar, Teacher and Politician.* New Haven: Yale University Press, 1991.)

Mayer, Hans. 1911. Eine neue Grundlegung der theoretischen Nationalökonomie. *Zeitschrift für Volkswirtschaft, Sozialpolitik und Verwaltung* 20: 181–209.

McCrea, R. C. 1913. Schumpeter's Economic System. *Quarterly Journal of Economics* 27.3: 520–29.

Meiners, R. E., and C. Nardinelli. 1986. What has Happened to the New Economic History? *Journal of Institutional and Theoretical Economics* 142.3: 510–27.

Meja, V., Misgeld, D., and Stehr, N., eds. 1987. *Modern German Sociology.* New York: Columbia University Press.

Menger, Carl. 1871. *Grundsätze der Volkswirtschaftslehre,* 2nd edn. Vienna: Wilhelm Braumüller, 1923. (*Principles of Economics.* J. Dingwall and B. F. Hoselitz, trans. New York: New York University Press, 1981.)

1883. *Untersuchungen über die Methode der Sozialwissenschaften und der Politischen Ökonomie insbesondere.* Leipzig: Duncker & Humblot. (*Investigations into the Method of the Social Sciences with Special Reference to Economics.* Francis J. Nock, trans. New York: New York University Press, 1985.)

1884. *Die Irrthümer des Historismus in der deutschen Nationalökonomie.* Vienna: Alfred Hölder.

Mensch, Gerhard. 1979. *Stalemate in Technology.* Cambridge, Mass.: Ballinger.

Mill, John Stuart. 1843. *A System of Logic. Collected Works of John Stuart Mill,* vols. 7 & 8. John M. Robson, ed. Toronto: University of Toronto Press, 1973.

1848. *Principles of Political Economy, with Some of Their Applications to Social Philosophy. Collected Works of John Stuart Mill,* vols. 2 & 3. John M. Robson, ed. Toronto: University of Toronto Press, 1965.

Minsky, Hyman P. 1992. Commentary to Yuichi Shionoya. In F. M. Scherer and M. Perlman, eds., *Entrepreneurship, Technological Innovation, and Economic Growth: Studies in the Schumpeterian Tradition,* 263–70. Ann Arbor: University of Michigan Press.

Mises, Ludwig von. 1949. *Human Action: A Treatise on Economics.* London: William Hodge.

1978. *Erinnerungen von Ludwig von Mises.* Stuttgart: Gustav Fisher Verlag. (*Notes and Recollections.* Hans F. Sennholz, trans. South Holland, Ill.: Libertarian Press, 1978.)

Mittermaier, K. H. M. 1992. Ludwig Lachmann (1906–1990): A Biographical Sketch. *South African Journal of Economics* 60.1: 7–23.

Morgan, Theodore. 1983. Letter to *The Economist,* 24 December 1983.

Morgenbesser, Sidney. 1969. The Realist-instrumentalist Controversy. In S. Morgenbesser, P. Suppes, and M. White, eds., *Philosophy, Science, and Method,* 200–18. New York: St. Martin's Press.

Morgenstern, Oskar. 1951. Obituary: Joseph A. Schumpeter, 1883–1950. *Economic Journal* 61.241: 197–202.

Morishima, Michio. 1994. Foreword. In Alfonso de Pietri-Tonelli and Georges H. Bousquet, *Vilfredo Pareto: Neoclassial Synthesis of Economics and Sociology,* xi–xxvi. London: Macmillan.

Mosca, Gaetano. 1896. *Elementi di Scienza Politica.* (*The Ruling Class.* H. D. Kahn, trans. New York: McGraw Hill, 1939.)

Moss, Laurence S., ed. 1996. *Joseph A. Schumpeter, Historian of Economics.* London: Routledge.

Mulkay, M. 1979. *Science and the Sociology of Knowledge.* London: George Allen & Unwin.

Müller, Klaus O. W. 1990. *Joseph A. Schumpeter: Ökonom der neuziger Jahre.* Berlin: Erich Schmidt Verlag.

Musgrave, Richard A. 1980. Theories of Fiscal Crisis: An Essay in Fiscal Sociology. In H. J. Aaron and M. J. Boskin, eds., *The Economics of Taxation*, 361–90. Washington D.C.: The Brookings Institution.

——— 1992. Schumpeter's Crisis of the Tax State: An Essay in Fiscal Sociology. *Journal of Evolutionary Economics* 2.2: 89–113.

Naderer, Bärbel. 1990. *Die Entwicklung der Geldtheorie Joseph A. Schumpeters: Statische und dynamische Theorie des Geldes im kapitalistischen Marktsystem.* Berlin: Duncker & Humblot.

Nagel, Ernst. 1961. *The Structure of Science: Problems in the Logic of Scientific Explanation.* New York: Harcourt, Brace & Co.

Negishi, Takasi. 1962. The Stability of a Competitive Economy: A Survey Article. *Econometrica* 30.4: 635–69.

Nell-Breuning, Oswald von. 1977. *Soziallehre der Kirche.* Vienna: Katholische Sozialakademie.

Newton, Isaac. 1713. Scholium Generale. In I. Bernard Cohen, *Introduction to Newton's "Principia."* Cambridge, Mass.: Harvard University Press, 1971.

Oakes, Guy. 1988. *Weber and Rickert: Concept Formation in the Cultural Sciences.* Cambridge, Mass.: MIT Press.

Oakley, Allen. 1990. *Schumpeter's Theory of Capitalist Motion: A Critical Exposition and Reassessment.* Aldershot: Edward Elgar.

O'Driscoll, Jr., G. P., and Rizzo, M. J. 1985. *The Economics of Time and Ignorance.* Oxford: Basil Blackwell.

Oldroyd, David. 1986. *The Arch of Knowledge: An Introductory Study of the History of the Philosophy and Methodology of Science.* New York: Methuen.

Osterhammel, Jürgen. 1987. Varieties of Social Economics: Joseph A. Schumpeter and Max Weber. In W. J. Mommsen and J. Osterhammel, eds., *Max Weber and His Contemporaries*, 106–20. London: Allen & Unwin.

Pareto, Vilfredo. 1896–97. *Cours d'économie politique*, 2 vols. Lausanne: Librairie de l'Université.

——— 1916. *Trattato di Sociologia Generale*, 4 vols. Florence: Barbera. (*The Mind and Society*, 4 vols. Arthur Livingston and Andrew Bongiorno, trans. New York: Harcourt, Brace & Co., 1935.)

Perroux, François. 1965. *La pense économique de Joseph Schumpeter: les dynamiques du capitalisme.* Geneve: Librairie Droz.

Pheby, John. 1988. *Methodology and Economics: a Critical Introduction.* London: Macmillan.

Pius XI. 1931. *Quadragesimo Anno.* (*On Reconstructing the Social Order.* Francis J. Haas and Martin R. P. McGuire, trans. 1942.)

Pohle, L. 1909. Book Review of J. A. Schumpeter, *Das Wesen und der Hauptinhalt der theoretischen Nationalökonomie*. *Zeitschrift für Sozialwissenschaft* 12: 332–58.

Poincaré, Henri. 1902. *La science et l'hypothèse*. Paris: Ernest Flammarion. (*The Foundations of Science*. George Bruce Halsted, trans. New York: Science Press, 1913.)

1905. *La valeur de la science*. Paris: Ernest Flammarion. (*The Foundations of Science*. George Bruce Halsted, trans. New York: Science Press, 1913.)

Popper, Karl. 1959. *The Logic of Scientific Discovery*. London: Hutchinson.

1963. *Conjectures and Refutations: the Growth of Scientific Knowledge*. London: Routledge & Kegan Paul.

1983. *Realism and the Aim of Science*. From the postscript to *The Logic of Scientific Discovery*. W. W. Bartley III, ed. London: Hutchinson.

Predöhl, Andreas. 1972. *Gustav Cassel, Joseph Schumpeter, Bernhard Harms: Drei richtungsweisende Wirtschaftswissenschaftler*. Göttingen: Vandenhoeck & Ruprecht.

Redlich, Fritz. 1955. Unternehmerforschung und Weltanschauung. *Kyklos* 8.3: 277–300.

Redman, Deborah A. 1991. *Economics and the Philosophy of Science*. New York: Oxford University Press.

Reichenbach, Hans. 1938. *Experience and Prediction: an Analysis of the Foundations and the Structure of Knowledge*. Chicago: University of Chicago Press.

1951. *The Rise of Scientific Philosophy*. Berkeley: University of California Press.

Rescher, Nicholas. 1973. *The Coherence Theory of Truth*. Oxford: Oxford University Press.

Rickert, Heinrich. 1899. *Kulturwissenschaft und Naturwissenschaft*, 6th edn. Tübingen: J. C. B. Mohr, 1926. (*Science and History: A Critique of Positivist Epistemology*. George Reisman, trans. New York: Van Nostrand, 1962.)

1902. *Die Grenzen der naturwissenschaftlichen Begriffsbildung*, 5th edn. Tübingen: J. C. B. Mohr, 1929. (*The Limits of Concept Formation in Natural Science: A Logical Introduction to the Historical Sciences*, Abridged edition. Guy Oakes, trans. Cambridge, UK: Cambridge University Press, 1986.)

Ringer, Fritz K. 1969. *The Decline of the German Mandarins: The German Academic Community, 1890–1933*. Cambridge, Mass.: Harvard University Press.

Robbins, Lionel. 1930. On a Certain Ambiguity in the Conception of Stationary Equilibrium. *Economic Journal* 40.158: 194–214.

1932. *An Essay on the Nature and Significance of Economic Science*, 2nd edn. London: Macmillan, 1935.

1955. Schumpeter's History of Economic Analysis. *Quarterly Journal of Economics* 69.1: 1–22.

Samuels, Warren J. 1983. The Influence of Friedrich von Wieser on Joseph A. Schumpeter. *History of Economics Society Bulletin* 4.2: 5–19.

Samuelson, Paul A. 1943. Dynamics, Statics, and the Stationary State. *Review of Economic Statistics* 25.1: 58–68.

1981. Schumpeter's *Capitalism, Socialism and Democracy*. In Arnold Heertje, ed., 1981, 1–21.

1982. Schumpeter as an Economic Theorist. In Helmut Frisch, ed., 1982, 1–27.

Santarelli, Enrico, and Pesciarelli, Enzo. 1990. The Emergence of a Vision: The Development of Schumpeter's Theory of Entrepreneurship. *History of Political Economy* 22.4: 677–96.

Scheler, Max. 1926. Probleme einer Soziologie des Wissens. In his *Die Wissensformen und die Gesellschaft*, 1–232. Leipzig: Neue-Geist Verlag. Reprinted in his *Gesammelte Werke*, vol. VIII. Bern: Francke Verlag, 1960. (Problems of a Sociology of Knowledge. In his *On Feeling, Knowing, and Valuing*, Harold J. Bershady, trans. 166–217. Chicago: University of Chicago Press, 1992.)

    1957. Vorbild und Führer. In his *Schriften aus dem Nachlass*, vol. I. *Gesammelte Werke*, vol. X, 255–318. Bern: Francke Verlag. (Exemplars of Person and Leaders. In his *Person and Self-Value: Three Essays*, 127–98. M. S. Frings, trans. Boston: Martinus Nijhoff Publishers, 1987.)

Schelting, A. von. 1922. Die logische Theorie der historischen Kulturwissenschaft von Max Weber und im besonderen sein Begriff des Idealtypus. *Archiv für Sozialwissenschaft und Sozialpolitik* 49: 623–752.

Scherer, F. M. 1992. Schumpeter and Plausible Capitalism. *Journal of Economic Literature* 30.3: 1416–33.

Schmitter, Philippe C. and Lehmbruch, Gerhard, eds. 1979. *Trends towards Corporatist Intermediation*. London: Sage Publications.

Schmoller, Gustav von. 1874. Die sociale Frage und der preussische Staat. *Preussische Jahrbücher* 33.4. Reprinted in Schmoller, 1890, 37–63.

    1883. Zur Methodologie der Staats- und Sozialwissenschaften. *Schmollers Jahrbuch* 7: 975–94. Reprinted as Die Schriften von K. Menger und W. Dilthey zur Methodologie der Staats- und Sozialwissenschaften, in Schmoller, 1888a, 275–304.

    1888a. *Zur Literaturgeschichte der Staats- und Sozialwissenschaften*. Leipzig: Duncker & Humblot.

    1888b. Wilhelm Roscher. In Schmoller, 1888a, 147–71.

    1890. *Zur Social- und Gewerbepolitik der Gegenwart*. Leipzig: Duncker und Humblot.

    1897. *Wechselnde Theorien und feststehende Wahrheiten im Gebiete der Staats- und Sozialwissenschaften und die heutige deutsche Volkswirtschaftslehre*. Berlin: Druck von W. Brüxenstein. Reprinted in Schmoller, 1898, 365–93.

    1898. *Über einige Grundfragen der Sozialpolitik und der Volkswirtschaftslehre*. Leipzig: Duncker & Humblot.

    1900. *Grundriss der allgemeinen Volkswirtschaftslehre*. 2 vols. Leipzig: Duncker & Humblot.

    1911. Volkswirtschaft, Volkswirtschaftslehre und -methode. In *Handwörterbuch der Staatswissenschaften*, 3rd edn., vol. 8, 426–501. J. Conrad, L. Elster, W. Lexis, and E. Loening, eds. Jena: Verlag von Gustav Fischer.

Schnädelbach, Herbert. 1974. *Geschichtsphilosophie nach Hegel: Die Problem des Historismus*. Freiburg: Verlag Karl Alber.

Schneider, Erich. 1951. Schumpeter's Early German Work, 1906–17. In S. E. Harris, ed., 1951, 54–58.

    1970. *Joseph A. Schumpeter: Leben und Werk eines grossen Sozialökonomen*. Tübingen: J. C. B. Mohr. (*Joseph A. Schumpeter: Life and Work of a Great Social Scientist*. W. E. Kuhn, trans. Lincoln: University of Nebraska-Lincoln, 1975.)

Schorske, Carl E. 1980. *Fin-de-Siècle Vienna: Politics and Culture*. New York: Alfred A. Knopf.

Schumpeter, Elizabeth B. 1940. *The Industrialization of Japan, Korea, and Manchuria, 1936–40.* New York: Macmillan.

1960. *English Overseas Trade Statistics, 1698–1808.* Oxford: Clarendon Press.

Schumpeter, Joseph Alois. 1906. Über die mathematische Methode der theoretischen Ökonomie. *Zeitschrift für Volkswirtschaft, Sozialpolitik und Verwaltung* 15: 30–49. Reprinted in Schumpeter, 1952, 529–48.

1908. *Das Wesen und der Hauptinhalt der theoretischen Nationalökonomie.* Leipzig: Duncker & Humblot.

1909. On the Concept of Social Value. *Quarterly Journal of Economics* 23: 213–32. Reprinted in Schumpeter, 1951c, 1–20.

1910a. Die neuere Wirtschaftstheorie in den Vereinigten Staaten. *Jahrbuch für Gesetzgebung, Verwaltung und Volkswirtschaft* 34.3: 913–63.

1910b. Über das Wesen der Wirtschaftskrisen. *Zeitschrift für Volkswirtschaft, Sozialpolitik und Verwaltung* 19: 271–325. Reprinted in Schumpeter, 1987, 227–74.

1912. *Theorie der wirtschaftlichen Entwicklung.* Lepzig: Duncker & Humblot.

1913. Eine "dynamische" Theorie des Kapitalzinses: Eine Entgegnung. *Zeitschrift für Volkswirtschaft, Sozialpolitik und Verwaltung* 22: 599–639. Reprinted in Schumpeter, 1952, 411–51.

1914a. *Epochen der Dogmen- und Methodengeschichte.* Tübingen: J. C. B. Mohr. (*Economic Doctrine and Method: An Historical Sketch.* R. Aris, trans. London: George Allen & Unwin, 1954c.)

1914b. Das wissenschaftliche Lebenswerk Eugen von Böhm-Bawerks. *Zeitschrift für Volkswirtschaft, Sozialpolitik und Verwaltung* 23: 454–528. Reprinted in Schumpeter, 1954b, 7–81.

1915. *Vergangenheit und Zukunft der Sozialwissenschaften.* Leipzig: Duncker & Humblot.

1916–17. Das Grundprinzip der Verteilungtheorie. *Archiv für Sozialwissenschaft und Sozialpolitik* 42: 1–88. Reprinted in Schumpeter, 1952, 320–407.

1917–18. Das Sozialprodukt und die Rechenpfennige. Glossen und Beiträge zur Geldtheorie von heute. *Archiv für Sozialwissenschaft und Sozialpolitik* 44: 627–715. Reprinted in Schumpeter, 1952, 29–117. (Money and the Social Product, A. W. Marget, trans. *International Economic Review* 1956, 6: 148–211.)

1918. *Die Krise des Steuerstaates.* Graz and Leipzig: Leuschner & Lubensky. Reprinted in Schumpeter, 1953, 1–71. (*The Crisis of the Tax State.* Wolfgang F. Stolper and Richard A. Musgrave, trans. In Schumpeter, 1991, 99–140.)

1918–19. Zur Soziologie der Imperialismen. *Archiv für Sozialwissenschaft und Sozialpolitik* 46: 1–39, 275–310. Reprinted in Schumpeter, 1953, 72–146. (The Sociology of Imperialisms. Heinz Norden, trans. In Schumpeter, 1951b, 3–130.)

1920. Max Webers Werk. *Der österreichische Volkswirt* 12: 831–34. Reprinted in Schumpeter, 1954b, 108–17. (Max Weber's Work. Guy Oakes, trans. In Schumpeter, 1991, 220–29.)

1920–21. Sozialistische Möglichkeiten von heute. *Archiv für Sozialwissenschaft und Sozialpolitik* 48: 305–360. Reprinted in Schumpeter, 1952, 465–510.

1921. Carl Menger. *Zeitschrift für Volkswirtschaft und Sozialpolitik* N.F., 1: 197–206. Reprinted in Schumpeter, 1954b, 118–27. (Carl Menger, Hans W. Singer, trans. In Schumpeter, 1951a, 80–90.)

1924. Der Sozialismus in England und bei uns. *Österreichischer Volkswirt*, 295–97, 327–330. Reprinted in Schumpeter, 1952, 511–26.

1925. Eugen von Böhm-Bawerk. *Neue Österreichische Volkswirt*, 1815–1918, vol. 2, 63–80. Reprinted in Schumpeter, 1954b, 82–99.

1926a. *Theorie der wirtschaftlichen Entwicklung: eine Untersuchung über Unternehmergewinn, Kapital, Kredit, Zins und den Konjunkturzyklus*, 2nd revised edn. Leipzig: Duncker & Humblot.

1926b. Gustav v. Schmoller und die Probleme von heute. *Schmollers Jahrbuch* 50: 337–88. Reprinted in Schumpeter, 1954b, 148–99.

1927a. Die sozialen Klassen in ethnisch homogenen Milieu. *Archiv für Sozialwissenschaft und Sozialpolitik* 57:1–67. Reprinted in Schumpeter, 1953, 147–213. (Social Classes in an Ethnically Homogeneous Environment. Heinz Norden, trans. In Schumpeter, 1951b, 133–221.)

1927b. Friedrich von Wieser. *Economic Journal* 37.146: 328–30. Reprinted in Schumpeter, 1951a, 298–301.

1928. The Instability of Capitalism. *Economic Journal* 38: 361–86. Reprinted in Schumpeter, 1951c, 47–72.

1929a. Ökonomie und Psychologie des Unternehmers. Vortrag in der 10. ordentlichen Mitgliederversammlung des Zentralverbandes der Deutschen Metallwalzwerks- und Hütten-Industrie E. V. in München. 1–15. Leipzig: Haberland.

1929b. Ökonomie und Soziologie der Einkommensteuer. *Der Deutsche Volkswirt* 4: 380–85. Reprinted in Schumpeter, 1985, 123–32.

1931a. The Present State of Economics or on Systems, Schools and Methods. *Kokumin Keizai Zasshi* 50: 1–27.

[1931b] 1982. The 'Crisis' in Economics – Fifty Years Ago. *Journal of Economic Literature* 20.3: 1049–59.

[1931c] 1982. Recent Developments of Political Economy. *Kobe University Economic Review* 28: 1–15.

[1931d] 1991. Recent Developments of Political Economy. In Schumpeter, 1991, 284–97.

[1932] 1952. Das Woher und Wohin unser Wissenschaft. In Schumpeter, 1952, 598–608.

1933a. The Common Sense of Econometrics. *Econometrica* 1.1: 5–12. Reprinted in Schumpeter, 1951c, 100–107.

1933b. Book Review of J. M. Keynes, *Essays in Biography. Economic Journal* 43: 652–57.

1934. *The Theory of Economic Development: an Inquiry into Profits, Capital, Credit, Interest, and the Business Cycle*. Redvers Opie, trans. Cambridge, Mass.: Harvard University Press.

1935a. Preface to *Theorie der wirtschaftlichen Entwicklung*, 4th edn. Leipzig: Duncker & Humblot.

1935b. Report from the Meetings of the Econometric Society in Chicago and Pittsburgh, December 1934. *Econometrica* 3.3: 345–50.

1936a. Book Review of Keynes, *General Theory. Journal of the American Statistical Association* 31: 791–95. Reprinted in Schumpeter, 1951c, 153–57.

[1936b]. Can Capitalism Survive? In Schumpeter, 1991, 298–315.

1937. Preface to the Japanese edition of *Theorie der wirtschaftlichen Entwicklung*. Tokyo: Iwanami Shoten. Reprinted in Schumpeter, 1951c, 158–63.

1939. *Business Cycles: a Theoretical, Historical and Statistical Analysis of the Capitalist Process*, 2 vols. New York: McGraw-Hill.

[1940] 1984. The Meaning of Rationality in the Social Sciences. *Zeitschrift für die Gesamte Staatswissenschaft* 140.4: 577–93. Reprinted in Schumpeter, 1991, 316–38.

[1941]. An Economic Interpretation of Our Time: the Lowell Lectures. In Schumpeter, 1991, 339–400.

1942. *Capitalism, Socialism and Democracy*. (2nd edn. 1947; 3rd edn. 1950). New York: Harper & Brothers.

1943. Capitalism in the Postwar World. In S. E. Harris, ed., *Postwar Economic Problems*, 113–26. New York: McGraw Hill. Reprinted in Schumpeter, 1951c, 170–83.

1946a. Capitalism. In *Encyclopaedia Britannica*, vol. 4: 801–7. Reprinted in Schumpeter, 1951c, 184–205.

1946b. L'avenir de l'entreprise privée devant les tendances socialistes modernes. In *Comment sauvegarder l'entreprise privée*. Premier Congres Patronals. (The Future of Private Enterprise in the Face of Modern Socialistic Tendencies. Michael G. Prime and David R. Henderson, trans. *History of Political Economy* 1975, 4.3: 293–98.)

1946c. The Decade of the Twenties. *American Economic Review* 36.2: 1–10. Reprinted in Schumpeter, 1951c, 206–15.

1947. The Creative Response in Economic History. *Journal of Economic History* 7: 149–59. Reprinted in Schumpeter, 1951c, 216–26.

1949a. Science and Ideology. *American Economic Review* 39.2: 345–59. Reprinted in Schumpeter, 1951c, 267–81.

1949b. The Communist Manifesto in Sociology and Economics. *Journal of Political Economy* 57.3: 199–212. Reprinted in Schumpeter, 1951c, 282–95.

1949c. The Historical Approach to the Analysis of Business Cycles. In *Conference on Business Cycles*, National Bureau of Economic Research, 149–62. Reprinted in Schumpeter, 1951c, 308–15.

1949d. Economic Theory and Entrepreneurial History. In Research Center in Entrepreneurial History, ed., *Change and the Entrepreneur: Postulates and Patterns for Entrepreneurial History*. Reprinted in Schumpeter, 1951c, 248–66.

1950a. *Capitalism, Socialism and Democracy*. 3rd edn. New York: Harper & Brothers.

1950b. The March into Socialism. *American Economic Review* 40.2: 446–56. Reprinted in Schumpeter, 1950a, 415–25.

1951a. *Ten Great Economists, from Marx to Keynes*. New York: Oxford University Press.

1951b. *Imperialism and Social Classes*. Heinz Norden, trans. New York: Augustus M. Kelley.

1951c. *Essays of J. A. Schumpeter*. Richard V. Clemence, ed. Cambridge, Mass.: Addison-Wesley Press.

1952. *Aufsätze zur ökonomischen Theorie*. Erich Schneider and Arthur Spiethoff, eds. Tübingen: J. C. B. Mohr.

1953. *Aufsätze zur Soziologie*. Erich Schneider and Arthur Spiethoff, eds. Tübingen: J. C. B. Mohr.

1954a. *History of Economic Analysis.* Elizabeth Boody Schumpeter, ed. New York: Oxford University Press.

1954b. *Dogmenhistorische und biographische Aufsätze.* Erich Schneider and Arthur Spiethoff, eds. Tübingen: J. C. B. Mohr.

1954c. *Economic Doctrine and Method: An Historical Sketch.* R. Aris, trans. London: George Allen & Unwin.

1970. *Das Wesen des Geldes.* Fritz Karl Mann, ed. Göttingen: Vandenhoeck & Ruprecht. (The first two chapters: Money and Currency. Arthur W. Marget, trans. appeared in *Social Research*, 1991, 58.3: 499–543.)

1985. *Aufsätze zur Wirtschaftspolitik.* Wolfgang F. Stolper and Christian Seidl, eds. Tübingen: J. C. B. Mohr.

1987. *Beiträge zur Sozialökonomik.* Stephan Böhm, ed. Vienna: Böhlau Verlag.

1991. *The Economics and Sociology of Capitalism.* Richard Swedberg, ed. Princeton: Princeton University Press.

1992. *Politische Reden.* Christian Seidl and Wolfgang F. Stolper, eds. Tübingen: J. C. B. Mohr.

1993. *Aufsätze zur Tagespolitik.* Christian Seidl and Wolfgang F. Stolper, eds. Tübingen: J. C. B. Mohr.

Seidl, Christian. 1984. Joseph Alois Schumpeter: Character, Life, and Particulars of His Graz Period. In Christian Seidl, ed., *Lectures on Schumpeterian Economics: Schumpeter Centenary Memorial Lectures Graz 1983*, 187–205. Berlin: Springer-Verlag.

Semmel, Bernard. 1993. *The Liberal Ideal and the Demons of Empire: Theories of Imperialism from Adam Smith to Lenin.* Baltimore: Johns Hopkins University Press.

Shionoya, Yuichi. 1986. The Science and Ideology of Schumpeter. *Rivista Internazionale di Scienze Economiche e Commerciali* 33.8: 729–62. Reprinted in Mark Blaug, ed., *Frank Knight (1885–1972), Henry Simons (1899–1946), Joseph Schumpeter (1883–1950).* Pioneers in Economics 37: 314–46. Aldershot: Edward Elgar, 1992.

1989a. Schmollers Forschungsprogramm: Eine methodologische Würdigung. In Jürgen Backhaus, Yuichi Shionoya, and Bertram Schefold, *Gustav von Schmollers Lebenswerk: Eine kritische Analyse aus moderner Sicht*, 55–76. Düsseldorf: Wirtschaft und Finanzen.

1989b. The Schumpeter Family in Třešt'. *Hitotsubashi Journal of Economics* 30.2: 157–66.

1990a. Instrumentalism in Schumpeter's Economic Methodology. *History of Political Economy* 22.2: 187–222. Reprinted in Bruce Caldwell, ed., 1993, vol. I, 239–74.

1990b. The Origin of the Schumpeterian Research Programme: a Chapter Omitted from Schumpeter's *Theory of Economic Development. Journal of Institutional and Theoretical Economics* 146.2: 314–27.

1991. Schumpeter on Schmoller and Weber: a Methodology of Economic Sociology. *History of Political Economy* 23. 2: 193–219.

1992a. Taking Schumpeter's Methodology Seriously. In Frederic M. Scherer and Mark Perlman, eds., *Entrepreneurship, Technological Innovation, and Economic Growth: Studies in the Schumpeterian Tradition*, 343–62. Ann Arbor: University of Michigan Press.

1992b. Max Webers soziologische Sicht der Wirtschaft. In Bertram Schefold, Guenther Roth, and Yuichi Shionoya, *Max Weber und seine »Protestantische Ethik,«* 93–119. Düsseldorf: Verlag Wirtschaft und Finanzen.

1995. A Methodological Appraisal of Schmoller's Research Program. In Peter Koslowski, ed., *The Theory of Ethical Economy in the Historical School: Ethics and Economics in Wilhelm Roscher, Lorenz von Stein, Schmoller, Dilthey and in the Present,* 57–78. Berlin: Springer-Verlag.

1996. The Sociology of Science and Schumpeter's Ideology. In Laurence S. Moss, ed., 1996, 277–300.

Shionoya, Yuichi and Perlman, Mark, eds. 1994. *Schumpeter in the History of Ideas.* Ann Arbor: University of Michigan Press.

Smithies, Arthur. 1951. Memorial, Joseph Alois Schumpeter, 1883–1950. In S. E. Harris, ed., 1951, 11–23.

Solterer, J. 1951. *Quadragesimo Anno*: Schumpeter's Alternative to the Omnipotent State. *Review of Social Economy* 9.1: 12–23.

Somary, Felix. 1955. *Erinnerung aus meinem Leben.* Zurich: Manesse Verlag.

Spann, Othmar. 1908. Der logische Aufbau der Nationalökonomie und ihr Verhältnis zu den Psychologie und zu Naturwissenschaften: Ein methodologischer Versuch. *Zeitschrift für die gesamte Staatswissenschaft* 64: 1–57.

1910. Die mechanisch-mathematische Analogie in der Volkswirtschaftslehre. *Archiv für Sozialwissenschaft und Sozialpolitik* 30: 786–824.

Spengler, Joseph J. 1968. Exogenous and Endogenous Influences in the Formation of Post-1870 Economic Thought: a Sociology of Knowledge Approach. In Robert V. Eagly, ed., *Events, Ideology and Economic Theory,* 159–87. Detroit: Wayne State University Press.

Spiethoff, Arthur. 1949. Josef Schumpeter: In Memoriam. *Kyklos* 3.4: 289–93.

Stark, Werner. 1959. The "Classical Situation" in Political Economy. *Kyklos* 12: 57–65.

Stevenson, Michael I. 1985. *Joseph Alois Schumpeter: a Bibliography, 1905–1984.* Westport, Conn.: Greenwood Press.

Stigler, George J. 1988. *Memoirs of an Unregulated Economist.* New York: Basic Books.

Stolper, Wolfgang F. 1982. Aspects of Schumpeter's Theory of Evolution. In Helmut Frisch, ed., 1982, 28–48.

1989. Spiethoff, Schumpeter und «*Das Wesen des Geldes*»: Comments and Additions. *Kyklos* 42.3: 435–38.

1994. *Joseph Alois Schumpeter: the Public Life of a Private Man.* Princeton: Princeton University Press.

Strachey, Lytton. 1918. *Eminent Victorians.* London: Chatto and Windus. Penguin Books, 1948.

1931. *Portraits in Miniature and Other Essays.* London: Chatto and Windus.

Streissler, Erich. 1982. Schumpeter's Vienna and the Role of Credit in Innovation. In Helmut Frisch, ed., 1982, 60–83.

1986. Arma virumque cano: Friedrich von Wieser, the Bard as Economist. In Norbert Leser, ed., *Die Wiener Schule der Nationalökonomie,* 83–106. Vienna: Hermann Böhlau.

Stump, David. 1989. Henri Poincaré's Philosophy of Science. *Studies in History and Philosophy of Science* 20.3: 335–63.

Suppe, Frederick, ed. 1977. *The Structure of Scientific Theories*. 2nd edn. Chicago: University of Illinois Press.

Swedberg, Richard. 1991a. *Joseph A. Schumpeter: His Life and Work*. Cambridge: Polity Press.

1991b. ed. Joseph A. Schumpeter: *The Economics and Sociology of Capitalism*. Princeton: Princeton University Press.

1992. Can Capitalism Survive? Schumpeter's Answer and its Relevance for New Institutional Economics. *Archives Européennes de Sociologie* 33: 350–80.

Sweezy, Paul. 1951. Editor's Introduction to J. A. Schumpeter, *Imperialism and Social Classes*, vii–xxv. New York: Augustus M. Kelley.

Tarascio, Vincent J. 1966. *Pareto's Methodological Approach to Economics: a Study in the History of Some Scientific Aspects of Economic Thought*. Chapel Hill: University of North Carolina Press.

Taylor, O. H. 1951. Schumpeter and Marx: Imperialism and Social Classes in the Schumpeterian System. *Quarterly Journal of Economics* 65.4: 525–55.

Taymans, A. 1949. George Tarde and Joseph A. Schumpeter: A Similar Vision. *Explorations in Entrepreneurial History* 1.4: 9–17.

Timmermann, Manfred, ed. 1987. *Die ökonomischen Lehren von Marx, Keynes, Schumpeter*. Stuttgart: Verlag W. Kohlhammer.

Tritsch, Walther. 1953. Schumpeter avant 1925 livré au hasard de ma mémoire. *Economie Appliquée* 6.4: 597–626.

1955. Ein Gespräch Joseph Schumpeters mit Max Weber. *Frankfurter Allgemeine Zeitung*, 27 August 1955. (A Conversation between Joseph Schumpeter and Max Weber. Gerd Schröter, trans. *History of Sociology* 6.1: 167–72. 1985.)

Tsuru, Shigeto. 1983. Schumpeter the Man (in Japanese). *Economic Seminar*, Supplement: 2–16.

Vecchi, Nicolò De. 1995. *Entrepreneurs, Institutions and Economic Change: the Economic Thought of J. A. Schumpeter (1905–1925)*. Aldershot: Edward Elgar.

Vercelli, A. 1985. Money and Production in Schumpeter and Keynes: Two Dichotomies. In R. Arena *et al.*, eds. *Production, circulation et monaie*, 31–45. Nice: Université de Nice.

Viner, Jacob. 1954. Schumpeter's History of Economic Analysis: a Review Article. *American Economic Review* 44.5: 894–910.

Wagener, H. J., and J. W. Drukker, eds. 1986. *The Economic Law of Motion of Modern Society: a Marx, Keynes, Schumpeter Centennial*. Cambridge, UK: Cambridge University Press.

Walras, Léon. 1874. *Eléments d'économie politique pure ou Théorie de la richesse sociale*. Lausanne: L. Corbaz. (*Elements of Pure Economics*. William Jaffé, trans. London: Allen & Unwin, 1954.)

Weber, Max. 1903–6. Roscher und Knies und die logischen Probleme der historischen Nationalökonomie. *Schmollers Jahrbuch* 27: 1181–222, 29: 1323–84, 30: 81–120. Reprinted in Weber, 1922a, 1–145.

1904. Die „Objektivität" sozialwissenschaftlicher und sozialpolitischer Erkenntnis.

Archiv für Sozialwissenschaft und Sozialpolitik 19: 22–87. Reprinted in Weber, 1922a, 146–214. ("Objectivity" in Social Science and Social Policy. In *The Methodology of the Social Sciences*. Edward A. Shills and Henry A. Finch, trans. 50–112. Glencoe, Ill.: Free Press, 1949.)

1908. Die Grenznutzlehre und das „psychophysische Grundgesetz." *Archiv für Sozialwissenschaft und Sozialpolitik* 27: 546–58. Reprinted in Weber, 1922a, 360–75. (Marginal Utility Theory and "The Fundamental Law of Psychophysics." Louis Schneider, trans. *Social Science Quarterly* 56.1: 21–36.)

1920–21. *Gesammelte Aufsätze zur Religionssoziologie*, 3 vols. Tübingen: J. C. B. Mohr.

1922a. *Gesammelte Aufsätze zur Wissenschaftslehre*. Tübingen: J. C. B. Mohr.

1922b. *Wirtschaft und Gesellschaft: Grundriss der verstehenden Soziologie*, 5th revised edn. Tübingen: J. C. B. Mohr, 1972. (*Economy and Society*, 2 vols. Guenther Roth and Claus Wittich, eds. Berkeley: University of California Press, 1978.)

Weintraub, E. Roy. 1983. On the Existence of a Competitive Equilibrium, 1930–1954. *Journal of Economic Literature* 21.1: 1–39.

1985. *General Equilibrium Analysis: Studies in Appraisal*. Cambridge, UK: Cambridge University Press.

1991. *Stabilizing Dynamics: Constructing Economic Knowledge*. Cambridge, UK: Cambridge University Press.

Wicksell, Knut. 1893. *Über Wert, Kapital, und Rente*. Jena: G. Fischer. (*Value, Capital, and Rent*. S. H. Frowein, trans. London: George Allen & Unwin, 1954.)

[1904]. Ends and Means in Economics. In Erik Lindahl, ed., *Selected Papers on Economic Theory*, 51–66. London: George Allen & Unwin, 1958.

Wieser, Friedrich von. 1889. *Der Natürliche Werth*. Vienna: Alfred Hölder. (*Natural Value*. W. Smart, trans. London: Macmillan, 1893.)

1910. *Recht und Macht: Sechs Vorträge*. Leipzig: Duncker & Humblot.

1911. Das Wesen und der Hauptinhalt der theoretischen Nationalökonomie: kritische Glossen. *Schmollers Jahrbuch* 35.2: 395–417. Reprinted in Wieser, 1929.

1914. *Theorie der gesellschaftlichen Wirtschaft*. Tübingen: Mohr-Siebeck. (*Social Economics*. A. F. Hinrichs, trans. New York: Greenberg, 1927.)

1926. *Das Gesetz der Macht*. Vienna: Springer.

1929. *Gesammelte Abhandlungen*, Friedrich A. von Hayek, ed. Tübingen: J. C. B. Mohr.

Windelband, Wilhelm. 1894. *Geschichte und Naturwissenschaft*. Rectoratsreden der Universität Strassburg. Strassburg: J. H. Ed. Heitz. Reprinted in his *Präludien*, vol. 2, 1924, 136–60. (History and Natural Science. Guy Oakes, trans. *History and Theory* 1980, 19.2: 165–85.)

Winterberger, G. 1983. *Über Schumpeters Geschichtsdeterminismus*. Tübingen: J. C. B. Mohr.

Wolff, Kurt H. ed. 1993. *From Karl Mannheim*, 2nd edn. New Brunswick: Transaction Publishers.

Wong, Stanley. 1973. The "F-Twist" and the Methodology of Paul Samuelson. *American Economic Review* 63.3: 312–25.

Wood, John Cunningham, ed. 1991. *Joseph A. Schumpeter: Critical Assessments*, 4 vols. New York: Routledge.

Yagi, Kiichiro. 1993. Schumpeter and Vienna University. *Research and Study*, Special Issue of *Economic Review*, Kyoto University 5: 63–83.

Index

DATE DUE
